PROFESSIONAL STANDARD
OF THE PEOPLE'S REPUBLIC OF CHINA

Code for Design of Medium and Low Speed Maglev Transit

CJJ/T 262 - 2017

Approval Department: Ministry of Housing and Urban-Rural Development
of the People's Republic of China
Implementation Date: November 1, 2017

China Architecture & Building Press

Beijing 2023

图书在版编目(CIP)数据

中低速磁浮交通设计规范：CJJ/T262—2017 = Code for Design of Medium and Low Speed Maglev Transit：英文 / 中华人民共和国住房和城乡建设部编译. — 北京：中国建筑工业出版社，2023.5

（中华人民共和国行业标准）

ISBN 978-7-112-28528-0

Ⅰ．①中… Ⅱ．①中… Ⅲ．①磁浮铁路—设计规范—中国—英文 Ⅳ．①U237-65

中国国家版本馆 CIP 数据核字(2023)第 048306 号

Chinese edition first published in the People's Republic of China in 2017

English edition first published in the People's Republic of China in 2023

by China Architecture & Building Press

No. 9 Sanlihe Road

Beijing，100037

www. cabp. com. cn

Printed in China by Beijing YanLinJiZhao printing CO.,LTD

ISBN 978-7-112-28528-0(40811)

NOTICE

This code is written in Chinese and English. The Chinese text shall be taken as the ruling one in the event of any inconsistency between the Chinese text and the English text.

Announcement of Ministry of Housing and Urban-Rural Development of the People's Republic of China

No. 1557

Announcement of Ministry of Housing and Urban-Rural Development on Publishing the Professional Standard of *Code for Design of Medium and Low Speed Maglev Transit*

This *Code for Design of Medium and Low Speed Maglev Transit* has been approved as a professional standard with the serial number of CJJ/T 262 – 2017, and it will be implemented from November 1, 2017.

Authorized by the Research Institute of Standard and Norms, this code is published and distributed by China Architecture & Building Press.

Ministry of Housing and Urban-Rural Development of the People's Republic of China

May 18, 2017

Foreword

According to the requirements of Document JIAN BIAO [2006] No. 77 issued by the Ministry of Housing and Urban-Rural Development (MOHURD) "Notice on Printing and Distributing the Development and Revision Plan of National Engineering Construction Standards (the first batch) in 2006", The Code Preparation Group based on comprehensive survey and research, summarization of practical experience and extensive solicitation of opinions, and reference was made to relevant national standards and foreign advanced standards.

Main technical contents of this code are as follows: 1. General Provisions; 2. Terms; 3. Vehicle; 4. Operational Organization and Operating Management; 5. Gauge; 6. Line; 7. Track; 8. Track Support Structure; 9. Station Building; 10. At-ground Structure; 11. Elevated Station Structure; 12. Underground Structure; 13. Structure Waterproof; 14. Ventilationing, Air Conditioning and Heating; 15. Water Supply and Drainage; 16. Power Supply; 17. Communication; 18. Operating Control System; 19. Elevator, Escalator and Autowalk; 20. Automatic Fare Collection System; 21. Fire Alarm System (FAS); 22. Building Automation System (BAS); 23. Integrated Supervisory and Control System; 24. Operation Control Center; 25. Vehicle Base; 26. Disaster Prevention; 27. Environment Protection.

This code is under the jurisdiction of The Ministry of Housing and Urban-Rural Development. Tongji University is in charge of the explanation of technical specifications. Any comments or suggestions collected in implementation may be forwarded to Tongji University (Address: Room 513, Tongxin Building, No. 4800 Cao'an Road, Jiading District, Shanghai, China, 201804).

Chief Development Organizations:

Tongji University

Beijing Enterprises Holdings Maglev Technology Development Co., Ltd.

Participating Development Organizations:

Shanghai Municipal Engineering Design Institute (Group) Co., Ltd.

The Third Railway Survey and Design Institute Group Corporation

National University of Defense Technology

Southwest Jiaotong University

China Railway Eryuan Engineering Group Co., Ltd.

CRSC Research & Design Institute Group Co., Ltd.

Shanghai Tunnel Engineering & Rail Transit Design and Research Institute

Shanghai Maglev Transportation Development Co., Ltd.

Guangzhou Metro Design & Research Institute Co., Ltd.

China Railway Shanghai Design Institute Group Co., Ltd.

China Railway sixth Bureau Group Co., Ltd.

China Railway Electrification Survey Design & Research Institute Co., Ltd.

China Railway Baoji Bridge Group Co., Ltd.

Tangshan Rail Bus Co., Ltd.

Laiwu Steel Group Co., Ltd.

Chief Drafting Staff:

Wu Xiangming, Wang Ping, Chen Xiaohong, Sun Jiliang, Wang Hongyu, Zhang Peizhu, Lin Guobin, Dou Zhongzan, Liu Wanming, Yan Peiliang, Long Zhiqiang, Li Aidong, Pan Guangxi, Zhu Ying, Luo Xiangping, Wang Zhirong, Tang Min, Yang Zhihao, Zhang Xingzhao, Xia Leng, Zhao Dongliang, Ji Minting, Gao Yanping, Yuan Shuqing, Shao Zhen, Qi Yuhua, Zeng Guofeng, Zhang Kunlun, Wang Jinyan, Zhu Shoujun, Wang Yonggang, Fang Hua, Wang Zhilong, Wang Yabin, Wang Kaijie, Wang Mingsheng, Wang Fenxian, Wang Jun, Tian Kun, Dai Jilong, Tian Liansheng, Tian Miaosheng, Jing Sinan, Lan Shugui, Feng Yun, Liu Wei, Sun Xianfeng, Zhu Hongxin, Yao Shengjun, He Dahai, Wu Song, Song Zhenhua, Zou Minghui, Zhang Ting, Zhang Xueshan, Zhang Huaying, Zhang Chunguang, Zhang Haibo, Song Wei, Zhang Peng, Li Jie, Li Jiangsuo, Li Meiling, Li Dexiu, Yang Zhen, Yang Jie, Yang Huili, Yang Caixia, Lu Jicheng, Chen Kejian, Chen Hao, Zhou Hua, Yi Sirong, Lin Zongliang, Luo Kun, Luo Shihui, Hong Shaozhi, Zhao Xiaomei, Suo Xiaoming, Guo Gongan, Xu Yinguang, Sheng Xiongwei, Huang Jian, Huang Jingyu, Zeng Guobao, Dong Decun, Yu Yi, Dou Guangzhan, Jin Shoujie, Teng Yibi, Yan Zhihua, Liu Haijian, Hou Guimin, Liu Qiang, Zhang Yalei

Chief Reviewers:

Shi Zhongheng, Yan Luguang, Qian Qingquan, Shen Jingyan, Shen Dachuan, Gao Jianqiang, Zhou Jian, Huang Guixing, Wang Yuefan, Bian Xiaochun, Mao Yufeng, Su Xiuyu, Gu Xiaoan, Shen Ping, Chen Wei

Translators:

Luo Li, Yan Peiliang, Yu Yi, Zeng Guobao, Sun Jiliang, Wang Zhirong, Wei Dehao, Zhao Dongliang, Jin Shoujie, Yang Zhihao, Li Jie, Zhang Yichen, Chen Xiaohong, Liu Haijian, Zhang Xueshan, Tang Min, Zhou Hua, Liu Lingzhi, Zeng Guofeng, Zhang Xingzhao, Xia Leng, Wang Liyan, Yan Wenfeng, Lin Guobin, Cheng Yanxia, Wu Yajing, Sun Chen, Mei Guangyu, Yun Zhaoguang, Li Xin

Contents

1 General Provisions

1.0.1 This code is prepared with a view to ensuring the safety, reliability, functional reasonability, economy and rationality, energy conservation, environment friendliness and technological advancement of medium and low speed maglev transit systems.

1.0.2 This code is applicable to the design of construction works of medium and low speed maglev transit system with the maximum running speed of 120 km/h that uses normal-conductive maglev technology for levitation and guidance and uses linear induction motor for traction and electric braking.

1.0.3 The design of medium and low speed maglev transit projects shall be in compliance with the overall urban planning and urban rail traffic network planning of the local regions. The rail route shall be determined based on passenger flow predication to attract maximum ridership.

1.0.4 The design years of medium and low speed maglev transit projects can be classified into initial, near-term and long-term years, which refer to the 3 years, 10 years and 25 years after completion respectively.

1.0.5 The design of medium and low speed maglev transit projects shall be planned in an overall manner. Near-term design and long-term design shall be planned in a coordinated way and implemented phase by phase. The construction scale, train formation, equipment capacity, and the land areas of depot and stabling yard shall be determined according to predicted long-term ridership and line carrying capacity. For constructions and equipment that may be built in stages, staged extension and addition shall be carried out.

1.0.6 The design service life of the main structure of medium and low speed maglev transit system shall be 100 years.

1.0.7 The medium and low speed maglev transit lines shall be fully enclosed.

1.0.8 The train formation in the initial, near-term and long-term periods shall be determined based on the predicted ridership, rated carrying capacity and train frequency for these periods.

1.0.9 Convenient transfer shall be realized among the medium and low speed maglev transit lines as well as between medium and low speed maglev transit line and other modes of transport.

1.0.10 The form of medium and low speed maglev transit lines shall be at-ground or elevated. In areas with special requirements, underground line may be also allowed.

1.0.11 The seismic fortification intensity of medium and low speed maglev transit projects shall be determined according to the seismic safety evaluation results approved by local government authorities.

1.0.12 The ground and elevated parts of medium and low speed maglev transit line across river or adjacent to a river shall be designed according to the flood frequency of 1/100 and anti-collision measures shall be considered for piers.

1.0.13 The electromechanical equipment and vehicles in medium and low speed maglev transit system shall meet the functionality requirements and shall be technologically advanced and economically feasible. They shall be gradually standardized and serialized.

1. 0. 14　In the design of medium and low speed maglev transit projects, the construction scale and system standard shall be strictly controlled without compromise on safety, reliability and functionality to reasonably control the construction cost and operating cost.

1. 0. 15　Medium and low speed maglev transit project shall be designed with protection measures against fire and other disasters, accidents and faults as well as evacuation and rescue routes and other relevant facilities in line sections.

1. 0. 16　In addition to the requirements stipulated in the design of medium and low speed maglev transit, those stipulated in the current relevant standards of the nation shall be complied with.

2 Terms

2.0.1 Medium and low speed maglev transit

Normal conductive maglev transit system driven by linear induction motor with stator placed on vehicle.

2.0.2 Medium and low speed maglev vehicle

Vehicle that uses normal conductive maglev technology to achieve levitation and guidance and uses linear induction motor to realize traction and electric braking.

2.0.3 Designed lifetime

A period during which the designed structure can be used for its intended purposes under normal maintenance conditions without major overhauls.

2.0.4 Operation routing

The process of designing each line sections in the round trip of train between turn-back points.

2.0.5 Traveling speed

Average speed of train running from starting station to terminal station (including station dwell time).

2.0.6 Monotonous passenger transport capacity

The upper limit of number of passengers passing through the cross section of line in a single direction per unit time, that is, the product of the rated passenger capacity and the upper limit of train frequency.

2.0.7 Gauge

Gauges are set to ensure the safe operation of urban rail transit, define the sectional dimensions of vehicle, limit the installation dimensions of the equipment along the rail, determine the effective net dimensions and profile of the buildings and structures along the rail, and determine the relevant positioning coordinates and parameters. Gauges can be classified into vehicle gauge, equipment gauge and structure gauge.

2.0.8 Vehicle profile

Envelopes of all cross sections of the vehicle.

2.0.9 Vehicle gauge

The maximum dynamic envelope of a vehicle running under normal operation condition along a straight line, used for vehicle manufacturing control and the positioning and sizing of platform and platform screen door.

2.0.10 Equipment gauge

The maximum dynamic envelope of a vehicle in faulty status, used for limiting the installation of equipment in operation area.

2.0.11 Structure gauge

The minimum size required for installing equipment and pipelines outside the equipment gauge.

2.0.12 Track structure

A complex structure in rail equipment or facilities, used for supporting and guiding the vehicle and transferring the load of vehicle to the substructure.

2.0.13 At-ground structure

Subgrade structure built at the ground.

2.0.14 F-type rail

A fundamental structural member that carries the levitation load, guidance load and traction load of maglev vehicles. It is composed of F-shaped steel and induction plates.

The inner F-shaped steel leg and outer F-shaped steel leg corresponding to the two magnetic pole plates of levitation electromagnet are respectively referred to as the inner and outer magnetic poles of the F-shaped rail. The end faces of the magnetic poles are called magnetic pole faces. The lower surface of the F-shaped steel web plate is called levitation inspection surface.

2.0.15 Reaction plate

A secondary component of the linear tractional induction motor, made of non-magnetic conductive material, mounted on F-type rail.

2.0.16 Reference

Reference is a measurement reference point that controls the size of each component of the vehicle and the relative position relationship between the vehicle and the rail. In theory, the levitation interface between the vehicle and the F-shaped rail should be taken as reference. But in practice, other positions are used for convenient measurement, such as the support surface of F-shaped rail or the top surface of sleeper. The midpoint of reference surface is the reference point.

2.0.17 Track gauge

The distance between the magnetic pole centerlines of F-shaped rails on both sides of rail beam.

2.0.18 Transport rail

A basic unit of the medium and low speed maglev transit line, responsible for supporting the maglev vehicle, bearing the levitation load, guidance load and traction load of the vehicle. Track panel consist of F-shaped rails, sleepers and fasteners and can be classified into the following categories:

    1 Linear rail, with a straight centerline.

    2 Circular curve rail, with a circular curve centerline.

    3 Transition curve rail, with a transition curve centerline.

    Note:1 The length of track panel refers to the length of rail centerline.

        2 The rail centerline refers to the symmetric center of two F-shaped rails.

2.0.19 Cross slope

A transverse slope provided to eliminate or reduce the transverse acceleration generated by the medium and low speed maglev vehicle running at curved section, with the slope angle expressed by the angle between the rail surface and the transverse ground line.

2.0.20 Medium and low speed maglev turnout

Route changing equipment of medium and low speed maglev line, composed of the switch, drive, locker, controlling system and signaling system. According to the structural composition and the status of the routes after route switching, turnouts can be classified into single turnout, three-way turnout, equilateral turnout, single crossover turnout and scissors crossover turnout.

2.0.21 Contact rail

A conductor rail on lateral side of rail beam, supplying power to medium and low speed maglev train via current collector.

2.0.22 Location and speed measuring system

A measuring system used for detecting the position, running direction and speed of the train.

3 Vehicle

3.1 General Requirements

3.1.1 1500 V DC power supply should be used for medium and low speed maglev transit vehicles. 750 V DC power supply may be used.

3.1.2 The types of medium and low speed maglev transit vehicles shall include end vehicles and intermediate vehicles. The technical specifications of the vehicles shall comply with the current professional standard CJ/T 375 *General Technical Specification for Medium and Low Speed Maglev Vehicles*.

3.2 Related Facilities

3.2.1 Mode of safe evacuation through side door shall be set for the medium and low speed maglev transit, and the vehicles of the train shall be interconnected with each other.

3.2.2 Regenerative braking energy absorption devices shall be used for the medium and low speed maglev transit, and the regenerative braking energy absorption devices shall be installed in the power supply system.

3.2.3 The communication facilities and functions of the train shall comply with the current national standard GB 50490 *Technical Code of Urban Rail Transit*.

3.3 Electrical Hazards and Equipment Protection

3.3.1 The vehicles shall be equipped with the grounding brushes which are compatible with the grounding devices in station and depot.

3.3.2 The vehicle protection against electrical hazards shall comply with the current national standard GB/T 21414 *Railway Applications - Rolling Stock - Protective Provisions against Electrical Hazards*.

3.3.3 The main protection system of vehicle shall be coordinated with the substation protection system and shall ensure safe breaking in case of vehicle fault.

4 Operational Organization and Operating Management

4.1 General Requirements

4.1.1 The passenger transport capacity of the system shall be designed to accommodate the forecasted long-term maximum monotonous section passenger flow in rush hour, with a 10% margin.

4.1.2 The operation statuses shall include normal operation condition, abnormal operation condition, and emergency operation status. The system must be operated under the conditions that all the staff and passenger access to the system and all the facilities of the system are safe.

4.2 Operational Organization

4.2.1 The design operation capacity shall be designed based on the turn-back mode, train formation and rated passenger transport capacity, thus determining a reasonable departing time interval to accommodate the predicted passenger flow and meet the demand of long-term maximum monotonous sectional passenger flow in rush hour.

4.2.2 Train formation and operation routing shall be determined based on the forecasted passenger flow and cross-section flow distribution for each design year.

4.2.3 The train departing time interval for each design year shall be determined based on the forecasted passenger flow, train formation and rated passenger capacity, which should not be larger than 2.5 min (24 pairs/ h) at minimum during the long-term rush hours and may be increased as appropriate for suburb lines based on the passenger flow forecast results.

4.2.4 The number of trains shall be configured based on the initial operation needs and increased as needed according to the near-term and long-term growth of passenger flow.

4.3 Operational Sidings

4.3.1 A parking line or transition line should be set at an interval of 3 stations to 5 stations or 8 km to 10 km along the line.

4.3.2 The departing/arriving line at vehicle base shall be connected with the upward and downward main lines, and the carrying capacity shall be determined and checked based on the long-term carrying capacity of the line and the operation requirements. The departing/arriving line at vehicle base should be intersected with the main line. A single departing/arriving line may be allowed where conditions are difficult due to limited space in stabling yard.

4.4 Operating Management

4.4.1 The medium and low speed maglev transit lines shall be of fully enclosed type, the train must operate under the monitoring and control of the safety protection system.

4.4.2 The operation time of medium and low speed maglev transit line should not be less than 18 h, the effective time for nighttime maintenance and repair shall not be less than 3 h.

4.4.3 The operation personnel quota of medium and low speed maglev transit should be controlled within 60 persons/km to 80 persons/km.

4.4.4 Crew shift system should be adopted, turn-back driver and service facilities should be provided at the turn-back station.

5 Gauge

5.1 General Requirements

5.1.1 The gauges for medium and low maglev transit shall be classified into vehicle gauge, equipment gauge, and structure gauge.

5.1.2 The clearance between structure gauge and equipment gauge shall allow for pipe installation. The clearance shall not be less than 200 mm, and in difficult sections, it shall not be less than 100 mm. A safety clearance of 50 mm should be reserved between the equipment gauge and the equipment to be installed.

5.1.3 For the adjacent lines, the safety clearance between the two equipment gauges shall not be less than 100 mm where no wall, column, or equipment exists between two lines, or shall be determined based on the structure gauge plus the width of wall or column and the construction error where there is wall or column between two lines.

5.1.4 The vehicle gauge and equipment gauge for straight sections should be calculated in accordance with Appendix A of this code, while that for curve sections should be calculated according to Appendix B in this code.

5.2 Basic Parameters

5.2.1 The basic vehicle parameters for calculating gauge should be determined based on the vehicle parameters in the current professional standard CJ/T 375 *General Technical Specification for Medium and Low Speed Maglev Vehicles*.

5.2.2 The parameters for calculating gauge shall be in accordance with the following requirements:

    1 The minimum radius of horizontal curve (stabling yard) shall be 50 m.

    2 The minimum radius of vertical curve shall be 1000 m.

    3 The maximum slope angle of cross slope of the track shall be 6° (rotating around the centerline of the track).

    4 The rate of twist of cross slope shall be 0.12°/m normally, and be 0.15°/m maximum.

    5 The crosswind load of elevated line or ground line shall be 400 N/m².

    6 The design speed for calculation at passing the station shall be 60 km/h.

5.2.3 The gauge coordinate system shall be a Cartesian coordinate with the reference point as the origin, the positive direction of Y-axis pointing upwards and the positive direction of X-axis pointing rightwards.

5.3 Structure Gauge

5.3.1 The structure gauges shall be classified into rectangular tunnel structure gauge, circular tunnel structure gauge, elevated and ground structure gauge, as well as station and vehicle base yard line structure gauge.

5.3.2 The structure gauge of rectangular tunnelshall be calculated in accordance with the following requirements:

1 For straight section of rectangular tunnel stucture gauge:

1) Width of structure gauge:

$$B_S = B_L + B_R \tag{5.3.2-1}$$

Clearance distance from the centerline of track to the left wall of tunnel:

$$B_L = X_S + b_L + c \tag{5.3.2-2}$$

Clearance distance from the centerline of line to the right wall of tunnel:

$$B_R = X_S + b_R + c \tag{5.3.2-3}$$

Where, B_S——Width of structure gauge for straight section of single-line rectangular tunnel (mm);

B_L——Distance from the centerline of line of the rectangular tunnel to the left side of the tunnel structure gauge (mm);

B_R——Distance from the centerline of line in rectangular tunnel to the right side of the tunnel structure gauge (mm);

X_S——Maximum width of equipment gauge in straight section (mm);

b_L——Maximum width of equipment or support on the left side of tunnel (mm);

b_R——Maximum width of equipment or support on the right side of tunnel (mm);

c——Safety clearance, in which the equipment installation error and measurement error are considered (mm).

2) Height of structure gauge: The equipment gauge shall be increased by 200 mm and no less than 100 mm at minimum on the top and no less than 200 mm at the bottom.

2 For curve section of rectangular tunnel stucture gauge:

1) Outer width of curve structure gauge:

$$B_a = X_{Ka} \cos\alpha - Y_{Ka} \sin\alpha + b_R (\text{or } b_L) + c \tag{5.3.2-4}$$

2) Inner width of curve structure gauge:

$$B_i = X_{Ki} \cos\alpha + Y_{Ki} \sin\alpha + b_L (\text{or } b_R) + c \tag{5.3.2-5}$$

3) Height of curve structure gauge:

$$B_u = X_{Kh} \sin\alpha + Y_{Kh} \cos\alpha + h_3 + 200 \tag{5.3.2-6}$$

Where, B_a——Outer width of structure gauge curve (mm);

B_i——Inner width of structure gauge curve (mm);

B_u——Height of structure gauge at curve section of rectangular tunnel (mm);

α——Cross slope angle of curve section (°);

h_3——Height of track structure (mm);

X_{Ka}——Horizontal coordinate of outer control point of equipment gauge curve before inclination of cross slope (mm);

Y_{Ka}——Longitudinal coordinate of outer control point of equipment gauge curve before inclination of cross slope (mm);

X_{Ki}——Horizontal coordinate of inner control point of equipment gauge curve before inclination of cross slope (mm);

Y_{Ki}——Longitudinal coordinate of inner control point of equipment gauge curve before inclination of cross slope (mm);

X_{Kh}——Horizontal coordinate of the maximum height point of equipment gauge curve before inclination of cross slope (mm);

Y_{Kh}——Longitudinal coordinate of the maximum height point of equipment gauge curve before inclination of cross slope (mm).

3 The structure gauge of rectangular tunnel at the transition curve section shall be calculated based on such factors as the radius of curvature and cross slope angle at the position of the curve.

4 The maximum height of the curve section should be taken as the height of structure gauge of the whole rectangular tunnel.

5.3.3 The structure gauge of a single-line circular tunnel shall be determined based on the minimum plane curve radius and the maximum cross slope angle of the section in which shield construction method is adopted throughout.

5.3.4 In the curve super-elevation section of circular tunnel, the centerline of the tunnel shall be deviated towards the inner side of the reference line of the line to solve the problem of uneven offset between inner and outer sides resulting from track super-elevation. The offset shall be calculated according to the following formula:

1 When the super-elevation is set up by rotating from the center:

$$x' = h_0 \sin\alpha \qquad\qquad (5.3.4\text{-}1)$$

$$y' = -h_0(1-\cos\alpha) \qquad\qquad (5.3.4\text{-}2)$$

2 When the super-elevation is set by raising one side of the F-shaped rail:

x' shall be calculated according to the formula (5.3.4-1) and y' shall be calculated according to the formula (5.3.4-3).

$$y' = (G \cdot \sin\alpha)/2 - h_0(1-\cos\alpha) \qquad\qquad (5.3.4\text{-}3)$$

Where, x'——Horizontal offset of tunnel centerline relative to inner side of track reference line (mm);

y'——Vertical offset of tunnel centerline (mm);

h_0——Height from tunnel centerline to the sliding surface of F-shaped rail (mm);

α——Cross slope angle of curve section (°);

G——Track gauge (mm).

5.3.5 The structure gauge for elevated line or ground line shall be in accordance with the following requirements:

1 The structure gauges for line sections and stations of elevated line and ground line shall be calculated based on the equipment gauge and equipment installation dimensions determined in Appendix A and Appendix B in this code.

2 Where no maintenance passage or pedestrian passage exists on one side of the line, the minimum clearance between structure gauge and equipment gaugeshall not be less than 200 mm. Where there is a maintenance passage or a pedestrian passage on one side, the safety clearance between the passage and the equipment gauge shall not be less than 50 mm.

3 Where sound barrier is provided on one side of the line, the safety clearance between the sound barrier and the equipment gauge shall not be less than 200 mm.

4 The height of structure gauge shall be determined based on the height of structure gauge of the rectangular tunnel.

5.3.6 The structure gauge of turnout section shall be widened respectively for super-elevation deficiency and curve track parameters calculated for the technical parameters for various types of turn-outs and vehicles on the basis of the structure gauge of straight line section.

5.3.7 Where fans and turnout drive equipment are installed in the tunnel, the gauge requirements shall be satisfied and local widening and heightening measures shall be taken for the structure gauge as necessary.

5.3.8 The structure gauge of straight section of the station shall be in accordance with the following requirements:

1 The surface of platform shall not be higher than the surface of carriage floor of the vehicle under non-levitation state with the air spring uninflated.

2 The distance between the platform edge within the calculation length of platform and the centerline of the line shall be designed not to intrude into the vehicle gauge. The clearance between the platform edge and the vehicle profile shall be in accordance with the following requirements:

    1) When sliding plug doors are used for the vehicle, the lateral clearance between the platform edge and the vehicle profile shall not be larger than $100 {}^{+5}_{0}$ mm;

    2) When containing doors or external doors are used, the lateral clearance between the platform edge and the vehicle profile shall be $70 {}^{+5}_{0}$ mm.

3 The distance between the platform edge outside the station's calculation length and the centerline of the line should be equal to the equipment gauge plus a safety clearance of not less than 50 mm.

4 For the structure gauges of other parts in the scope of the station, the structure gauge for the line section shall apply.

5 Where a platform screen door is set in the station, the installation dimensions of the platform screen door shall be designed to reserve a safety clearance of no less than 25 mm between the outermost protruding point of the platform screen door and the vehicle gauge.

5.3.9 The clearance between the curve station platform edge and the vehicle gauge shall not be larger than 150 mm.

5.3.10 For the structure gauge of flood gate and civil air-defense gate, a safety clearance of no less than 100 mm shall be reserved between the inner edge on top of the gate frame and the equipment gauge, and between the inner edge along the width of gate frame and the outermost protruding point of equipment gauge.

5.3.11 The structure gauge of vehicle base shall be in accordance with the following requirements:

1 For the structure gauge outside the garage at vehicle base, the structure gauge for the line section shall apply.

2 The transverse clearance between the garage gate of vehicle base and the equipment gauge shall not be less than 100 mm.

3 The minimum height of the garage gate of the vehicle base shall be equal to the height of vehicle plus a safety clearance of no less than 200 mm.

4 The safety clearance of 80 mm shall be reserved between the higher maintenance platform in the garage of vehicle base and the vehicle profile. For lower maintenance platforms, the safety clearance shall be determined using the same method for ordinary platforms.

6 Line

6.1 General Requirements

6.1.1 The medium and low speed maglev transit line shall be designed into a dual-line system with separated upward and downward routes. The train shall operate on the right-side route.

6.1.2 The medium and low speed maglev transit line shall be classified into the main line (including the branch line), siding, and yard line according to its position and role in operation.

6.1.3 The routing of the medium and low-speed maglev transit lines shall be determined taking into account the overall urban planning, geographical environment, terrain conditions, characteristics of the regions the line passes through, and the relevant requirements in terminologies of operation safety, fire protection, vibration reduction, noise reduction, landscape, energy conservation, emission reduction, and resident privacy.

6.1.4 The main line of medium and low speed maglev transit system should be laid in an elevated and fully enclosed way. The line plane position and elevation and the way of laying shall be determined by making comprehensive technical and economic comparison based on the current urban conditions and road planning, ground buildings, pipelines and other structures, cultural relics protection requirements, environment and landscape, topography, engineering geological and hydrogeological conditions, type of structure adopted, construction methods, and operation requirements.

6.1.5 The stations shall be located at the main passenger flow points, transportation hubs, and transfer points of rail transit.

6.1.6 Line, signaling, control, and measuring signs and markers shall be set for the stations, sections, and stabling yard along the whole line.

6.2 Plane of Line

6.2.1 The curve radius of the plane of line shall be reasonably determined according to the type of the line, traveling speed, and construction difficulty, taking into account the surrounding environment. The curve radius of the plane of line shall not be less than those specified in Table 6.2.1.

Table 6.2.1 Minimum Radius of Plane Curve (m)

Line	Under normal conditions	Under difficult conditions
Main line	150	100
Departing/arriving line, connecting line	100 (under the maximum gross weight)	75 (under the weight in readiness state)
Yard line	75	50

6.2.2 The line should be designed based on the track panel module of 1.2 m.

6.2.3 Compound curve should not be taken for the line.

6.2.4 Cross slope shall be set in curve section according to the train passing speed and the curve radius, which shall be in accordance with the following requirements:

    1 The cross slope angle shall be calculated according to the following formula:

$$\alpha = \frac{0.45V^2}{R} \qquad\qquad (6.2.4)$$

Where, α——Cross slope angle, degree (°);

      V——Train passing speed (km/h);

      R——Curve radius (m).

2 The maximum cross slope angle of the line shall not be larger than 6°.

3 The cross slope angle under the maximum allowable super-elevation deficiency shall not be larger than 2.3°.

4 Cross slope shall not be set at turn-outs.

5 The cross slope shall gradually change within the range of transition curve. The rate of twist of cross slope should not be larger than 5'/m in normal conditions, and shall not be larger than 7'12"/m under difficult conditions.

6.2.5 Transition curve shall be set between the circular curve and straight line of the plane of line according to the curve radius, cross slope setting, design speed, and other factors. The transition curve should be of cubic parabolic shape, and the length should not be less than those specified in Table 6.2.5.

6.2.6 For the associated curve of turn-out, transition curve may not be set, but the curve radius shall not be less than the lead curve radius.

6.2.7 The minimum length of the circular curve on the main line, connecting line, and the departing/arriving line in vehicle base should not be less than 18 m, orshall not be less than 14.4 m under difficult conditions. The yard line shall not be less than 3.6m. The minimum length of main line, connecting line, vehicle base departing/arriving line, and intermediate straight line between two adjacent curves without super-elevation shall be determined according to Table 6.2.7.

Table 6.2.5 Length of Transition Curve（m）

L / V → R ↓	100 N	100 D	95 N	95 D	90 N	90 D	85 N	85 D	80 N	80 D	75 N	75 D	70 N	70 D	65 N	65 D	60 N	60 D	55 N	55 D	50 N	50 D	45 N	45 D	40 N	40 D	35 N	35 D	30 N	30 D
3000	30	18	24	18	24	18	18		18		18		18		18		18		18		18		18		18		18		18	
2500	36	18	30	18	24	18	24	18	18		18		18		18		18		18		18		18		18		18	
2000	42	18	36	18	30	18	24	18	24	18	18		18		18		18		18		18		18		18		18	
1500	54	18	48	18	42	18	36	18	30	18	24	18	18		18		18		18		18		18		18		18	
1200	72	30	60	18	54	18	42	18	36	18	30	18	24	18	18		18		18		18		18		18		18	
1000	84	42	72	30	60	24	54	18	42	18	36	18	30	18	24	18	18		18		18		18		18		18	
800	108	60	90	48	78	36	66	30	54	18	42	18	36	18	30	18	24	18	18	18	18		18		18		18	
700	114	78	102	60	90	48	72	36	60	30	54	18	42	18	36	18	30	18	18	18	18		18		18		18	
650	114	84	108	72	96	54	78	42	66	30	54	24	42	18	36	18	30	18	18	18	18		18		18		18	
600	114	96	108	78	102	66	84	48	72	36	60	30	48	18	42	18	36	18	18	18	18		18		18		18	
550	114	108	108	90	102	72	96	60	78	42	66	30	54	24	42	18	36	18	18	18	18		18		18		18	
500	—	—	108	102	102	84	96	66	84	54	72	36	60	30	48	18	42	18	36	18	24	18	18		18		18		18	
450	—	—	—	—	102	96	96	78	90	60	78	48	66	36	54	24	42	18	36	18	24	18	18		18		18		18	

Table 6. 2. 5 (Continued)

R \ V	100		95		90		85		80		75		70		65		60		55		50		45		40		35		30	
	N	D	N	D	N	D	N	D	N	D	N	D	N	D	N	D	N	D	N	D	N	D	N	D	N	D	N	D	N	D
400	—	—	—	—	—	—	96	90	90	72	84	54	72	42	60	30	48	24	42	18	24	18	24	18	18		18		18	
350	—	—	—	—	—	—	—	—	90	90	84	72	78	54	66	36	54	30	48	18	30	18	24	18	18		18		18	
300	—	—	—	—	—	—	—	—	—	—	—	—	78	66	72	48	66	36	54	30	36	18	30	18	24	18	18		18	
250	—	—	—	—	—	—	—	—	—	—	—	—	—	—	72	66	72	48	66	36	42	24	36	18	30	18	24	18	18	
200	—	—	—	—	—	—	—	—	—	—	—	—	—	—	—	—	72	72	72	54	48	30	42	24	36	18	24	18	18	
150	—	—	—	—	—	—	—	—	—	—	—	—	—	—	—	—	—	—	—	—	54	48	54	36	42	24	36	18	24	18
100	—	—	—	—	—	—	—	—	—	—	—	—	—	—	—	—	—	—	—	—	—	—	54	42	48	30	36	18

N—normal; D—difficult.

Note: 1 R—Curve radius (m); V—Design speed (km/h); L—Length of transition curve (m);

2 Where a circular curve with large radius is selected, a transition curve with the length based on the calculation track super-elevation is used;

3 In the determination of transition curve, the deflection angle of the curve is not be larger than 24°.

Table 6. 2. 7 Minimum Length of Intermediate Straight Line (m)

Main line, connecting line, inlet/outlet line	Under normal conditions ($V \geqslant 36$)	0. 5V
	Minimum length under difficult conditions	18
Yard line	Adjacent curves with identical direction	3. 6
	Adjacent curves with reverse direction	14. 4

Note: V refers to the running speed of the train passing through the intermediate straight line (km/h).

6. 2. 8   The line segment in the calculation platform length of the station platform should be a straight segment. Where it is necessary to be a curve segment, the curve radius should not be less than 600 m.

6. 2. 9   The turnout should be close to the station. The distance from the end of buttress girder of the turnout to the end of calculation length of platform shall not be less than the length of one vehicle, or shall not be less than 5 m under difficult conditions (while shall be reduced the width of the platform).

6. 2. 10   The turnout shall be set on a straight line. The distance from the end of buttress girder of the turnout to the starting point of horizontal curve should not be less than 20 m for the main line, and not less than 5 m for the yard line.

6. 2. 11   The effective length of the turn back line and the faulty train parking line (excluding the length of buffer stop) shall not be less than those specified in Table 6. 2. 11.

Table 6. 2. 11 Effective Length of Turn Back Line and Faulty Train Parking Line (m)

Name of line	Effective length+Safety distance (excluding the length of buffer stop)
End type turn-back line, parking line	Long-term train length +50
Through type turn-back line, parking line	Near-term train length +64. 8

6. 3   Profile of Line

6. 3. 1   The designed slope gradient of the line shall be in accordance with the following requirements:

1 The maximum longitudinal slope gradient of the main line should not be larger than 60‰, provided that a maximum longitudinal slope gradient of 65‰ may be allowed in difficult sections. In special topographical areas of mountainous cities, the maximum slope gradient may be 70‰ where it is proved reasonable by technical and economic comparison.

2 The maximum slope gradient of connecting line and inlet/outlet line shall not be larger than 70‰ (any slope gradient allowance not considered). The maximum slope gradient of yard line shall not be larger than 3‰ outside the garage, and the slope gradient in the garage shall be zero.

6.3.2 The minimum slope gradient of the main line in a tunnel or cutting section should be 3‰, and 2‰ may be allowed under difficult conditions.

6.3.3 For an underground station, the slope gradient of the section in the calculation length of platform should be 2‰.

6.3.4 For the ground line or elevated line, the section in the calculation length of platform of the station should be set on a flat section. Where it is needed to set it on a ramp, the gradient shall not exceed 3‰.

6.3.5 The turn-back line and parking line should be arranged on a flat slope, or on a ramp no larger than 10‰ facing the buffer stop under difficult conditions.

6.3.6 The section in the calculation length of platform of the station shall be set on a ramp. Where conditions permit, the station should be arranged on a convex part of the vertical section and a reasonable energy conservation inlet/outlet slope is provided.

6.3.7 The turnout should be set on a flat section. Where it is necessary to set it on a slope, the gradient shall not be larger than 3‰.

6.3.8 The minimum slope length in the longitudinal section shall not be less than the long-term train formation length, and the length of intermediate straight line between two adjacent vertical curves shall not be less than 40 m.

6.3.9 When the algebraic difference of slope gradient of two adjacent slopes is larger than or equal to 2‰, they shall be connected by a vertical circular curve of which the radius shall not be less than those specified in Table 6.3.9. The vertical curve should not overlap with horizontal transition curve.

Table 6.3.9　Minimum Radius of Vertical Curve (m)

Line		Under normal conditions	Under difficult conditions
Main Line	Section	5000	2000
	Ends of station	3000	1500
Connecting line, inlet/outlet line		1500	
Yard line		1000	

6.3.10 Vertical curve shall not be set within the calculation length of the platform and in the range of turnout. The distance from the vertical curve to the end of the turnout shall not be less than 6 m.

6.3.11 At the main line sections where two straight lines are in parallel, the elevations of track surfaces should be designed to be identical.

7　Track

7.1　General Requirements

7.1.1　The structure of track shall have sufficient strength, stability, durability and appropriate elasticity to ensure safe, steady, fast operation of maglev train and passenger comfort.

7.1.2　The structure of track shall be built using commercially proven, advanced technologies and construction techniques.

7.1.3　The track structure should be uniform throughout the maglev line. The structure of track shall be simple and easy to maintain and repair under the premise that the functional requirements are met.

7.1.4　Tracks and turnouts within elevated and at-ground line sections shall be provided with lightning protection devices with the grounding resistance not larger than 10 Ω.

7.1.5　The main structure and support blocks of track shall be designed for a service life of not less than 100 years.

7.2　Track Panel and Composition

7.2.1　The standard length of track panel should be 12 m. The length of track panel less than 12 m should be a multiple of the track module 1.2 m and shall not be less than 3.6 m.

7.2.2　The sleeper spacing should be generally 1.2 m. Sleeper spacing at track panel joints should be 0.8m. In special cases, a spacing of 0.6 m to 1.2 m may be also allowed.

7.2.3　The determination of curve superelevation shall be in accordance with the following requirements:

　　1　Superelevation shall be calculated as follows:

$$h = \frac{D \cdot V_{\mathrm{C}}^2}{12.96g \cdot R} \tag{7.2.3}$$

Where, h——Superelevation (mm);

　　　　D——Track gauge (mm);

　　　V_{C}——Train running speed (km/h);

　　　　g——Gravitational acceleration (9.81 m/s^2);

　　　　R——Curve radius (m).

　　2　The angle between the plane passing through tracksurface at the maximum superelevation and the horizontal plane shall not exceed 6°.

　　3　The superelevation shall be gradually decremented within transition curve. In case of tough condition where there is no transition curve, it shall be decremented within the straight line segment.

　　4　The superelevation shall be achieved by elevating the outer track for half of the superelevation and lowering the inner track for the other half of the superelevation.

　　5　The superelevation slope rate should not be larger than 2‰. In case of tough conditions, it shall not be larger than 3‰.

7.2.4 The anti-corrosion coating of track panels shall comply with the current professional standard CJ/T 413 *Technical Specification for Low and Medium Speed Maglev Train Transport Rail Row*.

7.3 Substructure and Fastening

7.3.1 The design of track bearing platform shall be in accordance with the following requirements:

1 The track bearing platform should be of a reinforced concrete structure and the concrete grade should be C40.

2 Reinforcement measures shall be taken at the joint between track bearing platform and underlying pier and that between track bearing platform and bridge deck.

3 The height of track bearing platform shall meet the installation conditions of fasteners.

7.3.2 The track fasteners shall be in accordance with the following requirements:

1 The structures of fasteners shall be as simple as possible.

2 The fasteners shall have sufficient strength, fastening force, moderate elasticity.

3 The fasteners shall have good insulation performance and corrosion resistance.

7.3.3 The joint between track and track bearing platform shall be easy to maintain and repair.

7.4 Tectonic of Track Construction and Precision Requirements

7.4.1 The structure of track bed shall be in accordance with the following requirements:

1 The main lines should be supported by track beams. In special positions, track bearing beams may also be used.

2 Track beams should be used outside stabling yard and depot.

3 Track panels supported by columns should be used within stabling yard and depot.

7.4.2 The height of track structure shall be determined by calculation according to the structural type of track, the structural parameters of vehicle, the structural parameters of turnout and gauges.

7.4.3 The structural type of track shall be in accordance with the following requirements:

1 The track bearing beam shall be of reinforced concrete structure and the concrete grade should be C40.

2 The track bearing platform may be of reinforced concrete structure and the concrete grade should be C40. Steel structure may be also allowed.

3 Reinforcement measures shall be taken for the joint between track bearing platform and underlying piers and that between track bearing platform and bridge deck.

4 The structural height of track bearing platform shall meet the installation conditions of support blocks.

7.4.4 The geometric accuracy of track structure shall be in accordance with those specified in Table 7.4.4.

Table 7.4.4 Geometric Accuracy Requirements of Track Structure

Item	Allowable deviation
Track gauge (distance between centers of rails)	±3 mm
Flatness of magnetic pole face of track panel	±1.5 mm/3 m

Table 7. 4. 4 (Continued)

Item	Allowable deviation
Track height difference (rise in each 10 m length)	±3 mm/10 m
Track direction deviation (rise in each 10 m length)	±3 mm/10 m
Allowed track joint deviation (vertical/horizontal)	±1 mm/±1 mm

7. 5   Accessory Facilities of Track

7. 5. 1   Sliding type buffer stops should be used at the ends of the main line, auxiliary line and test line. Hydraulic buffer stops shall be used at the ends of underground line. Hydraulic buffer stops should be used for the line sections within stabling yard and depot.

7. 5. 2   The serial numbers of track panels shall be indicated at conspicuous positions on tracks.

7. 6   Joint

7. 6. 1   For continuously arranged bridge, where the spacing of fixed bearings is larger than 12 m, track panel joint shall be used as the guideway connection at beam gap. The expansion allowance of the track panel joint shall meet the thermal expansion requirement of bridge span.

7. 6. 2   The joint gap between track joints should be taken as 16 mm. The track gap reserved when laying track panels shall be determined based on the length of track panel and the work temperature of steel track.

7. 6. 3   Track joints shall be provided at the joint between bridges and the joint between bridge and abutment.

7. 7   Turnout

7. 7. 1   Turnout equipment shall be in accordance with the following requirements:

    1   The control circuits of turnout system shall comply with the *Failure-Safety Principles*.

    2   The control system and interface circuits of turnout system shall comply with the current professional standard CJ/T 412 *Technical Specification for Medium and Low Speed Maglev Turnout*.

    3   Surfaces of metallic components shall undergo anti-corrosion treatment. Turnouts used in cold areas shall be equipped with anti-freeze and heating facilities.

    4   The structure of turnout shall allow for easy operation and good maintainability.

    5   Turnout equipment shall be treated as Grade I power supply load.

    6   When integrated grounding system is used for turnout equipment, the grounding resistance shall not be larger than 1 Ω. When distributed grounding system is used, the grounding resistance shall not be larger than 4 Ω. The grounding resistance of lightning protection grounding system shall not be larger than 10 Ω.

    7   The turnout system shall be controlled by the signal system. In addition, the system shall provide centralized control mode, local control mode and manual control mode and shall have the functions of system inspection, fault diagnosis, protection and alarming.

    8   The turning time of the turnout shall not be larger than 15 s.

    9   When the turnout is switched to the lateral line, a speed limit of 25 km/h shall be applied. When the turnout is switched to the straight-running line, the maximum travel speed requirements of the train shall be met.

7.7.2   The installation of turnout shall be in accordance with the following requirements:

1   Installation of turnout equipment shall comply with the gauge requirements of Chapter 5 in this code.

2   Turnout shall be installed on solid and stable foundation. The turnout equipment at elevated line sections shall be installed on turnout bridge and that at at-ground line sections and in tunnel shall be installed on a dedicated turnout platform.

3   There shall not be expansion joints or settlement joints in turnout bridge or turnout platform.

4   The assembly deviation of turnout shall comply with the current professional standard CJ/T 412 *Technical Specification for Medium and Low Speed Maglev Turnout*.

5   Turnout zone shall be equipped with maintenance access, safety isolation facilities, power supply facilities for maintenance use and lighting facilities with the illuminance of not less than 50lx.

6   The power supply cables, communication and signal cables, and turnout control cables on turnout bridge and turnout platform shall be separately arranged in cable trough or cable trench depending on voltage level.

7   Video monitoring facilities should be installed in turnout zone.

8   Dedicated telephones should be provided in turnout zone.

7.8   Signs of Line and Signal

7.8.1   Maglev transit lines shall be provided with line signs and relevant signal signs.

7.8.2   The line signs shall mainly include 100 m sign, slope sign, curve element sign, curve start and end signs, vertical curve start and end signs, turnout serial number, expansion joint serial number and benchmark sign.

7.8.3   The relevant signal signs shall mainly include speed limit sign, speed limit cancellation sign and parking position sign.

7.8.4   100 m sign, slope sign, speed limit sign, parking position sign and fouling point sign should be made of reflective materials.

8 Track Support Structure

8.1 General Requirements

8.1.1 This chapter is applicable to the structural design of track supports, station track supports and elevated turnout bridges.

8.1.2 Track support structures shall be simple and elegant, and standardized and serialized design should be used. Their structural style and materials shall be beneficial to vibration and noise reduction and shall allow for easy construction, maintenance and operation. In addition, the structures shall also meet the requirements on vehicle operation safety and passenger comfort, and the architectural style and structure size shall be in good coordination with surrounding urban landscape. Prestressed concrete structure shall be used as thefirst option for track beams.

8.1.3 The span lengths of track beam bridge shall be determined according to the shape of cross section, bridge height and foundation depth while taking into consideration of economic indicators and other relevant factors. Medium-sized span length ($20\text{ m} \leqslant L \leqslant 30\text{ m}$) or small span length ($L < 20\text{ m}$) should be used. Where a span length of over 30 m is needed at the point where beam bridge crosses over a road or river, continuous beams, continuous rigid frame, tied arch structure or other combined bridge structures should be used.

8.1.4 For track beam bridges with medium span lengths ($20\text{ m} \leqslant L \leqslant 30\text{ m}$) or small span lengths ($L < 20\text{ m}$), simple supported beam structure shall be used preferably when conditions permit.

8.1.5 The layout of bridge piers in track support structure shall meet the requirements of urban planning. At railway or road crossovers, the clearance under the bridge shall meet the requirements of railway gauge and road gauge, and appropriate allowance for structure settlement, track bed elevation and road renovation height shall be considered. Line sections crossing flood discharge rivers shall be designed according to the flood frequency of $1/100$. The design of large bridges and extra-large bridges involving complicated technologies and great repair difficulties shall be checked according to the flood frequency of $1/300$. For line sections crossing navigable rivers, the clearance under bridge shall be determined in accordance with the grade of waterway and shall comply with the current national standard GB 50139 *Navigation Standard of Inland Waterway*.

8.1.6 The deformations of the reinforced concrete and prestressed concrete beam bridges under the static live load and temperature load of the train shall not exceed the allowable values in Table 8.1.6.

Table 8.1.6 **Allowable Deformations of Track Beam**

	Vertical deflection	Deformation due to temperature variation
Simply supported beam	$L/3800$	$L/6200$
Continuous beam	$L/4600$	$L/7600$

8.1.7 The horizontal deflection of beam body under the actions of train lateral guidance force, small-radius constraining force, centrifugal force, wind load and temperature stress shall not be larger than $1/2000$ of the design span of beam.

8.1.8 The vertical first-order inherent frequency of track beam shall be in accordance with the following requirements:

$$n_0 > 64/L \qquad (8.1.8)$$

Where, n_0——Vertical first-order inherent frequency of track beam (Hz);

L——Distance between bridge supporting points (m).

8.1.9 The horizontal elastic displacement of the top of track beam bridge piers under the actions of train load, lateral guidance force, centrifugal force, wind load and temperature stress shall be in accordance with the following requirements:

　　1 The displacement along the bridge shall be less than 10 mm.

　　2 The horizontal deflection angles of track beam ends caused by the horizontal displacement of pier shall not be larger than 1.5‰.

8.1.10 The settlement of track beam abutment shall be calculated according to dead load and shall be in accordance with the following requirements:

　　1 For external statically determinate structures, the difference between total settlement and the settlement during construction period shall not exceed the following allowable values:

　　　　1) Even settlement of the abutment: 30 mm.

　　　　2) Difference settlement between adjacent abutments: 5 mm.

　　2 For external statically indeterminate structures, the allowable difference settlement between adjacent abutments shall be determined according to the additional impacts of settlement on the structure.

8.1.11 The bridge intersection spacing should be designed to be 5 times the module of track panel, 6 m. In case of tough condition, the module of track panel may be taken as 1.2 m.

8.1.12 The guideway joints of medium and low speed maglev transit system at bridge beam gaps should be designed to be track panel joints with expansion couplings. The expansion and contraction of the expansion coupling shall be determined according to potential temperature change, concrete shrinkage and creep, shear deformation of bearing due to train braking force, installation temperature and other factors.

8.2 Loads

8.2.1 The structural design of supportingbeam bridge of medium and low speed maglev transit system shall be calculated according to the most unfavorable combinations of the loads listed in Table 8.2.1.

Table 8.2.1 Classification of Track Beam Bridge Loads

Type of load		Description of load
Primary loads	Dead load	Dead weight of structure; Dead weights of ancillary equipment and buildings; Prestress; Concrete contraction and creep impacts; Subgrade displacement impact; Earth pressure; Hydrostatic pressure and buoyancy

Table 8. 2. 1 (Continued)

Type of load		Description of load
Primary loads	Live load	Vertical static live load of train; Vertical dynamic action of train; Centrifugal force of train; Lateral guidance force of train; Small-radius constraining force; Earth pressure generated by live load of train; Crowd load
Additional forces		Train braking force or traction force; Wind load; Temperature load; Flowing water pressure
Special loads		Emergency braking force; Hits from ships or cars; Seismic force; Temporary construction load

Note: 1   If the main purpose of a member bar is to withstand a specific additional force, such additional force shall be treated as the main force in load calculations of the member bar.

 2   The lateral guidance force of the train is not be combined with centrifugal force and wind load.

 3   The flowing water pressure is not be combined with braking force or traction force.

 4   The combination of seismic force and other loads shall be made in accordance with the current national standard GB 50111 *Code for Seismic Design of Railway Engineering*.

 5   Other loads required to be considered in the calculation may be included in the corresponding load categories according to their nature.

8. 2. 2   In the design of track beam bridge, the combination of main forces and additional forces shall be made in accordance with the current professional standard TB 10002 *Code for Design on Railway Bridge and Culvert*.

8. 2. 3   Depending on the specific load combinations, the basic allowable stress of the material and the allowable bearing capacity of the substructure shall be multiplied by appropriate improvement factors. In calculation of strength and crack resistance of prestressed concrete structures, safety factors shall be used in accordance with the current professional standard TB 10002 *Code for Design on Railway Bridge and Culvert*.

8. 2. 4   When calculating the dead weight of structure, the unit weights of commonly used materials shall comply with the current professional standard TB 10002 *Code for Design on Railway Bridge and Culvert*. For the dead weights of ancillary equipment and buildings or the unit weights of materials, the relevant current national standards may apply.

8. 2. 5   The vertical static load of train shall be determined in accordance with the following requirements:

 1   The vertical static load diagram of train shall be determined according to the train's dead weight, maximum carrying capacity and the longest train formation in the near and long terminologies.

 2   In the design of the underlying track beam bridge, regardless of whether the rail consists of asingle line, double lines or more than two lines, the loads of train acting on each line shall be separately considered without any reduction.

3 In the calculation of loads on influence line, the live load diagram may be prepared at any cross section.

8.2.6 If the vertical live load of the train includes the dynamic action of the train, the vertical live load shall be the product of vertical static live load of the train multiplied by a dynamic factor φ. The dynamic factor shall be calculated according to the following formula:

$$\varphi = 1 + \Delta a_z / g \qquad (8.2.6\text{-}1)$$

$$\Delta a_z = \frac{V^2}{R_H} \sin\alpha \, \cos^2\beta + \left(g\cos\beta + \frac{V^2}{-R_V}\right)\cos\alpha - g \qquad (8.2.6\text{-}2)$$

Where, V——Design speed (m/s);

R_H——Horizontal curve radius (m);

R_v——Vertical curve radius (m), positive value for upward convex, negative value for downward concave;

α——Cross slope angle (°);

β——Longitudinal slope angle (°);

g——Gravitational acceleration.

8.2.7 The centrifugal force of the train onbeam bridge at curved line section shall be equal to the static live load of the train multiplied by the centrifugal force rate C. The centrifugal force shall be considered to be horizontally applied outwards to the center of gravity of the train. The centrifugal force rate C shall be calculated according to the following formula:

$$C = V^2 / (127R) \qquad (8.2.7)$$

Where, V——Design maximum train speed of the line (km/h);

R——Curve radius (m).

8.2.8 The lateral guidance force of the train shall be calculated according to the following specifications, with its application point the same as that of centrifugal force:

1 The maximum lateral guidance force of the train should be calculated to be 20% of static load.

2 The dynamic lateral guidance force of the train should be calculated according to the following formula:

$$P_y = \pm (1 + V/500) \qquad (8.2.8)$$

Where, P_y——Dynamic lateral force (kN/m);

V——design speed (km/h).

8.2.9 The small radius constraining force occurring within the range of transition curve should not be larger than 10 kN.

8.2.10 The train braking force or traction force shall be calculated in accordance with the following requirements:

1 The train braking force or traction force shall be calculated to be 15% of the vertical static live load of the train. Where centrifugal force is calculated together with it, it may be calculated as 10% of the vertical static live load.

2 The emergency braking force shall be calculated as 20% of the vertical static live load of the train.

3 In the case of a bridge carrying two lines, the braking force or traction force on one line shall be considered. In the case of a bridge carrying three or more lines, the braking force or traction force on two lines shall be considered.

4 For elevated maglev station and the double-line bridge within 100 m of the station, the braking force or traction force on both lines shall be considered, and the braking force or traction force on each line shall be calculated as 10% of the vertical static live load.

5 Braking force or traction force shall be applied to the center of gravity of the train above the track beam. But, in the calculation of abutment, it shall be moved to the center of bearing. In the calculation of rigid frame structure, it shall be moved to the centerline of the girder. In both cases, the torque generated by moving the applying point need not to be considered.

8. 2. 11 The wind load of track beam bridge shall comply with the current professional standard TB 10002 *Code for Design on Railway Bridge and Culvert*.

8. 2. 12 The effect of temperature change and concrete shrinkage may be considered in accordance with the current professional standard TB 10002 *Code for Design on Railway Bridge and Culvert*. When there is a temperature difference between the different lateral faces of cross section or between inner and outer faces of a structural member, the internal stress generated by the temperature gradient shall be taken into account.

8. 2. 13 If track beam bridge pier is likely to be hit by ship, anti-collision protection facilities shall be provided. Where anti-collision protection facilities are infeasible, the impact force of ship may be calculated according to the current professional standard TB 10002 *Code for Design on Railway Bridge and Culvert*.

8. 2. 14 Where track beam bridge pier is likely to be hit by automobiles, anti-collision protection facilities shall be provided. Where anti-collision protection facilities are infeasible, collision force shall be taken into account in the design of track beam bridge piers. The collision force is taken to be 1000 kN in the running direction of automobile, 500 kN in the direction perpendicular to the running direction of automobile, applied at 1. 20 m above the road.

8. 2. 15 The seismic load shall be calculated in accordance with the current national standard GB 50111 *Code for Seismic Design of Railway Engineering*.

8. 2. 16 The design of track beam bridge shall be checked according to the loads during various construction stages as well as the operation, maintenance and repair loads. For track beam that is erected by a bridge girder erection machine, the track beam and piers shall be checked separately according to the actual construction conditions.

8. 3 Structure Design

8. 3. 1 Reinforced concrete, prestressed concrete and steel structures shall be designed according to the allowable stress method. Their materials, allowable stress, structural safety factor, structural calculation method and structural requirements shall comply with the current professional standards TB 10092 *Code for Design of Concrete Structures of Railway Bridge and Culvert*, TB 10091 *Code for Design on Steel Structure of Railway Bridge*, and TB 10005 *Code for Durability Design on Concrete Structure of Railway*.

8. 3. 2 The design of prestressed and reinforced concrete track beams shall meet the requirements for laying equipment cables inside the beam or at the beam top.

8. 3. 3 For the purpose of checking the design of prestressed concrete structure against stresses and cracks during usage, the stress limits shall be determined in accordance with the current professional standard TB 10092 *Code for Design of Concrete Structures of Railway Bridge and Culvert*.

8. 3. 4 The design of concrete and masonry structures for trackbeam bridge shall be in accordance with the current professional standard TB 10092 *Code for Design of Concrete Structures of Railway Bridge and Culvert*.

8. 3. 5 The longitudinal horizontal force transferred from the simply supported beam to the abutment shall be calculated according to the following requirements:

1 100% of full beam for fixed bearing.

2 50% of full beam for sliding bearing.

3 25% of full beam for rolling bearing.

4 If fixed bearing and movable bearing are used on the same pier, shall be taken the sum of the above values. But in the case of unequal span girder, such sum shall not be larger than the longitudinal horizontal force of the fixed bearing of the largest span.

5 In the case of equal span girder, such sum shall not be larger than the longitudinal horizontal force of the fixed bearings of each span.

8. 3. 6 In addition to the current professional standard TB 10092 *Code for Design of Concrete Structures of Railway Bridge and Culvert*, the protective coating and reinforcement of concrete bridge structure shall also be in accordance with the following requirements:

1 The thickness of concrete cover between thesurface of prestressed rebar or pipes and the top and lateral surfaces of the structure shall not be less than the diameter of the pipe and in no case shall it be less than 50 mm.

2 The thickness of concrete cover on bottom side of the structure shall not be less than 60 mm.

8. 3. 7 The shrinkage, creep and deformation of concrete structure shall comply with the current professional standard TB 10092 *Code for Design of Concrete Structures of Railway Bridge and Culvert*.

8. 3. 8 The creep camber of prestressed concrete shall meet limit requirement. After the track is laid, the creep camber of track beam should not be larger than 5 mm.

8. 3. 9 The track beam bearing should use the spherical steel bearing with adjustable height. Where necessary, tensile bearing may be used.

8. 3. 10 The design of track beam bridge subgrade and the physical and mechanical indicators of the subgrade shall comply with the current professional standard TB 10093 *Code for Design on Subsoil and Foundation of Railway Bridge and Culvert*.

8. 4 Tectonic and Requirements of System Preinstall or Embedded Parts

8. 4. 1 Drainage system shall be provided at the track beam bridge piers, the lower girder structure of multipurpose bridge, turnout bridge and turnout platform.

8. 4. 2 Reinforced concrete and prestressed concrete track beams shall be provided with embedded pipes and parts to allow for subsequent installation of equipment such as signaling system, ring power supply cables and contact track.

8. 4. 3 The turnout bridge and turnout platform shall accommodate the arrangement of the turnout equipment and its control system.

8.4.4 The protections for the anchorage ends of prestressed concrete girders shall comply with the current professional standard TB 10005 *Code for Durability Design on Concrete Structure of Railway*.

8.4.5 The concrete parts of bridge piers erected on road in cold areas subject to rainwater erosion and the elevated structures erected in acid rain areas shall comply with the current national standard GB/T 50476 *Code for Durability Design of Concrete Structures*.

9　Station Building

9.1　General Requirements

9.1.1　The overall layout of the station shall conform to the requirements of urban planning, urban traffic planning, urban rail transit network planning, environmental protection and urban landscape, and its relationship with ground buildings, urban roads, underground pipelines, underground structures and traffic organization during constructions shall be properly coordinated to reduce house demolition and pipeline relocation.

9.1.2　The station design shall meet the demand of rush hour passenger flow, and ensure the safety of passengers during getting on/off, traffic evacuation, compact layout and easy management. Good ventilation, illumination, sanitation, disaster prevention and other facilities shall be equipped to provide passengers with a safe and comfortable riding environment.

9.1.3　The capacity of transfer facilities at transfer stations between various lines of medium and low speed maglev transit network and at the intersections with other rail transit lines shall meet the requirements of predicted long-term transfer passenger flow. The civil works of underground stations should be completed at one time, while the ground, elevated stations and related ground buildings may be constructed in stages.

9.1.4　The capacity of station concourse, platform, entrance/exit corridor, staircase, ticket office, ticket gate and other parts of the station shall be determined according to the long-term over-peak passenger flow. The over-peak design passenger volume shall be the predicted long-term peak hourly passenger volume of the station multiplied by the over-peak coefficient of 1.1 to 1.4.

9.1.5　The station design shall meet the functional requirements of the system, be reasonably arranged with equipment and management rooms, and should be standardized, modular, economic and centralized.

9.1.6　The station design should realize the comprehensive utilization of underground and above-ground space.

9.1.7　The design of station accessibility facilities shall comply with the requirements of the current national standard GB 50763 *Code for Accessibility Design*.

9.1.8　The station energy conservation design shall comply with the requirements of the current national standard GB 50189 *Design Standard for Energy Efficiency of Public Buildings*.

9.2　General Layout of Station

9.2.1　Island, side, or integrated island-side station shall be taken according to the conditions such as line features, operation requirements, ground and underground environment, and construction methods adopted in the station and section.

9.2.2　The transfer stations shall be set according to the factors such as medium-to-low-speed maglev transit network planning, route laying pattern, surrounding environment, transfer volume, etc. One station parallel transfer, one platform plane transfer, platform up-down parallel transfer, cross-shaped, T-shaped, L-shaped or H-shaped transfer between platforms and transfer through corridor is adopted and transfer should be arranged within the paid area.

9.2.3 Location of station entrance/exit and ventilation shaft shall be reasonably arranged according to the surrounding environment and urban planning requirements. Location of entrance/exit shall facilitate the access and evacuation of passenger flow. Location of the ventilation shaft shall meet the requirements of planning, environmental protection and landscape on the premise of meeting the functional requirements.

9.2.4 The space requirements of entrance and exit shall be considered in the station design, and non-motor vehicle parking areas should be established. Stations located in suburbs and outskirts may be equipped with P+R parking lots for parking and transfer.

9.3 Station Plane

9.3.1 The calculation length of the platform shall be the sum of effective length of the maximum formation of train and parking error. The effective length and parking error shall be in accordance with the following requirements:

1 As for the platform without platform screen doors, the effective length shall be the length between the outside of the cab doors of the first and last carriages of the train. As for the platform with platform screen doors, the effective length shall be the length between the outside of the passenger compartment doors at the end of the first and last carriages of the train.

2 The parking error in the absence of platform screen door should be 1 m to 2 m. The parking error in the existence of platform screen door shall not be larger than ± 0.3 m.

9.3.2 The platform width shall be calculated according to the current national standard GB 50157 *Code for Design of Metro*, but shall not be less than the requirements of Article 9.3.11 in this code.

9.3.3 The equipment and management rooms arranged at both ends of the platform level may be extended into the calculation length of the platform, but should not exceed the length of one carriage. They shall not be intruded into the calculation width of the side platform, and shall keep a distance of no less than 8 m from the escalator working point. The calculation width of the side platform at the intrusion point shall not be less than the requirements of Article 9.3.11 in this code.

9.3.4 The platform level of the elevated station may be equipped with power distribution room, duty room, cleaning room and air conditioned waiting rooms. Other equipment management rooms should not be arranged on the platform level.

9.3.5 According to the climatic conditions, open station shall be equipped with rain and snow awning on the platform, and in the design of awning size and shape, the requirements of urban landscape shall be considered.

9.3.6 Pedestrian stairs and escalators on the platform should be uniformly arranged along the longitudinal direction, and the distance between any point in the calculation length of the platform and the nearest stair passenger entrance shall not be larger than 50 m.

9.3.7 The total number of pedestrian stairs and escalators shall not only meet the requirements of passengers going up/down, but also satisfy the requirements of emergency evacuation time from platform not exceeding 6 min. Special fire-fighting escalators and elevators shall not be included in emergency evacuation facilities.

9.3.8 The emergency evacuation time at the platform level shall be calculated according to the following formula:

$$T = 1 + \frac{Q_1 + Q_2}{0.9[A_1(N-1) + A_2 B]} \tag{9.3.8}$$

Where, Q_1——Number of passengers on the train (person);

Q_2——Number of passengers on the platform (person);

A_1——Escalator carrying capacity [person/(min • each)];

A_2——Pedestrian stair carrying capacity [person/(min • m)];

N——Number of escalators;

B——Total width of pedestrian stairs (m).

9.3.9 A gathering space for passengers shall be reserved in front of the ticketing machine and fare collection machine. The gathering space shall not intrude into the pedestrian flow area.

9.3.10 The maximum carrying capacity of each part of the station should be in accordance with those specified in Table 9.3.10.

Table 9.3.10　Maximum Carrying Capacity of Each Part of the Station

Part Name			Number of passengers per hour (person)
1 m wide staircase	Upward		3700
	Downward		4200
	Two-way		3200
1 m wide corridor	One-way		5000
	Two-way		4000
Escalator	1 m wide	Conveying speed: 0.5 m/s	6720
		Conveying speed: 0.65 m/s	No larger than 8190
	0.65m wide	Conveying speed: 0.5 m/s	4320
		Conveying speed: 0.65 m/s	5265
Manual ticket office			1200
Automatic ticket vending machine			300
Manual ticket gate			2600
Automatic ticket checking machine	Two-bar type	Contactless IC card	1200
	Door leaf type	Contactless IC card	1800
	Two-way door leaf type	Contactless IC card	1500

9.3.11 The minimum dimensions of each part of the station and platform shall be in accordance with those specified in Table 9.3.11-1, Table 9.3.11-2.

Table 9.3.11-1　Minimum Width of Each Part of Station Platform

Name	Minimum width (m)
Island platform	8
Side platform of island platform	2.5
Side platform of side platform (stairs arranged along the length of the platform)	2.5
Side platform of side platform (corridor opening arranged perpendicular to the side platform)	3.5

Table 9. 3. 11-1 (Continued)

Name		Minimum width (m)
The calculation length of the platform shall not exceed 100 m and the staircase and escalator shall not extend into the calculation length of the platform	Island platform	6. 0
	Side platform	4. 0
Corridor or overpass		2. 4
One-way pedestrian staircase in public area		1. 8
Two-way pedestrian staircase in public area		2. 4
Pedestrian staircase arranged in parallel with escalators arranged in both upward and downward directions (under difficult circumstances)		1. 2
Special staircase for fire fighting		1. 2
Working staircase from platform to track area (also serve as evacuation staircase)		1. 1

Table 9. 3. 11-2　Minimum Height of Each Part of Station

Name	Minimum height (m)
Public area of underground station concourse (ground decoration surface to ceiling surface)	3. 0
Public area of elevated station concourse (ground decoration surface to ground beam surface)	2. 6
Public area of underground station platform (ground decoration surface to ceiling surface)	3. 0
Public area of ground, elevated station platform (ground decoration surface to weather shed)	2. 6
Platform and station concourse management rooms (ground decoration surface to ceiling surface)	2. 4
Corridor or overpass (ground decoration surface to ceiling surface)	2. 4
Pedestrian stairs and escalators (tread surface rim to ceiling surface)	2. 3

9. 3. 12　Stairs and escalators on the platform should be evenly arranged in the longitudinal direction.

9. 3. 13　In the absence of platform screen door, a longitudinal eye-catching safety line not less than 80 mm wide shall be set on the inner side of the safety protection belt 400 mm from the edge of the platform. The slip resistance of the ground within the scope of the safety protection belt shall comply with the requirements of the current professional standard JGJ/T 331 *Technical Specification for Slip Resistance of Building Floor*.

9. 3. 14　The clearance between the platform edge and the vehicle profile shall meet the requirements of Article 5. 3. 8 in this code.

9. 3. 15　The exit ticket gate should not be less than 5 m from the edge of the entrance/exit corridor, no less than 5 m from the stairway, and no less than 8 m from the escalator base point. The entrance ticket gate should not be less than 4 m from the staircase, and not be less than 7 m from the escalator base point.

9. 3. 16　The fare collection method may be manual, semi-automatic or automatic. In the case of phased implementation in near-term and long-term, fulfillment conditions shall be reserved.

9. 3. 17　The equipment and management rooms of underground station shall have a compact and reasonable layout, and the main management rooms shall be arranged in a concentrated manner. The fire pump room should be located beside the main corridor in the occupied area of equipment and management room or beside the evacuation exit passage in the equipment area.

9.3.18 The distance between structural columns, walls, etc. of the station beyond the calculation length of the platform and the edge of the platform must meet the gauge requirements.

9.3.19 Turnout areas and escalators shall be located away from structural induction joints and deformation joints.

9.3.20 The awning of the above-ground station platform shall be in accordance with the following requirements:

　　1 The awning shall have facilities to prevent rain and snow from falling on the platform.

　　2 Waterproof nodes of awning shall meet the structural requirements under train vibration and piston air.

　　3 The roof shall be equipped with facilities convenient for maintenance and cleaning at height.

9.4 Station Environment Design

9.4.1 The design of the station building shall be concise and take the best use of the structure and spatial form. The design of ground station and elevated station shall be adapted to local conditions, and should have smaller volume and good natural ventilation.

9.4.2 Class A materials shall be used for the decoration of the ceiling, wall and floor in the station; when using the raised floor, the quality of material shall be grade B1 or higher. Materials used for fixed service facilities such as advertising light boxes, rest chairs, telephone booths, ticket machine, etc. in the public areas of the station shall be low-smoke, halogen-free flame retardant materials. Floor materials shall be non-slip and wear resistant; safety glass shall be used when using glass materials.

9.4.3 The signs of station guidance accident evacuation and passenger service shall be set up in accordance with the national standard GB/T 18574 *The Passenger Service Signs for Urban Rail Transit*.

9.4.4 The lighting requirements of different areas in the station and the selection of illumination facilities shall comply with the current national standard GB/T 16275 *Urban Rail Transit Lighting*.

9.4.5 When setting up advertisement boards in the station, it shall not interfere with the signs of guiding, evacuating and passengers service.

9.4.6 For rooms with noise sources, sound insulation and sound absorption measures shall be taken by adopting soundproof doors for such rooms. Fireproof and soundproof doors shall be adopted when fire protection is required.

9.5 Station Entrances and Exits

9.5.1 The number of entrances and exits of stations shall be set up according to the requirements of attracting and evacuating passengers. At least two exits shall be set in each public area for going straight to the ground. The width of each entrance and exit shall be calculated by single direction design flow of future period or passenger flow control period multiplying non-uniformity coefficient from 1.1 to 1.25.

9.5.2 The entrances and exits of the station shall be in the same direction as the main passenger flow. They should be combined or connected with overpasses, underpass tunnel, underground streets and adjacent public buildings under unified planning, simultaneous or phased implementation. If they are also used as a pedestrian crossing, the passage width and the corresponding part of the station concourse shall take into consideration the passenger flow crossing the street, and isolation facilities for night shutdown shall be set up.

9.5.3 The entrances and exits on both sides of the road should be parallel or perpendicular to the authorized boundary line of the road. The distance from the authorized boundary line of the road shall meet the requirements of the local planning department. When the entrances and exits face the main roads of the city, assemble and evacuate spaces should be set up.

9.5.4 The floor elevation of the entrances and exits of the underground station shall be higher than the outdoor ground and shall meet the requirements for flood prevention.

9.5.5 The form of ground building at the entrances and exits shall be determined according to the specific location and planning requirements. The entrances and exits should preferably be built in the form of a joint construction with ground building or ventilation shaft, or otherwise may be built independently.

9.5.6 The entrance and exit passage should be short andstraight, and there should not be more than three bends with turning angle shall not be less than 90° for the passage. The length of the entrance and exit passage underground should not exceed 100 m. Otherwise, measures shall be taken to meet the fire evacuation requirements and ventilation facilities as well as a moving walkway should be installed.

9.6 Ventilation Shaft and Cooling Tower

9.6.1 The underground station shall be equipped with ventilation pavilions and cooling towers according to technological requirements, and the layout shall be coordinated with the ground environment and planning.

9.6.2 When the ventilation pavilion with side air vent is adopted, it shall be in accordance with the following requirements:

  1 The horizontal clearance between air inlet, air outlet and piston air vents shall not be less than 5 m, and the air inlet and air outlet, air inlet and piston air vents shall be arranged in different directions, or the air outlet, piston air vents shall be 5 m higher than the air inlet. When the air inlet, air outlet and piston air vents of the ventilation pavilion cannot be arranged in different directions and at different heights, the distance between ventilation pavilion vents shall meet the requirements of Items 1 and 2 of Article 9.6.3 in this code.

  2 There shall not be obstacles blocking the ventilation flow within 5 m of the ventilation pavilion vents.

  3 The height of bottom edge of the ventilation pavilion vents above ground shall meet the requirements of flood prevention. When the ventilation pavilion is located at roadside, its height shall not be less than 2 m. When the ventilation pavilion is located in green space, its height shall not be less than 1 m.

9.6.3 When the ventilation pavilion with top air vent is adopted, it shall be in accordance with the following requirements:

  1 The horizontal clearance between air inlet and air outlet, air inlet and piston air vents shall not be less than 10 m.

  2 The horizontal clearance between piston air vents and between piston air vent and air outlet shaft shall not be less than 5 m.

3 Fences with a width of not less than 3 m shall be provided around the ventilation pavilion. The minimum height of the air vent shall meet the requirements of flood prevention and shall not be less than 1 m.

4 The ventilation pavilion opening shall be provided with safety protection devices, and the bottom of the ventilation shaft shall be provided with drainage facilities.

9.6.4 When ventilation pavilion is used to exhaust smoke in emergency, the straight line distance between the opening of the outlet pavilion and the opening of the air inlet pavilion and the opening of the entrance/exit should be larger than 10 m. When the straight-line distance is less than 10 m, the opening of smoke exhaust pavilion should be 5 m higher than the opening of the air inlet pavilion and the opening of the entrance/exit.

9.6.5 The distance between ventilation pavilion opening and other buildings shall meet the requirements of fire prevention and environmental protection.

9.6.6 The shape, color and location of above-ground cooling tower of underground station shall conform to the requirements of urban planning, landscape and environmental protection.

9.6.7 In the case of restricted conditions, the cooling tower may be of sunken type or fully underground type on the premise of meeting technological requirements.

9.7 Stair, Escalator, Elevator, Platform Screen Door

9.7.1 Stairs used for passengers should be inclined at an angle of $26°34'$, and their width should not be less than 1.8 m for one-way traffic and 2.4 m for two-way traffic. When the width is larger than 3.6 m, center armrest shall be installed. Each staircase shall be no more than 18 steps, and the length of stair landing should be 1.2 m to 1.8 m.

9.7.2 Ascending and descending escalators shall be equipped to connect the station entrance/exit, platform with station concourse, and for the places with no conditions for setting up two-way escalators and with lifting height no larger than 10 m, only ascending escalator may be installed. Each station shall have at least one entrance/exit and at least one place connecting the platform and the station concourse must be equipped with ascending and descending escalators. Positions for escalators to be built in later stages shall be reserved.

9.7.3 The horizontal distance between the outer edge of the escalator handrail belt and the decorative surface of the parallel wall or edge of the floor opening shall not be less than 80 mm. The horizontal distance of the outer edge of handrail belts between two adjacent escalators arranged in crisscross or parallel manner shall not be less than 160 mm. When the outer edge of the handrail belt is less than 400 mm from any obstacle, collision prevention safety devices shall be installed.

9.7.4 The distance between working points of two oppositely arranged escalators shall not be less than 16m, and the distance between working points of escalators and obstacles affecting traffic in front shall not be less than 8 m. When the escalator is arranged opposite to pedestrian stairs, the distance between the working point of the escalator and the first step of the staircase shall not be less than 12 m.

9.7.5 Escalators for emergency evacuation shall be powered as Grade I load.

9.7.6 The installation positions of escalators and moving sidewalks should avoid the deformation joints of buildings, and corresponding structural measures shall be taken when crossing the joints.

9.7.7 The escalators for emergency evacuation of underground stations shall be powered as Grade I load and shall be able to realize automatic shutdown in case of fire or reverse operation after manual confirmation.

9.7.8 Pedestrian stairs shall be set between the station concourse and platform in the main management area of the station.

9.7.9 Machine-room-less elevators shall be selected.

9.7.10 The installation position of elevator shall avoid the induced joints and deformation joints of the civil structure.

9.7.11 Platform screen doors should be installed for the medium and low speed maglev transit stations. Platform screen doors shall be symmetrically and longitudinally arranged according to the center line of the calculation length of the platform, and sliding doors shall be arranged in one-to-one correspondence with train doors. The net opening width of sliding door shall not be less than the width of vehicle door plus parking error. The high screen doors of platform shall be of a height no less than 2.0 m, and the low screen doors of platform shall be of a height no less than 1.2 m.

9.7.12 The strength and rigidity of platform screen doors shall comply with the requirements of the current professional standard CJJ 183 *Technical Code for Platform Screen Door System of Urban Railway Transit*.

9.7.13 The installation of platform screen doors shall meet the requirements for gauge in Chapter 5 in this code.

9.7.14 Platform screen doors shall be powered as Grade I load, and the capacity of backup power source as power supply shall meet the requirement of opening/closing all sliding doors for 3 times within 30 min, and the capacity of the backup power source as control power shall meet the requirement of continuous working at full load for 30 min.

9.7.15 Platform screen doors shall have the function of manual opening or closing of each sliding door on the platform side or track side.

9.7.16 The end of the platform screen door shall be provided with an end door that opens to the inner side of the platform. Emergency doors shall be set along the length of the platform, and each side shall have at least 2 emergency doors.

9.7.17 The material of platform screen doors shall comply with the requirements of the current professional standard CJ/T 236 *Urban Railway Transportation Platform Screen Door System*. Platform screen doors shall not be used as fire separation measures for stations.

9.7.18 Corresponding structural measures shall be taken for platform screen doors located at deformation joints of civil works.

9.7.19 Platform screen doors shall have obvious safety signs and usage marks for use.

9.7.20 The insulation and grounding performance of platform screen door system shall comply with the requirements of the current professional standard CJJ 183 *Technical Code for Platform Screen Door System of Urban Railway Transit*.

9.7.21 Platform screen doors shall have obstacle detection function and shall comply with the requirements of the current professional standard CJJ 183 *Technical Code for Platform Screen Door System of Urban Railway Transit*.

9.8 Accessible Facilities

9.8.1 Station facilities for passenger service shall be designed as accessible facilities and shall comply with the requirements of the current national standard GB 50763 *Codes for Accessibility Design*.

9.8.2 The station shall be equipped with accessible elevators, which shall comply with the requirements of the current national standard GB 50763 *Codes for Accessibility Design*.

9.8.3 Accessible elevators shall be located in the paid area.

9.8.4 The depth of the waiting area in front of the accessible elevator should not be less than 1.8 m, the depth of elevator cage.

9.8.5 Anti-flooding measures shall be taken for the above-ground part of the accessible elevator shaft. Ramps shall be set up at the place with elevation difference between the elevator platform and outdoor ground, and shall comply with the requirements of the current national standard GB 50763 *Codes for Accessibility Design*.

9.8.6 The accessible passage facilities set up in the station shall be connected with the urban accessible system.

9.8.7 The station shall be equipped with accessible toilets.

9.9 Transfer Station

9.9.1 The transfer means shall be determined according to the direction of the planned road network and the route laying method.

9.9.2 The capacity of transfer facilities shall meet the requirements of transfer passenger flow in over-peak design.

9.9.3 At the transfer station, the manner of transfer within the pay area shall be preferred.

9.9.4 For reserved transfer nodes, the line positions of adjacent stations and corresponding sections shall be stable, and a margin no less than 500 mm shall be reserved on both sides of the transfer nodes.

9.9.5 For transfer stations implemented simultaneously, the resources such as station houses, equipment and facilities should be shared.

9.10 Economize Energy of Building

9.10.1 The above-ground stations shall adopt natural ventilation and natural lighting.

9.10.2 Above-ground stations should not be equipped with central air conditioning, but air-conditioned waiting rooms may be set up on the platform level according to climatic conditions.

9.10.3 The thermal design of retaining structure of equipment and management buildings of above-ground station shall comply with the current national standard GB 50189 *Design Standard for Energy Efficiency of Public Buildings*.

9.10.4 Thermal insulation measures shall be taken for the awning on the platform level of above-ground station.

9.10.5 According to the demand of passenger flow, underground stations shall be controlled in terminologies of scale and number of floors under the premise of meeting the functional requirements.

9.10.6 Warm air curtain shall be set at the entrance/exit of underground station located in severe cold area.

9.10.7 The lighting and power substation of underground station shall be located close to the station load center.

9. 10. 8 The thermal design of retaining structure of public buildings such as above-ground control center buildings and office buildings, training centers, apartments, canteens, etc. within the vehicle base shall comply with the current national standard GB 50189 *Design Standard for Energy Efficiency of Public Buildings*.

10 At-ground Structure

10.1 General Requirements

10.1.1 At-ground structure should not be used for subgrade sections with complex geological conditions, difficult-to-control post-construction settlement or high underground watertable, subgrade frost damage and other unstable factors. High embankment should not be used in at-ground structures of medium and low speed maglev transit.

10.1.2 The designer shall strengthen geological mapping, exploration and test work for at-ground structure, find out the geotechnical structure and physical and mechanical properties of subgrade, slope, support and other structures, identify the bad geological conditions and their distribution, and carry out design on the basis of obtaining reliable geological data.

10.1.3 The design of at-ground structures shall meet the requirements of environmental protection, pay attention to the greening design along the transit line, and shall be coordinated with the surrounding landscape.

10.1.4 Waterproof and drainage projects of subgrade shall be planned systematically and shall meet the waterproof and drainage requirements. Subgrade drainage equipment shall be connected to the drainage facilities of bridge culvert, tunnel, track and station, and shall be combined with water and soil conservation and comprehensive utilization of water conservancy facilities.

10.1.5 The design service life of retaining and bearing structures of subgrade shall be 100 years. The durability design of concrete structures shall comply with the current professional standard TB 10005 *Code for Durability Design on Concrete Structure of Railway*.

10.2 Design of Support Structure and Subgrade

10.2.1 Track bed shoulder shall be higher than the design water level height plus backwater height plus wave invasion height, or oblique local water surge height and then plus 1.0 m. For the values of the wave invasion height and the oblique local surge height, shall be selected the higher value.

10.2.2 The connection between at-ground structure and track should be installed with base plate which shall be designed according to the elastic foundation beam.

10.2.3 Post-construction settlement analysis shall be carried out for all at-ground structures. The non-uniform settlement within the 20 m length range of any section, faulting of slab ends caused by settlement difference, and the deflection angle of transition section between track bed and track bridge, the transition section between track bed and tunnel or any two subgrade sections caused by settlement difference shall be in accordance with those specified in Table 10.2.3.

Table 10.2.3 Post-construction Settlement Control Values

Post-construction settlement	Non-uniform settlement	Faulting of slab ends caused by settlement difference	Deflection dngle
≤30 m	≤20 mm/2 mm	≤5 mm	≤1/1000

10.2.4 Graded aggregate shall be used as the hardcore under the concrete subslab, the material shall be in accordance with those specified in Table 10.2.4-1, and the compaction standards of hardcore shall be in accordance with those specified in Table 10.2.4-2.

Table 10.2.4-1　Aggregate Size Grading

Side length of square hole (mm)	0.1	0.5	1.7	7.1	22.4	31.5	45
Screening percentage (by mass) (%)	0~5	7~32	13~46	41~75	67~91	82~100	100

Table 10.2.4-2　Graded Aggregate Compaction Standard

Materials	Compaction standards			
	Subgrade coefficient K_{30} (MPa/m)	Deformation modulus E_{v2} (MPa)	Dynamic deformation modulus E_{vd} (MPa)	Compaction coefficient
Graded aggregate	≥190	≥120	≥50	≥0.97

Note: At least two of K_{30}, E_{v2} and E_{vd} meet the requirements.

10.2.5 The cutting design shall reduce the damage to natural vegetation and mountains to prevent geological disasters.

10.2.6 The cutting slope form and slope rate shall be determined by mechanical analysis according to the engineering geology, hydrogeology, meteorological conditions, waterproof and drainage measures and construction methods.

10.3　Structure of Side Slope Retainer

10.3.1 The side slop retainer shall be constructed for at-ground structure in the following conditions:

　1　Steep slope section or weathered cutting slope section.

　2　Cutting sections where avoiding lots of excavation and reducing slope height are required.

　3　Slope, mountain, dangerous rock reinforcement or rock-fall block sections under adverse geological conditions.

　4　Sections for economizing land use and occupying less farmland and urban land.

　5　Sections for protecting existing important buildings and other special conditions.

10.3.2 Structure of side slope retainer shall be in accordance with the following requirements:

　1　Under a variety of designed loading combinations, structure of side slope retainer shall meet the requirements of stability, robustness and durability, structure type and location shall be safe and reliable, economic and reasonable, convenient for construction and maintenance, and the used materials shall be durable and corrosion resistant.

　2　During the design of structure of side slope retainer, the engineering geological and hydrogeological conditions of the mountain and foundation shall be carefully investigated.

　3　The seismic design of structure of side slope retainer shall comply with the relevant requirements of current national standard GB 50111 *Code for Seismic Design of Railway Engineering*.

　4　The connections of side slope retainers and abutment, tunnel portal and existing side slope retainers shall be smooth.

5 The waterproof and drainage design of side slope retainer shall be coordinated with the site drainage facilities to form a complete drainage system.

6 The positions at retaining wall sections shall be reserved where lighting poles and sound barriers are required to be built.

10.3.3 During the design of side slop retainer, the load system, load combinations, checking requirements, structural and material requirements should comply with the current professional standard TB 10025 *Code for Design on Retaining Structures of Railway Subgrade*, and the train loads shall be calculated according to the vertical loads generated by maglev vehicles.

10.3.4 If the side slope retainer has sound barriers or other ancillary facilities on it, wind load shall also be considered.

10.3.5 The light retaining structures such as cantilever type, buttress type, pile plate type and reinforced retaining wall, which are in harmony with the surrounding landscape, should be adopted around urban areas and scenic spots.

10.4 Drainage and Protection

10.4.1 The layout of site drainage facilities shall be in accordance with the following requirements:

1 Unilateral or bilateral drainage ditches may be built outside the natural berm of embankment.

2 Side ditches shall be built on both sides of road shoulder of the cutting.

3 Unilateral or bilateral gutter shall be built outside the cutting top.

10.4.2 The cross sections of gutter and side ditch shall have sufficient water passing capacity. The cross sections of gutter and side ditch designed according to flow rate shall be calculated according to the flow rate of 1/50 flood frequency, and the top of the gutter shall not be less than 0.2 m higher than the designed water level.

10.4.3 The distance between the inner edge of the gutter and the cutting top should not be less than 5 m. If the reinforced anti-seepage measures are taken in the gutter, the distance shall not be less than 2 m.

10.4.4 The site longitudinal drainage slope shall not be less than 2‰. For flat ground or counter-slope drainage sections, it may be 1‰.

10.4.5 The water in the side ditch of the cutting shall not be discharged through the tunnel.

10.4.6 The type, location and size of underground drainage facilities shall be determined according to engineering geology and hydro-geological conditions. If the groundwater level is high or there is no fixed aquifer, facilities such as open trench, drainage trough, seepage underdrain, slope seepage trench and supporting seepage trench should be used to remove the groundwater. When deeply buried groundwater or fixed aquifer endangers the subgrade, seepage tunnel, seepage well, seepage pipe or inclined borehole should be used to remove the groundwater.

10.4.7 For the side slopes prone to be damaged due to natural factors, appropriate protective measures shall be taken according to the soil quality, lithology, hydrogeological conditions, slope rate and height, environmental protection, water and soil maintenance requirements, and plant protection should be given priority.

11 Elevated Station Structure

11.1 General Requirements

11.1.1 The strength, rigidity and stability of elevated structure shall be calculated for construction and operation stages respectively.

11.1.2 The seismic design of the elevated structures shall comply with the current national standard GB 50111 *Code for Seismic Design of Railway Engineering*.

11.1.3 For integrated bridge-station structures, the structural design shall comply with the requirements of both this Chapter 11 and Chapter 8 in this code.

11.1.4 The building structure of the station shall meet the requirements for functions, vibration reduction and noise reduction, blending in the city view.

11.1.5 The design service life of main structure, non-replaceable components and secondary structural components of the station that are difficult to repair and replace shall be 100 years; those of other secondary structures may be 50 years.

11.2 Loads

11.2.1 The material weight shall comply with the current national standard GB 50009 *Load Code for the Design of Building Structures*.

11.2.2 The live load of the elevated station structure shall be in accordance with the following requirements:

   1 The train load shall be determined in accordance with Chapter 8 in this code.

   2 The standard values of the live loads of station concourse, stairs, platforms and bridges shall be 4 kN/m^2.

   3 The live load of the equipment room shall be based on factors such as actual weight, dynamic impact and the methods of installation and transportation, but shall not be less than 5.5 kN/m^2.

   4 The standard values of live loads of other rooms shall comply with the current national standard GB 50009 *Load Code for the Design of Building Structures*.

11.3 Structure Design

11.3.1 The safety level of elevated station structure shall be Grade I.

11.3.2 When the track beam structure is built completely separately from station structure to form an independent track beam bridge, the design of spans and structure shall be the same as the elevated structure within the same section. The elevated structures shall be designed in accordance with current national design codes for building structures.

11.3.3 For integrated bridge-station structural system, the track beam that directly bears the train load shall be designed in accordance with the design specifications of railway bridges and culverts, and its frame beams, columns and base below shall be calculated based on the current national building structure design specifications and the design specifications of railway bridges and culverts, for cross-sectional verification. The rest of beam slabs shall be designed in accordance with the current national building structure design specifications. The seismic design and structure of such frame shall comply with the current national standard GB 50111 *Code for Seismic Design of Railway Engineering*.

11.3.4 The structure of station should adopt the frame structure system of reinforced concrete or prestressed concrete. Steel structure should not be used for the elevated station rail beam and its supporting structure.

11.3.5 Deflection requirements and crack control levels of components that directly bear train loads shall meet the requirements of both building structure and line bridge.

11.3.6 When the structure is too long, the temperature influence shall be calculated in accordance with the current national standard GB 50009 *Load Code for the Design of Building Structures*.

11.4 Seismic Design

11.4.1 To build separated bridge elevated station, the seismic design of track beam bridge and station structure shall comply with current national standards GB 50111 *Code for Seismic Design of Railway Engineering* and GB 50011 *Code for Seismic Design of Buildings* respectively.

11.4.2 The seismic design of the elevated station with three or more transverse columns shall comply with the current national standard GB 50011 *Code for Seismic Design of Buildings*. The category of seismic fortification shall be Extremely Important.

11.4.3 The structural design of support track beams of elevated station with double transverse columns shall comply with the current national standard GB 50111 *Code for Seismic Design of Railway Engineering*, and its classification of seismic protection shall be B. When track beams and supporting track beams are in a whole frame structure, seismic design may also be carried out according to the current national standard GB 50011 *Code for Seismic Design of Buildings*, and the category of seismic fortification shall be Extremely Important.

11.4.4 For elevated station of frame structure with double transverse columns and a single span, no less than two different mechanical models shall be calculated, and the structural design of seismic performance shall be carried out according to the current national standard GB 50011 *Code for Seismic Design of Buildings*.

11.4.5 Long cantilever structure shall take account of the effects of vertical seismic force.

11.4.6 For bridge-integrated elevated station, the elastic horizontal displacement on the floor where track beams are located shall comply with the requirement that the horizontal displacement of the frame structure is not more than 1/550, and shall also meet the requirements of Article 8.1.9 in this code.

11.4.7 The seismic measures for the elevated station shall comply with the current national standard GB 50011 *Code for Seismic Design of Buildings*.

11.4.8 Non-load bearing components on the elevated station shall comply with the current national standard GB 50011 *Code for Seismic Design of Buildings*. Non-load bearing components and station main structure shall be reliably connected or anchored.

11.5 Tectonic Requirements

11.5.1 The elevated station structure shall comply with this code and the current national standard GB 50010 *Code for Design of Concrete Structures*.

11.5.2 When the independent track beam is simply supported on the beam of station structure, bearing shall be provided. Height-adjustable anti-vibration spherical steel bearing should be preferred.

11.5.3 If the elevated structural column (pier) is likely to be hit by cars and other motor vehicles, effective protection measures such as building anti-collision piers shall be taken. If it is not possible to take protection measures, the design of track beam pier column shall consider the impact of the car hitting on the pier column. The car crash forces shall be calculated as 1000 kN in the car travelling direction, 500 kN perpendicular to the car traveling direction, acting on the level of 1.20 m above the surface of the road.

11.5.4 The station and roof structures shall be possible to have repairing, maintenance and replacement.

11.6 Structure of Platfond, Entrances and Exits

11.6.1 The station roof should be of steel structure, or steel-concrete hybrid structure may be used.

11.6.2 The roof structure shall be designed with wind resistance. For open, semi-closed and complicated roof structures, if there is no reliable wind load value, wind tunnel tests should be carried out to determine wind load.

11.6.3 The roof structure shall be analyzed for overall structural stress together with the station structure, and the effect of temperature on the roof structure shall be taken into account.

11.6.4 The sectioning of roof structure should be consistent with the lower part, should not be staggered structure recommended.

11.6.5 The elevated structure of the station entrance and exit may be of reinforced concrete or steel structure. The entrance and exit structures should be independent of the main structure of the station. If the entrance and exit structures have a large span or need to go across the road, it may be in the form of beams and trusses. If the entrance and exit structures need to be directly supported by the main structure, the side beam of the main structure shall be provided with bearing. The calculation of the main structure shall take into account the load from the entrance and exit structures.

11.6.6 The entrance and exit structures shall meet the requirements for vertical vibration, and shall also take into account for the vertical seismic impact.

12 Underground Structure

12. 1 General Requirements

12. 1. 1 This chapter is applicable to the design of the following underground structures:

  1 Cut and cover structures built by side slope excavation method or retaining wall method.

  2 Mined structures built by shield method or mining method.

  3 Structures built by immersed tube method and other special methods.

12. 1. 2 In the design of underground structures, the scope and content of geotechnical investigation shall be determined based on the tasks and purposes of the specific design stage in accordance with the current national standard GB 50307 *Code for Geotechnical Investigations of Urban Rail Transit*. The classification of surrounding rocks of mined structures shall be determined in accordance with the current professional standard TB 10003 *Code for Design of Railway Tunnel*.

12. 1. 3 The design of underground structures shall minimize the adverse impact on environment during and after construction as well as the influence of surrounding environment changes due to urban planning on the structures.

12. 1. 4 In the design of underground structures, the construction technique and structure type shall be determined through comprehensive evaluation of technical and economic feasibility, environmental impact and application effect according to the site conditions along the line. Where aquifer is encountered, appropriate groundwater treatment and control measures shall be taken.

12. 1. 5 The durability design of underground structures shall be in accordance with the following requirements:

  1 Main structure and the structural members that cannot be replaced in service shall have a 100-year service life in line with the category of site environment.

  2 Minor structural members that can be replaced in service and could not affect the operation of maglev line should have a 50 year service life.

  3 The service life of temporary structures should be determined according to structural purposes and characteristics.

12. 1. 6 The durability design of underground structures should comply with the current national standard GB/T 50476 *Code for Durability Design of Concrete Structures*.

12. 1. 7 In the design of underground structure, the applicable structural design code and design method shall be determined according to the construction technique, the type of structure or structural member, the site conditions and loading characteristics.

12. 1. 8 The clearance of underground structure shall satisfy the structure gauge of medium and low speed maglev transit and other requirements of usage and construction techniques. Meanwhile, factors such as construction error, structural deformation and displacement shall be considered.

12. 1. 9 For soft soil tunnels, an overall dynamic analysis of maglev vehicles, tunnel structure and soil coupling effect should be conducted.

12. 1. 10 The type, length and installation method of the track support structure within tunnel shall be determined in combination with the actual construction conditions in the tunnel. Factors such as tunnel settlement and longitudinal uneven settlement shall also be considered.

12.1.11 The depth of underground structure and the distance to adjacent tunnel shall be reasonably determined in combination with the construction technique, structure type, sectional dimensions, engineering geological conditions, hydrogeological conditions and environmental conditions, and shall also be in accordance with the following requirements:

1 The overburden thickness of shield tunnels should not be less than the tunnel outer diameter.

2 The clear distance between parallel shield tunnels should not be less than the tunnel outer diameter.

3 The minimum overburden thickness of mined tunnels should not be less than the tunnel excavation width.

4 The minimum overburden thickness of mined station should be 6 m to 8 m.

12.1.12 The overburden thickness of immersed tube tunnel shall be determined in accordance with the anti-floating stability, river navigation requirements and the conditions of riverbed scour, shipwreck and ship anchor.

12.2 Loads

12.2.1 Loads on underground structures shall be determined based on factors such as possible changes during construction and in service life in accordance with the current national standard GB 50009 *Load Code for the Design of Building Structures* and other relevant standards. The loads may be classified according to Table 12.2.1.

Table 12.2.1 Classification of Loads on Underground Structure

Classification of load		Name of load
Permanent loads		Dead weight of structure
		Strata pressure
		Pressure from the facilities and buildings on the upper structure and within the range of wedge failure
		Hydrostatic pressure and buoyancy
		Shrinkage and creep of concrete
		Prestress
		Weight of fixed equipment
		Subgrade settlement
Variable loads	Basic variable loads	Load and dynamic action of ground vehicles
		Lateral earth pressure induced by loads of ground vehicles
		Load and dynamic action of vehicles in tunnel
	Other variable loads	Crowd load
		Temperature change impact
		Construction loads

Table 12. 2. 1 (Continued)

Classification of load	Name of load
Accidental loads	Seismic load
	Civil defense load
	Disastrous loads induced by shipwreck, explosion and ship anchor

Note: 1 Other loads to be considered in the design may be included in the above three categories of load according to their nature.

2 The loads in the above table not specified in this section may be determined according to other relevant national standards or according to actual conditions.

3 Tunnel loads include: loads of equipment during transportation and hoisting, loads from construction machines, apparatuses and crowd, stacking loads during construction, the influence of adjacent tunnel construction, jacking and grouting loads during shield tunneling or jacking construction, loads of immersed tubes during towage, sinking and hydraulic connection.

12. 2. 2 Pressure from strata shall be calculated according to the relevant formula or determined by comparison with similar projects based on the ambient engineering geological and hydrogeological conditions, the embedment depth and structural type of the underground structure.

12. 2. 3 The water pressure on underground structure shall be calculated according to the following rules based on the groundwater level change during construction and long-term use and the specific surrounding rock conditions:

1 Water pressure may be calculated as hydrostatic pressure, and the action of water pressure and buoyancy on the structure shall be calculated respectively based on the groundwater level for preventing up-floating and the maximum and minimum groundwater levels that may occur during construction and usage of the structure.

2 The lateral water and earth pressures of sandy soil strata shall be calculated separately.

3 The lateral water and earth pressures of viscous soil strata shall be calculated collectively in construction stage and calculated separately in usage stage.

12. 3 Engineering Material

12. 3. 1 The engineering materials of underground structures shall be determined according to the structure type, stress conditions, usage requirements and environment conditions of the structure while considering the materials' reliability, durability and economy. The main force bearing structure may be of reinforced concrete structure, composite structures such as steel pipe reinforced concrete structure, steel rib reinforced concrete structure and profiled steel reinforced concrete structure or metal structure.

12. 3. 2 The design strength grade of concrete under common environmental conditions shall not be less than those in Table 12. 3. 2 and shall comply with the material selection criteria specified in the current national standard GB 50010 *Code for Design of Concrete Structures*.

Table 12. 3. 2 Minimum Design Strength Grades of Underground Concrete Structures

Structural type		Concrete strength
Cut and cover method	Monolithic reinforced concrete structure	C35
	Prefabricated reinforced concrete structure	C35
	Diaphragm wall and cast-in-place piles serving as permanent structures	C35

Table 12.3.2 (Continued)

Structural type		Concrete strength
Shield method	Monolithic reinforced concrete lining	C35
	Prefabricated reinforced concrete lining segments	C50
Mining method	Shotcrete lining	C25
	Cast-in-place concrete or reinforced concrete lining	C35
Immersed tube method	Reinforced concrete structure	C35
	Prestressed concrete structure	C40

Note: Common environmental conditions refer to Grade I and Grade IIa environment in the current national standard GB 50010 *Code for Design of Concrete Structures*.

12.3.3 The rebar in ordinary reinforced concrete and shotcrete-bolt support structure and the non-prestressed rebar in prestressed concrete structures should be of HRB400 grade, and HRB500 or HPB300 grade rebar may also be used. For prestressed rebar in prestressed concrete structures, prestressed steel strands and steel wires should be adopted and heat treated rebar may also be used.

12.3.4 The connection mode and mechanical performance grade of threaded fasteners between reinforced concrete lining segments shall meet the structural requirements and structure load bearing requirements. The surfaces of the fasteners shall be treated against corrosion.

12.3.5 Shotcrete should be high-performance wet-mix shotcrete.

12.3.6 Steel structures and steel joints shall be treated against corrosion.

12.4 Structure Type and Inner Wall

12.4.1 Lining structure should be designed to be enclosed type. In Grade I and Grade II surrounding rocks without groundwater, there may be no floor slab, and a concrete cushion with a thickness of not less than 200 mm shall be laid.

12.4.2 The lining of cut and cover structures shall be in accordance with the following requirements:

1 Monolithic cast-in-place reinforced concrete lining should be used, or prefabricated reinforced concrete lining may be used locally.

2 The lining of main structure should be considered to be co-stressed jointly with retaining structure, and a separate lining structure may also be used. The diaphragm wall and the bored pile should be co-stressed jointly with the side wall of main structure, as part of the side wall of the main structure. The combination of the walls is be determined according to the specific usage and waterproof requirements, and superimposed or composite double lining may be used.

12.4.3 The lining of shield tunnels shall be in accordance with the following requirements:

1 The double reinforced concrete lining should firstly be used and the inner lining should be cast in place in the tunnel.

2 The prefabricated segmental lining at special sections such as cross passage may be made of steel, cast iron or steel-concrete composite material.

12.4.4 The structural lining of mined tunnels shall be in accordance with the following requirements:

1 The cross section shape and lining type of the structure shall be determined by comprehensive analysis of loading situation, surrounding rock stability and environmental

protection according to surrounding rock conditions, usage requirements, construction methods, sectional dimensions and other factors.

2 For interval tunnels in Grade Ⅲ to Ⅵ surrounding rock or tunnels with similar sectional dimensions, enclosed-type curved lining structure should be used, and the outer contour of lining's cross section should be round and smooth. Where site conditions are unfavorable such as stable surrounding rock, straight wall arched lining may be used, and in special cases, rectangular frame structure may also be used.

3 For station tunnels in Grade Ⅲ to Ⅵ surrounding rock or tunnels with similar sectional dimensions, multi-span structure should be used. The outer contour of the lining should be curved and smooth. Where site conditions are unfavorable such as stable surrounding rock, straight wall arched lining may be used, and in special cases, rectangular frame structure may also be used.

4 Tunnels in surrounding rock of Grade Ⅲ to Ⅵ should have an inverted arch design.

5 The determination of lining type shall be in accordance with the following requirements:

1) Mined tunnels shall use composite lining. In the case of single-track tunnel in Grade Ⅰ to Ⅱ surrounding rocks without groundwater and double-interval tunnel in Grade Ⅰ surrounding rock, one-pass monolithic cast-in-place concrete lining may also be used.

2) The primary lining of composite lining should be determined according to the surrounding rock condition, and the main types and application conditions shall be in accordance with those specified in Table 12.4.4.

Table 12.4.4　Types and Application Conditions of Primary Lining of Composite Lining

Type of primary lining	Application
Anchor rod+shotcrete	Rock-based strata able to keep stable in a long run
Anchor rod+steel arch+shotcrete	Rock-based strata unable to keep stable in a long run
Forepoling+steel arch+shotcrete	Soil-based strata

3) The secondary lining of composite lining shall be of reinforced concrete structure and a waterproof layer or isolating layer shall be laid between the inner and outer linings. Alternatively, prefabricated lining may also be used.

4) In the case of tunnels not intended for use by vehicles and passengers where surrounding rock is intact, stable, and free of groundwater and freezing potential, single-layer anchored shotcrete lining may also be used. The internal clearance of the anchored shotcrete lining shall meet the dimension requirements of the structures to be built subsequently.

12.4.5 The structure of immersed tube tunnel shall be in accordance with the following requirements:

1 The structural type of immersed tube tunnel shall be determined according to the functions and construction conditions. Multi-tube rectangular cross section should be used, and the cross section should be symmetrical.

2 The length and number of the elements shall be determined according to requirements including element fabrication, floating transportation, sinking and tunnel longitudinal slope while considering factors including navigation channel planning, geological conditions and riverbed landform. The length of each element should not be larger than 130 m.

12.5　Structure Design

12.5.1　The structural design shall be in accordance with the following requirements:

1　The underground structure shall be subject to structural strength, rigidity and stability calculations during the construction and normal operation stages. The concrete structure shall also be subject to crack width check in the operation stage. Where accidental load is combined, the crack width of the structure is not checked.

2　The allowable value of the maximum calculation crack width of ordinary reinforced concrete structures shall be determined according to such factors as the type of structure, operating requirements, environment in which it is located and the waterproofing measures.

3　For structures in normal environment, if the load effects are quasi-permanently combined and long-term effects are considered, the allowable value of the maximum calculation crack width should be controlled according to those specified in Table 12.5.1.

Table 12.5.1　Allowable Value of Maximum Calculation Crack Width

Type of structure		Allowable value (mm)	Remarks
Reinforced concrete segment		0.2	
Others	Underwater environment, oxygen-deficient environment in soil	0.3	
	Dry or wet environment in tunnel	0.3	Relative humidity of 45% to 80%
	Dry-wet alternating environment	0.2	

Notes: 1　In calculation, when the actual maximum thickness of concrete cover exceeds 30 mm, the calculation value of thickness of the concrete cover may be taken as 30 mm;

2　For the structures under adverse conditions such as thawing or erosive environment, the allowable value of the maximum calculation crack width shall be determined according to the specific conditions;

3　For the reinforced concrete structure with a thickness of not less than 300 mm, the effects of wetting and drying cycle may not be taken into consideration.

4　The calculation sketch shall be in accordance with the actual working conditions of the structure and reflect the interaction between the surrounding rocks and the structure. When the structure has double lining, the calculation model shall be selected based on the construction type, combination performance, and force transmission characteristics between the two passes of lining.

5　The underground structures shall be subject to stress calculation in the cross-sectional direction, and the longitudinal strength and deformation shall be analyzed under any of the following conditions:

　　1)　The overburden changes greatly in the longitudinal direction of the tunnel;

　　2)　Large local load exists above the structure, such as ground building (structure);

　　3)　The subgrade or foundation varies greatly;

　　4)　The subgrade suffers from uneven settlement in the longitudinal direction;

　　5)　Immersed tunnel structure;

　　6)　The structural form has significant change;

　　7)　Seismic effect is considered.

6　The sections with obvious spatial force effects should be analyzed as spatial structure.

7　In the design of structures in seismic zones, structural measures shall be taken based on the analysis that could reflect the seismic behavior according to the seismic fortification requirements, site conditions, structure type and depth. When the stratum contains liquefiable soil layer, measures for improving liquefaction resistance must be taken.

8 For the mined structure, hardenable slurry shall be injected in time into the backside of secondary lining when it reaches the design strength.

12.5.2 The design of cut and cover structure shall be in accordance with the following requirements:

1 The type of cut and cover structure shall be determined based on the safe and economical construction methods. The underground station should adopt a multi-level multi-span frame structure, and the cut and cover tunnel should adopt a single-span box culvert or an open structure. shall be met, the layout of station structures shall also meet the requirements for interval tunnel construction. For the interval tunnel constructed by shield method, both ends of the station shall be provided with shaft.

2 The cut and cover structure should be designed in such a way that the track beam and the abutment structure are completely separated form independent track beam bridge and independent station structure or interval structure. The track beam may also be directly supported by the cut and cover structure to form an integrated station structure or underground interval structure.

3 The design of track beam bridge with independent structure should be the same as that of the interval elevated structure. In the water-bearing stratum, reliable waterproof measures shall be taken at the connections between the cut and cover structure and the abutment of track beam bridge, and the gap width and settlement difference between the cut and cover structure and the abutment of track beam bridge shall satisfy the requirements for waterproof structure.

4 In the integrated structural system, the associated members of track beams and cut and cover station and interval structure shall be designed to meet the structural stress and deformation requirements in long-term operation. The overall deformation of the station shall meet the settlement control requirements of the track beam.

5 The influence of uneven settlement on the station structures shall be considered in the structural design. When the track beam is arranged independently, the influence of uneven settlement on the platform elevation shall be considered.

6 In the calculation, the cut and cover structure should be deemed as a structure with the bottom slab supported by elastic subgrade, and the long strip-shaped reinforced concrete structure may be deemed as a plane frame with the bottom slab supported by elastic subgrade for which the unit length is taken along the longitudinal direction. The compression effects of the columns and slabs should be considered in the calculation. When the girder is provided with inclined brackets, the influences of the inclined brackets should be taken into account.

7 The cut and cover structure should be calculated under various conditions according to the service conditions, construction requirements and geological and hydrogeological conditions. And the anti-floating, overall slip and foundation stability shall be analyzed according to the geological conditions, depth and construction methods.

8 If the side wall of cut and cover structure adopts composite linings, the interface between retaining wall and lining wall shall be treated and the shear bearing capacity of the interface shall satisfy the control requirements of shear stress.

9 The excavation engineering shall be designed in compliance with the current national specifications and codes for excavation design and shall be in accordance with the following requirements.

1) The excavation safety and environmental protection level, the maximum allowable ground settlement and the horizontal displacement control requirements of the retaining wall shall be determined according to the project characteristics, engineering geological and hydrogeological conditions, and construction conditions, and environmental protection requirements; and the excavation and groundwater treatment methods as well as excavation protection measures shall be proposed through comprehensive technical and economic comparison.

2) The excavation shall be subject to overall stability check against overturning and sliding, bottom soil mass stability check against uplift and seepage, and subsoil stability check against confined groundwater.

3) The depth of the retaining wall shall ensure the excavation stability and the safety of support system, and shall meet the requirements for stability against uplift, seepage and overturning.

4) All members of excavation support structure shall be subject to bearing capacity calculation for ultimate limit state. When the excavation support is taken as part of the main underground structure, it shall be checked to meet the requirements during the excavation period and the service period. Where seismic requirements are imposed for the main works during the service life, the seismic bearing capacity shall be calculated according to the design regulations of the underground structure of the main works.

5) The excavation support structure shall be checked for supporting capacity and deformation under the serviceability limit state and shall meet the allowable deformation value required for support structure and environmental conditions. If required, the structural members shall be subject to crack resistance or crack control check so as to meet the durability performance.

6) In the design of pile/wall type retaining structure, the internal force and deformation shall be calculated in stages by the elastic foundation beam model according to the given excavation conditions and construction sequence. When the supporting action is taken into account, the existing displacement of the wall and the elastic deformation of the supports at the time of setting each layer of support shall be included.

7) When the earth pressure on the lateral side of retaining wall of excavation is calculated, the calculation mode of lateral earth pressure shall be determined according to the factors such as plane shape, support, stress conditions, requirements on excavation deformation control, and the construction measures. The active earth pressure, passive earth pressure or static earth pressure shall be calculated respectively.

8) In the structural calculation, the factors such as segmentation, bracing and pre-stressing, and the time limit of each process during the excavation shall be taken into account to determine the construction parameters reasonably. The horizontal subgrade reaction coefficient of soft soil should be determined according to the structure type, ground characteristics and ground improvement method, construction method,

construction parameters, and the deformation under various construction conditions and load effects.

9) The bearing capacity of the intermediate piles shall be determined through calculation if cover and cut-bottom up method is adopted. Prior to the construction of structural bottom slab, the cumulative value of relative heaving/settlement of retaining wall and intermediate pile shall not be more than 0.003 L (L is the distance between the side wall and the column axis), and should not be more than 20 mm, and the effects shall be considered in the structural analysis.

12.5.3 The structure design of shield tunnel shall be in accordance with the following requirements:

1 The anti-floating safety factor of structure during construction and operation stages shall not be less than 1.1.

2 The tunnel should be a flexible structure with the joints having a proper rigidity and shall satisfy the structural stress and waterproof requirements. The deformation and joint opening under the load effects shall be limited. The calculation diameter deformation should not exceed 3‰ D (D is outer diameter of tunnel).

3 The calculation sketch of tunnel structure shall be determined according to the stratum conditions, lining structure characteristics and construction process.

4 The structure of segmental linings shall be in accordance with the following requirements:

1) Both the lining segments and rings should be connected by bolts;

2) The width of ring of the lining should not be less than 1000 mm;

3) The taper of wedged ring shall be determined according to the diameter of tunnel, width of lining ring and the curve radius of the tunnel, which should be taken in the range of 1 : 100 to 1 : 300;

4) The thickness of the lining shall be determined according to such factors as tunnel diameter, depth, geological and hydrogeological conditions, and the load conditions during construction and operation stages, which should be 0.04 to 0.06 times the outer diameter of the tunnel (smaller multiply should be taken for larger diameter tunnel);

5) The division of the lining ring shall be determined according to the requirements on segment fabrication, transportation, shield equipment, construction method and stress. The lining ring should be classified into 6 segments to 12 segments;

6) The selection of key segment should be based on the calculation mode and construction techniques;

7) The lining ring may be assembledby full longitudinal insertion, semi-longitudinal insertion and radial insertion methods according to the design requirements, shield equipment, practical experience, etc;

8) The width of end ribs and ring ribs of the segment shall satisfy the strength and crack resistance requirements under the stress condition of the bolt.

5 The fabrication, assembly and construction accuracy of segmental lining shall be in accordance with the following requirements:

1) Allowable errors for single segment: width: ±0.5 mm (or ±0.4 mm in the case of staggered assembling); thickness: ±1.0 mm; arc length and chord length: ±1.0 mm;

longitudinal and circumferential bolt hole diameter and position: ± 1.0 mm;

2) Allowable error for assembling of entire ring: torus gap of adjacent rings: not more than 1.0 mm; gap between adjacent segments along the longitudinal joint: not more than 1.5 mm; misalignment of corresponding circumferential bolt holes: less than 1mm; outer diameter of lining ring: $^{+3}_{-0}$mm; inner diameter: $^{+3}_{-0}$ mm;

3) The error for tunnel construction axis and design axis shall be less than 100 mm.

6 Rigid connection should be adopted for the tunnel and work shaft, and deformation joints should be set beyond the ground improvement area of the work shaft at intervals which varies from dense to sparse but still in normal spacing. Deformation joints shall also be provided where cross passage is built.

7 Measures against release of stress between the rings shall be taken at theTBM break-out section.

8 In the tunnel, the alignment shall set low and the supporting beam shall be secured on the primary bracing structure in the tunnel.

12.5.4 The mined structural design shall be in accordance with the following requirements:

1 For themined structure, the stability of the primary lining shall be judged in the pre-design and construction stages.

2 The primary lining of shotcrete-bolt lining and composite lining shall be designed based on the main force-bearing structure. The design parameters may be determined with the analogy method and corrected by means of monitoring and measuring during construction. The shallow-buried structures or those with large span, in complex rock or environmental conditions, or special type structures shall be checked through theoretical calculations.

3 The secondary lining of composite lining shall be determined according to such factors as the construction time, load changes after construction, geological and hydrogeological conditions, and requirements on depth and durability, and shall be in accordance with the following requirements:

1) For the shallow structures in the Quaternary soil layer and those passing through the rheological or swelling wall rock, the primary lining shall be designed with greater rigidity and strength, and the secondary lining should be provided in advance to bear the external load with the primary lining jointly;

2) During long-term service, the external load will be transferred to the secondary lining due to the degradation of material performance and rigidity of the primary lining;

3) The water pressure acting on the undrained structure is borne by the secondary lining;

4) For the shallow structures and those in Level V-VI surrounding rocks, reinforced concrete lining should be taken.

12.5.5 The structural design of immersed tube tunnel shall comply with the relevant provisions in the current national standard GB 50157 *Code for Design of Metro*.

12.6 Tectonic Requirements

12.6.1 The deformation joints shall be set in accordance with the following requirements:

1 The deformation joints of underground structure may be classified into expansion joints and settlement joints.

2 The spacing of the thermal deformation joints of underground structure may be determined according to the factors like structural characteristics, geotechnical conditions, construction technology, construction conditions, mode of combination between internal structure and retaining structure, operating conditions, and the changes in internal temperature during operation.

3 The settlement deformation joints should not be set in interval tunnel and station structure. Where great differential settlement may happen due to the changes in structure, ground or load, such methods as ground treatment, structural measures, setting construction joints or post-cast strip should be used to control settlement.

4 The deformation joints should be provided at the connection between station and entrance/exit passage or other auxiliary buildings.

5 Proper measures shall be taken to prevent the structures on either side of the deformation joint against any differential settlement that affects the safety of train operation and the normal use of the structures.

12.6.2 The transverse construction joints of cast-in-place concrete and reinforced concrete structures should be set on side wall, shall according to the form of structure, stress requirements, construction method, meteorological conditions, and the setting of deformation joints.

12.6.3 The thickness of concrete cover for reinforcement shall be in accordance with the following requirements:

1 The thickness of concrete cover for main bar shall not be less than the nominal diameter of the bar, the thickness of the minimum concrete cover for the outermost reinforcing bar in normal environment shall be in accordance with those specified in Table 12.6.3.

2 The thickness of the concrete cover shall also meet the requirements of the current national standard GB/T 50476 *Code for Durability Design of Concrete Structures*.

Table 12.6.3 Thickness of the Minimum Concrete Cover for the Outermost Reinforcing Bar in Normal Environment (mm)

Type of structure	Cut and cover structure														Reinforced concrete segment		Mined structure	
	Retaining structure			Main structure														
	Diaphragm wall		Cast-in-place pile	Roof slab		Floor slab	Bottom slab		Lining wall		Side wall		Column	Outer side	Inner side	Primary lining or shotcrete lining	Secondary lining
	Outer side	Inner side		Outer side	Inner side		Outer side	Inner side	Outer side	Inner side	Outer side	Inner side					
Thickness of concrete cover	70	70	70	45	35	30	45	35	40	30	45	35	35	35	25	35	40

Note: 1 The thickness of concrete cover for main bars of jacked tunnel and immersed tube tunnel may be as same as that of the cut and cover structure.

2 For the mined structure, the thickness of reinforcement concrete cover shall be 40 mm when the thickness of the secondary lining is larger than 500 mm.

3 In this table, the lining wall refers to the composite wall composed of diaphragm wall and lining wall. The thickness of the concrete cover of the bars on the inner side of the diaphragm wall may be 50 mm.

12.6.4 For the cut and cover structures, the reinforcement ratio of distribution bars in exposed surface on each side of the surrounding structural members and the intermediate slabs should not be less than 0.2%, and the spacing of distribution bars should not be larger than 150 mm. When the concrete strength grade is larger than C60, the minimum reinforcement ratio of distribution bars should be increased by 0.1%.

13 Structure Waterproof

13. 1 General Requirements

13. 1. 1 This Chapter is applicable to waterproofing design of cut and cover structures excavated with side slope or retaining wall, undermined structures excavated by shield method or mining method, immersed structures and other structures built by special methods for medium and low speed maglev transit lines.

13. 1. 2 Underground structure waterproofing shall be designed according to the specific climate condition, engineering geological and hydrological conditions, environmental protection requirements, structural characteristics, construction methods and application requirements.

13. 1. 3 Underground structural waterproofing grade shall be in accordance with the following requirements:

1 Underground station and the sections where mechanical and electrical equipment is concentrated shall be waterproof grade Ⅰ without seepage and wet stains on the structural surface.

2 Interval tunnels and other affiliated tunnel structures shall reach waterproof grade Ⅱ without leakage and tiny wet stains may be allowed on the structure surface. The total area of wet stains shall not be more than 2/1000 of entire waterproof area. There are less than three wet stains at any 100 m² waterproof area, and each stain shall not be larger than 0. 2 m²; the average leakage of tunnel structure shall not exceed 0. 05 L/m² · d and the leakage of any 100 m² waterproof area shall not exceed 0. 15 L/m² · d.

13. 2 Self-waterproof of Concrete Structure

13. 2. 1 The impermeability grade of waterproof concrete structure shall be dependent on its embedment depth and shall not be less than P8.

13. 2. 2 Waterproof concrete structure shall be in accordance with the following requirements:

1 Structural thickness shall not be less than 250 mm;

2 Crack width shall be in accordance with those specified in Table 12. 5. 1 in this code, and through cracks shall not be allowed.

13. 2. 3 Main technical measures for waterproofing and anti-crack of waterproof concrete shall comply with national standard of GB 50108 *Technical Code for Waterproofing of Underground Works*.

13. 3 Waterproof for Underground Station Structure

13. 3. 1 Underground station shall be provided with waterproof reinforced concrete and partially or wholly with additional waterproof layer according to structure type.

13. 3. 2 The additional waterproof layer may be waterproof membrane, waterproof coating, plastic waterproof sheet or bentonite waterproof layer, which shall be applied on the leading surface or within the composite lining.

13. 3. 3 Waterproof measures for stations built by cut and cover method shall be determined according to grade I waterproof requirement given in Table 13. 3. 3.

Table 13. 3. 3   Waterproof Measures for Cut and Cover Structure

Structural part	Major structure							Construction joint						Post-cast strip
Waterproof measure	Waterproof concrete	Waterproof Mortar	Waterproof coiled material	Waterproof coating	Bentonite waterproof material	Water swelling waterstop strip (sealant)	External adhesive waterstop tape	Embedded waterstop tape	Cement-based permeable crystalline waterproof coating	External waterproof mortar	External waterproof coating	Embedded grouting pipe		Shrinkage compensating concrete
Waterproof Grade	Grade I	Compulsory	One or two measures shall be selected					Two shall be selected						
	Grade II	Compulsory	One shall be selected					One or two shall be selected						

Structural part	Post-cast strip						Deformation joint (induced joint)					
Waterproof measure	External adhesive waterstop tape	Embedded grouting pipe	Waterproof coating	Water swelling waterstop strip (sealant)	Waterproof sealing material	Embedded waterstop tape	External adhesive waterstop tape	Detachable waterstop tape	Waterproof sealing material	External adhesive roll type membrane	External waterproof coating	Embedded grouting pipe
Waterproof Grade	Compulsory	Two shall be selected					Compulsory	Two or three shall be selected				
	Compulsory	One or two shall be selected					Compulsory	One or two shall be selected				

Note: Water swelling waterstop strip (sealant) shall be slow swelling type.

13. 3. 4   The underground station built by side slope excavation method and the underground station structure with composite side wall shall be protected by waterproof concrete and fully-covered flexible waterproof layer.

13. 3. 5   The waterproof design of diaphragm wall as the single wall of main structure shall be in accordance with the following requirements:

1   Single diaphragm wall shall not be directly used as underground structural wall with waterproof Grade I.

2   Single wall used for underground structure shall be applied with high-molecular polymer protective material and non-dispersive underwater concrete.

3   Water seepage shall be prohibited at joints between panels of diaphragm walls.

4   Embedded parts of supports shall be provided with waterstops or water swelling waterstop strips. Cracks, holes and other defects in supports and walls shall be repaired in time with waterproof mortar. Water seepage at joints between panels of diaphragm wall shall be treated by grouting or elastic sealing material filling.

5   Diaphragm wall shall be provided with inner waterproof layer.

6   The connection surface of wall with roof slab, bottom slab and intermediate floor slab shall be chiseled, cleaned and provided with one to two water swelling waterstop strips (sealants), the connectors should be sealed by cement-based permeable crystalline waterproof material or high-permeability modified epoxy coating.

7   The leading surface of station roof slab shall be provided with a flexible waterproof layer and the rigid-flexible transition area shall be sealed.

13. 3. 6   Where diaphragm wall or bored secant pile is used as retaining structure and forms a superimposed structure together with lining wall, the anti-permeability grade may be one grade lower than that of the lining wall concrete but shall not be less than P8; where the diaphragm wall or bored secant pile lining wall constitutes a separate structure, anti-permeability grade may be not compulsory.

13.3.7 Where retaining structure and lining wall constitute a composite wall structure to jointly bear loads, their waterproof design shall be in accordance with the following requirements:

1 If diaphragm wall is used as retaining structure, cracks, holes or other defects in supports and walls shall be repaired in time by waterproof mortar; seepage at joints between panels of diaphragm wall shall be treated by grouting or elastic sealing material filling.

2 The leading surface of station roof slab should be provided with flexible waterproof layer and the rigid-flexible connection transition area shall be well sealed.

3 The surface of diaphragm wall shall be chiseled and cleaned, and waterproof treatment shall be made before casting waterproof concrete as lining where necessary.

13.3.8 Waterproof design of the compound wall structure shall be in accordance with the following requirements:

1 The waterproof layer of the leading surfaces of station roof slab and bottom slab and the interlayer waterproofing between side wall retaining structure and lining wall should be an integral water seal layer; and suitable protective layer is be provided at different positions.

2 The connection between underground station and interval tunnel may use rigid joint, but the gap should be sealed by flexible materials, meanwhile, the surrounding ground should be improved.

3 Materials selected for underground station and interval tunnel shall be able to be mutually bonded or welded.

13.3.9 Waterproof measures for mined underground station shall be determined according to grade I waterproof requirement in Table 13.3.9.

Table 13.3.9 Waterproof Measures for Mined Underground Structure

Structural parts	Waterproof measures	Waterproof grade	
		Grade I	Grade II
Main structure	Waterproof concrete	Compulsory	Compulsory
	Plastic waterproof board	One or two shall be applied	One shall be applied
	Waterproof membrane		
	Bentonite waterproof material		
Lining construction joint	External adhesive waterstop strip	Two shall be applied	One or two shall be applied
	Water swelling waterstop strip (sealant)		
	Waterproof sealing material		
	Embedded waterstop strip		
	Embedded grouting pipe		
Lining deformation joint	Embedded waterstop strip	Compulsory	Compulsory
	External adhesive waterstop strip	Two shall be applied	One or two shall be applied
	Detachable waterstop strip		
	Waterproof sealing material		
	Embedded grouting pipe		

13.3.10 Waterproof measures for deformation joints shall meet the waterproof sealing requirements of differential settlement and longitudinal expansion and contraction of both sides of joints.

13. 4 Waterproof for Tunnel Structure

13. 4. 1 Waterproof measures forinterval tunnel built by cut and cover method shall be determined according to the waterproof Grade II requirement in Table 13. 3. 3 in this code.

13. 4. 2 Waterproof designof diaphragm wall used as the single wall of interval tunnel shall meet the requirements of Article 13. 3. 5 in this code.

13. 4. 3 Waterproof methods for composite wall shall meet the requirements of Article 13. 3. 7 in this code.

13. 4. 4 Waterproof methods for compound wall structure shall meet the requirements of Article 13. 3. 8 in this code.

13. 4. 5 Water measures for interval tunnels built by mining method and tunnel affiliated structures shall be determined in accordance with the Grade II waterproof requirement in Table 13. 3. 9 in this code.

13. 4. 6 Waterproof measures for shield tunnels shall be in accordance with the following requirements:

 1 Lining segments of shield tunnels shall be made of waterproof concrete with an anti-permeability grade shall not less than P10 and chloride ion diffusion coefficient should not larger than 3×10^{-12} m^2/s (RCM test, 56d test pieces). Waterproof coating should be applied over the external surface of the lining which is tested to be unqualified.

 2 Anti-corrosive waterproof coating should be applied over the external surface of lining structure in case the tunnel is exposed to medium or above level of corrosive medium.

 3 Waterproof measures for the shield tunnel lining shall be in accordance with those specified in Table 13. 4. 6.

Table 13. 4. 6　Waterproof Measures for Shield Tunnel

Waterproof grade measures taken waterproof measures	High-precision lining segment	Waterproof measures for joints				Concrete lining or other linings	External waterproof coating
		Gasket	Caulking	Inject sealant	Bolt hole sealing washer		
Grade I	Compulsory	Compulsory	Throughout the tunnel or locally used shall be selected	Optional	Compulsory	Recommended	Recommended
Grade II	Compulsory	Compulsory	Locally used should be selected	Optional	Compulsory	Local use is recommended	Recommended for strata imposing medium and above level corrosion on concrete

 4 The lining segment joints must be provided with at least one gasket groove. The specification and technical performance of waterproof materials and waterproof measures for screw hole and caulking groove shall comply with the current national standard GB 50108 *Technical Code for Waterproofing of Underground Works* besides design requirements.

5 The gasket of lining segment joint shall ensure that no leakage occurs at the joint when it expands and dislocates to the maximum under design water pressure. The gasket shall undergo the straight or T-shaped joints water pressure test and shall reach such a criteria that no leakage occurs when the joint expands to the design maximum opening and predicted maximum displacement under three times the water pressure at the maximum depth of tunnel.

14 Ventilationing, Air Conditioning and Heating

14.1 General Requirements

14.1.1 The internal air environment of medium and low-speed maglev transit line shall include the station concourse, platform, entrance and exit passages, equipment and management rooms in the station, interval tunnels and other auxiliary buildings.

14.1.2 The function of the ventilation and air-conditioning systems of the underground line shall comply with the current national standard GB 50490 *Technical Code of Urban Rail Transit*.

14.1.3 Ventilation and air conditioning systems for elevated and ground lines should preferably adopt natural ventilation. However, when natural ventilation does not meet the air environmental requirements, the mechanical ventilation or air conditioning systems may be used.

14.1.4 The ventilation and air conditioning systems shall be designed according to the predicted maximum passenger flow and throughput, but the equipment shall be implemented in phases according to the short-term and long-term configuration.

14.1.5 The energy conservation design of ventilation and air-conditioning systems shall comply with the current national standard GB 50189 *Design Standard for Energy Efficiency of Public Buildings*.

14.1.6 The layout of equipment, piping and fittings for ventilation and air conditioning systems shall comply with the current national standard GB 50736 *Design Code for Heating Ventilation and Air Conditioning of Civil Buildings*. HVAC system and smoke exhaust system equipment should not be installed above the tracks. In case the equipment has to be set above the track, reliable anti-shedding measures shall be taken.

14.1.7 Class A non-combustible materials shall be used for pipes, insulation materials and sound-absorbing materials for HVAC system. When it is difficult to use Class A non-combustible materials in a local part, Class B1 nonflammable materials may be used. Pipe and insulation materials shall be moisture-proof, anti-corrosive, anti-insect, anti-aging and non-toxic.

14.2 Design Standards

14.2.1 The design standards for public areas of stations shall be in accordance with the following requirements:

  1 Outdoor air calculation parameters shall be in accordance with the following requirements:

    1) For ground and elevated stations, the outdoor air temperature and relative humidity for HVAC system calculations shall comply with the current national standard GB 50736 *Design Code for Heating Ventilation and Air Conditioning of Civil Buildings*;

    2) For underground station, the calculation dry bulb temperature of summer air conditioning outdoor air shall be the dry bulb temperature with 30 h non-guaranteed per year at rail transit peaks in the summer of the last 20 years;

    3) For underground station, the calculation wet bulb temperature of summer air conditioning outdoor air shall be the wet bulb temperature with 30 h non-guaranteed per year at rail transit peaks in the summer of the last 20 years;

4) For underground station, the calculation temperature of the summer ventilation outdoor shall be average value of the average temperature of the hottest months in the past 20 years;

5) Calculation temperature of the winter ventilation outdoor shall be average value of the average temperature of the coldest months in the past 20 years.

2 Indoor air calculation parameters shall be in accordance with the following requirements:

1) For ground and elevated stations, when the station concourse is ventilated, the calculation summer temperature in the station concourse shall not be higher than the outdoor calculation temperature by 3 ℃, but the maximum shall not exceed 35 ℃;

2) For ground and elevated stations, when the air conditioning system is required in the station concourse, the summer design temperature in the station concourse shall be 29 ℃ to 30 ℃, and the relative humidity shall not be greater than 70%;

3) For underground stations, when the station adopts a ventilation system, the calculation summer air temperature in the station should not be higher than the outdoor calculation temperature by 5 ℃, and shall not exceed 30 ℃;

4) For the underground station, when the station adopts the air conditioning system, the summer air conditioning design temperature in the station concourse shall be 2 ℃ to 3 ℃ lower than the outdoor calculation dry bulb temperature, and shall not exceed 30 ℃, and the relative humidity should be 40% to 70%;

5) For the underground station, when the station adopts the air conditioning system, the summer air conditioning design temperature on the station platform shall be 1 ℃ to 2 ℃ lower than the design temperature of the station concourse, and the relative humidity should be 40% to 70%;

6) For ground and elevated stations, when the heating system is installed in the station, the design temperature shall be 12 ℃;

7) For underground stations, the winter design temperature in the station shall not be greater than the natural temperature of the local ground floor, but the minimum temperature shall not be less than 12 ℃.

3 The fresh air volume shall be in accordance with the following requirements:

1) When the ventilation system operates in an open mode, the amount of fresh air required per passenger per hour shall not be less than 30 m³; when in the closed mode, the fresh air volume shall not be less than 12.6 m³, and the fresh air volume of the system shall not be less than 10% of the total air inlet;

2) When the station adopts the air conditioning system, the fresh air volume required per passenger per hour in the public area of the station shall not be less than 12.6 m³, and the fresh air volume of the system shall not be less than 10% of the total air inlet.

4 Air quality shall be in accordance with the following requirements:

1) The average daily concentration of CO_2 in the station shall be less than 1.5‰;

2) The average daily concentration of respirable particulate matter in the air of the station shall be less than 0.25 mg/m³.

5 The instantaneous wind speed of the station concourse and platform should be less than 5 m/s.

14. 2. 2 Design standards of equipment and management rooms in underground station shall be in accordance with the following requirements:

1 Outdoor air design parameters shall comply with the current national standard GB 50736 *Design Code for Heating Ventilation and Air Conditioning of Civil Buildings*.

2 Interior design parameters of main equipment and management rooms shall be in accordance with those specified in Table 14. 2. 2; other equipment rooms shall be equipped with ventilating, air conditioning and heating systems according to process requirements. Design temperature shall be determined by the process requirements.

Table 14. 2. 2 Interior Air Calculating Parameters of Main Equipment and Management Rooms in Underground Station

No.	Rooms	Winter	Summer		Air circulation ratio (time/h)	
		Design temperature (℃)	Design temperature (℃)	Relative humidity (%)	Intake air	Exhaust air
1	Stationmaster's room, station attendant room, duty room, station lounge	18	27	<65	6	6
2	Station central control room, broadcasting room, control room	18	27	40~60	6	5
3	Booking office, ticketing room	18	27	40~60	6	5
4	Automatic fare collection (AFC) room	16	27	40~60	6	6
5	Communication equipment room, communication power supply room, signal equipment room, signal power room, integrated monitoring equipment room	16	27	40~60	6	5
6	Rectifier substation, lighting and power substation, main substation	—	36	—	Ventilation capacity is calculated based on exhausted residual heat	
7	Switching room, machine room	16	36	—	4	4
8	Battery room	16	30	—	6	6
9	Locker room, repair room, cleaners room	18	27	<65	6	6
10	Public security room, meeting and shift room	18	27	<65	6	6
11	Telecommunication cable room, signal cable room	—	—	—	4	4
12	Tea room	—	—	—	—	10
13	Washing room, station supplies room	—	—	—	4	4
14	Cleaning tools room, gas cylinders room, storeroom	—	—	—	—	4
15	Sewage pump room, waste water pump room, fire-pump room	5	—	—	—	4
16	Turn line maintaining room	12	30	—	—	6
17	Environment control machine room	—	—	—	6	6
18	Toilet	>5	—	—	—	Discharge air

Note: 1 Air flow rate in toilet is calculated by 100 m³/h, and air should be exhausted no less than 10 times per hour;

2 Air changing rate per hour means room minimum air changing rate under ventilating condition.

3 The fresh air per staff per hour shall not be less than 30 m³. And total fresh air volume shall not be less than 10% of the total air inlet.

4 Air quality of station equipment and management rooms shall conform to following specifications:

1) Daily average CO_2 concentration shall be lower than 1‰.

2) Daily average concentration of inhalable particle in the air shall be lower than 0.25 mg/m^3.

14.2.3 Design standard of the underground sections shall be in accordance with the following requirements:

1 Outdoor air calculation parameters shall be in accordance with the following requirements:

1) For ventilating in summer, the outdoor design temperature shall adopt the highest monthly average temperature in the past 20 years.

2) For ventilating in winter, the outdoor design temperature shall adopt the lowest monthly average temperature in the past 20 years.

2 Air design parameters of underground sections shall be in accordance with the following requirements:

1) When there is no air conditioner in train compartments, the maximum temperature shall not be higher than 33 ℃;

2) When there are air conditioners working in train compartments and there are no totally-enclosed platform screen door in the station, the maximum average temperature shall not be higher than 35 ℃;

3) When there are air conditioners working in train compartments and there are totally-enclosed platform screen doors in the station, the maximum temperature in train compartments shall not be higher than 40 ℃;

4) For interval tunnel, winter average temperature shall not be higher than natural temperature of local stratum, bus shall not be lower than 5 ℃.

14.2.4 Noise from air conditioning and ventilating equipment to other areas shall be in accordance with the following requirements:

1 Noise level reaching the station concourse and platform shall be no higher than 70dB (A).

2 Noise level reaching the working rooms and the lounge shall be no higher than 60dB (A).

3 Noise level in the air conditioner and ventilator room shall be no higher than 90dB (A).

4 Noise level reaching the ground ventilating shaft through the ventilating shaft shall conform to the current national standard GB 3096 *Environmental Quality Standard for Noise*.

14.3 Underground Station and Tunnel

14.3.1 Air ventilating and conditioning system of underground station shall take in air directly from outdoor air and exhaust air directly to the ground.

14.3.2 When calculating the flow of air required to remove residual heat, the amount of heat transferred from the station and the tunnel to the soil surrounding the stratum shall be calculated.

14.3.3 Ventilation system should be installed at the heat generation part of the train when it stops at the underground station.

14.3.4 When piston air has a significant impact on the station, a venting shaft or a circulation tunnel shall be provided at both ends of the station.

14.3.5 Ventilation or other cooling measures shall be adopted at entrance/exit passages with a continuous length of more than 60 m or long passages of underground station.

14. 3. 6 Where a central air shaft is to be installed, the shaft should be located at the midpoint of the tunnel. In exceptional cases, it may be located at a point not less than 1/3 of the overall tunnel length away from tunnel end, but the distance should not be less than 400 m.

14. 3. 7 The public zone of underground station and interval tunnel may not be installed with heating system. When the equipment management room at underground station needs heating, local heating may be employed.

14. 3. 8 Underground substation shall be provided with a mechanical ventilation system, and the ventilation capacity of the system shall be calculated according to the residual heat to be removed. Where the capacity of mechanical ventilation is insufficient to remove residual heat, cold air system may be installed.

14. 3. 9 The mechanical ventilation system shall be provided in the room where gas fire extinguishing is used and the gas shall be directly exhausted to the ground.

14. 3. 10 The toilet shall be provided with an independent ventilation system with mechanical air outlet and natural air intake, in which air shall be directly exhausted to the ground.

14. 3. 11 When ventilation systems of end line or turn-back line equipment and management rooms need to induce draft from tunnel, the air inlet shall be set on the side where the train enters the station while the air outlet shall be set on the side where the train exits. The air inlet shall be provided with a dust filter and the average daily concentration of the inhalable particulate matter in the filtered air shall be less than 0. 25 mg/m^3.

14. 4 Ground and Elevated Station

14. 4. 1 Natural ventilation should be adopted for the station concourses and platforms of at-ground and elevated stations. Mechanical ventilation or air conditioning system may be installed in station concourse. Communication equipment room, signaling equipment room, transformer room and automatic fare collection (AFC) room should be equipped with independent mechanical ventilation system and independent air conditioning system.

14. 4. 2 Ground substation should adopt natural ventilation to reduce temperature. Where natural ventilation cannot meet the work environment requirement of equipment, mechanical air outlet and natural air intake may be adopted.

14. 4. 3 The temperature, humidity and air quality of other equipment and management rooms in the station shall comply with the requirements of Article 14. 2. 2 of this code.

14. 4. 4 For the management rooms of at-ground and elevated stations in heating areas, local heating may be adopted, and the indoor design heating temperature should be 18 ℃.

14. 4. 5 When air conditioner is used in station concourse, air curtains should be provided at the stairway entrance, escalator entrance and accesses connecting station concourse and platform.

14. 4. 6 For areas where the average outdoor temperature in the coldest month is greater than −10 ℃, heating system may not be installed in the station concourse and platform of at-ground and elevated stations.

14. 4. 7 For the cold areas where the average outdoor temperature in the coldest month is less than −10 ℃, heating system should be installed in the station concourse but not in the platform.

14. 4. 8 When heating system is installed in station concourse, warm air curtain shall be provided at the stairway entrance, escalator entrance and accesses connecting station concourse and platform.

14.5 Colding Source, Water System and Heating Source

14.5.1 The design of cold source of air-conditioner shall be in accordance with the following requirements:

1 The cold source of air conditioning system should be a natural cold source. If there is no natural cold source, artificial cold source may be used.

2 Air-conditioner cold source equipment in underground line shall be of electric compression type, and absorption-type chiller shall not be adopted.

3 The chiller shall be chosen according to the load condition, operation time and operation adjustment requirements of the air conditioning system, combined with the type of refrigerant, installed capacity and energy saving effect.

4 In areas where time-of-use electricity price is implemented and the price during peak load period differs greatly from that during valley load period, cool storage system may be adopted if technological and economic comparison shows it is feasible.

14.5.2 The design of refrigerator room shall be in accordance with the following requirements:

1 Each station should be equipped with a refrigerator room, which shall be located close to the load center of air conditioning system and should be integrated with air-conditioner room.

2 In the refrigerator room, the space required for transportation, installation, maintenance, overhaul and measurement of the refrigeration equipment shall be reserved under the premise of considering various air flues and pipelines in the room, and water drainage facilities shall be installed as well.

3 The ventilation facilities of the refrigerator room shall comply with the current national standard GB 50736 *Design Code for Heating Ventilation and Air Conditioning of Civil Buildings*.

4 The pressure relief pipe of refrigerant's safety valve shall be connected to an outdoor safe area.

5 Local lighting shall be provided in the instrument centralized area of the refrigerator room.

6 There should not be less than 2 chillers in the refrigerator room, and stand-by chiller may not be provided. When only one chiller is employed, multi-head joint-control chiller should be used.

14.5.3 The design of chilled water system shall be in accordance with the following requirements:

1 Chilled water system shall adopt closed water system.

2 The make-up water flow shall be 1% of the water capacity of the system, and the water make-up point should be set at the inlet of the chilled water pump.

3 The lift of the chilled water make-up pump shall be 3 m to 5 m higher than the pressure of the make-up point, and the chilled water flow per hour should be 4% to 5% of the water capacity of the system.

4 The chilled water pump should match with the chiller.

5 The thickness of cold insulation layer of chilled water pipe shall be calculated according to the method for calculating the thickness of the cold insulation layer provided for preventing surface condensation in the current national standard GB/T 8175 *Guide for Design of Thermal Insulation of Equipment and Pipes*.

14.5.4 The design of cooling system shall be in accordance with the following requirements:

1 Cooling water shall be recycled.

2 The water quality of cooling water shall comply with the current national standard GB 50050 *Code for design of Industrial Circulating Cooling Water Treatment*.

3 The cooling water makeup flow shall be 1% to 2% of the circulating water flow of the system.

4 When the temperature of the cooling water is lower than the allowable water temperature of the chiller, the water temperature shall be controlled.

5 Cooling water pump should match with the chiller.

6 Cooling water pipes shall be thermally insulated according to local climatic conditions.

14.5.5 The cooling tower shall be in accordance with the following requirements:

1 The cooling tower shall be located in a draughty place and in harmony with the surrounding environment. Its noise level shall comply with the current national standard GB 3096 *Environmental Quality Standard for Noise*.

2 When more than one cooling towers are used, they should be identical in type. Connecting pipes shall be provided under the water collecting tray and electric valves shall be provided in inlet and outlet pipes.

14.5.6 The accessories of air conditioning water system shall be in accordance with the following requirements:

1 Large-sized air conditioning water systems should be equipped with water separator and water collector.

2 Filter or dirt separator shall be installed at the inlet of equipment such as chiller and pump.

3 Air conditioning water system shall be equipped with accessories such as pressure gage and thermometer.

4 Water seal shall be installed if surface air cooler is on the suction side.

14.5.7 Nearby heat supply network shall be utilized as the heat source. Other unpolluted heat sources may be used in case there is no heat supply network.

14.6 System Control

14.6.1 Air conditioning and ventilation equipment for at-ground and elevated stations should adopt two-level control mode: local control and station control.

14.6.2 Ventilation system of underground interval tunnel should adopt three-level control mode: local control, station control and central control.

14.6.3 The ventilation system for the public area of underground station should adopt three-level control mode: local control, station control and central control.

14.6.4 The ventilation and air conditioning systems of underground station equipment and management rooms should adopt two-level control mode: local control and station control.

14.7 Air Duct, Air Shaft and Air Pavilion

14.7.1 The design air flows of air duct and air pipe should be in accordance with the following requirements:

1 The design air flows of air duct and air shaft should not exceed 8 m/s.

2 The design air flows of the exhaust air duct at the bottom of station platform and the exhaust air duct at the top of the train should not exceed 15 m/s.

3 The design air flow of air pavilion grille should not exceed 4 m/s.

14.7.2 The design of air shaft and air pavilion shall be in accordance with the following requirements:

1 The at-ground air inlet pavilion shall be located in a place with clean air and should be on the windward side of air outlet pavilion.

2 The opening of air outlet pavilion should keep clear of the local most-frequent wind direction in the year.

14.8 Rooms for Equipment Management and Others

14.8.1 The temperature, humidity and air quality of the equipment management room shall meet the requirements of Article 14.2.2 in this code.

14.8.2 Rectifier substation, lighting and power substation and high voltage substation shall be equipped with mechanical ventilation system, the ventilation flow of which is calculated according to the residual heat to be removed. If the residual heat exceeds the capacity of mechanical ventilation, cold air system may be used.

14.8.3 Toilet shall be provided with an independent ventilation system with mechanical air exhaust and natural air intake, in which air shall be directly exhausted to the ground.

14.8.4 The ventilating, air conditioning and heating system of control center shall meet the requirements of Section 24.7 in this code. The ventilating, air conditioning and heating systems of the comprehensive maintenance base and process equipment room shall comply with the current national standard GB 50019 *Design Code for Heating Ventilation and Air conditioning of Industrial Buildings*.

14.8.5 The air conditioning and ventilating system of underground equipment management room should have the function of fire smoke extraction.

15　Water Supply and Drainage

15.1　General Requirements

15.1.1　The water supply system shall be designed to meet the flow, pressure, and quality requirements of production, living, and fire water.

15.1.2　The drainage system shall be designed to collect and drain the living wastewater, production wastewater, structure leakage and seepage, flushing wastewater, fire wastewater and rainwater and the wastewater and sewage shall be discharged in compliance with the current national standard GB 8978 *Integrated Wastewater Discharge Standard*.

15.1.3　The water supply system and drainage system shall be designed to provide convenience for the construction and installation, operation and management, maintenance and inspection, and personal protection.

15.1.4　Information technology shall be taken in the water supply and drainage design to monitor the operating state of the systems, and reliable automation devices shall be used to realize automatic control of the operation process, reduce manual operations, and improve system performance.

15.1.5　The design of water supply and drainage systems shall comply with the current national standards GB 50015 *Code for Design of Building Water Supply and Drainage*, GB 50016 *Code for Fire Protection Design of Buildings*, and GB 50555 *Standard for Water Saving Design in Civil Building*.

15.2　Water Supply

15.2.1　The municipal water supply system shall be preferred for medium and low speed maglev transit, or other reliable water sources shall be used if it is impossible to access to the municipal water supply system along the line.

15.2.2　The water supply system shall be selected according to quality, pressure, and consumption requirements of production water, living water, and fire water and comply with the following provisions:

　　1　The production and living water supply systems shall be connected from the municipal water supply system and pressurization devices or water reservoir shall be provided when the water pressure or flow could not meet the requirements.

　　2　The indoor production and living water systems of the station shall be separated from the fire water system and metering facilities shall be provided according to the requirements of local water supply company.

　　3　Where urban miscellaneous water system is available around the station and the water quality meets the requirements for cooling water and flushing water, separate quality water supply system should be used in which the miscellaneous water of station shall be separated from other water supply systems and measures for avoiding drinking shall be taken.

　　4　Two water supply pipes should be led from the municipal water supply systems to be used as the water sources of vehicle base. For the production, living and outdoor fire water supply pipes, common ring pipe network water supply system should be used. When one water supply pipe is available from the municipal water supply system, the production, living, and outdoor fire water systems shall be separated. The indoor and outdoor fire water supply systems shall be shared only if justified by technical and economic comparison.

15.2.3 The design quota of water consumption shall be in accordance with the following requirements:

1 The living water consumption of working personnel shall be controlled within 30 L per person per shift to 60 L per person per shift, with the hourly variation coefficient of 2.5 to 2.0.

2 The flushing water consumption for common areas of the station shall be controlled within 1 L/m^2 per time to 2 L/m^2 per time (one flushing lasting for 1 h every day). The flushing water consumption for the vehicles of depot, stabling yard and comprehensive maintenance base shall be 1 m^3 per vehicle to 1.5 m^3 per vehicle, with the hourly variation coefficient of 1.5 to 1.2.

3 The water consumption for the public toilets of the station shall be calculated based on the hourly consumption of the sanitary wares.

4 The make up water consumption of cooling water cycling system shall be determined based on 1% to 2% of the circulating water flow.

5 The production water consumption and variation coefficient shall be determined according to the requirements of the production process.

6 The fire water consumption shall meet the requirements of Chapter 21 in this code.

7 The water consumption for public buildings, road washing and greening shall comply with the current national standard GB 50015 *Code for Design of Building Water Supply and Drainage*.

8 The piping leakage loss and unpredicted water consumption shall be 10% to 15% of the comprehensive water consumption.

15.2.4 The quality of living water shall comply with the current national standard GB 5749 *Standard for Drinking Water Quality*.

15.2.5 The pressure of living water shall comply with the current national standard GB 50015 *Code for Design of Building Water Supply and Drainage*. The pressure of production water shall be determined according to the requirements of production process and that of the fire water shall meet the requirements of Chapter 21 in this code.

15.2.6 The arrangement and laying of the water supply piping shall be in accordance with the following requirements:

1 The production and living water systems of the station should be designed to form dendritic pipeline network, and one water supply pipe shall be led from the main water supply pipe of the station to connect to the production and living water supply pipes of the station.

2 The production, living and fire water supply pipes of underground station should be connected from the air duct or pedestrian walkway.

3 The water supply pipes in the station or along the track of tunnel section should be laid on the side with less electrical equipment and the pipe valves and fire hydrants installed shall not intrude into the structure gauge.

4 The water supply pipes running through the main structure shall be provided with waterproof casing.

5 The spacing of hydrants set in the tunnel sections should not be greater than 100 m while that for the station stabling yard and comprehensive maintenance base should not be greater than 60 m.

6 The fire water supply pipe led from the municipal water supply pipe network shall be installed with backflow preventer.

7 The water supply pipe shall not run through the substation, communication signaling equipment room, station control room, and power distribution room.

8 Where the water supply pipe is installed in a place subject to possible freezing or condensation, antifreeze or anti-condensation and insulation facilities shall be taken. The plastic water supply pipe laid outdoors in an exposed way shall be provided with proper measures to avoid direct sunlight.

9 The expansion compensator of pipeline shall be determined based on the ambient temperature and the change of water temperature in the pipe. However, pipe expander and shear deformation devices shall be installed when the pipe runs through the structural expansion joint, deformation joint and settlement joint.

10 Steel plastic compound pipe, copper pipe or thin-walled stainless steel pipe and others that meet the relevant national regulations should be used for the indoor production and living water supply pipes. For the outdoor water supply pipes, plastic pipe, cast iron pipe with lining, and steel pipe with reliable protection treatment may be used. The safety of living and drinking water distribution equipment and protective materials shall comply with the current national standard GB/T 17219 *Standard for Hygienic Safety Evaluation of Equipment and Protective Materials in Drinking Water*.

15.3 Drainage

15.3.1 The municipal drainage system shall be preferred as the receiving system of wastewater, sewage, and rainwater. Sewage and wastewater shall be treated to meet the requirements of the current national standard GB 8978 *Integrated Wastewater Discharge Standard*.

15.3.2 The design of drainage system shall be in accordance with the following requirements:

1 Separate drainage system with the sewage and rainwater collected and treated separately shall be used.

2 Gravity flow drainage shall be used for the ground or elevated stations. The drainage of underground station should be centralized by class and a lifting pump station shall be provided where the gravity flow mode is impossible.

3 Water reclaim facilities shall be provided for water-deficient cities and areas and the projects for which conditions for water reclaim facilities are met.

4 Where rainwater is taken as the source or make-up source of reclaimed water, reliable storage capacity and overflow discharge facilities shall be provided.

15.3.3 The design amount of drainage shall be in accordance with the following requirements:

1 The amount of drainage of living wastewater shall be determined as 95% of the living water consumption, with the hourly variation coefficient of 2.5 to 2.0.

2 The amount of drainage of production water and variation coefficient shall be determined according to the process requirements.

3 The amount of drainage of flushing and fire wastewater shall be equivalent to the water consumption.

4 The seepage of underground structure should be calculated based on 0. 5 $L/(m^2 \cdot d)$ to 1 $L/(m^2 \cdot d)$.

5 For the rainwater pump station, drainage ditch, and drainage pipe/channel of elevated section, open entrance/exit, open air duct and tunnel entrance/exit, the drainage capacity shall be calculated based on the intensity of 50-year return period rainstorm and the design rainfall duration shall be determined by calculation.

6 The design return period of roof drain piping of ground station and elevated station shall be calculated based on the intensity of local 10-year return period rainstorm and the design rainfall duration shall be taken as 5 minutes. The total drain capacity of the roof rainwater facilities and overflow facilities shall not be less than the rainfall of 50-year return period.

15. 3. 4 The arrangement of drain pump station (house) shall be in accordance with the following requirements:

1 The main drain pump station in the interval tunnel shall be set at the actual lowest point of slope of the line. The length of the section served by each pump station should not be greater than 3km (for single line) or 1. 5km (for double line). The main drain pump station is mainly used for draining the water seepage of structures, flushing wastewater and fire wastewater. Where the length of the section served by the pump station exceeds the required value and the amount of drainage is high, an auxiliary drain pump station should be provided or other effective measures should be taken.

2 The drain pump house of underground station should be located at the downslope end of the line.

3 The local drain pump house of underground station should be located near the foundation pit of the escalator connecting the ground to the station concourse, at the end of the vehicle maintenance pit of turn-back line, under the plates of platform of the underground station, in the elevator shaft, or in any other low-lying places where water may be accumulated and drainage by gravity flow is impossible.

4 The drain pump station shall be provided at an appropriate position of the tunnel entrance where the rainwater could not be drained by gravity flow.

5 The drain pump station shall be equipped with 2 pumps to 3 pumps, in which one serves as the standby pump. The drain pump should be designed as self-priming pump or submersible pump. The submersible pump should be equipped with backwashing devices. The times of automatic startup of the drain pump under automatic control should not be greater than 6 per hour.

6 No less than two pressure outlet pipes shall be provided for the drain pump station and stilling well should be set at the position where the pressure outlet pipe is connected to the ground piping.

7 Where the discharged water contains rainwater or fire wastewater, the amount of drainage should be designed based on the maximum pump flow of 5 mm to 10 mm. While under any other conditions, the amount of drainage should be designed based on the maximum pump flow of 10 mm to 20 min.

15.3.5 The arrangement and laying of the drainage pipes/ditches shall be in accordance with the following requirements:

1 One DN75 to DN100 floor drain should be installed at an interval of 50 m along the side wall of hall and equipment rooms of the underground station, and the drainage riser shall be connected to the drainage ditch of the line. At the joint where the pedestrian passage leading from the ground to the station concourse is connected to the station concourse floor, transverse ditch should be set and drainage riser leading to the line ditch at the platform level should be installed in the ditch.

2 An open drainage ditch with the longitudinal slope gradient no less than 3‰ should be provided in the tunnel, along which manholes shall be set at an interval of 20 m.

3 Drainage facilities shall be provided at the low-lying positions of ground station, stabling yard, train repair garage, inspection and repair shed and test line.

15.3.6 The pipe materials selected shall be in accordance with the following requirements:

1 For gravity flow drain pipe, flame retardant hard PVC pipes and fittings should be used.

2 For forced drain pipe, hot-dip galvanized steel pipe or steel-plastic compound pipe should be used.

3 For siphon forced drain pipe, pressurized plastic or stainless pipe should be used.

4 Plastic pipe should be used for outdoor drain pipe.

15.4 Monitoring of Water Supply and Drainage

15.4.1 The information on the operation, manual/auto mode, and fault status of production and living water supply and drainage equipment shall be displayed in the control room of the station.

15.4.2 Level auto control and local control modes shall be used for the drain pump while remote control in the control room of the station shall be used for the main drain pump of station and section and the rainwater pump at entrance.

15.4.3 The production and living water pressurization equipment should be equipped with automatic speed regulation or pressure regulation devices. For the pump sets in other pump stations (houses), the start and shutdown shall be automatically controlled and both manual control and remote monitoring functions shall be available.

15.4.4 The monitoring of water supply and drainage shall be incorporated into the Building Automation System (BAS), and that of the fire water supply system shall be incorporated to the Fire Alarm System (FAS).

16 Power Supply

16.1 General Requirements

16.1.1 Power supply system shall consist of power system, traction power supply system, low voltage system, the Power Supervisory Control and Data Acquisition (PSCADA) system and integrated grounding system. Power system shall consist of external power source, high voltage substation (or power supply switching station) as well as medium voltage distribution network; traction power supply system shall consist of rectifier substation and contact line; low voltage system shall consist of lighting and power substation and low voltage distribution system.

16.1.2 Power source shall meet the power supply requirement of Grade I load; the power supply scheme of external power source shall be designed by combining with rail transit network planning and urban power network planning. The centralized power supply mode by constructing high voltage substation should be adopted preferably, and the distributed power supply mode by constructing power supply switching station may also be adopted. Resource sharing of external power source shall be prioritized where available.

16.1.3 Power supply system shall meet the basic requirement of safety, reliability and economy. Power supply system shall be designed with scale and capacity in accordance with the rush hour load of long-term transportation and may be constructed as a whole or by stages.

16.1.4 In the case of centralized power supply, the voltage grade of the medium voltage power supply network should be 35 kV; in the case of distributed power supply, the voltage of the medium voltage power supply network shall be compliant with the voltage of urban power grid.

16.1.5 Traction loads shall be treated as Grade I load. Non-traction power loads shall be classified into Grade I load, Grade II load and Grade III load according to load characteristics.

16.1.6 Grade I load shall be supplied by two independent power sources, either one of which breaks down shall not affect normal supply of the other one. Fo rmost important loads in Grade I loads, in addition to the two power sources, there shall be one more emergency power source installed which must not be connected with other loads.

16.1.7 When there is only one power source working or the power supply capacity is not enough in power supply system, Grade III load may be permitted to be automatically cut off.

16.1.8 The following power sources should be taken as the emergency power sources:

1 Generator sets independent of the normal supply.

2 A separate feeder of the supply network that is effectively independent of the normal feeder.

3 Batteries.

16.1.9 Every one of the various power substations in power supply system shall have two reliable power sources, where the high voltage substation and power supply switching station shall have at least one dedicated power source. The capacity of every power source shall meet the power demand of all Grade I load and Grade II load of the power substation. Under normal operation, the two power sources work simultaneously and back up each other.

16. 1. 10 Both traction power and non-traction power shall be served by the medium voltage power supply network in power supply system, which should adopt the same mode of double-circuit ring network. The capacity of the medium voltage network shall be designed in accordance with the long-term train service headway. The two circuits are standby to each other where Circuit A fails, Circuit B shall take charge of Grade Ⅰ and Grade Ⅱ loads of both Circuits A and B. The voltage deviation at the end of the medium voltage network should not exceed 5%.

16. 1. 11 The traction load shall be determined according to the line information, the service headway and train density in rush hours, train formation, and vehicle performance. The location, quantity and capacity of the rectifier substation shall meet the power supply demand of long-term rush hour operation.

16. 1. 12 The power supply mode of contact line shall be in accordance with the following requirements:

    1   Under normal condition contact line of the main line shall be bi-feed by two rectifier substations adjacent.

    2   The contact line in depot or stabling yard should be supplied separately.

    3   The power supply support mode between the depot or stabling yard and the main line contact line shall be determined in accordance with the requirement and capacity of power supply system.

16. 1. 13 The nominal voltage of the contact line should be 1500 V DC.

16. 1. 14 The distortion rate of sinusoidal waveform of grid voltage caused by harmonic wave generated by the DC traction power supply system and nonlinear electric equipment shall be controlled and comply with the current national standard GB/T 14549 *Quality of Electric Energy Supply Harmonics in Public Supply Network*.

16. 1. 15 Energy feedback or absorption device for regenerative braking of train shall be set in power supply system, the design of which shall be determined after comprehensively comparison of techno-economics.

16. 1. 16 Reactive power compensation at 0. 4 kV side of each lighting and power substation or centralized compensation of high-voltage substation shall be determined after comprehensively comparison of techno-economics according to the reality of the power supply system.

16. 1. 17 Power supply workshop which manage and maintain the power supply equipment shall be set in vehicle base.

16. 2　Substation

16. 2. 1 Substation shall be classified into high voltage substation (or power supply switching station), rectifier substation and lighting and power substation. The rectifier substation and lighting and power substation at the same station (vehicle base or stabling yard) should be built into one hybrid substation. The lighting and power substation shall be installed at the heavy duty side of the station.

16. 2. 2 The quantity and locations of substations along the line shall be determined by power supply calculation, network planning and local environment of the place where the substations are installed.

16. 2. 3 High voltage substation and rectifier substation of vehicle base should be designed to be unattended substations with watchmen. The remaining substations shall be designed to be unattended substations without watchmen.

16. 2. 4 The main transformer with on-load voltage regulation should be adopted for high voltage substation. The quantity and capacity of main transformers shall be determined based on short-term and long-term loads and should be installed by stages. In case that one main transformer is out of operation, the remaining transformers shall be capable to undertake the Grade Ⅰ and Grade Ⅱ loads within its power supply range.

16. 2. 5 Harmonic monitoring devices should be applied and an area for harmonic control devices should be reserved at the supply side in high voltage substation. Some harmonic controlling devices should be distributed in rectifier substation and lighting and power substation.

16. 2. 6 The capacity of transformer-rectifier units shall be determined based on short-term and long-term loads. Their power supply capacity shall meet the requirements that once a rectifier substation is out of operation, the adjacent rectifier substations shall be capable to undertake the traction load within their power supply scope.

16. 2. 7 The load characteristics of transformer-rectifier units shall be in accordance with those specified in Table 16. 2. 7.

Table 16. 2. 7 The Load Characteristics of Transformer-rectifier Units

Load	100 % rated current	150% rated current	300% rated current
Time of duration	Continuous	2 h	1 min

Note: The 1 minute's 300% rated current is added to 2 hours' 150% rated current.

16. 2. 8 The capacity of distribution transformer in lighting and power substation shall be such that, when one transformer is out of operation, the other transformer shall be capable to undertake the Grade Ⅰ and Grade Ⅱ loads within both their power supply ranges.

16. 2. 9 The siting of substation shall be in accordance with the following requirements:

   1 shall be close to load center.

   2 shall be convenient for incoming and outgoing of cable lines.

   3 shall be convenient for transportation.

   4 The independent substation shall be close to medium and low speed maglev transit line and in harmony with urban planning.

16. 2. 10 Dedicated cable channels should be provided between power substations and medium and low speed maglev transit line.

16. 2. 11 The main circuit wiring of substations shall be reliable. The sectionalized single-bus configuration should be adopted for the MV AC bus in the high voltage substation, rectifier substation and lighting and power substation. The AC side of rectifier unit at rectifier substation shall be connected to the MV AC bus in the same section, while the bus on DC side should adopt single bus configuration.

16. 2. 12 The minimum width of the gangways for all power distribution devices between 35 kV and 110 kV installed indoor shall comply with the current national standard GB 50060 *Code for Design of High Voltage Electrical Installation (3 to 110 kV)*. The minimum width of the passages for all power distribution devices bellow 20 kV installed indoor shall comply with the current national standard GB 50053 *Code for Design of 20 kV and Below Substation*.

16.2.13 All equipment rooms of the substation shall be centrally arranged.

16.2.14 The layout of the substation shall be accompanied with operation passage, repair and maintenance passage and transportation passage, and shall meet the requirements of convenient operation and maintenance and smooth cable laying paths. In case that the devices in the substation cannot be directly carried through outdoor roads, transportation passages and lifting openings shall be provided, and lifting equipment shall be reserved.

16.2.15 Package devices should be adopted for AC and DC auxiliary panels whose power supply shall be fed from low-voltage buses of the substation. The battery panels shall have sufficient capacity to achieve requirement of 2 h continuous power supply in case failure of the substation.

16.2.16 Integrated automation system with hierarchical and distributed structure shall be adopted for the substations. The protection relays shall meet the requirements of reliability, selectivity, sensitivity and speed of operation.

16.2.17 The integrated automation system of the substation shall have the following functions:

    1 Protection, control, signaling and measurement.

    2 Compatible interface with PSCADA.

    3 Program control.

    4 Standard interfaces and open protocol.

    5 Online self-diagnose for failures.

16.2.18 Appropriate protection devices shall be provided for the medium-voltage AC power supply against phase-to-phase fault and phase-to-earth fault or abnormal operation.

16.2.19 The dry-type transformer shall be installed with corresponding protections to prevent failures or abnormal operation as follows:

    1 The phase-to-phase short circuit of winding and its outgoing lines, andthe single-phase grounding short circuit on the solidly grounded (or low resistance grounding) side of neutral point.

    2 The turn-to-turn short circuit of winding.

    3 Overcurrent caused by external phase fault.

    4 Overload.

    5 The temperature rise of transformer exceeds threshold.

16.2.20 The traction rectifier shall be applied with corresponding protections to prevent failures or abnormal operations as follows:

    1 Overcurrent caused by external phase-to-phase short circuit.

    2 Internal short circuit.

    3 Component failure.

    4 The temperature rise of component exceeds threshold.

16.2.21 The DC traction incoming line shall be applied with direct overcurrent release and overcurrent relay when circuit breaker is adopted as incoming line switch in case of failures or abnormal operations.

16.2.22 In case of failures or abnormal operation, DC traction feeder shall be applied with protection devices as follows:

    1 Direct overcurrent release.

    2 Overcurrent protection.

    3 Rate of rise (dI/dt) and ΔI relay.

4 Bilateral intertrip relay.

16. 2. 23 DC traction power supply devices shall be applied with frame leakage protection. The regenerative braking energy feedback or absorption device should be separately applied with frame leakage protection.

16. 2. 24 The earth-leakage protection shall be installed between DC negative bus and ground grid of the rectifier substation.

16. 2. 25 The bus-sectionalizing switches at all substations shall be applied with standby power supply automatic switching device.

16. 2. 26 The DC traction feeders of the substation shall be applied with auto-reclose with line test device.

16. 3　Traction Power Network

16. 3. 1 The contact line of medium and low speed maglev transit line shall be in accordance with the following requirements:

　　1 The contact line shall consist of positive contact rail and negative contact rail, which shall be respectively connected with DC buses of the rectifier substation by feeding and return cables.

　　2 The contact line shall meet the requirements of train traffic flow in long-term rush hours and minimum network voltage.

　　3 The contact rail shall be capable to continuously supply power to the train and ensure that it can reliably feed to the current collector of the train within specified operation speed.

　　4 The layout of contact rail of medium and low speed maglev transit line which adopts turning spur shall meet the requirements of the polarity conversion of power supply for returning train.

　　5 The sizes and models of positive contract rail and negative contact rail shall be the same. The ways of current collection and rail type of the contact rail shall be determined after technical and economic comparison and verification.

16. 3. 2 The installation of the contract rail shall be in accordance with the following requirements:

　　1 The positive contract rail and negative contact rail shall be installed at both sides of track beam.

　　2 The supporting components of the contract rail shall meet the requirements of mechanical strength, insulation and voltage resistance.

　　3 The contact rail shall be free to expand and contract in the case of temperature changes.

　　4 The installation location and error of the contact rail shall meet the requirements of vehicle and equipment gauges.

16. 3. 3 The plane layout of the contact rail shall be in accordance with the following requirements:

　　1 The length of the free expansion segmentation of the contact rail shall be determined based on its expansion capacity at the maximum temperature difference and the expansion of track beam.

　　2 The contact rail at movable turnout shall be installed independently, the contact rail between main line and side line shall use mechanical sectioning for track switching.

　　3 The midpoint anchor shall be installed in the middle of every independent free expansion segmentation.

4 Contact rail mechanical sectioning realized by expansion elements shall be adopted between free expansion sections. The terminal elbow shall be installed at the mechanical sectioning of turnout contact rail and the terminal of the contact rail.

16.3.4 The installation of the electrical sectioning device of contact rail shall be in accordance with the following requirements:

1 The arrival terminal (i. e. , the idle running terminal of the train) of the station where rectifier substation is located shall be equipped with contact rail electrical sectioning device.

2 The contact rail between main line and vehicle maintenance base shall be installed with electrical sectioning device.

3 Electrical sectioning devices shall be provided between up and down contact rails on the main line.

16.3.5 The section insulator or insulating material should be adopted for the electrical sectioning of contact rail.

16.3.6 The vehicle repair base shall be installed with several power supply sections of contact rail.

16.3.7 The minimum clear distance between the live parts of the contact rail and structure body/ train body shall be in accordance with those specifications in Table 16.3.7.

**Table 16.3.7 The Minimum Clear Distance (mm) between the Live Parts of the
Contact Rail and Structure Body/Train Body**

Nominal voltage	Static	Dynamic	Absolute minimum, dynamic
750 V DC	25	25	25
1500 V DC	150	100	60

16.3.8 Lightning arresters shall be installed in the following areas of the contact rail:

1 At an interval of 300 m in ground and elevated segmentations.

2 At connecting point between feeder line and contact rail in ground and elevated segmentations.

3 Tunnel entrance.

16.3.9 The power frequency ground resistance of lightening arrestor shall not be greater than 10 Ω.

16.3.10 The rigidity of the current collecting face of contact rail shall be greater than that of the part where current collector of maglev train contacts with the contact rail.

16.4 Cable

16.4.1 The halogen-free flame-retardant cable with low smoke shall be adopted for the power cable and control cable used in power supply system. The fire resistant copper cable or mineral insulated fire resistant cable shall be adopted for distribution line that need keep normal power supply in case of fire accidents.

16.4.2 The single core cable should be adopted for the power cable with cross section larger than 150 mm² in medium-voltage power supply network.

16.4.3 The cables should be distributed at one side of the line or the dedicated cable passage under the track when they are installed in tunnels or via elevated sections.

16.4.4 The cable laying shall meet the limit requirements of structure gauges in station and section.

16.4.5 The main grounding wire of the station or section shall be reliably electrically connected with each metal cable bracket, hanger or cable tray. And its terminals shall be connected with the ground grid of the substation.

16.4.6 When the cable tray is adopted for cable laying, an expansion gap of not less than 20 mm should be reserved whenever the straight-line segment of the cable tray reaches 15 m (steel) or 30m (aluminum alloy or glass fiber reinforced plastics). The compensation of cable tray may be equipped with expansion compensation of main grounding line. The semicircular compensation loop with a radius of 100 mm should be adopted for the compensation of main grounding line. When cable is laid in the section or station, relevant sizes and distances shall be in accordance with those specified in Table 16.4.6.

Table 16.4.6　The Relevant Sizes and Distances of Cable Laying (mm)

Cable bracket configuration and passages		Cable passage		Cable trench	
		Horizontal	Vertical	Horizontal	Vertical
The net width of the passage with brackets installed on both sides		≥1000	—	≥300	—
The net width of the passage with bracket installed on one side		≥900	—	≥300	—
Spacing of cable bracket layers	Power cable	—	≥200	—	≥250
	Control cable	—	≥100	—	120
Spacing of cable brackets	Power cable	1000	1500	1000	—
	Control cable	800	1000	800	—
The net height of cable passage below the platform of the station		—	≥1900	—	—
		—	≥1300	—	—
The net height of cable passages in the substation		—	≥1900	—	—
The clear distance between power cables		≥35	—	≥35	—

Note: Where power cable and control cable are laid together, the control cable standard should be adopted for the distance between cable brackets.

16.4.7 The hangers, clamps for fixing single core AC power cable shall be non-magnetic material such aluminum alloy. The cable bracket, hanger, cable tray and clamp shall be capable of corrosion resistance or treated with anti-corrosion measures.

16.4.8 The cable laying shall be in accordance with the following requirements:

1 The trefoil formation should be adopted for medium-voltage single-core power cable in single loop. The flat-touching formation should be adopted for DC power cable and the close or multi-layer superimposition arrangement may be adopted for ELV cable such as control cable and signal cable.

2 During the laying of multiple layers of brackets on the same side, cables shall be arranged in the sequence of power cables from high voltage class to low voltage class, control cables, signal cables and communication cables, etc.

3 During the laying of multiple layers of brackets on the same side, when the number of bracket layers is restricted by space, the adjacent voltage classes of power cables up to 35 kV may be arranged on the same bracket layer. The power cable up to 1 kV may be laid on the same layer of bracket with ELV cables.

4 The cables of main and backup essential circuit shall be installed on different layers of brackets.

16.4.9 The grounding method and requirements for the metallic screen of medium-voltage AC power cables shall meet the requirements of current national standard GB 50217 *Code for Design of Cables of Electric Engineering*.

16.4.10 The active cross section of the metallic screen of medium-voltage AC power cable shall meet the requirements that the temperature rise shall not exceed the permitted maximum average temperature rise for the short circuit between insulation and outer sheath under the prospective short circuit current.

16.4.11 In some buildings such as stations, where there are a lot of cables in vertical direction, cable shaft laying method should be adopted.

16.4.12 The fixtures shall be installed in accordance with the requirements of current national standard GB 50217 *Code for Design of Cables of Electric Engineering* during power cable laying.

16.4.13 The expansion joints should be installed at the terminals of medium-voltage power cable and the area where intermediate joint is connected with the cable. Both sides of the joint without expansion joint should be rigidly fixed or laid in a zigzag shape within a proper length range.

16.4.14 Direct buried cable must not be directly above or below the underground pipelines. The allowable minimum distance between cables or between cable and pipelines, roads or buildings shall be in accordance with those specified in Table 16.4.14.

Table 16.4.14 The Allowable Minimum Distance between Cables or between Cable and Pipelines, Roads or Buildings (mm)

Positional relationship of buried cables		Parallel	Intersected
Spacing between control cables		—	500①
Spacing between power cables or between power cable and control cable	Power cable of 10 kV and below	100	500①
	Power cable above 10 kV	250②	500①
Clearance from communication lines		150	50
Spacing between cables used by different departments		500②	500①
Spacing between cable and underground pipe ditch	Heat pipe ditch	2000③	500①
	Oil or inflammable gas pipeline	1000	500①
	Other pipelines	500	500①
Spacing between cable and building foundation		600③	—
Spacing between cable and road edge		1000③	—
Spacing between cable and drainage ditch		1000③	—
Spacing between cable and tree trunk		700	—
Spacing between cable and overhead line pole below 1 kV		1000③	—
Spacing between cable and overhead line tower base above 1 kV		4000③	—

Note: ① The allowable minimum distance may be 250 mm when pipeline is separated by partitioning plate or cable runs through pipeline;

② The allowable minimum distance may be 100 mm when pipeline is separated by partitioning plate or cable runs through pipeline;

③ The allowable minimum distance shall not be less than half for special circumstances.

16.4.15 The fire-retardant blocking measures shall be implemented at the entrance of power cables from outdoor to indoor, the access to cable shaft, the openings where cables run through partition walls and floors of building as well as the openings where cables from power supply devices run through cable mezzanine.

16.5 Power and Lighting

16.5.1 The classification of power and lighting equipment for medium and low speed maglev transit shall be made in accordance with the following requirements:

1 The Grade Ⅰ loads shall mainly include emergency lighting, operational power supply of substation, FAS equipment, firefighting system equipment, fireman's elevator, the lighting of underground station concourse and platform, the lighting of underground sections, fans and electrically operated valves of smoke extraction system, communications system equipment, signaling system equipment, turnout system equipment, PSCADA system equipment, BAS equipment, AFC equipment, escalator (also serving for evacuation), platform screen door, protective door, flood gate, rain pump, and water discharge pumps for underground station and sections. Among them, emergency lighting, operational power supply of substation, automatic AFC equipment, communications system equipment, and signaling system equipment are the most important loads.

2 The Grade Ⅱ loads shall mainly include the lighting of aboveground station concourse and platform, the lighting of auxiliary rooms, passenger information system, the power supply used during repair and maintenance of substation, ordinary fans, sewage pumps, elevator and escalator.

3 The Grade Ⅲ loads shall mainly include air-conditioning, refrigeration and water system equipment, power socket in auxiliary rooms, advertising lighting, cleaning equipment, electric heating equipment and maintenance equipment.

16.5.2 The power supply modes of the power and lighting loads shall be in accordance with the following requirements:

1 The Grade Ⅰ loads must be powered by two independent power supplies, which shall be able to be switched at the load side. The most important loads may be fed by additional battery or other independent power supply as a third power source.

2 The Grade Ⅱ loads should be powered by two power supplies, which may be switched at the 0.4 kV bus of the substation.

3 The Grade Ⅲ loads may be powered by a single power supply.

16.5.3 The exclusive power supply circuit shall be adopted for the electrical equipment used for firefighting and other disaster prevention. The power distribution equipment for firefighting shall be marked with red characters.

16.5.4 The coefficient method shall be adopted to calculate the power and lighting loads.

16.5.5 The radial power distribution should be adopted for large capacity equipment and the electric equipment with critical load nature. The trunk-shaped power distribution should be adopted for small and medium capacity power equipment. The chain-shaped power distribution may be adopted for the secondary electrical equipment with intensive energy consumption and small capacity. There should not be more than 5 pieces of equipment connected with the same chain, and their total capacity shall not exceed 10 kW.

16.5.6 The reactive-power compensation devices of power and lighting equipment should be intensively installed in the substation. The local compensation should be independently installed for the electrical equipment with large capacity, stable loads and frequent use. The space for reactive-power compensation device may be reserved during construction.

16.5.7 The allowable voltage derivation for the lighting within line sections shall be -10% to $+5\%$. The allowable voltage derivations at the terminals of other electrical equipment shall comply with the current national standard GB 50052 *Code for Design Electric Power Supply Systems*.

16.5.8 The lighting equipment shall be installed in the cable passages, with voltage shall not higher than 36V.

16.5.9 The electric equipment may be controlled in the following ways based on demands:

    1 Local control, either manual ormotorized.

    2 Station control.

    3 Central control.

16.5.10 The lighting of station may be classified into normal lighting, emergency lighting, on-duty lighting, safety lighting, sign lighting and advertising lighting based on function. The normal lighting shall include the normal lighting in public areas and the lighting in auxiliary rooms. The emergency lighting shall include standby lighting and evacuation lighting. The safety lighting shall include the lighting of cable interlayers of the substation, the lighting beneath platform board and the lighting of maintenance accesses under escalator. The lighting distribution boxes should be intensively installed. The station lighting shall be controlled in groups.

16.5.11 The power supply time for emergency lighting shall comply with the current national standard GB/T 16275 *Urban Rail Transit Lighting*.

16.5.12 The underground sections and turnouts shall be installed with exclusive power supply facilities for fixed lighting and the mobile electrical appliances used for repair and maintenance. The station concourse and platform shall be installed with the power sockets for mobile electrical cleaning appliances.

16.5.13 The socket circuit of power and lighting equipment shall have the function of leakage protection.

16.5.14 The electric stove, electric heater and distributed air-conditioning system at station should be provided with independent power supply circuit.

16.5.15 The emergency lighting shall be installed for the entrances and exits of the station, station concourse, platform, station control room, duty room, public security room, power substation, power distribution room, signal machinery room, fire-pump room and underground sections.

16.5.16 The energy conservation lamps should be adopted for the lighting of the station concourse and platform. The gas discharge lamp with good color rendering property and high luminous intensity should be adopted for the lighting of at-ground line sections and tall tunnels.

16.5.17 The illumination, the unified glare rating and color rendering index in all places shall comply with current national standards GB/T 16275 *Urban Rail Transit Lighting* and GB 50034 *Standard for Lighting Design of Buildings*.

16.6 Power Monitoring

16.6.1 The design of PSCADA system shall be in accordance with the following requirements:

1 The PSCADA system shall meet the requirements for operator to monitor, control and measure the operation status of the major equipment of high voltage substation (or power supply switching station), traction power supply system and low voltage system at control center so that the power supply system can run in a safe, reliable and economical manner.

2 The PSCADA system shall consist of the master station (at control center), slave stations (at substations) and communication channel.

3 The design of the master station of PSCADA system shall include: the position of master station, the configuration scheme for master station system equipment, the functions, types and requirements of all equipment, system capacity, and the formats to record telecontrol data and the requirement of the man-machine interface.

4 The design of the communication channels of PSCADA system shall include: the structure mode of the channels, the configuration of primary/standby channel, the interface of the transmission channel of telecontrol data and the performance requirements of the channels.

5 Ethernet communication should be adopted for the master station of the PSCADA system.

6 The PSCADA system shall meet the requirements of real-time capability, reliability, maintainability and scalability.

7 The redundant configuration shall be adopted for the communication channel, system server and dispatcher workstation of PSCADA system.

16.6.2 The PSCADA system shall have the following functions:

1 Remote operation of the remotely controlled and dispatched objects.

2 Real-time monitoring and fault alarming on the operation status of power supply system.

3 Real-time monitoring on the major operating parameters of the power supply system.

4 Accident recall function.

5 Automatic detection and patrol inspection.

6 Report printing.

7 Password management.

8 System maintenance.

9 Switch between main and standby channels.

10 Synchronization of system clock.

11 Training.

16.6.3 The monitoring scope of PSCADA system shall include the remote control, remote signaling and telemetering for the equipment of high voltage substation (or power supply switching station), rectifier substation, lighting and power substation, and contact line.

16.6.4 The objects under remote control shall include the following switch devices:

1 The circuit breakers, load switches and electric disconnectors rated 10 kV and above in substations.

2 Low-voltage incoming breakers, bus tie breakers, the main switch of tertiary loads and tertiary load switches with large capacity in lighting and power substation.

3 DC fastcircuit breakers and electric disconnectors in rectifier substation.

4 Electric disconnector on contact rail.

16.6.5 The objects under remote signaling shall include the following signals:

1 The position signals of objects controlled remotely.

2 Fault trip signals of high and medium-voltage breakers and DC fast circuit breakers.

3 The fault signals of transformer and rectifier units.

4 The fault signals of substation's AC/DC power supply system.

5 The fault-inducedtrip signals of low-voltage incoming breakers and bus tie breaker in lighting and power substation.

6 The disconnection signal of switch control circuit.

7 The action signals of automatic devices.

8 The PT and CT fault signals of protection and measurement circuits.

9 The abnormality alarms in substation.

10 Control modes.

16.6.6 The objects under telemetering shall include the following basic items:

1 The voltage, current, active-energy and reactive-energy of incoming line in switching station.

2 The current and voltage of AC bus in power substation.

3 The current of incoming and outgoing lines of AC ring network in power substation.

4 The current, active-energy, reactive-energy and active power of AC feeder line in substation.

5 The voltage of buses of AC/DC auxiliary power supply system in power substation.

6 The voltage of buses of DC tractive power supply system.

7 The current of DC incoming line, the current of negative return system and the current of feeder line.

8 The current and power factor of 400 V incoming line.

9 The current and voltage of 400 V bus.

10 The current of grounding circuit.

16.6.7 The hardware of master station shall include the following devices:

1 Computer (include RAID) and computer network.

2 Man-machine interface device.

3 Record printing and screen copying devices.

4 Communication processing device.

5 Mimic panel and other display devices.

6 Uninterrupted power supply (UPS) device.

7 Debugging terminal equipment and printer.

16.6.8 The hardware of maintenance and dispatch management system shall include the following devices:

1 Computer (host) and computer network.

2 Man-machine interface device.

3 Record printing and screen copying devices.

4 Communication processing device.

5 Uninterrupted power supply (UPS) device.

6 Debugging terminal equipment and printer.

16.6.9 The main technical indicators of the system shall be in accordance with the following requirements:

1 The accuracy of remote signaling shall not be less than 99.99%.

2 The transmission time of remote control commands shall not be larger than 3 s.

3 The transmission time of position change remote signaling commands shall not be larger than 3 s.

4 The automatic switch time between primary and standby devices shall not be larger than 30 s.

5 The display response time for the screen shall not be larger than 3 s.

6 The telemetering error shall not be larger than 1.5%.

7 The load rate of the server shall not be larger than 50%.

8 The load rate of the network should not be larger than 30%.

9 The network communication velocity of master station shall not be less than 100 Mbps.

10 The mean time between failures (MBTF) shall not be less than 20000 h.

11 The mean time to repair of the equipment shall not be larger than 1 h.

16.7 Grounding

16.7.1 The exposed conductive part of electrical devices and facilities in the power supply system shall be grounded unless otherwise specified.

16.7.2 The interconnected grounding system should be adopted for the power supply system, whose grounding resistance shall not exceed the minimum value required by the equipment connected with the system.

16.7.3 The grounding resistance of electrical devices shall comply with the current national standard GB/T 50065 *Code for Design of AC Electrical Installations Earthing*.

16.7.4 The neutral point on the secondary side of main transformer in high voltage substation should be grounded via low resistance. The neutral point on the secondary side of power transformer in lighting and power substation shall be directly grounded. The type of low-voltage system grounding should be TN-S system.

16.7.5 The positive and negative contact rails of DC traction power supply system and the DC equipment in rectifier substation shall be insulated.

16.7.6 The safe grounding device for train body shall be installed in station and vehicle base. At the accesses where personnel enter or exit the train, the train body shall be grounded through the safe grounding device, which shall have a grounding resistance of not larger than 4 Ω.

16.7.7 The contact rails of train repair lines in the depot shall be installed with safe grounding devices required during maintenance.

17 Communication

17.1 General Requirements

17.1.1 Communications system shall meet the requirements of improving transport efficiency, ensuring train operation safety, improving modern management level and transmitting various voice, data, image, and text information. The system shall be reliable, functional, with mature equipment and advanced technology, and economical and practical.

17.1.2 The communications system shall meet the communication requirements for emergency response and emergency rescue in the event of a disaster or accident.

17.1.3 The communications system should be composed of the special communications system, the civil communications system and the public security communications system.

17.1.4 Special communications system should consist of transmission system, radio system, service telephone system, direct line telephone system, public address system, clock system, closed circuit television system, office automation system, passenger information system and other subsystems.

17.1.5 Private communications system shall meet the communications requirements in normal operation mode and emergency operation mode. In the normal operation mode, the Private communications system shall offer the communication required for operation management. In the case of emergency operation, the special communications system shall offer the communication required for the command of disaster prevention, rescue and handling.

17.1.6 Civil communications system shall meet the requirement of public communication service, and the mobile communications system of the telecommunication operator should be incorporated into the underground space.

17.1.7 The public security communications system shall meet the communication requirements of the public security department in the area of medium and low speed maglev transit line, and shall provide communication for the emergency dispatch command of the public security department in case of emergency.

17.1.8 Special communications system, civil communications system and public security communications system should realize resource sharing.

17.1.9 The main equipment and modules of communications system shall have self-check function and realize automatic switching and alarm in case of a fault. The operation control center may monitor and collect the operation results and the detection results of station equipment.

17.1.10 The communications facilities along the line must not intrude into the equipment gauge. The on-board wireless antenna must not go beyond the vehicle gauge.

17.1.11 The electromagnetic compatibility of communications system equipment shall comply with the current national standard GB/T 24338.5 *Railway Applications-Electromagnetic Compatibility-Part 4: Emission and Immunity of the Signaling and Telecommunications Apparatus*.

17.2 Transmission System

17.2.1 The transmission system shall meet the requirements for information transmission of the communication subsystems and signal, integrated monitoring, PSCADA, BAS and AFC systems, and a margin not less than 30% shall be reserved according to the long-term requirements.

17.2.2 The transmission system shall form a self-healing protection ring by using two channels of different paths.

17.2.3 Transmission equipment shall be based on optical synchronous digital transmission system or other broadband optical digital transmission system, and shall meet the bandwidth requirements for system access.

17.2.4 The communication cable and optical cable should be installed along the wall in the section tunnel, and laid in a hidden mode for the parts in the station. The power cable and optical cable for the elevated section should be laid in the cable tray under the track girder or in the cable trench with evacuation route. The ground power cable and optical cable should be laid in pipes or in the direct burial method. If the direct burial method is taken, the buried depth at the top of the pipeline should not be less than 0.8 m or shall not less than that specified in Table 17.2.4-1 under difficult circumstances, and the clearance from other underground pipelines and buildings shall not be less than that specified in Table 17.2.4-2. When erected along the wall, the clearance from other pipes shall not be less than that specified in Table 17.2.4-3.

Table 17.2.4-1 Burial Depth from Top Surface of Pipe to Pavement for Special Sections (m)

Type of pipe	Minimum depth from road surface to pipe top		Minimum depth from road surface (base surface) to pipe top	
	Under the sidewalk	Under the roadway	Under the tramline	under the railway
Concrete pipe or plastic pipe	0.5	0.7	1.0	1.3
Steel pipe	0.2	0.4	0.7(plus the insulation)	0.8

Table 17.2.4-2 Minimum Clearance of between Pipe and Other Buried Facilities and Buildings (m)

Facility name		Minimum clearance	
		Parallel	Cross
Power cable	Voltage<35 kV	0.5	0.5
	Voltage≥35 kV	2.0	0.5
Other communication cable		0.75	0.25
Water supply pipe	Pipe diameter<0.3 m	0.5	0.15
	Pipe diameter≥0.3 m	1.0	0.15
Gas pipe	Pressure≤300 kPa	1.0	0.3
	300 kPa<Pressure<800 kPa	2.0	0.3
Big tree outside the city		2.0	—
Big tree in the city		0.75	—
Heat pipe, drain pipe		1.0	0.15
Drainage ditch		0.8	0.5
House building's boundary line (or foundation)		1.0	—

Table 17.2.4-3 Minimum Clearance between the Cable Erected Along the Wall and Other Pipelines (m)

Type of pipeline	Minimum clearance	
	Parallel	Vertical cross
Power cable	0.15	0.05
Lightning lead	1.00	0.30
Protection grounding cable	0.05	0.02
Heat pipe (not enclosed)	0.50	0.50
Heat pipe (enclosed)	0.30	0.30
Water supply pipe	0.15	0.02
Gas pipe	0.30	0.02

17.2.5 Communication backbone cables and optical cables shall be made of non-halogen, low-smoke, flame retardant and anti-electrical interference materials. The outer layer of the cable at elevated sections shall be protected against sunlight radiation. The cables laid in the station shall be halogen-free, low-smoke, and flame-retardant cables with shielded plastic sheath.

17.2.6 Shielding grounding cable should not be provided for optical cable, but the metal sheath and metal reinforcement on both sides of the joint shall be insulated from each other. Insulated joints shall be used for the cable led into the room.

17.3 Public Service Telephone System

17.3.1 The service telephone system shall meet the needs of voice exchange and communication for official affairs and business connection required for medium and low speed maglev transit.

17.3.2 Fully automatic calling relay mode should be adopted for the connection between private branch exchange network and public network local telephone office, and shall be incorporated into the public network local telephone network unified numbers.

17.3.3 Service telephone system shall have the function of Integrated Services Digital Network (ISDN), and the function of data information service should be reserved.

17.3.4 Private branch exchange shall take unified user numbers, which should be as follows in the switch network:

1 "0" or "9" indicates calling a number of local call.

2 "1" is the first number of special business and new business.

3 2 to 8 represent the first number of medium and low speed maglev transit users.

17.4 Dedicated Telephone System

17.4.1 The direct line telephone system shall meet the requirements of the operation control center dispatcher and the on-duty operators at station, depot, and stabling yard to organize the train operation and carry out operation management.

17.4.2 Direct line telephone system shall integrate the dispatch telephones, inter-station train operation telephones, and direct line telephones in station/depot/stabling yard and for sections.

17.4.3 The dispatching telephone system shall integrate the dispatching telephones for train operation system, power system, and BAS.

17.4.4 The control center dispatching station should be set in the control center dispatching hall. The train operation dispatching extensions shall be set at the places of the on-duty operators for train operation at each station and the signaling building at vehicle base.

17. 4. 5 Power dispatch telephone extension shall be set in the main control room and LV power distribution room of each substation.

17. 4. 6 BAS dispatch telephone extensions shall be set in each station, comprehensive control room of depot, and fire-fighting control room of depot.

17. 4. 7 The dispatching telephone shall be in accordance with the following requirements:

1 The dispatching telephone terminal shall enable select call, group call and full call of the extensions, and no blockage shall occur under any circumstances.

2 The dispatching telephone extensions may provide general calls and emergency calls to the dispatching telephone terminals.

3 Inter-office communication and other functions shall be realized between the control center dispatching telephone terminals.

4 The dispatching telephone system shall have recording function.

17. 4. 8 The direct line telephone inside station shall enable the on-duty operator for train operation or the station master to communicate with the personnel involved in the operation affairs of the station. At the turnouts under the jurisdiction of the station, direct line telephone to the on-duty operator at the station may be provided. The direct line telephones at vehicle base may include train operation command telephone, crew affairs telephone, intra-depot dispatching command telephone and vehicle maintenance telephone.

17. 4. 9 The inter-station train operation telephone shall enable the on-duty operators of adjacent stations to communicate with each other for train operation affairs, and shall be installed in the places where the on-duty operators are located.

17. 4. 10 Section telephones for the drivers and section maintenance personnel to contact the on-duty operators of adjacent stations and related departments may be set according to operational needs. The section telephones should be set at every 150 m to 200 m.

17. 5 Broadcasting System

17. 5. 1 The broadcasting system shall consist of main line operation public address system and vehicle base public address system.

17. 5. 2 For the main line operation public address system, train operation and disaster prevention broadcasting consoles shall be provided for the control center and stations. The control center broadcasting console may make complete coverage broadcasting based on station selection and route selection, and the station broadcasting console may broadcast within the jurisdiction of this station based on route selection.

17. 5. 3 The train operation broadcast and disaster prevention broadcast of the main line public address system shall cover the same regions. Disaster prevention broadcast shall have priority over train operation broadcast.

17. 5. 4 When the train enters the station, the station may automatically broadcast the passenger guidance information, and the train arrival information should be provided by the Automatic Train Control system.

17. 5. 5 For the main line operation public address system, devices should be provided at the station platform for passenger service personnel to join the station public address system for targeted broadcasting at any time. The station load areas of the main line operation public address system should be classified into platform floor, station concourse floor, entrance/exit corridor, office areas and sections directly related to train operation. The broadcast sound shall be clear and stable at each point of load area.

17.5.6 Vehicle base public address system shall enable the train operation dispatchers in the vehicle base to issue operation instructions and relevant safety information to the production personnel directly relevant to train operation. The vehicle base public address system may access the operation public address system.

17.5.7 The total capacity of power amplifier equipment in public address system shall be determined according to the sum of rated power of all broadcasting load areas and line attenuation. The power amplifier shall adopt N+1 hot standby mechanism, and the system shall have automatic power amplifier detection and switching function.

17.5.8 Train broadcasting equipment shall be compatible with the associated devices of vehicle. Train broadcasting equipment shall have both automatic and manual broadcasting modes. Besides, it may receive the voice broadcast of control center dispatcher to the passengers in the running train through wireless communications system.

17.6 Clock System

17.6.1 The clock system shall be able to provide uniform standard time information for operation and uniform timing signals for other systems. The clock system shall be composed of central master clock (abbreviated as primary master clock), station and depot master clock (abbreviated as secondary master clock), and time display unit (abbreviated as slave clock).

17.6.2 The primary master clock shall be installed in the operation control center, secondary master clocks shall be installed in each station and depot, and slave clocks shall be installed in the central dispatching room, station comprehensive control room, duty room of rectifier substation, station concourse, platform floor and other offices directly related to train operation.

17.6.3 Primary master clock shall be able to receive reference signal calibration from external global positioning system (GPS) and may be able to receive signal calibration from Beidou satellite positioning system. The primary master clock regularly sends time coded signal to the secondary master clock for calibration. The secondary master clocks generate time signal and provide the signal to the slave clock of the station.

17.6.4 The self-timekeeping accuracy of primary master clock shall be above 10^{-7} and that of secondary master clock shall be above 10^{-6}.

17.6.5 Primary master clock and secondary master clock shall be equipped with digital and pointer type multi-output interface. Primary master clock shall be equipped with data interface and may provide timing signals to other systems.

17.7 Image Monitoring System

17.7.1 The CCTV system shall be able to provide visual information on train operation, disaster prevention, disaster relief and passenger evacuation for control center dispatcher, attendants of all stations and train drivers.

17.7.2 The CCTV system shall consist of central control equipment, station control equipment, image capture, image display, recording and video signal transmission, etc.

17.7.3 The CCTV system shall be installed with surveillance cameras in the following places:
—Fare collection hall;
—Concourse;
—Upward and downward platforms;
—Escalators and other public places;
—Places with firefighting equipment, turnout equipment and substation equipment installed.

17.7.4 The CCTV system shall provide control and monitoring devices at places attended by control center train operation dispatchers, disaster prevention dispatchers, station train operation attendants and station disaster prevention attendants. Driver monitoring device shall be installed in the parking space of the platform or the cab.

17.7.5 Outdoor cameras shall be equipped with all-weather protective covers, and shall adapt to the minimum illuminance of 0.2 lx. Indoor cameras shall adapt to the minimum illuminance of 1 lx.

17.7.6 The CCTV system shall have the functions of monitoring, priority control, cyclic display, random freeze-frame and locking, image selection, video recording at any time, camera range control, character superposition, remote power supply control, etc.

17.7.7 The real-time video captured by all cameras shall be saved for a period of time in accordance with the requirements of current national standard GB/T 26718 *Technical Requirements for Safety System of Urban Mass Transit*. Videos may be retrievable from the center and the stations.

17.7.8 Analog or digital transmission mode may be adopted for long-distance transmission of video signals in CCTV system. Video coaxial cable should be adopted for local video signal transmission.

17.7.9 Cities or regions with public security monitoring requirements shall provide the public security monitoring center with monitoring images of public areas of stations according to the requirements of public security departments.

17.8 Radio Communication System

17.8.1 Radio system shall meet the requirements of train operation safety and emergency rescue, and shall have dispatching communication functions such as selective call, group call, general call, emergency call, call priority authority, etc., as well as storage and monitoring functions, etc.

17.8.2 Radio system should adopt digital trunking-based mobile communications system.

17.8.3 Radio system shall adopt transmission mode combining wired and wireless forms. The central wireless equipment is connected with wireless base stations in stations, vehicle bases and stabling yards through optical digital transmission systems or optical fibers, and each base station establishes the communication with mobile station via antenna space wave propagation or radiation through leaky coaxial cable.

17.8.4 Radio system may be equipped with train operation dispatching, disaster prevention dispatching, comprehensive maintenance, public security, vehicle base dispatching and other systems according to operation requirements.

17.8.5 Radio system shall have dispatching communication functions such as selective call, group call, general call, emergency call, call priority authority, etc., as well as storage function.

monitoring function, etc.

17.9 Passenger Information System

17.9.1 The passenger information system should have passive multimedia passenger guidance information acquisition and active media inquiry service functions.

17.9.2 In addition to operation-related information shall be provided, passenger information system should also provide public information such as news, weather forecast, road traffic information, as well as public service advertisements.

17.9.3 The passenger information system shall have full digital transmission function, and the information acquisition, transmission and display should be in full digital mode.

17.9.4 The passenger information system shall support the priority level definition function of data transmission and data display, and data defined with high priority level shall be prioritized.

17.9.5 For terminal display devices which shall display various types of information simultaneously, multi-region screen segmentation function shall be available, with each segment being independently controlled, and separate broadcast list function shall be provided.

17.9.6 Passenger information system should be classified into control center subsystem, station subsystem, on-board subsystem, network subsystem and advertisement management subsystem.

17.9.7 The control center subsystem should be equipped with facilities such as central server, video server, consultation server, operator workstation, network management workstation, broadcast control workstation, audio/video switching matrix, video encoder/decoder, broadcast format preview device, etc.

17.9.8 The station subsystem should be equipped with data server, operator workstation and various kinds of terminal display equipment. The display configuration shall be in accordance with the following requirements:

 1 Display equipment shall be provided on each side of the station platform.

 2 The station concourse should be provided with no less than four displays.

 3 Entrance/exit corridors and transfer corridors should be provided with displays.

 4 The station entrance and exit should be provided with display equipment.

 5 The station concourse and platform should be equipped with multimedia touch inquiry equipment.

17.9.9 The on-board subsystem should be equipped with on-board controller, on-board wireless client, image storage equipment, network equipment and carriage terminal display screen.

17.9.10 The transmission network of passenger information system should be built on communications system. The station local area network and line section wireless network should be independently constructed by the passenger information system. The wireless network shall meet the requirements of seamless switching during train operation.

17.9.11 The passenger information system should be provided with interfaces with internal systems such as clock system, signal system and comprehensive monitoring system, and should be provided with interfaces with external information such as digital television, wireless television and wired television.

17.9.12 The data cable of passenger information system shall be of halogen-free and low-smoke flame retardant type.

17. 9. 13 The data cable and power cable of passenger information system shall not be shared and shall be laid in different metal pipes.

17. 10 Public Mobile Communication Access System

17. 10. 1 Civil communications system should be composed of civil communication transmission system, mobile communications system, centralized monitoring and alarm system, civil communication power supply system, etc.

17. 10. 2 The civil communication transmission system shall offer transmission channel for mobile communication access and centralized monitoring and alarm system. When conditions permit, the civil transmission system may be combined with the dedicated communication transmission system.

17. 10. 3 The mobile communications system shall combine and distribute network for various civil wireless signals, may provide and reserve radio frequency signal combiner of different systems, and realize signal coverage in underground station and tunnel space through antenna feeder and leaky coaxial cable.

17. 10. 4 Centralized monitoring and alarm system should be composed of equipment in monitoring center and equipment in controlled termination stations.

17. 10. 5 The civil communication power supply system shall meet the power supply demands of facilities such as civil communication transmission system, mobile communications system, centralized monitoring and alarm system, etc.

17. 10. 6 The civil communications system shall reserve the conditions for leading optical cables outside the station to the computer room inside the station, and arranging cables and equipment inside the station.

17. 11 Police Communication System

17. 11. 1 Public communications system should consist of public security closed circuit television (CCTV) system, public security wireless communications system, public security data network, power supply system, etc.

17. 11. 2 Public security video monitoring system shall meet the requirements of the public security department on station-wide monitoring, and the monitoring may be conducted in public security rail transit sub-bureaus, rail transit police stations and station public security duty rooms. Where conditions permit, the public security video monitoring system may be integrated with dedicated communication video monitoring system.

17. 11. 3 Public security wireless communications system shall cover the underground stations and tunnel space within the scope of medium and low speed maglev transit.

17. 11. 4 Public security wireless communications system shall be compatible and interconnected with the existing urban public security wireless communications system.

17. 11. 5 Public security data network shall meet the requirements of data transmission between urban rail transit public security sub-bureaus, police stations and station public security duty rooms, and may be connected to the urban public security data network.

17. 11. 6 Public security power supply system shall meet the power supply requirements of facilities such as public security video monitoring system, public security wireless communications system, public security data network, etc. , and should be set up independently.

17. 12　Office Automation System

17. 12. 1　Office automation system shall offer an information platform for teleworking, information release, daily operation and management, resource management and personnel communication for operation and management.

17. 12. 2　The platform development of office automation software should be planned and implemented in a unified way according to the demands of the operating unit.

17. 12. 3　Office automation system may provide data network equipment in the control center, station and vehicle base of each line, and in the offices related to the operation of medium and low speed maglev transit, user terminal equipment shall be installed.

17. 12. 4　Office automation should use transmission system as the backbone transmission network, and user terminal equipment may access the network equipment through integrated wiring system.

17. 12. 5　Office automation system shall be provided with network security measures.

17. 13　Power Supply System and Grounding

17. 13. 1　Communication power supply system should adopt independent power supply equipment or be integrated into comprehensive power supply system. It shall have functions of centralized monitoring and management, and ensure uninterrupted power supply for communication equipment without instantaneous change. The backup power supply time of communication power supply shall not be less than 2 h.

17. 13. 2　Communication equipment shall be powered as Class Ⅰ load. AC power of double-power double-circuit line is led from the substation to AC distribution panel of communication machine room. When one circuit in use fails, it shall be automatically switched to the other circuit.

17. 13. 3　Communication equipment requiring DC power supply should use high-frequency switching power supply in centralized mode and shall be in accordance with the following requirements:

　　1　DC power supply system shall consist of DC switchboard, high-frequency switching rectifier module, DC converter, inverter and valve-regulated sealed lead-acid battery pack combined rack, and shall have remote communication, telemetry and remote control capabilities and standard interfaces and communication protocols.

　　2　The base voltage of DC power shall be -48 V, while for other DC power, DC converter shall be used.

17. 13. 4　For communication equipment requiring AC uninterruptible power supply, the power supply mode may be chosen from inverter power supply or AC uninterruptible power supply (UPS) depending on the load capacity.

17. 13. 5　The capacity of power supply equipment shall be in accordance with the following requirements:

　　1　The capacity of DC power distribution equipment shall be configured according to the long-term load.

　　2　The capacity of rectifier, DC converter, inverter and AC uninterruptible power supply equipment shall be configured according to the near-term load.

3 The capacity of battery pack shall be configured according to the near-term load and should be in accordance with the following requirements.

    1) Two battery packs in parallel should be provided, the capacity of each pack shall be 1/2 of the total capacity.

    2) One battery pack should be provided for AC uninterruptible power supply equipment.

17. 13. 6 The grounding system of communication equipment shall be designed to ensure the safety of personnel and communication equipment, as well as normal operation of communication equipment.

17. 13. 7 Communication equipment should adopt comprehensive grounding system with the grounding resistance shall not be larger than 1 Ω.

17. 13. 8 The separate grounding system shall consist of grounding body, grounding lead-in, grounding plate and indoor grounding wiring.

17. 13. 9 The distance between different grounding bodies set as separate grounding system shall be larger than 20 m.

18 Operating Control System

18.1 General Requirements

18.1.1 For the Automatic Train Control (MATC) system, communication based train control (CBTC) system should be used.

18.1.2 The MATC system shall be composed of train operation command equipment and automatic train control equipment. Fault monitoring and alarm equipment shall be provided.

18.1.3 The MATC system shall be highly reliable, available and safe.

18.1.4 The equipment circuits and interfaces of the MATC system which involve train operation safety shall follow the fail-safe principle. The safety systems and equipment used shall pass the required safety certification.

18.1.5 The MATC system shall meet the requirements of maglev transit for train operation organization and management to ensure the operation safety and improve the operation efficiency.

18.1.6 The MATC system shall be designed based on the maximum carrying capacity of train and meet the requirements of operation under the maximum traveling speed of 120 km/h, high traffic volume, high density and various train formation conditions.

18.1.7 The MATC system shall have the required electromagnetic compatibility.

18.1.8 The normal operation of maglev train shall be under the automatic control of the MATC system.

18.1.9 The Safety Integrity Level (SIL) of Automatic Train Protection (ATP) subsystem and Computer Interlocking (CI) subsystem shall reach Level 4.

18.1.10 The on-board equipment of the MATC system must not go beyond the vehicle gauge, while the ground equipment must be forbidden to intrude into the equipment gauge.

18.1.11 The MATC system and equipment shall be integrated, modular, intelligent, extendable, and upgradable.

18.1.12 The MATC system and equipment installed for the elevated or ground lines shall be coordinated with the urban landscape.

18.2 Maglev Automatic Train Control (MATC) System

18.2.1 The MATC system shall be consists of the following subsystems:

    1 Automatic Train Supervision (ATS) subsystem.

    2 Automatic Train Protection (ATP) subsystem.

    3 Automatic Train Operation (ATO) subsystem.

    4 Computer Interlocking (CI) subsystem.

18.2.2 The block modes of MATC system may be classified into moving block type and quasi-moving block type.

18.2.3 The MATC system may realize train to wayside communication by wireless free wave, waveguide, leaky coaxial cable or inductive loop.

18.2.4 The MATC system shall offer the following control levels:

1 Automatic control by control center.

2 Automatic control by control center, with manual intervention.

3 Automatic control in station.

4 Manual control in station.

18.2.5 The MATC system may offer driveless mode, ATO driving mode, ATP driving mode, restricted manual driving mode, and not restricted manual driving mode.

18.2.6 The MATC system and equipment shall be able to ensure the safe operation of trains in the case of failure of communication, power supply, and other related systems and equipment. It shall also be capable of degraded operation, fail-soft operation and fault recovery.

18.2.7 The design capacity of the MATC system shall be in accordance with the following requirements:

1 The monitoring and control coverage of the MATC system for the stations, depots, and stabling yards shall match up with the determined construction scale for the line, while the monitoring and control capability shall adapt to the long-term conditions of the line.

2 The minimum number of trains monitored, controlled, and managed by the MATC system shall be determined based on that to be configured for the long-term period, with a margin no less than 30% reserved. When a new line is designed, the actual number of on-board MATC equipment should be determined according to the number of trains to be configured for the initial and near-term periods.

3 The carrying capacity of train should be designed according to the long-term demand and the turn-back capacity shall meet the long-term operation demand.

4 The MATC system shall have interfaces with the communication, PSCADA, disaster prevention and alarm, environmental monitoring, vehicle, turnout and other systems.

18.3 Automatic Train Supervision (ATS) System

18.3.1 The ATS system shall have the following functions:

1 Automatic train identification, tracking and train number display.

2 Preparation and management of train diagram.

3 Automatic or manual control of route.

4 Automatic adjustment of train operation.

5 Automatic monitoring of train operation and equipment status.

6 Operation and data logging, playback, output and statistics.

7 Vehicle repair program and crew management.

8 System fault recovery.

9 Train operation simulation and training.

18.3.2 Redundancy techniques shall be used for the computers and network of the ATS system, and dispatcher workstation, chief dispatcher workstation, train diagram edit workstation and system maintenance workstation may be set.

18.3.3 The monitoring and control scope of the ATS system shall cover the stations, sections, and turn-back lines on the line.

18.3.4 The departing and arriving trains in the depots and stabling yards shall not interfere with the operation of trains on the main line.

18.3.5 The control of train route shall be based on the interlocking table and realized according to the train working diagram, train ID, etc.

18.4 Automatic Train Protection (ATP) System

18.4.1 The ATP System shall deliver the following functions:

1 Detect the train position to control thetrain interval.

2 Monitor the traveling speed of train to realize overspeed protection and control.

3 Prevent unexpected movement of train, such as rolling away.

4 Provide safety supervision information for the opening/closing of train doors and platform screen doors.

5 Daily inspection of on-board ATC equipment.

6 Logging of driver's operations.

18.4.2 The basic requirements for the ATP system shall be in accordance with the following requirements:

1 The ATP system shall consist of wayside equipment and on-board equipment.

2 The information transmission channel between the internal devices of the ATP system shall follow fail-safe principle.

3 The safety interval for train operation shall be determined through train operation simulation.

4 The ATP system shall adopt continuous control mode and should adopt speed-distance brake mode.

5 The ATP system should share the speed measurement devices with the trains.

6 The ATP system should offer multiple train location detection abilities. Inductive loop and balise techniques may be used for train positioning, supplemented by speed sensor, Doppler radar, and acceleration meter.

18.4.3 As the top safety criteria, ATP system shall be able to trigger train stop. In the event of train-to-wayside communication interruption, train integrity circuit interruption, train overspeed, unwanted train movements, and vital faults of on-board equipment, etc., ATP system shall implement emergency baking and stop.

18.4.4 When ATP system executes emergency braking and stop control, it shall cut off the traction until the train stops without braking release.

18.4.5 On-board equipment of the ATP system shall include on-board computer equipment, speed measuring equipment, human-machine interface display equipment, train-to-wayside communications equipment, and associated interface equipment.

18.4.6 The information displayed by the human-machine interface display equipment of ATP system shall at least include the actual speed of train, target speed, and target distance.

18.4.7 The cables of ATP on-board equipment and vehicle interface circuit shall be laid separately from the HV cables of the main circuit and be provided with protection. Isolation measures shall be provided for the interfaces with the vehicle electrical equipment.

18.5 Automatic Train Operation (ATO) System

18.5.1 The ATO system shall have the following main functions:

1 Automatic inter-station operation.

2 Fixed-point stopping in station.

3 Automatic turn-back by ATO or unmanned driving system.

4 Monitoring of train door and platform screen door.

5 Automatic adjustment of train operation.

6 Energy conservation control of train.

18. 5. 2 The MATO system shall be able to offer multiple section operation modes and shall adapt to different train operation intervals and operation adjustment.

18. 5. 3 The precision of fixed-point stopping of the ATO system shall be determined according to the platform length, train performance, and setting of platform screen doors. The fixed-point stopping precision at platform should be ±0.30m.

18. 5. 4 The control process of ATO system shall meet the comfort and punctuality requirements of train operation.

18. 5. 5 The ATO system shall be able to control the train to realize station passing operation.

18. 6　Computer-based Interlocking (CI) System

18. 6. 1 CI system and equipment should be used. The CI system shall adopt a "2×2 out of 2" or "2 out of 3" redundant structure.

18. 6. 2 The CI system shall enable interlocking of the turnouts, signal and sections. The route must not be open where the interlocking conditions are not met. Conflicting routes must be double inspected to prevent simultaneous opening.

18. 6. 3 The CI system shall enable setting of train route and shunting route, and protection route shall be set as needed.

18. 6. 4 Route release by section should be adopted.

18. 6. 5 The interlocked turnouts shall be able to enable independent operation and route selection functions.

18. 6. 6 Platform emergency stop button following the fail-safe principle shall be provided in the station platform and station control room.

18. 6. 7 The CI system may be able to enable the fallback mode of ATC system through automatic inter-station block and route block.

18. 6. 8 The main control items of the station CI system shall include train route, calling-on route, route release and cancel, signal at stop and at clear, turnout operation and lock, temporary speed limit in section, train holding and cancel, remote control and local control, platform emergency stop and cancel.

18. 6. 9 The CI system shall be capable of the required detection, voice or audible alarm, and self-diagnosis for the indoor and outdoor interlocking equipment.

18. 6. 10 The CI system shall be easy to operate, and any single operation shall not constitute an effective operation command.

18. 7　Base of Vehicle and Stabling Yard

18. 7. 1 The MATC system for depot and stabling yard shall include the following main equipment:

1 ATS equipment.

2 CI equipment.

3 Test line equipment.

4 Micro-computer monitoring equipment.

5 Training, routine maintenance and detection equipment.

18.7.2 The MATC system for depot and stabling yard shall be in accordance with the following requirements:

1 Yard/depot entry/exit signal shall be provided on the switch track connecting the main line with the depot and stabling yard, and shunting signal shall be provided as needed in the depot and stabling yard. The depot/yard entry/exit signal and shunting signal shall display prohibition signal for positioning.

2 The entry signal should be controlled in the depot, and the exit signal should be controlled in the station or control center.

3 According to the size and operation characteristics of depot and stabling yard, the depot and stabling yard may be partially or wholly incorporated into the control scope of MATC system. The setting of signals shall be determined according to the operation requirements and control mode.

4 The train should be controlled as shunting route in the depot and the interlock equipment shall be able to check the interlock conditions according to the operation characteristics in the depot.

18.8 Others

18.8.1 The power supply of the MATC system shall be in accordance with the following requirements:

1 The power supply load shall be grade I load and two circuits of independent power supplies shall be provided. The on-board equipment shall be powered directly by the on-board DC power supply.

2 The power supply equipment of the MATC system shall be provided with voltage stabilizing equipment.

3 The MATC equipment should be powered by intelligent power supply panel, for which Uninterruptable Power System (UPS) and maintenance-free batteries should be used. The UPS for the MATC equipment of station, depot, and stabling yard including the control center and signal shall be designed with the same backup time and the power supply time should no be less than 30 min.

4 Dedicated AC and DC power supplies of the MATC equipment shall be insulated from ground.

18.8.2 The MATC equipment shall be provided with working grounding cable, protection grounding cable, shielding grounding cable and lightning protection grounding cable. The MATC system shall be connected with the integrated earthing system with the earthing resistance no larger than 1 Ω.

18.8.3 The lightning protection for the MATC system equipment shall comply with the current national standard GB 50343 *Technical Code for Protection of Building Electronic Information*

System against Lightning.

18.8.4　The electromagnetic compatibility of the MATC system equipment shall comply with the current national standard GB/T 24338. 5 *Railway Applications-Electromagnetic Compatibility-Part 4: Emission and Immunity of the Signaling and Telecommunications Apparatus*.

18.8.5　The house for MATC system equipment shall satisfy the requirements for normal operation of the equipment, with a proper margin reserved. The equipment house shall be provided with air conditioner and anti-static floor.

18.8.6　The indoor wires and cables used for the MATC system should be of flame retardant type, and shielded wires or cables shall be used for the parts of electronic equipment subject to interference.

18.8.7　Proper protection measures shall be taken for the equipment and apparatuses used in wet, severe cold, and white-ants areas.

18.8.8　The circuit of MATC system shall be separated from the power line, and shall be provided with protection measures when it crosses over the power line.

19 Elevator, Escalator and Autowalk

19.1 Elevator

19.1.1 Passenger/freight elevators without machine room shall be used for medium and low speed maglev transit. Where it is impossible to install the elevator without machine room, hydraulic elevator should be used.

19.1.2 The elevators shall be monitored and controlled by station BAS.

19.1.3 The elevators shall realize three-party intercom system among maglev station control room, lift car and control cabinet or machine room.

19.1.4 The wall, floor and roof of the lift car shall be constructed of non-combustible, sturdy, dust-free materials.

19.1.5 Elevator pits shall be provided with water drainage facilities to prevent leakage or seepage. If hydraulic elevator is used, an oil collecting device shall be installed at the pit.

19.1.6 Where hydraulic elevator is used, the machine room should be located on the lateral side of elevator shaft and shall comply with the current professional standard JG 5071 *Hydraulic lift*. If hydraulic elevator is installed outdoors, anti-freezing thermal insulation device shall be installed over the hydraulic part.

19.1.7 Each facility of the elevator shall comply with the current national standard GB 50763 *Code for Accessibility Design*.

19.1.8 Where elevator is also used as a fire elevator, its facilities shall comply with the functional requirements of fire elevator and shall be treated as Grade I power load.

19.1.9 Video monitoring devices shall be installed inside the elevators.

19.1.10 The rated load carrying capacity of the elevators shall not be less than 800 kg.

19.1.11 The rated speed of the elevators shall not be less than 0.63 m/s.

19.1.12 The elevator door should not be less than lm in width and central opening door should be used.

19.1.13 The electric wires and cables used for elevators shall meet the requirements of Article 16.4.1 in this code.

19.1.14 The elevator shafts should be of reinforced concrete structure or other suitable structural types.

19.1.15 When an elevator without machine room is used and the top of the elevator shaft is exposed to the outdoors, the exposed part of the shaft should not be made of transparent materials.

19.1.16 Fittings, holes, grooves and lifting rings shall be embedded in the civil structure construction of elevator shaft according to the product requirements of elevator.

19.1.17 The installation position of the elevator shall keep clear of the induced joints and deformation joints in civil structures.

19.2 Escalator and Autowalk

19.2.1 Escalators and autowalk shall be of public transport type.

19. 2. 2 Escalators and Autowalk shall be capable of variable frequency speed control, which is conducive to energy conservation.

19. 2. 3 Escalators used outdoors shall be of outdoor product type, and anti-slip measures shall be taken at both the upper and lower platforms. In cold areas, appropriate measures shall be taken to prevent snow and ice accumulation.

19. 2. 4 Escalators and moving walks shall be monitored by the BAS.

19. 2. 5 Video monitoring devices shall be provided wherever escalator and moving walk are arranged.

19. 2. 6 Escalators for emergency evacuation shall be treated as Grade Ⅰ power load.

19. 2. 7 Escalator and moving walk pits shall be provided with gravity drainage. Where gravity drainage conditions are not met, a sump and drainage facilities shall be provided outside the machine pit. Escalators shall be equipped with oil-water separator.

19. 2. 8 The continuous running time of escalators and moving walks shall not be less than 20 h per day, or 140 h per week. The escalators shall be able to run continuously at 100% braking load for 1h in every 3h.

19. 2. 9 Elevators and moving walks shall be provided with local-level and station-level control systems.

19. 2. 10 The gearing devices, structural members and decorative parts of escalators and moving walks shall be made of materials in compliance with the current national standard GB 50490 *Technical Code of Urban Rail Transit*.

19. 2. 11 Electric wires and cables of escalators and moving walks shall be made of flame retardant materials.

19. 2. 12 The rated speed of escalators and moving walks shall not be less than 0. 5 m/s, and 0. 65 m/s should be used.

19. 2. 13 The inclination angle of escalator shall not be larger than 30% and that of moving walk shall not be larger than 12°.

19. 2. 14 The net tread width of moving walk should not be less than 1 m.

19. 2. 15 If the rated running speed of escalator is 0. 5 m/s and the lifting height is not more than 6 m, there shall be at least 2 horizontal steps at both the top and bottom ends of the escalator. If the rated running speed of escalator is 0. 5 m/s and the lifting height is more than 6 m, there shall be at least 3 horizontal steps at both the top and bottom ends of the escalator. If the rated speed of escalator is 0. 65 m/s, there shall be at least 3 horizontal steps at both the top and bottom ends of the escalator. If the rated speed of escalator is higher than 0. 65 m/s, there shall be at least 4 horizontal steps at both the top and bottom ends of the escalator.

19. 2. 16 Escalators and moving walks shall be provided with embedded parts and reserved lifting conditions.

19. 2. 17 Elevators and moving walks should keep clear of the inducing joints and deformation joints in structures.

20 Automatic Fare Collection System

20.1 General Requirements

20.1.1 The design capacity of AFC system shall meet the requirements of over-peak passenger flow. The allocation number of terminal equipment in stations shall be calculated and determined in accordance with near-term ultra-peak passenger flow. And equipment locations and installation conditions shall be reserved in accordance with long-term ultra-peak passenger flow.

20.1.2 The system shall be designed with availability, reliability, security, maintainability and extendibility.

20.1.3 Station control room shall be equipped with emergency control button, which shall be interlinked with FAS. In case that station is in the state of emergency or power outage, the retention device of automation ticket checking machine shall be in the state of clearance.

20.1.4 The system shall meet the requirements of all operation modes of medium and low speed maglev transit line.

20.1.5 The terminal equipment of the system shall provide friendly operation interfaces and clear message alerts so that it can be quickly and effectively used by passengers.

20.1.6 In case that central computer system is out of order or transmission network breaks off, the computer system and terminal equipment of station shall be capable to run independently with a capability of data export.

20.1.7 The system equipment shall be capable of 24 hours continuous operation.

20.1.8 The electromagnetic compatibility of the system shall comply with the current national standard GB/T 20907 *Technical Requirements for Automatic Fare Collection System of Urban Rail Transit*.

20.1.9 The interfaces between AFC system and relevant systems shall be installed.

20.2 Management Mode and Type of Ticket

20.2.1 Three-level management mode should be adopted for AFC system, i. e. , Line-Network Ticket Center, Line Ticket Center and Station.

20.2.2 Fare clearing system should be included in the fare clearing system of local urban rail transit.

20.2.3 The centrally monitored and integrated ticket management model shall be adopted for AFC system.

20.2.4 Fare system may include integrated fare system, regional fare system (region-based system), distance-and-time-based fare system, distance-based and time-limited fare system and frequency-based fare system.

20.3 System Composition

20.3.1 AFC system shall consist of fare clearing system, line central computer system, and station computer system as well as station terminal equipment.

20.3.2 Fare clearing system should be installed in the rail transit clearing center. The rail transit clearing center shall be constructed in accordance with relevant local standards, in which relevant design interfaces and necessary disaster recovery system shall be reserved.

20.3.3 Line central computer system shall consist of redundancy-configuration central server, communication server, data storage equipment, communication encryption machine, versatile work stations, fare coding machine, network equipment, Uninterrupted Power Supply (UPS) and printing devices.

20.3.4 Station computer system should be installed in the station control room, which shall consist of station server, operating workstation, network equipment, emergency button, Uninterrupted Power Supply (UPS) and printing devices.

20.3.5 Station terminal equipment shall consist of automation ticket vending machine, semi-automation ticket vending machine, automation ticket checking machine, automation value-added machine and portable ticket verifying machine.

20.3.6 The battery standby time of the uninterrupted power supply for line central computer system should not be less than 2 hours. The battery standby time of the uninterrupted power supply for station computer system and station terminal equipment should not be less than 0.5 hours.

20.4 System Function

20.4.1 The functions of fare clearing system shall include:

1 Fare clearing system shall be capable of fare clearing between medium and low speed maglev transit lines, between medium and low speed maglev transit line and rail transit line as well as between medium and low speed maglev transit and local urban transit card clearing system.

2 The core functions of fare clearing system shall include fare and card issuing, information management, safety management, accounting management and the supply of relevant statistical information.

3 The basic functions of fare clearing system shall include fare and card utilization management, fare data management, parameter management, mode management, operation supervision, statistical reports, system maintenance and access test.

20.4.2 The functions of line central computer system shall include:

1 To issue instructions and commands to station computer system and station terminal equipment.

2 To receive the information about original fare transaction, equipment operation status and equipment repair uploaded by station computer system.

3 To categorize data, statistically analyze passenger flow, print reports as well as automatically back up and recover important data.

4 To include functions of fare tracking, management and sorting code assignment and blacklist management.

5 To include system management function like user management, access management, communication monitoring, clock management, equipment maintenance and network management.

20.4.3 The functions of station computer system shall include:

1 To receive instructions and commands like system operation parameters, operation mode and blacklist issued by line central computer system and pass down these instructions and commands to station terminal equipment.

2 To collect data about the transactions, operation status and equipment maintenance of station terminal equipment and upload these data to line central computer system.

3 To monitor station terminal equipment in a real-time manner, visually display the information about communication, operation status and failures of the equipment and initiate emergency mode through station computer or emergency button.

4 To accomplish a variety of fare management of station systems, automatically manage all intraday data and documents and provide a variety of statistical analysis reports.

20.4.4 The functions of station terminal equipment shall include:

1 The general functions of station terminal equipment shall include:

1) To receive system operation parameters, operation mode and blacklist issued by station computer system.

2) To automatically store the data about the original transaction, operation status and equipment maintenance of the equipment and upload to station computer system.

3) To be capable to work under different operation modes. In case that the communication outage with station computer system occurs, it shall be capable to work standalone and store data.

4) To provide friendly man-machine interface, precautionary measures and error reminder as well as efficient and convenient operation methods.

5) The modular and universal components that can be cycled and maintained shall be adopted for all terminal equipment.

6) The metal shell of station terminal equipment shall be reliably grounded.

2 Automation ticket vending machine shall be installed in the non-payment area of the station and operated with banknote and coin by passengers. The machine shall be capable to automatically issue multiple one-way tickets for the same destination for once and provide changes with banknote and coin.

3 Semi-automation ticket vending machine shall be operated by personnel through keyboard or mouse to automatically issue tickets while being capable to issue replacement tickets and verify tickets.

4 Automation ticket checking machine shall be installed at the junction of payment area and non-payment area of the station, which shall automatically verify the validity of tickets, control retention devices on aisles and lead passengers for check in and check out. The emergency mode may be initiated through station computer system and emergency button.

5 Automation value-added machine shall be installed in the non-payment area of the station and operated with banknote by passenger. The machine shall recharge stored-value tickets and verify a variety of tickets but without the function to provide changes.

6 Portable ticket verifying machine shall be used to check the authenticity and validity of tickets held by passengers. The data exchange can be conducted after it is connected with station computer. The machine shall be capable to check tickets.

20.5 Terminal Equipments Allocation Rules

20.5.1 Centralized layout of station terminal equipment shall be ensured in accordance with passenger flow organization and construction layout of the station.

20.5.2 The allocation number of station terminal equipment shall be calculated in accordance with short-term passenger flow and fare processing capability of all equipment.

20.5.3 The redundancy configuration of station terminal equipment shall be ensured in accordance with the principle of non-interruptible passenger flow.

1 Each payment area shall be equipped with one or two semi-automation ticket vending machines to issue replacement tickets during check out.

2 The allocation number of ticket checking machines for check in and check out equipped in each ticket gate should not be less than 3.

3 Each independent payment area shall be equipped with at least one two-way gangway automation ticket checking machine. The net width of gangway automation ticket checking machine should be 900mm.

4 Each non-payment area shall be equipped with at least two automation ticket vending machines and one automation value-added machine.

20.5.4 The stations with great changes in passenger flow for check in and check out in different time periods should be equipped with a certain number of two-way ticket checking machines.

20.6 Others

20.6.1 The transaction data of all tickets shall be uploaded to fare clearing system for transaction clearing, and the transaction clearing between local urban transit card clearing system shall be realized through the clearing system.

20.6.2 Station terminal equipment shall be properly located with embedded anchor channel in accordance with the requirements of passenger flow organization.

20.6.3 All stations, control centers and maintenance bases of depot shall be properly equipped with equipment room and management room.

20.6.4 The electrical load of clearing system, disaster recovery system, line central computer system, and station computer system as well as station terminal equipment shall be Grade I load, and the electrical load of maintenance and testing system should be Grade II load.

20.6.5 The integrated grounding pattern shall be adopted for the system. The ground resistance shall not be greater than 1 Ω.

20.6.6 The time of the system shall be synchronized with that of fare clearing system.

21 Fire Alarm System (FAS)

21.1 General Requirements

21.1.1 The line stations, interval tunnels, control center, stabling yard, high voltage substation, and vehicle base of medium and low-speed maglev transit shall be equipped with FAS. The design of FAS shall comply with the current national standard GB 50116 *Code for Design of Automatic Fire Alarm System*.

21.1.2 FAS shall exert direct control over fire protection equipment. FAS may exert automatic control over the equipment that requires operation under both normal and fire conditions via BAS or the integrated supervision and control system.

21.1.3 The fire resistance ratings of underground structures, access passageways and air shafts shall be Grade Ⅰ. The fire resistance ratings of at-ground buildings at entrance/exit, at-ground stations, elevated stations and elevated line sections shall not be lower than Grade Ⅱ.

21.1.4 The fire resistance rating of control center shall be Grade Ⅰ. If the control center is integrated with other buildings, independent accesses shall be provided.

21.2 System Composition and Function

21.2.1 FAS shall consist of a center-level supervision and control layer, station-level (including station, vehicle base, control center building and stabling yard) supervision and control layer, local control layer and the relevant communication network. The supervision and control management layers should be integrated with the integrated supervision and control system. The local control layer of FAS shall be configured independently.

21.2.2 The center-level supervision and control management layer of FAS shall be composed of central management computer, maintenance computer, communication network, printer, uninterruptible power supply and display screen. It shall have the following functions:

    1 Communicate with station-level FAS, operator workstations and communication network.

    2 Receive, display, and store the information on fire incidents throughout the maglev line.

    3 Confirm fire conditions, give firefighting, evacuation and disaster relief commands, and issue evacuation information to passengers via fire communications system and fire broadcast system.

    4 Keep an archive of history data on fire incidents.

    5 Receive, display, store, collate, query and print the status information on major fire alarm devices and firefighting equipment.

21.2.3 Attended buildings should be equipped with FAS station-level supervision layer, which should be present in the station control center of each station and the fire control center in vehicle base or control center building. FAS station-level supervision layer shall be composed of fire alarm control units, graph indicator, printer, uninterruptible power supply and automatic control equipment and manual control panel. FAS station-level supervision layer shall have the following functions:

1 Communicate with the central supervision layer of FAS and the local control layer of the station.

2 Receive, display, store and forward the fire alarm information within the control area to control center.

3 Confirm fire conditions, give control commands to fire protection equipment in connection with fire protection and disaster relief within the control area, and issue disaster relief and safe evacuation instructions across the control area via fire communications system and fire broadcast system.

4 Receive, display, store and forward the operating status information on the main fire-fighting equipment in the control area.

5 Carry out manual control over the important interlocked fire-fighting equipment in the control area.

6 Store and print event records and operator's operation records.

21.2.4 The local control layer shall consist of the input/output module, fire detector, manual call point, fire telephone and local network, and shall have the following functions:

1 Monitor fire condition and collect fire information within the control area.

2 Monitor the low-frequency patrol inspection signals, operating status, equipment failures, and pipe pressure signals of fire pumps.

3 Monitor the operating status of fire power supply.

4 Monitor the work status of all firefighting and disaster relief equipment at the station.

21.2.5 The fire alarm and automatic control information throughout the maglev line should be transmitted via communication network. The local control layer of FAS shall be configured independently.

21.2.6 The configuration of fire communication facilities shall meet the requirements of Section 26.5 in this code.

21.3 Automatic Control System for Fire Protection

21.3.1 The fire control equipment in station control center and fire control center shall have the following functions:

1 Control the start and stop of fire equipment and display its work status.

2 Station-level FAS controls the switching on/off of electric valve of main fire water pipe and displays its work state.

3 Station-level FAS displays the alarms, confirmed alarms, faults, gas release, the status of fans and gas valves, manual/automatic mode and other status data within the protection zone of automatic gaseous fire extinguishing system.

21.3.2 The control over smoke prevention and exhaust system shall be in accordance with the following requirements:

1 Fires shall be confirmed by FAS, which shall in turn issue the commands in the preset smoke prevention and exhaust mode.

2 The smoke prevention and exhaust system shall be directly controlled by FAS or may be automatically controlled by BAS or the integrated supervision and control system according to received commands.

3 After fire control command is received, BAS or the integrated supervision shall firstly carry out mode conversion and then send a command execution feedback signal.

4 The operating mode and status shall be indicated by graph indicator.

21.3.3 When fire occurs, the station FAS (or BAS) shall disconnect the non-fire power supplies in power distribution room or substation to the areas involved in the fire, switch on the power supplies to emergency lighting and evacuation identification lights, and monitor their work status.

21.3.4 The station FAS shall be able to switch the automatic ticket checking machine and access control system to open status by means of automatic control.

21.3.5 For fire hydrant pumps, in addition to the automatic control via station-level FAS, manual control shall also be provided at station control room. For smoke prevention and exhaust equipment, in addition to the automatic control via BAS, manual/automatic mode control device shall also be provided.

21.3.6 When fire occurs, the station-level FAS shall forcedly switch the broadcast system to fire emergency broadcast status by means of automatic control.

21.3.7 When fire occurs, the station-level FAS shall automatically control the fire shutter to close up and display its work status.

21.3.8 When fire occurs, the station-level FAS (or BAS) shall be able to control the operation of elevators according to evacuation requirements and display their work status, and shall be in accordance with the following requirements:

1 The fire automatic controller shall have the function of issuing automatic control signal to force all elevators to stop at the first floor or at transfer floor.

2 The elevator running status information and the feedback signal showing whether elevator stops at the first floor or transfer floor shall be transmitted to fire control center for displaying. A dedicated telephone allowing direct communication with fire control center shall be provided in elevator car.

21.3.9 The control over the fire hydrant system shall be in accordance with the following requirements:

1 FAS shall be able to control the start and stop of fire hydrant pumps.

2 For buildings equipped with fire hydrant pumps, fire hydrant buttons shall be provided at fire hydrants.

3 Fire control center shall be able to display the working/faulty status of fire pumps, the status of manual/automatic switch and the status of fire hydrant buttons.

21.4 Layout of Fire Detector

21.4.1 The alarm zones shall be divided in line with the division of fire zones and the configuration of equipment.

21.4.2 In the case of large spaces such as station concourse and platform, fire detection zones shall be divided according to the division of smoke prevention zones.

21.4.3 The Layout of fire detectors shall be in accordance with the following requirements:

1 The arrangement of fire detectors shall be in line with the fire protection rating of the protected object.

2 At underground stations, there shall be fire detectors at the station concourse, platform, equipment rooms, warehouse, duty room, offices, corridors, power distribution room, cable tunnel or mezzanine and access passageways longer than 60m.

3 At control center and vehicle base, there shall be fire detectors in the stabling yard, vehicle maintenance yard, important equipment houses, combustible gases storage and usage rooms, combustible materials warehouses, power transformation and distribution rooms and other places with high fire hazard.

4 Rooms with automatic gaseous fire extinguishers shall be equipped with two types of fire detectors.

5 There shall be fire detectors in the enclosed station concourses, equipment rooms, management rooms, power distribution room, cable tunnel or mezzanine of ground station and elevated station.

21.4.4 Underground interval tunnels and the access passageways longer than 30m shall be provided with manual call point. The position of manual call point in underground section should be determined in conjunction with the position of fire hydrant.

21.4.5 Wherever there is fire detector, manual call point shall be installed.

21.4.6 Audible alarm devices should not be installed in the public activity area for passengers. Alarm bells shall be installed at corridors in office area.

21.5　Fire Protection Control Room

21.5.1 The central control and management system of FAS shall be provided in the dispatch hall of control center.

21.5.2 Station fire control center shall be provided in conjunction with the station's integrated control room. The fire control center shall be equipped with fire alarm controller, fire automatic controller, and fire graphic display device.

21.5.3 Fire control centers at transfer station should be arranged in a centralized manner. Fire control centers for different lines shall be able to transmit and display status information between each other, but mutual control should not be recommended.

21.5.4 Fire control center shall allow for supervision and controlling of the fire protection-related systems in protection zone, including fire alarm and automatic control system, fire hydrant system, automatic fire extinguishing system, smoke prevention and exhaust system, fire door and roller shutter system, fire power supply, fire emergency lighting and evacuation indication system and fire communications system as well as the various fire protection facilities in these systems. It shall also display the dynamic information and fire management information on the fire protection facilities.

21.5.5 The fire control center shall be able to control the work status of audible or optical fire alarm.

21.6　Power Supply and Cabling

21.6.1 FAS shall be provided with main power supply and standby DC power supply. The main power supply shall be designed as grade I power load.

21.6.2 The standby DC power supply of FAS should be powered by a dedicated battery or a centrally-arranged battery pack. The capacity of the standby DC power supply shall be able to maintain continuous power supply for 3 hours after the main power supply is interrupted. Where battery pack is used, the power supply circuit of fire alarm controller shall be wired separately.

21.6.3 Leakage circuit breaker shall not be used for electrical protection of FAS's main power supply.

21.6.4 The data transmission line, power supply line and control line of FAS shall be in accordance with the following requirements:

    1 Where FAS's data transmission line, power supply line and control line are laid underground, halogen-free, low-smoke insulation and sheath shall be used for these lines. Where these lines are laid on the ground, low-halogen, low-smoke insulation and sheath should be used.

    2 FAS's power supply lines and fire automatic control lines shall be fire-resistant copper-core wires and cables. The transmission lines such as alarm bus, fire emergency broadcast line and fire telephone line shall be flame-retardant or flame-retardant, fire-resistant wires and cables.

    3 Cables of different voltage ratings shall not be routed in the same protective conduit. Where it is unavoidable to run cables of different voltage ratings via the same conduit, the conduit shall be divided by partitions.

    4 Where concealed wiring is required, FAS lines shall be run through conduits and laid in incombustible structures, with a protective cover of at least 30mm. Where surface wiring is required (including wiring in suspended ceiling), FAS lines shall be run through metal pipe or enclosed metal raceway and fire protection measures shall be taken.

    5 Where fire-retardant or fire-resistant cables are used as FAS lines laid in cable wells or cable trenches, additional fire protection measures may be omitted.

21.6.5 If cable shaft is used for laying FAS lines, the cable shaft should be independent of the low-voltage distribution line shafts for supplying industrial power and lighting power. If a common cable shaft has to be used due to restriction of poor conditions, the two types of cables shall be arranged separately on both sides of the shaft.

22 Building Automation System (BAS)

22.1 General Requirements

22.1.1 BAS shall be provided for the medium and low speed maglev transit.

22.1.2 The BAS shall be designed with the same standards as the monitored objects, and the interfaces among various systems shall be coordinated.

22.2 Principle of System Design

22.2.1 The BAS shall be designed to be a layered and distributed computer control system which shall be composed of central, station and local level monitoring and control equipment as well as the related communication network equipment.

22.2.2 If FAS exerts linkage control over the equipment that requires operation under both normal and fire conditions via BAS highly reliable communication interfaces shall be set between FAS and BAS. In the case of fire, the FAS shall issue the fire mode command, and the BAS shall perform the fire control program in priority.

22.2.3 The equipment shared by the smoke control system and the normal ventilation system shall be under the centralized monitoring and control of the BAS in case of fire.

22.2.4 The BAS shall monitor and control the following systems:

1 HVAC system.

2 Water supply and drainage system.

3 Lighting system.

4 Emergency power supply (EPS) and Uninterrup table Power Supply (UPS) systems.

5 Passenger information and indication system.

6 Escalators and elevators.

7 Platform screen door, civil defense door.

8 Environmental parameters such as temperature and relative humidity.

22.2.5 For the monitored equipment, manual operation shall have priority over automatic operation.

22.3 Basic Function of System

22.3.1 The BAS shall have the following basic functions:

1 Monitor the electromechanical equipment.

2 Execute the disaster protection and blockage mode.

3 Monitor the station environment.

4 Measure the energy consumption of system.

5 Management and control of energy conservation operation of equipment.

6 Management of station environment and equipment.

7 System maintenance.

22.3.2 The monitoring of electromechanical equipment shall have the following functions:

1 Central level and station level monitoring.

2 The control commands of BAS may be manually issued from the central workstation, station workstation and the station integrated backup panel (UBP) or executed by the program automatically. Skip-level control function shall be provided.

3 Sign-in and permission setting.

22.3.3 The disaster protection and blockage mode shall have the following functions:

1 Receive the automatic or manual fire mode command issued from the station and execute the smoke prevention and exhaust mode for the station.

2 Receive the signal about the train location in the section, and execute the tunnel smoke control and exhaust mode according to train fire location information.

3 Receive train blockage information in the section and execute the blockage ventilation mode.

4 Monitor the escape signage system and emergency lighting system of station.

5 Monitor the dangerous water level of drain pump houses.

22.3.4 The BAS shall have the following management functions:

1 Make statistics of the environmental and other parameters of the station.

2 Make statistics and analysis of the energy consumption data.

3 Make statistics of the operating conditions of the equipment, optimize the operation of equipment, and forecast the maintenance management trend.

22.3.5 System maintenance shall have the following functions:

1 Monitor the operation of all BAS equipment along the line, and carry out central monitoring and management on the system equipment.

2 When necessary, backup operations and confirm silence of global alarms along the line.

3 Carry out maintenance, configuration, definition of operating parameters, building of system database, modification and addition of users and operation screens for all software of BAS along the line, and make records of the operations.

4 Judge the failure of hardware equipment and notify the maintenance personnel in time to ensure the system engineer can monitor and maintain the system in real time in the maintenance workshop.

22.3.6 The monitoring item of BAS shall meet the actual operational requirements, and the configuration shall comply with the current national standard GB 50314 *Standard for Design of Intelligent Building*.

22.4 Basic Requirement for Hardware

22.4.1 Industrial equipment shall be used for the BAS, and redundancy design shall be adopted for the monitoring of emergency ventilation and smoke control system.

22.4.2 The configuration of central level hardware shall be in accordance with the following requirements:

1 Two operation workstations shall be provided for parallel operation or redundant hot standby.

2 One maintenance workstation may be provided to monitor the operation of all BAS equipment along the line.

3 Two redundant servers may be provided.

4 At least one emergency information printer and one report printer shall be provided.

5 Online uninterruptible power supply with the backup time no less than 1 h shall be provided.

6 A mimic panel or large screen projection system may be provided and its design shall coordinate with surrounding systems.

7 The central level hardware shall be synchronized with the communication clock system.

8 When the BAS is integrated with the integrated monitoring system, the central level hardware equipment shall be set up by the integrated monitoring system.

22.4.3 The configuration of station level hardware shall be in accordance with the following requirements:

1 Industrial control computer should be used as station-level operation workstation, or it may be configured uniformly by the integrated monitoring system.

2 Online uninterruptible power supply shall be provided with the backup time no less than 1 h.

3 One printer should be provided to serve as both history printer and report printer, or it may be configured uniformly by the integrated monitoring system.

4 Integrated backup control panel (IBP) in station control room shall be provided to serve as the backup for automatic control of fire conditions of BAS, of which the operation priority shall be higher than that of the station and central workstation. The panel shall mainly display the fire conditions and the operation procedures shall be simple. When the BAS is integrated with the integrated monitoring system, the IBP may be configured by the integrated monitoring system.

5 The operation workstation shall not serve as gateway concurrently.

22.4.4 The configuration of field-level hardware shall be in accordance with the following requirements:

1 Programmable logic controller (PLC) should be used for the field control device of BAS.

2 The controller should be of modular structure that is scalable and maintainable, and has the remote programming function.

3 The input/output (I/O) module should have the hot plug function.

4 For the sensors, transmitters, and actuators, products with standard electrical signal output or supporting open bus protocol shall be used.

5 The system shall be designed with the measures to suppress frequency converter harmonics and noise interference.

22.5 Basic Requirement for Software

22.5.1 The software system shall be compatible with the configuration of the hardware system. Application software shall be developed based on a mature, reliable and open software platform of monitoring system and adapt to the functional requirements of medium and low speed maglev transit.

22.5.2 The software system shall adopt modular structure and be open and highly expandable.

22.5.3 The application software shall be designed as three-level architecture, that is, central level, station level, and field level.

22.5.4 The software system shall be designed with complete system maintenance and diagnostic functions, as well as a user-friendly human-machine interface.

22.6 Network Structure of System and Functions

22.6.1 The network structure shall be in accordance with the following requirements:

1 The transmission network between the central level and the station level may rely on the communications system, alternatively an independent industrial Ethernet may be set up.

2 The functional requirements of central level and station level monitoring shall be met.

3 The requirements on centralized management and distributed control shall be met.

4 The system shall be designed to be highly reliable, open, and scalable.

22.6.2 The network of BAS shall be composed of the communication transmission network, central and station level monitoring network (local area network), and field-level control network.

22.6.3 The central level network shall have the following functions:

1 The central monitoring network shall be connected to the station-level monitoring network via the communication transmission network. The outage of any station workstation or central workstation shall not lead to the interruption of network communication.

2 The communication rate of the data transmission network of BAS should not be less than 100Mbps.

22.6.4 The station level network shall conform to the standard communication protocol.

22.6.5 The field level control network of BAS shall have the following functions:

1 It may enable the system to realize distributed control.

2 It may connect with intelligent instruments.

3 It may connect with remote I/O and controllers.

22.7 Cabling and Grounding

22.7.1 The cables used for underground stations and sections shall meet the requirements of Article 16.4.1 in this code.

22.7.2 The cables of BAS shall be arranged to allow for convenient maintenance and overhaul, and prevent external mechanical damage.

22.7.3 The signal cable of BAS shall not be shared with the power cable, and they shall not be arranged in the same metal conduit.

22.7.4 The cables of all field control boxes and cabinets should be led in from the lower part. Where they are led in from the upper part, proper sealing measures must be taken.

22.7.5 Where shielded cabling system is used, the shielding layer of the system shall keep continuous.

22.7.6 The cable shielding layer of BAS should be grounded at the same point.

22.7.7 All field cabinets of the BAS shall be grounded.

22.7.8 The controllers and computer devices of BAS should be grounded at one point or adopt floating grounding depending upon the requirements of the related products or systems.

22.7.9 The overall grounding resistance shall not be larger than 1 Ω.

23　Integrated Supervisory and Control System

23.1　General Requirements

23.1.1　Medium and low speed maglev transit should be equipped with an integrated supervision and control system (ISCS).

23.1.2　ISCS shall be a system that combines real-time monitoring and control with transaction and data management.

23.1.3　ISCS shall be of an integrated, interconnected design. The scope of integration and interconnection shall be in accordance with the following requirements:

1　PSCADA system and BAS shall be integrated into ISCS.

2　FAS should be integrated into ISCS.

3　Signal system, closed circuit television system, broadcast system, passenger information system, AFC system, access control system, platform screen door system and clock system should be interconnected with ISCS.

4　The ATS system should be integrated into ISCS as appropriate depending on the needs of technical development and operational management.

23.1.4　ISCS shall provide information to the operation control center of line network, providing coordination in operation management of the network.

23.2　System Setting Requirements

23.2.1　ISCS shall consist of a central-level ISCS and station-level ISCS.

23.2.2　The central-level ISCS shall be interconnected with station-level ISCSs via a track network to form a system network.

23.2.3　Communications system should be used as the backbone network for ISCS transmission. Building a separate ISCS transmission network may be also allowed. In the latter case, redundant ring-shaped industrial Ethernet should be used.

23.2.4　The local equipment monitored by ISCS should be connected to the station network equipment or communication processor of ISCS via Ethernet or fieldbus.

23.2.5　Both central-level ISCS network and station-level ISCS network shall use redundant industrial Ethernet.

23.2.6　ISCS shall be equipped with a network management system and should be equipped with an equipment maintenance management system.

23.2.7　ISCS shall be equipped with a training management system and a software test platform, which should be shared by other systems.

23.2.8　The control center building, vehicle base, and stabling yard may be equipped with ISCS, which should be designed according to station level.

23.2.9　The design of interface shall comply with the requirements on ISCS interface as stated in current national standard GB 50636 *Technical Standard for Urban Rail Transit Integrated Supervision and Control System Engineering*.

23.3　Basic Function of System

23.3.1　ISCS shall be capable of monitoring and management of the system integrated by it as well as data acquisition and linkage control of the systems interconnected by it.

23.3.2　ISCS shall realize operation management and equipment monitoring and control of the systems integrated by it at both central level and station level.

23.3.3　ISCS shall have the following functions:

　　1　Controlling.

　　2　Monitoring.

　　3　Alarms management.

　　4　Trend recording.

　　5　Reports generation.

　　6　Authority management.

　　7　System configuration.

　　8　File management.

　　9　Network functions.

　　10　System maintenance and diagnosis.

　　11　Training management system.

　　12　System backup and recovery.

23.3.4　ISCS shall have the following linkage control functions:

　　1　Under normal working condition, automatic broadcasting of station opening/closing and train arrival and other linkage control functions;

　　2　Under fire condition, smoke prevention and exhaust mode control in case of fire at line sections, smoke prevention and exhaust mode control in case of fire at stations, fire emergency broadcast, video monitoring of station fire scenes, and fire and evacuation information issue of passenger information system and other linkage control functions;

　　3　Under blockage condition, start the ventilation equipment of the relevant stations and interval tunnels;

　　4　Under emergency condition, start the related systems and the equipment under control.

23.3.5　The integrated backup panel (IBP) should have the following functions:

　　1　Stop trains at platform in case of emergency.

　　2　Detain and release trains at platform.

　　3　Enable the emergency mode of ventilation and smoke exhaust system.

　　4　Enable the release mode of automatic ticket checking.

　　5　Enable the release mode of door access control system.

　　6　Shut down escalator.

　　7　Open platform screen doors.

　　8　Other functions needing control.

23.4　Requirements of Hardware

23.4.1　The central ISCS shall mainly consist of network devices, real-time server, history server, data storage equipment, dispatch workstation, integrated display screen, printer, UPS and communication processor. Among them, the network devices, real-time server, history server and communication processor shall be in redundant configuration.

23.4.2 Station-level ISCS shall mainly consist of network devices, server, workstation, communication processor, UPS, integrated backup panel and printer. Among them, the network devices, server and communication processor shall be in redundant configuration.

23.4.3 The local equipment of building automatic subsystem shall comply with the provisions of Chapter 22 in this code. The configuration of local equipment of PSCADA and control subsystem shall meet the requirements of Chapter 16 in this code. The configuration of local equipment of fire alarm subsystem shall meet the requirements of Chapter 21 in this code.

23.5 Basic Requirement of Software

23.5.1 The software of ISCS shall be in accordance with the following requirements:

1 The software shall be of a layered, distributed architecture.

2 The software shall be of a modular structure.

3 The software shall be an open system based on standard programming language and compiler, support multiple hardware configurations, and be capable of integrating products from different manufacturers (including interface protocol, data, work mode, etc.).

23.5.2 The software of ISCS shall be scalable and allow access by upper-level information management system.

23.6 System Performance Index

23.6.1 The system monitoring and control shall be in accordance with the following requirements:

1 Real-time data uplink response time shall not exceed 2 s.

2 Real-time data downlink control time shall not exceed 2 s.

23.6.2 The time for switching to redundant equipment shall be in accordance with the following requirements:

1 The time for switching to redundant server shall not exceed 2 s.

2 The time for switching to redundant network shall not exceed 0.5 s.

3 The time for switching to redundant communication processor shall not exceed 1 s.

23.6.3 The mean time between failures (MTBF) of the system shall not be less than 10,000 h.

23.6.4 The mean time to repair (MTTR) of the system shall not exceed 1 h.

23.6.5 The system availability shall be greater than 99.98%.

23.7 Power Supply, Protection Agasint Lightning and Grounding

23.7.1 ISCS equipment shall be treated as Grade I power load.

23.7.2 The emergency power supply shall be an online UPS with the battery pack capacity supporting at least 1 hour's continuous power supply.

23.7.3 ISCS shall be designed with lightning-induced overvoltage protection. At terminals connecting electronic equipment and outdoor lines, lightning protection measures shall be taken.

23.7.4 ISCS equipment grounding measures shall include working ground wire, protective ground wire, shielding ground wire and lightning protection ground wire.

23.7.5 The grounding resistance of integrated grounding system shall not be greater than 1 Ω, and that of separate grounding system shall not be greater than 4 Ω.

23.8 Equipment Room and Arrangement

23.8.1 Equipment room shall be placed adjacent to station control room and should be close to other low-current devices rooms.

23.8.2 The area of equipment room shall accommodate long-term equipment capacity and shall facilitate future equipment upgrade.

23.8.3 The net height of equipment room shall not be less than 2.8 m.

23.8.4 Equipment room shall be dust-proof, moisture-proof and sound-insulating and shall have anti-static measures. The temperature and humidity in equipment room shall reach Grade B as stated in the current national standard GB 50174 *Code for Design of Data Centers*.

23.8.5 The equipment layout of ISCS shall be in accordance with the following requirements:

  1 Any two face-to-face cabinets shall not be less than 1.5 m apart.

  2 The front, rear and lateral sides of cabinet shall not be be less than 0.8 m apart from adjacent walls.

23.9 Laying of Cable and Conduit

23.9.1 The cables used in ISCS shall meet the requirements of Article 16.4.1 in this code.

23.9.2 Measures against electromagnetic interference shall be taken for the cables.

23.9.3 Power line communication shall not be used and power line and signal line shall not be laid in the same metal conduit.

23.9.4 Where shielded cables are used, the shielding layer shall be kept continuous and should be grounded at a single point.

23.9.5 Cables of central control room and those of station equipment room shall be laid in a concentrated manner.

24　Operation Control Center

24.1　General Requirements

24.1.1　Operation Control Center (OCC) shall be set up for the medium and low speed maglev transit system.

24.1.2　The OCC should be located at a central place near the medium and low speed maglev transit line, stations, and the objects to be monitored. When an integrated OCC is built for several lines, the center should be located in a place enabling the monitoring and controlling over all the lines.

24.1.3　Through the OCC, the operation dispatch and command functions including train operation dispatch, power dispatch, BAS dispatch, disaster protection dispatch, passenger transport management, passenger information management, equipment repair, and information management shall be available, and centralized monitoring, control and management over the whole operation process of the medium and low speed maglev transit shall be realized.

24.1.4　Serving as the disaster protection and emergency command center concurrently, the OCC shall have the required functions for disaster protection and emergency command.

24.1.5　The general layout of the OCC shall be designed in the principles of safety and reliability, to provide convenience for operation, maintenance, and management, and reduce the operation costs. The size, level, operation management mode, and decoration standards shall be determined economically and reasonably according to the line operation and management mode, the number and length of lines under control, the required system configuration, as well as the equipment type and quantity. Conditions for further development shall be reserved as appropriate.

24.1.6　The multi-line OCC shall be protected against the risk of global failure of multiple lines. Where it is impractical to prevent, control, and isolate the risk, off-site disaster recovery measures should be taken. The equipment, rooms, and other associated facilities of the disaster recovery center may be configured according to the minimum requirements for train operation command.

24.2　Function Section and General Layout

24.2.1　The OCC should be classified into operation monitoring area, operation management area, equipment area, maintenance area, and auxiliary equipment area by function. The functional areas shall be set up based on the actual operation and management modes. The operation monitoring area shall be adjacent to the operation management area. The equipment areas shall be arranged centrally on a floor close to the operation monitoring area, and be separated from the operation management area. The maintenance area should be arranged on the floor close to the equipment areas.

24.2.2　The operation monitoring area shall be taken as a separate safety zone, in which central control room and emergency command room shall be set up. A buffer area with security facilities shall be provided in front of the entrance to the central control room. In the operation monitoring area, shift handover room, printing room, necessary duty and management rooms as well as living and sanitation facilities should be provided.

24.2.3 The equipment layout and design of the central control room shall be in accordance with the following requirements:

1 The equipment and dispatch consoles in the central control room shall be arranged orderly, compactly, neatly, and allow for convenient movement and evacuation of the dispatchers.

2 The mimic panels and dispatch consoles in the central control room shall be arranged based on the needs of train operation command and facilitate the information communication among train operation dispatcher, power dispatcher, BAS dispatcher (and disaster protection dispatcher), maintenance dispatcher, and the general dispatcher.

3 The mimic panels and dispatch consoles should be arranged to form an arc shape. The position on the mimic panel that displays the professional information shall correspond to the position of the dispatch console for the profession.

4 The mimic panels configured for the systems should be uniform. Adequate visual space and repair space shall be reserved in front of and behind the mimic panels.

5 The passage from dispatch console to mimic panel should be larger than 2.0m wide, and the space in front of and behind each dispatch console should be larger than 1.6 m.

6 Where the dispatch console equipment is arranged by layer in a sector shape, taking the central position of the sector as the reference for observing the mimic panels, the elevation angle of the vertical line of sight should be less than 15° and the horizontal extending angle should be less than 120°.

7 When the central control room is designed to be used for multiple maglev transit lines, the functional areas should be divided by dispatch post or may be divided by line.

8 The dispatch consoles shall be designed ergonomically, facilitate equipment arrangement on and under the dispatch consoles, and meet the requirements for heat dissipation.

9 The central control room shall have the functions required for the emergency command center.

10 In the central control room, the monitoring and control system and operation terminal equipment related to the operation shall be provided.

24.2.4 The equipment layout and design in the equipment area shall be in accordance with the following requirements:

1 The equipment rooms may be divided by system or line. Either enclosed or open layout (separated by glass curtain wall) may be allowed.

2 Heavy-current equipment with high power shall be installed and arranged separately from the weak-current equipment. Water pipe shall not pass through the equipment rooms of electrical system. Fire damper shall be installed where any air duct passes through the equipment rooms of electrical system.

24.2.5 Office, management and living facilities may be provided in the operation management area according to the production and living needs.

24.2.6 System test room, maintenance test room, spare parts room, and tools room should be set up in the maintenance area. The system test room and maintenance test room shall meet the requirements of maintenance procedures for replacement or that below minor repair. Each system may have its own maintenance test room and tools room, alternatively the systems may share one.

24.2.7 The equipment layout and design of equipment rooms in the auxiliary equipment area shall be in accordance with the following requirements.

1 In the auxiliary equipment area, rooms for the auxiliary equipment like power supply and LV distribution system, ventilation and air-conditioning system, FAS, fire-fighting system, and water supply and drainage system should be set;

2 The rooms for equipment and facilities of power supply and LV distribution system, air-conditioning system, as well as water supply system shall be kept far away from the central control room. They should be placed in the basement.

24.3 Building and Decoration

24.3.1 The OCC shall be highly safe and reliable and should be built as a separate building. Where it is integrated with other buildings, separate access (including elevator and fire access) shall be provided to facilitate evacuation in the case of emergency.

24.3.2 The central control room and equipment areas should not be arranged in the top floor or underground floor of the building.

24.3.3 The central control room shall be in accordance with the following requirements:

1 The central control room shall satisfy the technical requirements of the process.

2 The clearance in the central control room shall be determined based on the room size and visual requirements, which should not be less than 4 m.

3 Passage should be provided among the dispatch consoles in the central control room. At least two exits leading to the outside shall be provided for the central control room, among which at least one shall be designed as 1.2 m in width and 2.3 m in height and meet the requirements of relevant disciplines.

4 In the central control room, fixed double-layer window shall be installed for the purpose of sealing, sound insulation, and thermal insulation, special design requirements for fire protection and explosion proof, where applicable, shall be met, and shielding measures shall be provided for the equipment exposed to direct sunlight.

5 Indoor ground shall be installed with anti-static raised floor, with due consideration given on the system interface and power socket of each dispatch console. The equipment shall not be directly installed on the raised floor.

6 Ceiling should be installed in the central control room and conditions shall be provided for installation of ventilation ducts and pipelines. The ceiling should be made of lightweight refractory materials.

24.3.4 For the equipment rooms in the equipment areas, the clearance should not be less than 3.0m. The floor should be designed according to the specific technical requirements of each system. When the incoming cables are led in at the lower part, raised floor shall be installed, and load-bearing, fixing and lifting devices shall be installed for the equipment according to the installation requirements.

24.4 Structure

24.4.1 The structural design of the OCC shall be in accordance with the following requirements.

1 The service life of main structure shall be 100 years.

2 In the structural design, strength, deformation and other calculations shall be performed during the construction stage and the use stage respectively, and the requirements on environmental protection, fire protection, waterproofing, anti-corrosion and lightning protection shall be met.

3 The load values for the OCC shall be determined according to the nature of the premise and shall be in accordance with those specified in Table 24. 4. 1.

4 The standard value of construction load shall be taken as 2kPa and meet the requirements of transportation and installation under the most adverse conditions.

Table 24. 4. 1　Load Values for OCC

Item	Standard value of live load
Dispatch hall	6. 0 kN/m²
Equipment room, power source room	8. 0 kN/m² − 10. 0 kN/m²
Power source and battery room	16. 0 kN/m²
Other systems room	4. 0 kN/m²
Workshop and spare parts room	2. 0 kN/m²
Office, conference room	2. 0 kN/m²
Floor of other equipment room	Depending upon the actual dead weight and operating conditions of equipment

24. 5　Cabling

24. 5. 1 Integrated cabling and integrated pipe laying modes should be adopted for the OCC.

24. 5. 2 Vertical cables should be laid by cable shaft and shall meet the requirements of heavy-current, weak-current, and fire protection disciplines.

24. 5. 3 Horizontal cables should be laid by cable vault, while cable trays or cable troughs shall be set up by layer and section according to the specific conditions of vault. Power cables shall be separated from weak-current cables.

24. 5. 4 The cables, wires, and conduits in the central control room should be laid in a concealed way.

24. 6　Power Supply, Protection Against Lightning and Grounding

24. 6. 1 The OCC should be provided with a separate lighting and power substation in which two power transformers shall be installed and connected with two mutually independent power supplies. The requirements of Grade I, Grade II, and Grade III loads in the OCC shall be met. When one transformer is out of operation, the other transformer should meet the requirements of all Grade I and Grade II loads.

24. 6. 2 The lightning protection and grounding systems of the OCC shall comply with the current national standard GB 50057 *Code for Design Protection of Structure against Lightning*, and the protection level shall not be lower than that of Class 2 lightning protection buildings.

24. 6. 3 The OCC shall be installed with an integrated grounding electrode for the heavy-current and weak-current systems. The integrated grounding resistance shall not be larger than 1 Ω and shall meet the requirements for current diffusion of the weak-current system.

24.7   Ventilationing, Air Conditioning and Heating

24.7.1   The ambient temperature in the central control room should be controlled to 16 ℃～27 ℃. The temperature change per hour in the central control room and each system equipment room should not exceed 3 ℃. The temperature in the system equipment room shall comply with the current national standard GB 50174 *Code for Design of Data Centers* and should not be lower than Class B.

24.7.2   Positive pressure shall be maintained in the central control room and equipment rooms.

24.7.3   Separate air conditioning systems shall be installed respectively for the central control room, operation management area, and equipment area.

24.7.4   The ventilation and air conditioning system should be monitored and controlled by the BAS.

24.8   Lighting and Emergency Lighting

24.8.1   The OCC shall be equipped with general lighting system and emergency lighting system. The lighting fixtures used shall comply with the current national standard GB/T 16275 *Urban Rail Transit Lighting*. The arrangement of the lighting fixtures should be coordinated with the building decoration and equipment layout.

24.8.2   The design of lighting system of the central control room shall be in accordance with the following requirements:

   1   The light in the central control room shall be soft, uniform, and free of glare. The lighting fixtures should be arranged reasonably and neatly, and reach the maximum illumination required for the mimic panel and operation console. The lighting fixtures shall be embedded in the ceiling to form a light strip. There shall be no shadow on the operation console. The illumination uniformity should not be less than 0.7 and dimming control and zone control shall be adopted.

   2   Where mosaic mimic panel is used in the central control room, the illumination should be 150 lx～200 lx at 0.8 m above ground in front of the mimic panel and operation console.

   3   Where projection type mimic panel is used in the central control room, the illumination should be 100 lx～150 lx at 0.8 m above ground in front of the mimic panel and operation console, and local lighting should be provided.

24.8.3   The illumination in the equipment room, maintenance room, office management room and other places shall comply with the current national standard GB/T 16275 *Urban Rail Transit Lighting*.

24.8.4   The illumination of the emergency lighting system for the OCC shall not be less than 10% of the normal illumination, while that in the central control room shall not be less than 50% of the normal lighting. The emergency lighting system shall be able to supply power continuously for no less than 1 h.

24.9   Fire Protection and Security

24.9.1   The OCC shall be equipped with FAS, BAS, fire accident broadcast system, automatic fire extinguishing system, water fire-fighting system, smoke prevention and exhaust system, and other systems. Automatic fire extinguishing system shall be provided in the multi-line central control room.

24. 9. 2 Fire control center shall be set up in the OCC.

24. 9. 3 The OCC should be installed with such security systems as CCTV and security access control system, and monitoring and automatic recording facilities should be installed at each area's entrance/exit, room, and main passageway.

24. 9. 4 The OCC should be provided with a watch room integrated with the fire control center.

25 Vehicle Base

25.1 General Requirements

25.1.1 Vehicle bases shall include depot (stabling yard), comprehensive maintenance center, central warehouse, training center and other production, living and office facilities.

25.1.2 Vehicle bases shall be designed in an overall manner considering the initial, short-term and long-term plans and constructed by phase. Vehicles shall be configured according to the initial plan. Station tracks, buildings, structures and mechanical and electrical equipment shall be designed according to the short-term plan. The range of land use shall be determined according to the long-term plan.

25.1.3 The functions, layout and facilities configuration of vehicle bases shall be determined according to the operational needs of the project, the layout planning for vehicle bases in urban rail transit network and the functions and distribution of the existing vehicle bases.

25.1.4 The siting of vehicle base shall be in accordance with the following requirements:

1 Vehicle bases shall be sited in line with the overall urban planning and coordinated with the surrounding environment and landscape.

2 Vehicle base shall be convenient to be connected with station to reduce the travelling distance of empty train.

3 Vehicle base should keep clear of areas with poor engineering geology and hydrogeology.

4 Vehicle base shall have good water drainage conditions.

5 Vehicle bases shall be convenient to be connected with utility facilities, including power grid, water supply network, gas supply network, cable TV line, rainwater and sewage pipelines, and municipal roads.

6 Vehicle base shall have sufficient site area to meet both current use and long-term development.

25.1.5 The general layout of vehicle base, the design of buildings and the selection of materials and equipment shall comply with the current national standard GB 50016 *Code for Fire Protection Design of Buildings*.

25.1.6 There shall be transport roads and fire lanes in vehicle base, and there shall be at least two accesses to external roads. The design of transport roads shall allow smooth delivery of new maglev vehicles or return of repaired maglev vehicles.

25.2 Function, Scale and General Layout of Depot

25.2.1 Vehicle base shall be designed according to the following scope of work:

1 Train parking, formation, routine inspection, fault elimination, cleaning and washing, regular disinfection and other routine maintenance activities.

2 Regular repairs and intermediate repairs (workshop repairs) of vehicles.

3 Temporary troubleshooting of vehicles.

4 Repair of equipment, apparatuses and tools used in vehicle base and reconditioning and repair of special vehicles.

5　Management of drivers and crew and the relevant operations.

25.2.2　Stabling yard shall be designed in accordance with the scope of work as stated in Items 1, 3 and 5 of Article 25.2.1 in this code.

25.2.3　The design size of vehicle base shall be comprehensively determined by calculation according to the relevant basic data such as the design number of trains to be serviced, the vehicle maintenance mechanism and the distribution of vehicle bases.

25.2.4　The design of vehicle base shall be based on the technical parameters of maglev vehicles. The maintenance mechanism for maglev vehicles shall combine routine maintenance and regular repairs. The grades and interval of repairs shall be determined by vehicle manufacturer.

25.2.5　The general layout of vehicle base shall be in accordance with the following requirements:

1　The general layout shall be reasonably designed according to the operation and maintenance requirements of maglev vehicles, the storage of materials and spare parts, the arrangement of maintenance facilities and equipment, the layout of roads and pipelines, as well as the requirements on greening, fire protection and environmental protection.

2　In the layout of production buildings, the running shed and maintenance shed shall be taken as the core buildings. The auxiliary production buildings shall be arranged by zone according to nature of production. Auxiliary production buildings closely related to the running and maintenance of vehicles should be placed in or near the lateral span of vehicle base. Buildings with the same or similar functions and nature should be integrated.

3　Power houses such as air compressor room, power transformation and distribution substations, water supply station and boiler room shall be placed near load center.

4　Air compressor room, battery room, boiler room should be built separately.

25.2.6　The design of departing/arriving line in vehicle base shall be in accordance with the following requirements:

1　The minimum plane curve radius of the departing/arriving line should not be less than 100m, and, in case of difficult conditions, it should not be less than 75 m. The minimum length of circular curve shall not be less than the length of a single train car.

2　The maximum slope of the departing/arriving line shall not exceed 70‰.

3　Where the algebraic difference of slope gradients of two adjacent sloped sections is greater than or equal to 2‰, vertical curve connection shall be used, and the vertical curve radius shall not be less than 1500m. The vertical curve shall not overlap with plane curves and there shall not be vertical curves within turnout.

4　The access line shall be connected to track at station.

25.2.7　There shall be testing lines in depot. The design of the testing lines shall be in accordance with the following requirements:

1　The testing lines should be built on straight lines. Where condition is unfavorable, the testing line may be designed to be a plane curve line as appropriate depending on the length of the line, theoretical test speed, terrain conditions and other factors.

2　The minimum length of circular curve of testing line should not be less than 18 m. In case of unfavorable conditions, it shall not be less than the length of a single train car.

3　The length of straight line between two adjacent curves (excluding superelevation slope) should not be less than 18 m. In case of unfavorable conditions, it shall not be less than the length of a single train car.

25.2.8 The design of lines within vehicle base shall be in accordance with the following requirements:

1 The minimum curve radius of lines in vehicle base should not be less than 75 m, and, in case of unfavorable condition, it shall not be less than 50m. The lines in sheds shall be built at flat slopes. Where conditions do not permit, they may be built at slopes not greater than 1.5‰.

2 Where conditions are unfavorable, the length of straight section of yard line between curves in the same direction shall not be less than 3.6 m, and that between curves in opposite direction shall not be less than the length of a single train car.

3 Turnouts shall be built at straight line sections. The distance between the end of buttress beam in the front of turnout and the end of the adjacent curve segment shall not be less than the length of a single train car. The distance between the end of buttress beam at the rear of turnout and the end of the adjacent curve segment in the same direction shall not be less than 3.6 m (length and modulus requirements of a single bogie, excluding the length of superelevation slope segment). The distance between the end of buttress beam at the rear of turnout and the end of the adjacent curve segment in the opposite direction shall not be less than the length of a single train car.

4 The distance between two adjacent buttress beams shall not be less than the length of a single train car.

5 There shall not be vertical curves within turnout. Any vertical curve shall be at least 6 m away from the end of turnout buttress beam.

6 Lines in maintenance shed should be arranged to be dead-end tracks.

7 Lines in running shed and maintenance shed shall be designed to be flat, straight lines. The length of straight line segment in front of the shed shall not be less than the length of a single train car.

8 The spacing of lines in sheds should be 9.0 m to 10.5 m. The outmost track in shed should be 6.0 m to 7.5 m away from the axis of adjacent side wall.

25.3 Facilities for Vehicle Running and Servce

25.3.1 Depot shall be equipped with vehicle serving facilities such as stabling hall (shed), daily servicing workshop (shed), monthly servicing workshop, and train cleaning and washing equipment. Office and living houses may be built depending upon production needs. The size and type of daily servicing workshop (shed) shall be in accordance with the following requirements:

1 The sizes of stabling hall (shed) and daily servicing workshop (shed) shall be determined according to near-term plan, with space reserved for long-term development. If the near-term design size does not differ greatly with long-term design size or future expansion is difficult, they may be built at a time according to long-term design size.

2 The stabling hall (shed) and daily servicing workshop (shed) shall be designed according to local meteorological conditions and operational requirements. Shed should be used in hot and rainy areas, and workshop should be used in cold or windy areas. Where outdoors parking has no adverse impact on operations, open air yard may be allowed.

3 The lines in stabling hall (shed) and daily servicing workshop (shed) shall be arranged according to the type of the structure. If the structure is of dead end type, each line in it should be arranged in two rows according to long-term formation plan. If the structure is of run-through type, each line in it should be arranged in three rows according to long-term formation plan.

25.3.2 The contact rails in workshops shall be built by section, and safety protection measures, acoustic and optical alarm devices that give alarm when the contract rail supplies power and display devices indicating energized status shall be installed. At sections where personnel, equipment and vehicles pass through transversely, there shall be no contact rails.

25.3.3 The design of stabling hall, daily servicing workshop and monthly servicing workshop shall be in accordance with the following requirements:

1 The length of stabling hall should not be less than the value calculated by the following formula. The length of tracks in hall should be designed on the basis of the module of 12 m:

1) Length of stabling hall (shed):

$$L_{tk} = N_t \times (L_c + 2) + (N_t - 1) \times 6 + 18 \qquad (25.3.3-1)$$

Where, L_{tk}——Calculation length of stabling hall (m);

N_t——Number of trains to be stabled on each line;

L_c——Length of train (m);

2——Parking error;

6——Width of passageway between stabling positions;

18——Additional length (the front end of train is 6 m from end wall, the rear end of train is 6 m from buffer stop (including the buffer stop and the relevant structure), and the buffer stop is 6 m from end wall).

2) Lengths of daily servicing workshop and monthly servicing workshop:

$$L_{ry} = N_{yl} \times (L_c + 2) + (N_{yl} - 1) \times 6 + 18 \qquad (25.3.3-2)$$

Where, L_{ry}——Calculation length of daily/monthly servicing workshop (m);

N_{yl}——Number of trains to be stabled on each line;

L_c——Length of train (m);

2——Parking error;

6——Width of passageway between stabling positions;

18——Additional length (the front end of train is 6 m from end wall, the rear end of train is 6 m from buffer stop (including the buffer stop and the relevant structure), and the buffer stop is 6 m from end wall).

2 The clear height of workshop gate shall meet the equipment gauge requirements for vehicles.

3 The track supports of each line in the workshop should be designed to be column type, and the elevations of track surface and inner and outer ground shall be determined in combination with operational requirements.

4 The column type track supporting structure in workshop shall be provided with fixed lighting, auxiliary power sockets and other facilities.

25.3.4 Vehicle washing facilities shall be provided in vehicle base, and manual cleaning platforms or mechanical washing facilities may be provided depending on the needs of operations. Mechanical wash facilities shall include vehicle washer, vehicle wash line and auxiliary production houses, its design shall be in accordance with the following requirements:

1 The vehicle washer should be able to properly clean both lateral sides and end part (cab) of vehicle and allow use of chemical detergent.

2 The vehicle wash line should be arranged in a run-through pattern. Where terrain condition is unfavorable, dead end arrangement may be allowed.

3 Vehicle wash facilities shall be designed according to the wash process requirements of wash equipment.

4 The effective length of vehicle wash line should be designed on a basis of the module of 12 m and shall be calculated according to the following formula:

1) The effective length of fixed, dead-end, mechanical vehiclewash line:

$$L_{xj} = L_a + 2L_c + 10 \qquad (25.3.4\text{-}1)$$

Where, L_{xj}——Effective length of vehicle wash line (m);

L_a——Required safe length of vehicle washer (m);

$2L_c$——Length of a train before and after vehicle washer (m);

10——Safety distance at the terminal of vehicle wash line (m).

2) The effective length of fixed, run-through, mechanical vehicle wash line:

$$L_{xg} = L_a + 2L_c + 12 \qquad (25.3.4\text{-}2)$$

Where, L_{xg}——Effective length of vehicle wash line (m);

L_a——Required safe length of vehicle washer (m);

$2L_c$——Length of a train before and after vehicle washer (m);

12——Additional length required for signal device (m).

3) The effective lengths of dead-end, mobile, mechanical vehicle wash line and manual vehicle wash line:

$$L_{xy} = L_c + 12 \qquad (25.3.4\text{-}3)$$

Where, L_{xy}——Effective length of vehicle wash line (m);

L_c——Length of train (m);

12——Safety distance at both ends of wash line+auxiliary work length.

5 The vehicle wash line shall be equipped with auxiliary production houses according to the requirements of vehicle wash equipment.

25.3.5 Vehicle base shall be provided with lead tracks. The effective length of lead track shall not be less than the value calculated by the following formula:

$$L_q = L_a + L_c + 10 \qquad (25.3.5)$$

Where, L_q——Effective length of lead track (m);

L_a——Safe length between train parking point and turnout (m);

L_c——Total length of train to be led out (m);

10——Safety distance at the terminal of lead track (m).

25.4 Facilities for Vehicle Reqaire and Maintenance

25.4.1 Vehicle bases shall be provided with servicing shed and auxiliary production houses according to the specific servicing process requirements. The size of servicing shed shall be determined according to the specific servicing work load and time.

25.4.2 The design of servicing hall should be in accordance with the following requirements:

1 The length of servicing hall should be calculated according to the following formula, and may be adjusted as appropriate depending upon the combination mode of workshops, the design of process plan, buildings and structures and the servicing process requirements:

$$L_{jk} = L_c + (N_b - 2) \times 1 + (N_d - 1) \times 6 + 18 \qquad (25.4.2)$$

Where, L_{jk}——Length of servicing shed (m);

L_c——Length of a train (m);

N_b——Number of trains to be serviced;

N_d——Number of vehicle groups to be serviced;

1——Minimum spacing of vehicle groups of a train that is fully disassembled for Servicing (1 m);

6——Spacing of vehicle groups required for batch disassembly and assembly of bogies (to improve the disassembly and assembly efficiency and provide necessary safety distance in the maintenance of vehicle groups);

2——In the formula, the 6 m spacing coincides with the 1 m spacing of vehicle groups, so two 1 m spacings need to be removed;

18——Additional length (the front end of train is 6 m from end wall, the rear end of train is 6 m from buffer stop, including the buffer stop and the relevant structure, and the buffer stop is 6 m from end wall).

2 The height of servicing hall shall allow for assembly of vehicles and replacement of large parts.

3 A detachable track should be installed at the joint of two adjacent vehicles on each line. The length of the detachable track shall be determined comprehensively according to the length of levitation bogie.

4 The servicing hall shall be equipped with hoisting equipment and its carrying capacity shall meet the tonnage requirement of vehicles.

25.4.3 The auxiliary houses required for vehicle servicing shall be equipped with parts inspection, repairing, cleaning, testing and flaw detection devices.

25.4.4 Each servicing area and test room shall be designed with air conditioning and ventilation system, power system, lighting, water supply and drainage facilities and fire protection facilities according to the specific technical requirements.

25.4.5 Battery room should be provided independently. The size of battery room shall meet the servicing and charging requirements of maglev vehicles as well as the on-board battery maintenance requirements of other transport vehicles and special engineering vehicles in vehicle base.

25.5 Power and Maintenance Facilities of Depot

25.5.1 The equipment servicing and power facilities of depot shall be configured in accordance with the following requirements:

1 Intermediate and minor repairs of mechanical and electrical equipment throughout the depot.

2 Repair of production tools throughout the depot.

3 Technical renovation and modification within the depot and fabrication and maintenance of small non-standard equipment.

25.5.2 Air compressors at compressed air station shall be of low-noise, energy conservation type. Their rated pressure and capacity shall be determined according to the requirements of air consuming equipment. The number of air compressors shall not be less than two.

25.5.3 The equipment servicing workshop in depot shall be equipped with metal cutting and machining equipment, electric welding and gas welding equipment, electrical equipment testing equipment, pipeline repair equipment and hoisting equipment as appropriate depending upon the maintenance and servicing requirements of the electrical and mechanical equipment and power facilities in the depot.

25.6 Integrated Maintenance Center

25.6.1 The integrated maintenance center shall meet the servicing and maintenance requirements of all tracks (including turnout), at-ground structures, bridges, tunnels, buildings, roads and other facilities, as well as the maintenance requirements of power supply equipment, communications equipment, automatic train control electromechanical equipment and automation equipment.

25.6.2 The integrated maintenance center shall be equipped with production houses, warehouses, offices and living houses according to operational needs. The layout of the houses shall be reasonably designed according to the nature of work activities and the actual conditions.

25.6.3 The urgent repair tools storage points and work areas should be arranged in accordance with the following requirements:

1 Urgent repair tools for mechanical and electrical equipment, signal system, tracks and power supply system may be provided at stations according to maintenance and urgent repair needs.

2 Track (turnout) maintenance work areas should be integrated with stations with turnout and those with urgent repair tools storage point.

3 Maintenance work area for tractive power supply system should be integrated with rectifier substation.

4 Other maintenance work areas may be built in vehicle base.

25.6.4 The maintenance center shall be equipped with rail-guided, special engineering vehicles for inspection, maintenance, urgent repair and troubleshooting of maglev tracks and contact rails according to actual operational requirements. Parking lines and parking garages shall also be provided for engineering vehicles.

25.7 Storehouse

25.7.1 Vehicle base shall be provided with a storehouse to satisfy the purchase, storage, distribution and management requirements of the materials, accessories, equipment, machines, tools and labor protection articles throughout the system.

25.7.2 The sizes of the storehouse and sub-storehouse shall be determined according to the categories and quantity of materials, accessories and equipment to be stored. The materials stacking sites shall use hardened ground.

25.7.3 Materials and equipment of different natures should be placed separately. Storehouse storing inflammable materials should be provided separately and shall comply with the current national standard GB 50016 *Code for Fire Protection Design of Buildings*.

25.7.4 The storehouse shall be equipped with hoisting equipment for loading and unloading of materials, accessories and equipment as well as transport vehicles such as motor vehicles and battery-powered vehicles.

25.7.5 The storehouse shall allow for outward transportation and shall have accesses to main roads in vehicle base and external public roads.

25.8 Training Center

25.8.1 Where there are training centers in the existing urban rail transit network or there have been good social education resources, these resources should be appropriately shared by the vehicle base.

25.8.2 The training center should be located in vehicle base.

25.8.3 The training center shall be equipped with classrooms, laboratories, library, reading room and offices and living rooms for faculty as well as teaching equipment and supporting facilities.

25.9 Others

25.9.1 The vehicle base shall have a rescue office and shall be equipped with appropriate rescue equipment and facilities. The rescue office shall be under the command of the OCC.

25.9.2 The rescue office shall include a duty room. The duty room shall be equipped with an electric clock, automatic telephone, wireless communication equipment, and a disaster prevention dispatch telephone directly connected to the OCC.

25.9.3 Vehicle base shall be equipped with dedicated at-ground engineering vehicles and command vehicles.

25.9.4 The elevation of the grade of vehicle base shall be determined according to factors including groundwater level, level of accumulated surface water, the 1/100 tide levels of nearby rivers, site drainage conditions, the elevations of nearby roads, and the specific earthwork requirements.

26　Disaster Prevention

26. 1　General Requirements

26. 1. 1　The medium and low speed maglev transit shall be provided with the facilities for protection against fire, flood, windstorm, snow and ice disaster, lightning, earthquake, and abnormal shutdown accidents, especially fire.

26. 1. 2　The fire protection system shall be designed based on the consideration that one fire accident occurs to one line at one time.

26. 1. 3　Commercial facilities shall not be set up in the passenger evacuation area of station concourse, platform, and evaluation passage.

26. 1. 4　When underground commercial facilities are developed, the commercial areas shall be divided into different fire compartments from the station concourse and the fire protection design shall comply with the current national standard GB 50016 *Code for Fire Protection Design of Buildings*.

26. 1. 5　The station and line section shall be provided with disaster prevention, evacuation, and rescue facilities, and the vehicle base and comprehensive base shall be provided with disaster prevention and rescue facilities.

26. 1. 6　The OCC shall take full responsibility for the disaster prevention dispatch and command, evacuation, and rescue.

26. 2　Building Fire Prevention

26. 2. 1　The fire resistance rating of main structures (such as underground station section and substation), entrance/exit passage and air ducts shall reach Class I, and that of the auxiliary buildings (including at-ground entrance/exit and air pavilion), ground station, elevated station, and elevated section structures shall not be lower than Class II.

26. 2. 2　The fire resistance rating of the OCC buildings shall be Class I and separate access shall be set up for the OCC when it is integrated with other buildings.

26. 2. 3　Fire separation facilities must be installed for the medium and low speed maglev transit where it adjoins to any ground or underground shopping mall or buildings.

26. 2. 4　The division of fire compartments shall be in accordance with the following requirements:

　1　For the underground station, the platform and station concourse public areas shall be divided into one fire compartment, while the maximum allowable usable area of the fire compartments in other parts shall not exceed 1500 m².

　2　When the station concourse is shared by the underground transfer station, the station concourse public area shall not exceed 2. 5 times that of the standard station for a single line.

　3　The fire compartment of at-ground station shall not exceed 2500 m².

　4　The division of fire compartments in vehicle base and OCC shall comply with the current national standard GB 50016 *Code for Fire Protection Design of Buildings*.

26. 2. 5　Any two adjacent fire zones shall be separated by the fire wall with the fire resistance rating of 3h and grade A fire door. Where an observation window is installed on the fire wall, grade A fire window shall be used. The floor slab of fire compartment shall have a fire resistance rating no less than 1.5h.

26.2.6 For the underground station, the train operation duty room or station control room, and the important equipment rooms like substation, power distribution room, communication and signal room, ventilation and air-conditioner room, fire pump room, fire extinguishing agent cylinder room shall be separated from other parts by the partition wall and floor slab of which the fire resistance ratings are not less than 3h and 2h respectively. The ceiling shall be made of non-combustible material and the doors and windows in the partition wall shall reach Class A.

26.2.7 Smoke barrier shall be installed at the landing of staircase from the station concourse to the platform. The vertical distance from the lower edge of the smoke barrier to the step surface of the staircase shall not be less than 2.3 m, and the height of the smoke barrier shall not be less than 0.5 m.

26.2.8 The decoration materials of the station shall be in accordance with the following requirements:

1 For the underground station, the ceiling, wall and floor decoration materials and garbage bins in the public area, equipment rooms, and management rooms shall be incombustible materials with the burning behavior rating of Class A.

2 For the at-ground station, the wall and ceiling decoration materials and garbage bins in the public area shall be Class A incombustible material and the floor shall be inflammable materials no lower than Class B1. The decoration materials of the equipment management area shall comply with the current national standard GB 50222 *Code for Fire Prevention in Design of Interior Decoration of Buildings*.

3 The fixed service facilities such as advertising light boxes, guiding signs, rest chairs, telephone booths and ticket vending/checking machine in the public areas of at-ground and underground stations shall be made of inflammable materials no less than Class B1. Asbestos, fiberglass or plastic decoration materials shall not be used.

26.2.9 The gap between the fire shutter and the building and the positions where the pipes, cables and air ducts pass through the fire wall, floor slab and fire partition shall be tightly sealed by fireproof sealing material.

26.2.10 The setting of safety entrances/exits of the station shall be in accordance with the following requirements:

1 The number of safety exits for the public areas of each station concourse of the station shall be determined by calculation, and at least two entrances/exits leading directly to the ground shall be provided.

2 For the underground single-story side platform, the number of safety exits on each side of the platform shall be determined by calculation and at least two safety exits leading directly to the ground shall be provided.

3 For the equipment room and management room areas of the underground station, at least two safety exits shall be set up and one leading directly to the ground shall be provided for the attended fire compartment.

4 The safety entrances and exits shall be set up in a de-centralized manner. For two entrances/exits set in the same direction, the clear distance between them shall not be less than 10 m.

5 Shaft, ladder, elevator, fire access, and track-crossing passage between the two side platforms shall not be taken as safety exit.

6 The transfer passage of underground transfer station shall not be taken as safety exit.

26.2.11 The distance from any point in the platform and station concourse public areas to the entrance of evacuation staircase or passage shall not exceed 50 m. Each end of the platform shall be installed with stair leading to the line section.

26.2.12 The fences for the paid area and free area of the public area shall be provided with evacuation door with opening devices that are automatically released in case of disaster. The gross width of the evacuation door shall be calculated according to the following formula:

$$L \geqslant \frac{0.9[A_1(N-1)+A_2B]-A_3}{A_4} \qquad (26.2.12)$$

Where, A_1——Carrying capacity of escalator (person/min/unit);

A_2—— Carrying capacity of staircase (person/min/m);

A_3——Total passing capacity of automatic ticket checking machine (person/min);

A_4——Total passing capacity of evacuation door (person/min/m) which may be taken as 80 persons/min/m;

B——Gross width of staircase (m);

L——Gross width of evacuation door (m).

26.2.13 The evacuation capacity of staircase and escalator used for personnel evacuation shall be calculated at 90% of that under normal conditions.

26.2.14 The setting of safety exits, staircases and evacuation passages shall be in accordance with the following requirements:

1 The width of the exit staircase and evacuation passage for personnel evacuation shall be calculated in accordance with the provisions of Chapter 9 in this code.

2 The minimum clear width of the safety exits, staircases and evacuation passages in the equipment area and management area of the station shall be in accordance with the following requirements:

　　1) The safety exit and staircase of equipment room and management room areas of the station shall not be less than 1.2 m wide;

　　2) The evacuation passage of the room arranged on one side shall not be less than 1.2 m;

　　3) The evacuation passage of the room arranged on two sides shall not be less than 1.5 m.

3 The distance from the evacuation door of the equipment room and management room directly leading to the evacuation passage to the nearest safety exit shall not exceed 40 m. For the rooms on the sides or at the end of the passage with enclosed end, the distance from the evacuation door to the nearest safety exit shall not exceed 22 m.

26.2.15 The length of underground access passage should not exceed 100 m, otherwise, measures shall be taken to meet the fire protection requirements for evacuation.

26.2.16 Connecting passage shall be set up between two single-route tunnels of underground line section. The spacing between the adjacent two connecting passages shall not exceed 600 m. Class A fire doors arranged in parallel and opened in reverse direction shall be installed in the connecting passage, and the doors shall not intrude into the gauge when opened.

26.3 Water Supply for Fire Protection and Extinguish Fire

26.3.1 Municipal tap water system shall be preferred for supplying fire water.

26.3.2 The fire water supply system shall be in accordance with the following requirements:

1 For the fire water supply system of underground station and tunnel, two water supply pipes shall be led from the municipal tap water system and connected to the ring pipeline network of the station or line section. Each water supply pipe shall be capable of supplying all the fire water required. Fire pumps and fire pool shall be provided when the municipal tap water system is of dendritic pipeline.

2 The fire water supply system of at-ground or elevated station shall comply with the current national standard GB 50974 *Technical Code for Fire Protection Water Supply and Hydrant Systems*.

3 When the municipal tap water system could supply adequate water for fire protection but fail to reach the required pressure for fire water, fire water pressure boosting and stabilization facilities shall be installed.

26.3.3 The underground station and its connected underground sections, entrance/exit passages of more than 20 m in length, and section tunnel with a length greater than 200 m shall be installed with indoor fire hydrant water supply system. The setting of indoor fire hydrants of at-ground or elevated station shall comply with the current national standard GB 50016 *Code for Fire Protection Design of Buildings*.

26.3.4 The water consumption of fire hydrants shall be in accordance with the following requirements:

1 Shall not lower than 20L/s for the fire hydrants for underground station (including transfer station).

2 Shall not lower than 10L/s for the fire hydrants for underground turn-back line and underground tunnel.

3 The water consumption of fire hydrants for at-ground station and elevated station shall comply with the current national standard GB 50016 *Code for Fire Protection Design of Buildings*.

26.3.5 The arrangement of fire water supply pipes shall be in accordance with the following requirements:

1 The fire water supply pipeline of underground station and section shall be designed to be ring pipeline.

2 Each underground station shall be installed with two fire water supply pipes, each connecting the municipal tap water system with the ring pipeline of the station. The upward route and downward route of underground section shall each be installed with one fire water supply pipe to connect to the ring pipeline of station at the end of the station.

3 The connecting pipe between the two main water supply pipes of the underground section shall be determined through technical and economic comparison.

4 The fire water system shall be designed to ring pipeline network if more than 10 indoor fire hydrants are installed for the at-ground and elevated stations, and the outdoor fire water consumption is greater than 15L/s.

5 The number of fire hydrants set on the dendritic fire water pipe shall not exceed four.

26.3.6 The setting of indoor fire hydrants shall be in accordance with the following requirements:

1 The diameter of fire hydrant shall be $DN65$; the diameter of fire nozzle shall be 19 mm; the length of each hose shall be 25 m; the height of hydrant outlet above ground or floor shall be 1.1 m.

2 In the public places of station such as station concourse and platform, the fire hydrants and fire extinguishers should share the box in which hoses and nozzles, self-rescue fire hose reels and fire extinguishers are installed. For the fire hydrant box in other parts of the station, the self-rescue fire hose reel may not be provided. When double-outlet, double-valve fire hydrant box is provided, a 25-meter hose may be equipped in the box.

3 The fire hydrants shall be arranged in such a way that two nozzles with full water spout may reach any part in the room simultaneously. The full water spout of nozzle shall not be less than 10 m. The spacing of the fire hydrants shall be determined by calculation, which, however, shall not exceed 30 m for single-outlet, single-valve fire hydrants or not exceed 50 m for double-mouth, double-valve fire hydrants. The spacing of fire hydrants in underground tunnel (single culvert) shall not exceed 50 m and that in the passage shall not exceed 30 m.

4 The hydrostatic pressure at the hydrant port shall not exceed 0.8 MPa, and outlet pressure at the outlet of fire hydrant shall not ex ceed respectively 0.5 MPa.

5 Fire hydrant without fire hydrant box and water hose may be installed for the underground tunnel, but the water hose shall be provided in the special fire box near the end of the station.

6 For the station with fire pump house, pump startup button shall be installed at the fire hydrant.

26.3.7 Water pump adapters shall be installed at obvious positions of the entrance/exit of underground station and mouth of ventilation pavilion, and outdoor fire hydrants shall be installed within the range of 15 m to 40 m. The setting of water pump adapters for the at-ground or elevated station shall comply with the current national standard GB 50974 *Technical Code for Fire Protection Water Supply and Hydrant Systems*.

26.3.8 When fire pumps and fire pool are needed for the station, the effective volume of the fire pool shall meet the consumption demand of fire water. The water demand of fire hydrant system shall be calculated based on 2h (duration of fire accident), from which the water that may be made up in the fire duration may be deducted if adequate makeup water is available.

26.3.9 The underground communication and signal room (including power room), substation (including control room), integrated monitoring equipment room, battery room, and HV substation shall be provided with automatic fire extinguishing system. The at-ground OCC, communication and signal room, comprehensive monitoring equipment room, AFC room and computer data center shall be provided with automatic fire extinguishing system. The setting of automatic fire extinguishing system for at-ground or elevated station and vehicle base shall comply with the current national standard GB 50016 *Code for Fire Protection Design of Buildings*.

26.3.10 The setting of fire extinguishers shall comply with the current national standard GB 50140 *Code for Design of Extinguisher Distribution in Buildings*.

26. 4　Smoke Prevention, Smoke Exclude and Emergency Ventilation

26. 4. 1　The underground station and line section tunnel must be provided with smoke prevention, smoke exclude and emergency ventilation systems.

26. 4. 2　Mechanical smoke exclude facilities shall be installed at the following parts of medium and low speed maglev transit.

1　Equipment rooms and management rooms of underground station which are located in the same fire compartment and have the total area exceeding 200 m², or a single constantly occupied room with the area exceeding 50 m².

2　Inner walkway with the straight-line distance from the farthest point to the public area of underground station exceeding 20 m; underground passage and entrance/exit passage with the continuous length exceeding 60 m.

26. 4. 3　When the smoke prevention, smoke exclude, and emergency ventilation system is integrated with the normal ventilation and conditioning system, the latter shall be provided with fire prevention measures and the function enabling fast switching to the smoke prevention and smoke exclude system in case of emergency conditions shall be available.

26. 4. 4　The smoke prevention, smoke exclude and emergency ventilation shall have the following functions:

1　Exclude the smoke in the direction opposite to the passenger evacuation and deliver fresh air in the passenger evaluation direction when a fire occurs in the tunnel.

2　Prevent and exclude the smoke and ventilate when fire occurs in the station concourse or platform of underground station.

3　Perform ventilation effectively for the blocked section when the train is blocked in the tunnel of line section.

4　Exclude the smoke when fire occurs to the at-ground or elevated station.

5　Prevent and exclude the smoke and ventilate when fire occurs to the equipment room and management room;

26. 4. 5　The public areas and equipment and management rooms of underground station shall be classified into smoke compartments not crossing the fire compartments. The floor area of each smoke compartment in the public areas of station concourse and platform should not exceed 2000 m², and that in the equipment and management rooms should not exceed 750 m².

26. 4. 6　The smoke zones should be separated by smoke barriers and other facilities. The suspended height of smoke barriers should not be less than 500 mm.

26. 4. 7　The smoke exhaust volume in case of fire in the platform and station concourse of underground station shall be calculated at 1 m³/m² · min based on the floor area of one smoke compartment. When the smoke exhaust equipment serves for two or more smoke compartments, the equipment capacity shall be adequate to exhaust the smoke in the two biggest smoke compartments simultaneously. When the fire occurs to the platform of station, downward air flow no less than 1. 5 m/s shall be delivered at the landing of staircase or escalator from the station concourse to the platform.

26. 4. 8　The smoke exhaust capacity of interval tunnel shall be calculated based on that the smoke exhaust flow of single-cavity interval tunnel is not less than 2 m/s, larger than the calculated critical wind speed, and not larger than 1 m/s.

26.4.9 The smoke exhaust fans in interval tunnel and other auxiliary equipment through which the smoke flows, such as air valves and silencers, shall be able to work effectively for one continuous hour under the temperature of 150 ℃.

26.4.10 The smoke exhaust fans and other auxiliary equipment through which the smoke flows in the hall, platform and equipment and management rooms of underground station, such as air valves and silencers, shall be able to work effectively for one continuous hour under the temperature of 250 ℃.

26.4.11 When the train is blocked in interval tunnel, the air inlet capacity shall be calculated based on that the air speed at the section of interval tunnel is not less than 2 m/s, the tunnel temperature at the most adverse point of the train top is less than 45 ℃, and the air speed shall not be larger than 11 m/s.

26.4.12 The air speed at the exhaust vent should not exceed 10 m/s.

26.4.13 When the main exhaust pipe is metal pipe, the air speed in the pipe shall not be larger than 20 m/s; when non-metal pipe is used, the air speed in the pipe shall not be larger than 15 m/s.

26.4.14 Fire dampers shall be installed on the air ducts at the following positions of the ventilation and air conditioning system:

    1 Where the pipes pass through the fire wall and floor of fire compartment.

    2 Interconnection of horizontal main pipe and vertical main pipe at each floor.

    3 Where the pipe passes through the deformation joint and a partition wall is set.

26.4.15 The smoke prevention and exhaust system of at-ground and elevated substations shall be designed to comply with the current national standard GB 50016 *Code for Fire Protection Design of Buildings*.

26.5　Communication for Disaster

26.5.1 The program-controlled telephone of the public communications system shall have the function of automatically switching to "119" of the local telephone network when a fire alarm occurs, and be equipped with wireless communication equipment for rescuers'communication in the event of disaster.

26.5.2 The control center shall be equipped with a wireless control console for disaster prevention. In the driver cabin, a wireless communication console shall be installed. In the station control room, station master's office, watch room and depot duty room, wireless communication equipment shall be provided.

26.5.3 For the disaster prevention dispatch telephone system, dispatch telephone switchboard shall be set up in the control center, and extensions shall be installed in the train station, stabling yard and vehicle base.

26.5.4 Fire control telephones shall be provided in the control center, stations stabling yards and vehicle bases.

    Disaster prevention broadcast consoles shall be installed in the control center and in the fire control rooms at each station, stabling yard and vehicle base.

26.6 Disaster Prevention Power Supply and Evacuation Indicator Sign

26.6.1 The electrical equipment for disaster prevention shall be considered as Grade I load, and automatic switching devices shall be provided at the last distribution box. The switching time shall comply with the current national standard GB 17945 *Fire Emergency Lighting and Evacuate Indicating System*.

26.6.2 The continuous power supply duration of emergency lighting shall not be less than 60 min.

26.6.3 The distribution equipment of disaster-prevention electrical equipment shall have obvious signs.

26.6.4 When the indicated high temperature part of illuminator is close to any combustible materials, heat insulation and dissipation as well as other disaster protection measures shall be taken. High-temperature illuminators shall not be installed in the warehouses storing combustible goods.

26.6.5 Lighting evacuation indication signs shall be set up at the following locations:

1 Station concourse, platform, escalator, moving walk, and landing.

2 Evacuation passage and safety exits, such as walkway in the auxiliary buildings of station.

3 Interval tunnel.

4 Evacuation staircase, evacuation passage, and safety exit of building in vehicle base, and control center building.

26.6.6 Emergency lighting shall be set up at the following locations:

1 Station concourse, platform, escalator, moving walk, and staircase.

2 Evacuation passage, such as walkway in the auxiliary buildings of station.

3 Interval tunnel.

4 Single building in vehicle base, and the evacuation staircase, evacuation passage, and fireman's elevator lobby (including miniature chamber) of control center building.

26.6.7 The power cable and control cable of the disaster prevention power supply system shall meet the requirements of Article 16.4.1 in this code.

26.7 Evacuation Platform

26.7.1 Evacuation platform shall be set up in the elevated line section of medium and low speed maglev transit.

26.7.2 The minimum width of the evacuation platform shall be in accordance with those specified in Table 26.7.2.

Table 26.7.2　Minimum Width of Evacuation Platform (mm)

Position	Inside Tunnel		Outside Tunnel	
	General Conditions	Difficult Conditions	General Conditions	Difficult Conditions
Single Route (on one side)	700	550	700	550
Double-route	1000	800	1000	800

26.7.3 The evacuation platform shall not be higher than the carriage floor surface of the train when the train is under non-levitation state and the air spring of train is not loaded with air.

26. 7. 4 The setting of the evacuation platform shall meet the gauge requirements of Chapter 5 in this code.

26. 8　Other Disaster Prevention

26. 8. 1 The flooding protection measures at the station entrances/exits and open low air shafts shall comply with flood control requirements.

26. 8. 2 The flood prevention measures for the entrance and open entrances/exits shall be carried out in accordance with the requirements of Section 15. 3 in this code.

26. 8. 3 The seismic design of the structures shall comply with the current national standard GB 50111 *Code for Seismic Design of Railway Engineering*.

26. 9　Other Disaster Alarms

26. 9. 1 Dangerous water level alarm devices shall be installed at all drainage pump stations, rainwater pump stations and sewage pump stations at the stations and along the line.

26. 9. 2 The medium and low speed maglev transit system shall have the function of receiving weather forecast from local meteorological department.

26. 9. 3 The medium and low speed maglev transit system shall have the function of receiving telephone alarm or network communication alarm from the local earthquake forecast department.

27 Environment Protection

27. 1 General Requirements

27. 1. 1 Environment protection measures shall be designed, constructed and put into use simultaneously with the main project.

27. 1. 2 The siting of medium and low speed maglev transit lines shall avoid sensitive areas such as environment sensitive areas, cultural relics, nature reserves, scenic spots, water source conservation areas and ecological function areas and other areas requiring special protection.

27. 1. 3 Environment protection measures shall include equipment vibration reduction and noise reduction measures, air pollution control measures, wastewater treatment measures and electromagnetic influence prevention measures.

27. 1. 4 Environment protection facilities shall be designed according to the design service life, predicted long-term ridership and maximum throughput of maglev line. These measures may be taken completely from the beginning according to the long-term plan or may be implemented by phase, i. e., near-term plan is implemented in the early stage with implementation conditions reserved for long-term plan.

27. 1. 5 The environment protection equipment shall use clean production processes and technologies, have high energy efficiency, and be easy to maintain and use. Use of equipment and materials that may lead to serious pollution to environment must be forbidden.

27. 2 Noise

27. 2. 1 The noise pollution control design for medium and low speed maglev transit shall comply with the current national standards GB 3096 *Environmental Quality Standard for Noise*, GB 12348 *Emission Standard for Industrial Enterprises Noise at Boundary* and GB/T 15190 *Technical Specifications for Regionalizing Environmental Noise Function*.

27. 2. 2 The siting of maglev line and stations shall be in line with the local urban environment planning and functional zoning, and avoid the existing, under-construction and planned areas and buildings sensitive to noise.

27. 2. 3 The noise control of station equipment shall be in accordance with the following requirements:

  1 For the ventilation and air conditioning system of underground station, local ventilation and air conditioning systems and the ventilation systems of interval tunnels, low-noise equipment in compliance with the relevant national standards shall be preferably used. In addition, silencers shall be installed at both air inlet and air outlet of air fans in accordance with the noise limit requirements of the corresponding areas as stated in the current national standard GB 3096 *Environmental Quality Standard for Noise*.

  2 Power equipment that produces noise pollution shall be arranged in dedicated equipment rooms and well isolated from station concourse and the public areas of platform.

  3 Depending on noise characteristics, power equipment such as fans and pumps shall be

equipped with rubber vibration isolation pads or vibration dampers at the bottom of their pedestals or foundations, while flexible joints and elastic hangers and supports shall be used for the inlet and outlet pipes directly connected to the equipment.

27.2.4 Environmental noise control of station platform, station concourse and management rooms shall be in accordance with the following requirements:

1 In the absence of maglev trains, the equivalent sound level of station platform and station concourse shall not exceed 70dB (A), and that of management rooms shall not exceed 60dB (A).

2 The average equivalent sound levels of maglev trains entering and exiting the station shall comply with the current national standard GB 14227 *Acoustical Requirement and Measurement on Station Platform of Urban Rail Transit*.

27.2.5 Environment noise control of maglev lines shall be in accordance with the following requirements:

1 Where there are noise-sensitive buildings along maglev line, the noise level of maglev train shall comply with the noise limits of the corresponding areas as stated in the current national standard GB 3096 *Environmental Quality Standard for Noise*.

2 Where an elevated or at-ground maglev line is adjacent to noise-sensitive areas, the line shall be provided with acoustic barriers and sound insulating walls.

3 The acoustic barriers shall be close to the line and meet the gauge requirements of the line.

4 The points where maglev train enters or exits tunnel, air shaft and cooling tower shall keep clear of or keep back on to noise-sensitive buildings. The noises of air pavilion and cooling tower shall comply with the current national standard GB 3096 *Environmental Quality Standard for Noise*.

27.2.6 Depot and stabling yard shall be sited in non-noise-sensitive areas, and their boundary noise shall meet the noise limit requirements of the corresponding areas as stated in the current national standard GB 12348 *Emission Standard for Industrial Enterprises Noise at Boundary*.

27.3 Vibration

27.3.1 The design to control environmental vibrations generated by running maglev trains shall comply with the current national standard GB 10070 *Standard of Environmental Vibration in Urban Area*.

27.3.2 The control of train-induced vibration shall be in accordance with the following requirements:

1 The plane position and depth of underground maglev line shall be determined according to the structures and types of at-ground buildings and the environmental protection requirements of environment functional division. At existing urban areas, underground maglev line shall be kept away from environmental protection targets such as vibration-sensitive areas and important sensitive buildings. The ground vibration generated by running maglev trains shall comply with the current national standard GB 10070 *Standard of Environmental Vibration in Urban Area*;

2 Where the vibration of nearby sensitive areas brought by maglev train exceeds the limit specified in current national standard GB 10070 *Standard of Environmental Vibration in Urban Area*, the plane position of the line shall be adjusted or appropriate vibration mitigating measures shall be taken.

27.3.3 The vibration mitigating measures for the ventilation and air conditioning system of station, local ventilation and air conditioning systems and the ventilation systems of interval tunnels shall comply with the relevant requirements of the current national standard GB 50736 *Design Code for Heating Ventilation and Air Conditioning of Civil Buildings*.

27. 4   Air Polution

27. 4. 1   The design of air pollution prevention and control shall comply with the current national standards GB 14554 *Emission Standards for Odor Pollutants*, GB 13271 *Emission Standard of Air Pollutants for Boiler* and GB 18483 *Emission Standard of Cooking Fume*.

27. 4. 2   The interior decoration materials of maglev line station shall meet the hazardous emission limits specified in the relevant national standards.

27. 4. 3   In underground station, the concentration of CO_2 shall be lower than 1. 5‰ and the daily average concentration of inhalable particulate matters shall be lower than 0. 25 mg/m^3.

27. 4. 4   Around air pavilions, shrubs good at absorbing harmful gases such as CO_2, NO_x and CO and particulate matters should be planted.

27. 4. 5   The air pollution control of depot shall be in accordance with the following requirements:

1   Vehicle bases in cold regions requiring heating shall be connected to the utility urban heating network. Where access to utility urban heating network is not available, clean energy heating equipment shall be used;

2   Coal-fired boilers used for heating shall be equipped withdedusting and desulfurization equipment. The emission concentrations of major air pollutants from the boilers shall comply with the current national standard GB 13271 *Emission Standard of Air Pollutants for Boiler*;

3   The food handling room of dining hall of vehicle base shall be installed with fume purification facilities and the fume emission concentration shall comply with the current national standard GB 18483 *Emission Standard of Cooking Fume*.

27. 5   Effluent

27. 5. 1   The design of effluent pollution prevention and control shall comply with the relevant provisions of the *Water Pollution Prevention and Control Law*. The design of effluent discharge shall comply with the current national standard GB 8978 *Integrated Wastewater Discharge Standard*.

27. 5. 2   Where there is no municipal sewage system in the vicinity, the domestic sewage and production effluent from maglev station and vehicle base shall be treated in accordance with the current national standard GB 8978 *Integrated Wastewater Discharge Standard*.

27. 5. 3   The industrial effluent from vehicle base should be recycled after treatment.

27. 6   Electromagnetic Environment

27. 6. 1   The electromagnetic environment of medium and low speed maglev transit system shall mainly include the electromagnetic environment generated by HV substation and that generated by running train.

27. 6. 2   The electromagnetic environment generated by HV substation and running train shall comply with the current national standard GB 8702 *Controlling Limits for Electromagnetic Environment*.

27. 6. 3   When field strength for receiving TV signal reaches the specified value, the signal-to-noise ratio of the signal shall not be less than 35dB ($\mu V/m$).

Appendix A   Calculation Methods of Dynamic Vehicle Envelope and Equipment Gauge for Beeline Section

A. 1   General Requirements

A. 1. 1   The vehicle gauge of straight line section shall refer to the maximum dynamic envelope of medium and low speed maglev train running normally on straight line sections, which is determined taking into account factors including the geometric deviation of the line, vehicle manufacturing errors, magnetic pole spacing, vehicle vibration, transverse acceleration, eccentric load, crosswind and downward levitation deviation.

A. 1. 2   The equipment gauge of straight line section shall refer to a control line formed by adding a safety clearance to vehicle gauge. The safety clearance shall include the deviation of medium and low speed maglev vehicle from its normal running position at the time of failure and the safety margins for unrecognized factors.

A. 1. 3   Failures of maglev vehicle shall be classified into the following two categories:

1   Air springs on one side overinflated, those on the other side underinflated + levitation gap out of control + transverse geometric ultimate displacement of magnetic pole;

2   Air springs at the front or rear end overinflated or underinflated + levitation gap out of control + transverse geometric ultimate displacement of magnetic pole.

A. 2   Definition of Design Gauge Parameters

A. 2. 1   The design gauge parameters shall be as defined in Table A. 2. 1.

Table A. 2. 1   Definition of Design Gauge Parameters

S/N	Symbol	Description
1	ΔX_{cj}	Dynamic traverse displacement of levitation bogie relative to the magnetic poles of F rail (mm)
2	ΔM_{BX}	Transverse manufacturing error of maglev vehicle (mm)
3	ΔM_{BY}	Vertical manufacturing error of maglev vehicle (mm)
4	$\Delta\omega$	Normal transverse deformation of maglev vehicle relative to levitation chassis at ♯2 and ♯5 track bearing platforms within straight line sections (mm)
5	δ_w	Vertical wear of skid (mm)
6	f_{1dx}	Empty-to-load elastic deflection change of levitation bogie (mm)
7	f_2	Height adjustment error of air spring (mm)
8	Δf_{pcj}	Dynamic variation of levitation air gap of magnetic pole (mm)
9	Δf_{smax}	Deflection of air spring due to lateral roll (maximum value in the presence of various factors during normal operation), (mm)
10	$\Delta f'_{smax}$	Dynamic deflection of air spring due to floating and sinking (mm)
11	ΔM_{qc}	Upwarp/downwarp of vehicle outside pin (mm)
12	Δ_c	Transverse deviation of F rail centerline (mm)
13	δ_c	Vertical deviation of F rail centerline (mm)
14	Δh_1	Transverse height difference of F rail (mm)

Table A. 2. 1 (Continued)

S/N	Symbol	Description
15	Δ_e	Transverse elastic deformation of F rail (mm)
16	δ_e	Vertical elastic deformation F rail (mm)
17	Δh_2	Transverse elastic height difference of F rail (mm)
18	a	Longitudinal spacing between ♯2 and ♯5 track bearing platforms of levitation bogie (mm)
19	n	Center distance between design section and ♯2 and ♯5 track bearing platforms of the adjacent levitation bogie (mm)
20	h_{cs}	Height from the upper supporting surface of air springs and the rail surface (mm)
21	ΔM_{tX}	Transverse manufacturing error of levitation bogie (mm)
22	ΔM_{tY}	Vertical manufacturing error of levitation bogie (mm)
23	R	Horizontal curve radius (depot line) (m)
24	R_V	Vertical curve radius (minimum) (m)
25	θ_{ac}	Maximum cross slope angle of F rail (°)
26	θ_{dc}	Superelevation deficiency rate
27	V	Maximum running speed of vehicle (km/h)
28	f_{XF}	Levitation height (mm)
29	Δf_{SD}	Decline due to underinflated air spring or rise due to overinflated air spring (mm)
30	Δf_{sk}	Out-of-control limit of unilateral levitation gap (mm)
31	$\Delta X'_{cj}$	Transverse geometric extreme displacement of magnetic pole (mm)
32	L	Track gauge (mm)
33	Δf_{hq}	Vertical deflection of skid (mm)
34	h_{cp}	Height of F rail acting surface relative to sliding rail surface (mm)
35	b_s	Transverse spacing of air springs (mm)
36	θ_{px}	Offset angle (maximum) of vehicle as a result of asymmetric arrangement of passengers (rad)
37	$\Delta \omega_{max}$	Maximum transverse deformation of vehicle relative to levitation bogie at ♯2 and ♯5 track bearing platforms (mm)
38	a'	Longitudinal spacing of ♯1 and ♯6 track bearing platforms of levitation bogie (mm)
39	n'	Center distance between the design cross section and ♯1 or ♯6 track bearing platforms of levitation bogie (mm)
40	L_{xfj}	Effective length of levitation bogie (mm)

A. 2. 2 Deflection of air spring due to lateral roll (maximum value in the presence of various factors during normal operation) shall be calculated according to the following formula:

$$\Delta f_{smax} = 0.5 b_s \times \sqrt{[A_w \cdot P_w(1+S_2)(h_{sw}-h_{cs})/k_{\Phi s}]^2 + [m_j \cdot a_B(1+S_2)(h_{sc}-h_{cs})/k_{\Phi s}]^2}$$

$$(A. 2. 2)$$

Where, $A_w \cdot P_w$——Wind load (N);

$\quad\quad A_w$——Windward area (m²);

$\quad\quad P_w$——Wind pressure (N/m²);

$\quad\quad m_j$——Design weight of vehicle (AW3) (kg);

$\quad\quad a_B$——Transverse acceleration (m/s²);

$\quad\quad h_{sw}$——Centroid height of windward area (mm);

$\quad\quad h_{sc}$——Height of center of gravity of vehicle (mm);

$k_{\Phi s}$——Anti-roll rigidity of secondary springs throughout vehicle (N · mm/rad);

S_2——Additional coefficient of gravity angle $=m_j g[(h_{sc}-h_{cs})/k_{\Phi s}]$ (rad).

A. 2. 3 Offset angle of vehicle as a result of asymmetric arrangement of passengers shall be calculated according to the following formula:

$$\theta_{px} = [100 m_z g(1+S_2)/k_{\Phi s}] \leqslant 2f_2/b_s \qquad (A. 2. 3)$$

Where, m_z——2/3 passenger capacity (AW$_2$) (kg).

A. 3 Calculation of Vehicle gauge

A. 3. 1 The deviations of vehicle and the components installed on vehicle should be calculated according to the following formulas considering two cases: the transverse deviation and lateral roll of vehicle are in the same direction or in reverse direction.

1 Where the transverse deviation and lateral roll of vehicle are in the same direction:

1) Transverse deviation

$$\Delta X_{BP} = \sqrt{\Delta X_{cj}^2 + \Delta w^2} \times \frac{2n+a}{a} + \Delta_e + \theta_{px}|Y - h_{cs}| + \Delta M_{BX}$$

$$+ \sqrt{\Delta_c^2 + \left[\frac{\Delta h_1}{L} \cdot Y\right]^2 + \left[\frac{\Delta h_2}{L} \cdot Y\right]^2 + \left[2 \times \frac{\Delta f_{pcj}}{L}(Y - h_{cp})\right]^2 + \left[2 \times \frac{\Delta f_{smax}}{b_s}(Y - h_{cs})\right]^2} \qquad (A. 3. 1-1)$$

2) Upward vertical deviation

$$\Delta Y_{BPu} = \Delta M_{BY} + \Delta M_{qc} + f_2 + f_{XF} + \delta_c - X\theta_{px}$$

$$- \sqrt{[2 \times \Delta f_{pcj} \times X/L]^2 + [2 \times \Delta f_{smax} \times X/b_s]^2 + \left[\frac{\Delta h_1}{L}X\right]^2 + \left[\frac{\Delta h_2}{L}X\right]^2}$$

(If less than 0, take 0.) $\qquad (A. 3. 1-2)$

3) Downward vertical deviation

$$\Delta Y_{BPd} = \Delta M_{BY} + \Delta M_{qc} + f_{1dx} + f_2 + \delta_e + X\theta_{px} - f_{XF}$$

$$+ \sqrt{\delta_c^2 + [2 \times \Delta f_{smax} \times X/b_s]^2 + [2 \times \Delta f_{pcj} \times X/L]^2 + [\Delta h_1 \times X/L]^2 + [\Delta h_2 \times X/L]^2} \qquad (A. 3. 1-3)$$

2 Where the transverse deviation and lateral roll of vehicle are in the reverse direction:

1) Transverse deviation

$$\Delta X_{BP} = \sqrt{\Delta X_{cj}^2 + \Delta w^2} \times \frac{2n+a}{a} + \Delta_e + \Delta_c - \theta_{px}|Y - h_{cs}| + \Delta M_{BX}$$

$$- \sqrt{[\Delta h_1 \cdot Y/L]^2 + [\Delta h_2 \cdot Y/L]^2 + [2 \times \Delta f_{pcj}(Y - h_{cp})/L]^2 + [2 \times \Delta f_{smax}(Y - h_{cs})/b_s]^2} \qquad (A. 3. 1-4)$$

2) Upward vertical deviation

$$\Delta Y_{BPu} = \Delta M_{BY} + \Delta M_{qc} + f_2 + f_{XF} + X\theta_{px}$$

$$+ \sqrt{\delta_c^2 + [2 \times \Delta f_{pcj} X/L]^2 + [2 \times \Delta f_{smax} \times X/b_s]^2 + [\Delta h_1 \times X/L]^2 + [\Delta h_2 \times X/L]^2} \qquad (A. 3. 1-5)$$

3) Downward vertical deviation

$$\Delta Y_{BPd} = \Delta M_{BY} + \Delta M_{qc} + f_{1dx} + f_2 + \delta_e - X\theta_{px} - f_{XF}$$

$$- \sqrt{\delta_c^2 + [2 \times \Delta f_{smax} \times X/b_s]^2 + [2 \times \Delta f_{pcj} \times X/L]^2 + [\Delta h_1 \times X/L]^2 + [\Delta h_2 \times X/L]^2}$$

$$\text{(If less than 0, take 0)} \qquad (A.3.1\text{-}6)$$

3 Transverse deviation and levitation:

1) Transverse deviation

$$\Delta X_{BP} = \sqrt{\Delta X_{cj}^2 + \Delta w^2} \times \frac{2n+a}{a} + \Delta_e + \Delta M_{BX} + \Delta_c \qquad (A.3.1\text{-}7)$$

2) Upward vertical deviation

$$\Delta Y_{BPu} = \Delta M_{BY} + \Delta M_{qc} + f_2 + f_{XF}$$
$$+ \sqrt{\delta_c^2 + \left[\Delta f_{pcj} \times \frac{2n'+a'}{a'}\right]^2 + \left[\Delta f'_{smax} \times \frac{2n'+a'}{a'}\right]^2}$$

$$(A.3.1\text{-}8)$$

3) Downward vertical deviation

$$\Delta Y_{BPd} = \Delta M_{BY} + \Delta M_{qc} + f_{1dx} + f_2 + \delta_e - f_{XF} +$$
$$\sqrt{\delta_c^2 + \left[\Delta f'_{smax} \times \frac{2n'+a'}{a'}\right]^2 + \left[\Delta f_{pcj} \times \frac{2n'+a'}{a'}\right]^2}$$

$$(A.3.1\text{-}9)$$

4) Downward levitation deviation

$$\Delta Y_{BPdx} = \Delta M_{BY} + \Delta M_{qc} + f_{1dx} + f_2 + \delta_e + \delta_w$$
$$+ \sqrt{\delta_c^2 + \left[\Delta f'_{smax} \times \frac{2n'+a'}{a'}\right]^2 + \left[\Delta f_{hq} \times \frac{2n'+a'}{a'}\right]^2}$$

$$(A.3.1\text{-}10)$$

A.3.2 The deviations of levitation bogie and the components installed on it should be calculated according to the following formulas:

1 Transverse deviation

$$\Delta X_t = \Delta X_{cj} + \Delta_e + \Delta M_{tX} + \sqrt{\Delta_c^2 + [\Delta h_1 \times Y/L]^2 + [\Delta h_2 \times Y/L]^2 + \left[2 \times \frac{\Delta f_{pcj}}{L}(Y - h_{cp})\right]^2}$$

$$(A.3.2\text{-}1)$$

2 Upward vertical deviation

$$\Delta Y_{tu} = \Delta M_{tY} + f_{XF} + \sqrt{[2 \times \Delta f_{pcj} \times X/L]_{\geqslant \Delta f_{pcj}}^2 + \delta_c^2 + [\Delta h_1 \times X/L]^2 + [\Delta h_2 \times X/L]^2}$$

$$(A.3.2\text{-}2)$$

3 Downward vertical deviation

$$\Delta Y_{td} = \delta_e + \Delta M_{tY} - f_{XF} + \sqrt{[2 \times \Delta f_{pcj} \times X/L]_{\geqslant \Delta f_{pcj}}^2 + \delta_c^2 + [\Delta h_1 \times X/L]^2 + [\Delta h_2 \times X/L]^2}$$

$$(A.3.2\text{-}3)$$

4 Downward levitation

$$\Delta Y_{tdx} = \delta_e + \Delta M_{tY} + \delta_w + \sqrt{[\Delta f_{hq}]^2 + \delta_c^2 + [\Delta h_1 \times X/L]^2 + [\Delta h_2 \times X/L]^2}$$

$$(A.3.2\text{-}4)$$

A.4 Calculation of Equipment gauge at Straight Sections

A.4.1 In the calculation of equipment gauge, the dynamic deviations shall be calculated according to the two fault conditions as stated in article A.1.3 of this code. The maximum deviation plus an appropriate margin shall be taken as the equipment gauge.

A.4.2 The deviation of vehicle and the components installed on it under ♯1 fault condition should be calculated according to the following formula:

1 Where the transverse deviation and lateral roll of vehicle are in the same direction:

1) Transverse deviation

$$\Delta X_{\text{BPS}} = (\Delta X'_{\text{cj}} + \Delta w_{\text{max}}) \times \frac{2n+a}{a} + \Delta_{\text{e}} + \Delta M_{\text{BX}}$$

$$+ 2 \times \frac{\Delta f_{\text{SD}}}{b_{\text{s}}} |Y - h_{\text{cs}}| + \frac{(2 \times \Delta f_{\text{sk}} + \delta_{\text{w}})}{L} |Y - h_{\text{cp}}| \qquad \text{(A. 4. 2-1)}$$

$$+ \sqrt{\Delta_{\text{c}}^2 + \left[\frac{\Delta h_1}{L} \cdot Y\right]^2 + \left[\frac{\Delta h_2}{L} \cdot Y\right]^2}$$

2) Upward vertical deviation

$$\Delta Y_{\text{BPuS}} = \Delta M_{\text{BY}} + \Delta M_{\text{qc}} + f_{\text{XF}} + \delta_{\text{c}}$$

$$- 2 \times \Delta f_{\text{SD}} \times X/b_{\text{s}} - (2 \times \Delta f_{\text{sk}} + \delta_{\text{w}}) \times X/L$$

$$- \sqrt{\left[\frac{\Delta h_1}{L} X\right]^2 + \left[\frac{\Delta h_2}{L} X\right]^2}$$

(If less than 0, take 0) \qquad (A. 4. 2-2)

3) Downward vertical deviation

$$\Delta Y_{\text{BPdS}} = \Delta M_{\text{BY}} + \Delta M_{\text{qc}} + f_{\text{1dx}} + \delta_{\text{e}} - f_{\text{XF}}$$

$$+ 2 \times \Delta f_{\text{SD}} \times X/b_{\text{s}} + (2 \times \Delta f_{\text{sk}} + \delta_{\text{w}}) \times X/L$$

$$+ \sqrt{\delta_{\text{c}}^2 + [\Delta h_1 \times X/L]^2 + [\Delta h_2 \times X/L]^2} \qquad \text{(A. 4. 2-3)}$$

2 Where the transverse deviation and lateral roll of vehicle are in the reverse directions:

1) Transverse deviation

$$\Delta X_{\text{BPS}} = (\Delta X'_{\text{cj}} + \Delta w_{\text{max}}) \times \frac{2n+a}{a} + \Delta_{\text{e}} + \Delta_{\text{c}} + \Delta M_{\text{BX}}$$

$$- 2 \times \Delta f_{\text{SD}} |Y - h_{\text{cs}}|/b_{\text{s}} - (2 \times \Delta f_{\text{sk}} + \delta_{\text{w}}) |Y - h_{\text{cp}}|/L \qquad \text{(A. 4. 2-4)}$$

$$- \sqrt{[\Delta h_1 \cdot Y/L]^2 + [\Delta h_2 \cdot Y/L]^2}$$

2) Upward vertical deviation

$$\Delta Y_{\text{BPuS}} = \Delta M_{\text{BY}} + \Delta M_{\text{qc}} + f_{\text{XF}}$$

$$+ 2 \times \Delta f_{\text{SD}} \times X/b_{\text{s}} + (2 \times \Delta f_{\text{sk}} + \delta_{\text{w}}) \times X/L \qquad \text{(A. 4. 2-5)}$$

$$+ \sqrt{\delta_{\text{c}}^2 + [\Delta h_1 \times X/L]^2 + [\Delta h_2 \times X/L]^2}$$

3) Downward vertical deviation

$$\Delta Y_{\text{BPdS}} = \Delta M_{\text{BY}} + \Delta M_{\text{qc}} + f_{\text{1dx}} + \delta_{\text{e}} + \delta_{\text{c}} - f_{\text{XF}}$$

$$- 2 \times \Delta f_{\text{SD}} \times X/b_{\text{s}} - (2 \times \Delta f_{\text{sk}} + \delta_{\text{w}}) \times X/L$$

$$- \sqrt{[\Delta h_1 \times X/L]^2 + [\Delta h_2 \times X/L]^2}$$

(If less than 0, take 0) \qquad (A. 4. 2-6)

A. 4. 3 The deviation of levitation and the components installed on it under ♯1 fault condition should be calculated according to the following formula:

1 Transverse deviation

$$\Delta X_{\text{tS}} = \Delta X'_{\text{cj}} + \Delta_{\text{e}} + \Delta M_{\text{tX}} + \frac{(2 \times \Delta f_{\text{sk}} + \delta_{\text{w}})}{L} |Y - h_{\text{cp}}|$$

$$+ \sqrt{\Delta_{\text{c}}^2 + [\Delta h_1 \times Y/L]^2 + [\Delta h_2 \times Y/L]^2} \qquad \text{(A. 4. 3-1)}$$

2 Upward vertical deviation

$$\Delta Y_{\text{tuS}} = \Delta M_{\text{tY}} + f_{\text{XF}} + [(2 \times \Delta f_{\text{sk}} + \delta_{\text{w}}) \times X/L]_{\geqslant \Delta f_{\text{sk}}}$$

$$+ \sqrt{\delta_c^2 + [\Delta h_1 \times X/L]^2 + [\Delta h_2 \times X/L]^2} \qquad \text{(A. 4. 3-2)}$$

3 Downward vertical deviation

$$\Delta Y_{tdS} = \delta_e + \Delta M_{tY} + [(2 \times \Delta f_{sk} + \delta_w) \times X/L]_{\geqslant(\Delta f_{sk} + \delta_w)} - f_{XF}$$

$$+ \sqrt{\delta_c^2 + [\Delta h_1 \times X/L]^2 + [\Delta h_2 \times X/L]^2}$$

$$\text{(A. 4. 3-3)}$$

A. 4. 4 The transverse and vertical deviations of vehicle under ♯ 2 fault condition should be calculated according to the following formula:

1 Transverse deviation

$$\Delta X_{BPS} = (\Delta X_{cj} + \Delta w_{max}) \times \frac{2n + a}{a} + \Delta_e + \Delta M_{BX} + \Delta_c \qquad \text{(A. 4. 4-1)}$$

2 Upward vertical deviation

$$\Delta Y_{BPuS} = \Delta M_{BY} + \Delta M_{qc} + f_{XF} + \Delta f_{SD} \times \frac{n' + a'}{a'} + \Delta f_{sk} \times \frac{n' + a'}{a'}$$

$$+ \sqrt{\delta_c^2 + \left[\Delta f_{pcj} \times \frac{n'}{a'}\right]^2 + \left[\Delta f'_{smax} \times \frac{n'}{a'}\right]^2}$$

$$\text{(A. 4. 4-2)}$$

3 Downward vertical deviation

$$\Delta Y_{BPdS} = \Delta M_{BY} + \Delta M_{qc} + f_{1dx} + \delta_e - f_{XF}$$

$$+ \Delta f_{SD} \times \frac{n' + a'}{a'} + (\Delta f_{sk} + \delta_w) \times \frac{n' + a'}{a'}$$

$$+ \sqrt{\delta_c^2 + \left[\Delta f_{pcj} \times \frac{n'}{a'}\right]^2 + \left[\Delta f'_{smax} \times \frac{n'}{a'}\right]^2 + \left[\Delta f_{hq} \times \frac{n'}{a'}\right]^2}$$

$$\text{(A. 4. 4-3)}$$

4 Downward levitation deviation

$$\Delta Y_{BPdxS} = \Delta M_{BY} + \Delta M_{qc} + f_{1dx} + \delta_e + \delta_w + \Delta f_{SD} \times \frac{n' + a'}{a'}$$

$$+ \sqrt{\delta_c^2 + \left[\Delta f'_{smax} \times \frac{n'}{a'}\right]^2 + \left[\Delta f_{hq} \times \frac{2n' + a'}{a'}\right]^2}$$

$$\text{(A. 4. 4-4)}$$

Appendix B Calculation Methds of Equipment Gauge for Curved Section

B. 0. 1 The equipment gauge of curved section shall be determined by appropriately widening or heightening the equipment gauge of straight sections according to the geometric deviation of vehicle at curved sections.

B. 0. 2 The geometric deviation of vehicle at curved sections should be calculated according to the following formula:

    1 Widening of transverse gauge of vehicle:

        1) Outer side of curve:

$$T_a = 1000 \left[4n \left(n + a \right) + 4m \left(m + p \right) \right] / 8R \qquad \text{(B. 0. 2-1)}$$

        2) Inner side of curve:

$$T_i = 1000 \left[4n \left(a - n \right) - 4m \left(m + p \right) \right] / 8R \qquad \text{(B. 0. 2-2)}$$

    2 Heightening or lowering of vertical gauge of vehicle:

        1) Outside ♯2 and ♯5 track bearing platforms:

$$T_a' = 1000 \left[4n \left(n + a \right) + 4m' \left(m' + p' \right) \right] / 8R_V \qquad \text{(B. 0. 2-3)}$$

        2) Inside ♯2 and ♯5 track bearing platforms:

$$T_i' = 1000 \left[4n \left(a - n \right) - 4m' \left(m' + p' \right) \right] / 8R_V \qquad \text{(B. 0. 2-4)}$$

The above two formulas are based on the premise is that the height of valve-controlled air spring is adjusted according to the heights of ♯2 and ♯5 track bearing platforms.

    3 Widening of transverse gauge of levitation bogie:

        1) Outer side of curve:

$$T_{ba} = 1000m'' \left(m'' + p \right) / 2R \qquad \text{(B. 0. 2-5)}$$

        2) Inner side of curve:

$$T_{bi} = 1000m' \left(p - m' \right) / 2R \qquad \text{(B. 0. 2-6)}$$

Where, a——Longitudinal spacing of ♯2 and ♯5 track bearing platforms of levitation bogies (m);

    m——Longitudinal distance between the centerline of ♯2 and ♯5 track bearing platforms and the transverse position limit device of adjacent levitation magnet (m), $m = \left(\dfrac{a}{3} - p \right) / 2$ (m);

    m'——Longitudinal distance between the centerline of ♯2 and ♯5 track bearing platforms and the vertical air gap sensor of adjacent levitation magnet (m);

    m''——Longitudinal distance between the design cross section and the transverse position limit device of adjacent levitation magnet (m);

n——Centerline distance between the design cross section and $\sharp 2$ and $\sharp 5$ track bearing platforms of adjacent levitation bogie (m);

p——Longitudinal spacing of transverse position limit devices of levitation magnet (m),

$$p = \frac{3}{5} \times L_{xfj};$$

p'——Longitudinal spacing of vertical position limit devices of levitation magnet (m);

R——Horizontal curve radius (m);

R_V——Vertical curve radius (m).

Explanation of Wording in This Code

1 Words used for different degrees of strictness are explained as follows in order to mark the differences in executing the requirements in this code:

    1) Words denoting a very strict or mandatory requirement:

    "Must" is used for affirmation; "must not" for negation.

    2) Words denoting a strict requirement under normal conditions:

    "Shall" is used for affirmation; "shall not" for negation.

    3) Words denoting a permission of a slight choice or an indication of the most suitable choice when conditions permit:

    "Should" is used for affirmation; "should not" for negation.

    4) "May" is used to express the option available, sometimes with the conditional permit.

2 "Shall comply with..." or "Shall meet the requirements of..." is used in this code to indicate that it is necessary to comply with the requirements stipulated in other relative standards and codes.

List of Quoted Standards

1 GB 50009 *Load Code for the Design of Building Structures*

2 GB 50010 *Code for Design of Concrete Structures*

3 GB 50011 *Code for Seismic Design of Buildings*

4 GB 50015 *Code for Design of Building Water Supply and Drainage*

5 GB 50016 *Code for Fire Protection Design of Buildings*

6 GB 50019 *Design Code for Heating Ventilation and Air Conditioning of Industrial Buildings*

7 GB 50034 *Standard for Lighting Design of Buildings*

8 GB 50052 *Code for Design Electric Power Supply Systems*

9 GB 50053 *Code for Design of 20kV and Below Substation*

10 GB 50057 *Code for Design Protection of Structures against Lighting*

11 GB 50060 *Code for Design of High Voltage Electrical Installation* (3－110kV)

12 GB/T 50065 *Code for Design of AC Electrical Installations Earthing*

13 GB 50108 *Technical Code for Waterproofing of Underground Works*

14 GB 50111 *Code for Seismic Design of Railway Engineering*

15 GB 50116 *Code for Design of Automatic Fire Alarm System*

16 GB 50139 *Navigation Standard of Inland Waterway*

17 GB 50140 *Code for Design of Extinguisher Distribution in Buildings*

18 GB 50157 *Code for Design of Metro*

19 GB 50174 *Code for Design of Data Centers*

20 GB 50189 *Design Standard for Energy Efficiency of Public Buildings*

21 GB 50217 *Code for Design of Cables of Electric Engineering*

22 GB 50222 *Code for Fire Prevention in Design of Interior Decoration of Buildings*

23 GB 50307 *Code for Geotechnical Investigations of Urban Rail Transit*

24 GB 50314 *Standard for Design of Intelligent Building*

25 GB 50343 *Technical Code for Protection against Lightning of Building Electronic Information System*

26 GB/T 50476 *Code for Durability Design of Concrete Structures*

27 GB 50490 *Technical Code of Urban Rail Transit*

28 GB 50555 *Standard for Water Saving Design in Civil Building*

29 GB/T 50636 *Technical Standard for Urban Rail Transit Integrated Supervision and Control System*

30 GB 50736 *Design Code for Heating Ventilation and Air Conditioning of Civil Buildings*

31 GB 50763 *Code for Accessibility Design*

32 GB 50974 *Technical Code for Fire Protection Water Supply and Hydrant Systems*

33 GB 3096 *Environmental Quality Standard for Noise*

34　GB 5749　*Standard for Drinking Water Quality*

35　GB/T 8175　*Guide for Design of Thermal Insulation of Equipment and Pipes*

36　GB 8702　*Controlling Limits for Electromagnetic Environment*

37　GB 8978　*Integrated Wastewater Discharge Standard*

38　GB 10070　*Standard of Environmental Vibration in Urban Area*

39　GB 13271　*Emission Standard of Air Pollutants for Boiler*

40　GB 14227　*Acoustical Requirement and Measurement on Station Platform of Urban Rail Transit*

41　GB/T 14549　*Quality of Electric Energy Supply Harmonics in Public Supply Network*

42　GB 14554　*Emission Standards for Odor Pollutants*

43　GB/T 15190　*Technical Specifications for Regionalizing Environmental Noise Function*

44　GB/T 16275　*Urban Rail Transit Lighting*

45　GB/T 17219　*Standard for Hygienic Safety Evaluation of Equipment and Protective Materials in Drinking Water*

46　GB 17945　*Fire Emergency Lighting and Evacuate Indicating System*

47　GB 18483　*Emission Standard of Cooking Fume*

48　GB/T 18574　*The Passenger Service Signs for Urban Rail Transit*

49　GB/T 20907　*Technical Requirements for Automatic Fare Collection System of Urban Rail Transportation*

50　GB/T 21414　*Railway Applications-Rolling Stock – Protective Provisions against Electrical Hazards*

51　GB/T 24338. 5　*Railway Applications-Electromagnetic Compatibility-Part 4: Emission and Immunity of the Signaling and Telecommunications Apparatus*

52　GB/T 26718　*Technical Requirements for Safy System of urban Mass Transit*

53　CJJ 183　*Technical Code for Platform Screen Door System of Urban Railway Transit*

54　JGJ/T 331　*Technical Specification for Slip Resistance of Building Floor*

55　TB 10002　*Code for Design on Railway Bridge and Culvert*

56　TB 10091　*Code for Design on Steel Structure of Railway Bridge*

57　TB 10092　*Code for Design of Concrete Structures of Railway Bridge and Culvert*

58　TB 10093　*Code for Design on Subsoil and Foundation of Railway Bridge and Culvert*

59　TB 10003　*Code for Design of Railway Tunnel*

60　TB 10005　*Code for Durability Design on Concrete Structure of Railway*

61　TB 10025　*Code for Design on Retaining Structures of Railway Subgrade*

62　CJ/T 236　*Urban Railway Transportation Platform Screen Door System*

63　CJ/T 375　*General Technical Specification for Medium and Low Speed Maglev Vehicles*

64　CJ/T 412　*Technical Specification for Medium and Low Speed Maglev Turnout*

65　CJ/T 413　*Technical Specification for Low and Medium Speed Maglev Train Transport Rail Row*

66　JG 5071　*Hydraulic Lift*

PROFESSIONAL STANDARD
OF THE PEOPLE'S REPUBLIC OF CHINA

Code for Design of Medium and Low
Speed Maglev Transit

CJJ/T 262 - 2017

Explanation of Provisions

Notes to Preparation

CJJ/T 262 – 2017 *Code for Design of Medium and Low Speed Maglev Transit* was published and approved upon the Ministry of Housing and Urban-Rural Development of the People's Republic of China through No. 1557 announcement on May 18, 2017.

In the development of this code, the drafting panel carried out extensive investigation and studies and summarized the engineering research achievements and project practical experience in the field of medium and low speed maglev transit in China to figure out the important technical parameters of maglev line, track and track support.

To facilitate relevant personnel of design, construction, scientific research, school and other entities to correctly understand and implement the provisions of this Code, the Preparation Group of *Code for Design of Medium and Low Speed Maglev Transit* has prepared the explanation on provisions for this code in the sequence of chapter, section and article, clarifying the purpose and basis of provisions and relevant matters to which attention should be paid during implementation. However, the explanation of provisions does not have the same legal effect as the text of this Code. It only provides references for users to understand and grasp the provisions of this code.

Contents

1　General Provisions

1. 0. 2　This article is proposed in accordance with the maximum speed requirement (120km/h) of medium and low speed maglev vehicle in CJ/T 375 − 2011 *General Technical Specification for Medium and Low Speed Maglev Vehicles*.

For other rail transit lines with a maximum speed of more than 120km, this code can only be used as a reference, for technical requirements are different.

1. 0. 3　The overall urban planning is a legally valid document approved by government to provide programmatic guide to urban development and construction. The urban rail traffic network planning, developed in combination with the overall urban planning, is a legally valid programmatic document approved by government to provide guide to the development and construction of urban rail transit systems. The medium and low speed maglev transit lines, as a part of urban rail traffic network planning, must comply with the overall urban planning and the urban rail traffic network planning. The determination of rail routes shall be based on passenger flow predication to attract the maximum ridership, so that the routes can fully play their roles as backbone members in urban traffic network and create the greatest social and economic benefits.

1. 0. 4　The ridership of rail transit systems may gradually increase with urban development. Taking the commercial operation year of project as the reference year, the design period of urban rail transit project can be classified into initial, near-term and long-term periods. The initial period refers to the third year after completion; the near-term period refers to the 10th year; the long-term period refers to the 25th year. The purpose of such division is to realize phased, economically rational investment and construction.

1. 0. 5　Structures that are difficult to expand in subsequent stages or those that are adverse to surrounding environment if they are constructed in stages shall be completed at a time, such as underground station, underground tunnel, storage line, turn-back line, elevated bridge, etc.

For structures that can be completed by stage and equipment that can be provided by stage, phased implementation shall be considered to save initial investment. But conditions for those phased implementation project and equipment installation must be reserved, such as stabling yard, vehicles, power supply system, operation automation system and AFC system.

1. 0. 7　To realize high passing capacity and safe operation, the rail line shall be designed into a fully-enclosed double-line system with separated upward and downward routes.

1. 0. 10　The medium and low speed maglev transit system is featured by low noise, small turning radius (50 m to 75 m) and high climbing ability (65‰ to 70‰). Its route selection should give full play to its advantages. The rail is generally elevated or built at ground, which may help improve line adaptability, reduce land acquisition and demolition efforts, and save construction cost.

Underground structure may be used at special areas such as those where elevation and ground laying are unsuitable (such as among buildings), where elevation and ground laying are infeasible due to limitation of clearance, and where same-platform transferring with other underground rail transit system is required.

In the case of large spans, if simply supported beam structure does not meet requirements, other forms of bridge construction may be used.

1.0.11　According to the *Law of the People's Republic of China on Protecting Against and Mitigating Earthquake Disasters*, *Regulations on the Administration of Seismic Safety Evaluation* and the Article 7.4.7 of GB 50490 – 2009 *Technical Code of Urban Rail Transit*, medium and low speed maglev transit projects must undergo seismic safety evaluation. The approved seismic safety evaluation result shall be used as the basis for seismic fortification design of the projects.

1.0.12　Medium and low speed maglev transit lines are part of the urban backbone transit systems. Flood erosion and scouring and the collision of drifting objects and ship on piers could bring unsafe impact or even devastating impact to system operation. In addition, arduous repair efforts and high repair cost are needed if they are damaged. Therefore, it is specified that the at-ground and elevated parts of medium and low speed maglev transit system crossing river or adjacent to river shall be designed according to the flood frequency of 1/100 and anti-collision measures shall be considered for piers.

3　Vehicle

3. 1　General Requirements

3. 1. 1　As the mature and proved power supply technologies for urban rail transit in China, 1500V DC and 750V DC power supplies are also applicable for medium and low speed maglev transit vehicles.

3. 1. 2　Table 1 gives the main vehicle parameters specified in the professional standard CJ/T 375 – 2011 *General Technical Specification for Medium and Low Speed Maglev Vehicles*. The medium and low speed maglev transit technology is at the early stage now. With its further development, the vehicle types and parameters will be further optimized.

Table 1　Main Vehicle Parameters in CJ/T 375 – 2011 *General Technical Specification for Medium and Low Speed Maglev Vehicles*

No.	Item	Type of vehicle	
		End vehicle	Intermediate vehicle
1	Basic length of vehicle (mm)[a]	15600	14600
2	Basic length of vehicle body (mm)	15000	14000
3	Basic width of vehicle body (mm)	3000	
4	Maximum height of vehicle (mm)[b]	≤3700	
5	Clear height in vehicle (mm)	≥2100	
6	Height of floor in vehicle (mm)	≤950	
7	Gross area of seating (m^2)	10. 8	12. 3
8	Gross area of standing (m^2)	20. 4	21. 8
9	Effective area in vehicle (m^2)[c]	31. 2	34. 1
10	Seating capacity (persons)	24	28
11	Rated capacity (persons/vehicle)[d]	146	159
12	Overload (persons/vehicle)[e]	208	224
13	Weight of vehicle in readiness state (t)	22. 5	21. 5
14	Maximum loading capacity of vehicle (t)	12. 5	13. 5
15	Maximum gross weight of vehicle (t)	35	35
16	Number of doors (pairs)	2—3	
17	Startup acceleration	≥0. 9 m/s^2	
18	Normal braking deceleration	≥1. 1 m/s^2	
19	Emergency braking deceleration	≥1. 3 m/s^2	

Note：[a]　Distance between the two coupling surfaces；

　　　[b]　From top of rail to vehicle top；

　　　[c]　Effective area in vehicle ＝ Gross area of seating ＋ Gross area of standing；

　　　[d]　Seating capacity ＋ Standing capacity at 6 persons/m^2；

　　　[e]　Seating capacity ＋ Standing capacity at 9 persons/m^2.

3.2 Related Facilities

3.2.1 This article describes the lateral safe evacuation mode of medium and low speed maglev transit.

Due to the nature of elevated line of medium and low speed maglev transit, walking on the line is dangerous and less efficient for evacuation. Instead, lateral evacuation by laying a longitudinal evacuation platform is safer and practical. At present, it is required in the special technical requirements for Beijing S1 line that evacuation platforms shall be provided along the line.

3.2.2 This article requires that regenerative braking energy absorption device shall be provided for the medium and low speed maglev transit, and sets out the position requirements.

Installed in the power supply system, the regenerative braking energy absorption device is used to reduce the dead weight of medium and low speed maglev transit vehicle, the equipment carried by the vehicle, and the power consumption for traction. To deploy such device, install a box on the ground power supply system which contains the electrical components for consuming the electrical energy. The traction rail is connected to the box to absorb the electric energy generated in the process of regenerative braking.

3.2.3 The passenger information system of the train consists of the broadcasting system, wireless communications system, information display system, and emergency voicing device for passengers and driver. Among them, the wireless communications systems and information display system are related to engineering design.

3.3 Electrical Hazards and Equipment Protection

3.3.1 This article requires that grounding plates shall be provided for the station or base.

The grounding plates of the station or base work with the grounding protection devices of the vehicle to ensure the passengers and the maintenance personnel in the garage are not exposed to dangerous potential when getting on and off the vehicle.

3.3.3 According to the basic requirements of power system protection and equipment protection and the design and operation experience in urban rail transit, the main protection of medium and low speed maglev transit vehicles shall be coordinated with the DC traction feeder protection in the following basic principles:

1 Main protection shall be provided for the vehicle, which shall be able to act reliably when the vehicle suffers from an internal short-circuit fault at any place;

2 The DC traction feeder protection shall extend to the vehicle to serve as backup for the main protection of vehicle. When the main protection fails, the DC traction feeder protection acts as the backup protection.

To ensure "coordinated protection" between the main protection system of vehicle and the rectifier substation protection system, the protection parameters of the main protection system of vehicle shall be determined based on the short-circuit parameters provided by the power supply system design department and the protection scheme for the rectifier substation, and adjusted as necessary in consultation with the power supply system design department and based on the test results.

4 Operational Organization and Operating Management

4. 1 General Requirements

4. 1. 2 The operation states of medium and low speed maglev transit include normal operation state, abnormal operation state, and emergency operation state.

Under abnormal operation state, the system is able to operate under de-rated state going beyond the normal range, which will not directly endanger the safety of passengers or cause extensive serious damage to the vehicles and equipment, including train delay, short-term jam in section, passenger congestion at station, line equipment failure, train failure, and failure of system and equipment along the line.

Emergency operation state refers to a situation that directly endangers the life safety of passengers, serious natural disaster or a major accident in the system which results in failure of operation, including fire, earthquake, train operation accident, and major equipment accident.

As a kind of public transportation system, the medium and low speed maglev transit system shall ensure the operation safety not only under normal conditions of system equipment and environment, but also under system equipment failure or other emergency conditions. Any operation mode shall be designed to ensure all passengers and staff accessing the system and all system facilities are safe.

4. 2 Operational Organization

4. 2. 1 The designed carrying capacity depends upon various factors such as the technical performance of vehicle and signal system, line conditions, and the organization and management level of train operation. The signal tracking interval of urban rail transit in China is generally designed as 100s and the train operation interval is generally designed as 120s (the interval is 95s in Hong Kong subway, 90s in Moscow, and 85s in Paris).

The operation control of medium and low speed maglev transit train has no significant difference from that of metro train but the action time of turnout. According to CJ/T 412 – 2012 *Technical Specification for Medium and Low Speed Maglev Turnout*, the action time of turnout for medium and low speed maglev transit shall not exceed 15s. The time for passenger getting on/off is 15s to 20s. Therefore the maximum carrying capacity will be 24 pairs/hour when the minimum train operation interval is 2. 5 min at the turn-back at switch mode. When the mode of turn-back by return line is taken, the minimum train operation interval is 2 min and the maximum carrying capacity will not be less than 30 pairs/hour. The carrying capacity will be improved further with the technical development and the improvement of operation management.

According to CJ/T 375 – 2011 *General Technical Specification for Medium and Low Speed Maglev Vehicles*, for a medium and low speed maglev transit vehicle with the track gauge of 2000 mm and vehicle width of 3000 mm, the passenger carrying capacity (under rated capacity, that is seating volume + standing volume at 6 persons/m²) shall be 146 (for end vehicle) and 159 (for intermediate vehicle).

4.2.3 The operation interval of train is related to the passenger flow, train formation and carrying capacity, and system transportation efficiency, which is also an important indicator to reflect the service level. With reference to the design requirements on the minimum operation interval of train in long-term rush hours of subway, straddle-type monorail, and other urban rail transit systems and considering the technical characteristics of medium and low speed maglev transit, the minimum operation interval of medium and low speed maglev transit train in the long-term peak time should not be larger than 2.5 min, which may be increased as appropriate for suburban lines.

4.2.4 The design period can be classified into initial, near-term and long-term periods. The initial period refers to the third year after completion.

The trains are configured according to the initial operation demand to meet the operation needs after construction completion and save the initial investment, while the fast growing of passenger flow in the initial years is also considered. The vehicles may be increased since the end of the initial period according to the changes in passenger flow.

The number of trains in operation may be calculated according to the following formula. It shall be calculated separately when long and short routings are set.

$$M_{(n)} = m \cdot \left[\left(\frac{2L_R \cdot 60}{V_{travel}} + t_{turn\text{-}back\ 1} + t_{turn\text{-}back\ 2} \right) / t_{interval} \right] \tag{1}$$

Where,　　　　$M_{(n)}$——Number of vehicles in operation;

　　　　　　L_R——Length of train routing (km);

　　　　　　V_{travel}——Traveling speed (km/h);

$t_{turn\text{-}back\ 1}$, $t_{turn\text{-}back\ 2}$—— Turn-back time of train between two turn-back stations at ends (including the parking time);

　　　　$t_{interval}$——Minimum train operation interval of one routing (min).

　　　　　m——Number of vehicles for train formation.

4.3 Operational Sidings

4.3.1 With a more distributed power system, each medium and low speed maglev transit vehicle is equipped with 5 levitation bogies and 10 linear motors, which contributes to its lower probability of operation faults than wheel-rail system, higher fault tolerance, and less parking lines required than urban rail transit.

The parking line guides the faulty train to leave the main line in time to minimize the interference and allow for normal operation of other trains, which, however, would increase the civil construction of station and lead to higher investment accordingly. Therefore, the distribution density and quantity of parking lines shall be controlled as appropriate.

4.3.2 A single inlet/outlet line is allowed where the space of stabling yard is limited (less than 30% of the assigned trains) and the conditions for setting inlet/outlet lines are difficult.

4.4 Operating Management

4.4.1 Considering its moderate traveling speed, large carrying capacity, and high departing frequency, the medium and low speed maglev transit line shall be fully enclosed and laid at an elevated level.

The trains must operate under the monitoring and control of the safety protection system in order to ensure safety.

4.4.3 According to Item 3 of Article 82 in JB[2008] No. 104 *Construction Standard of Urban Railway Transit Project*, the urban railway transit operator may estimate and calculate the rated carrying capacity based on 80 persons/km to 100 persons/km. It is required in Article 6.6.3 of CJJ 167 – 2012 *Code for Design of Urban Rail Transit By Linear Motor* that the long-term operation management and maintenance personnel for the first line should be controlled within 60 persons/km to 80 persons/km. Article 3.5.4 in GB 50157 – 2013 *Code for Design of Metro* provides for that "the system operation personnel of the first metro line should not be larger than 80 persons/km and that for each subsequent line should not exceed 60 persons/km". Considering the technical characteristics of medium and low speed maglev transit, the maintenance workload shall be less than the traditional urban rail transit. It is tentatively estimated as 60 persons/km to 80 persons/km as less operation and maintenance experience is available.

5 Gauge

5.1 General Requirements

5.1.2 Structure gauge refers to the minimum effective section with the equipment and pipeline installation dimensions taken into account based on the equipment gauge. Optimization of layout helps to reduce the dimensions of structure gauge. A safety clearance of 50 mm is reserved between the equipment and the equipment gauge, which is only used to allow for measurement error. Such safely clearance shall be gradually reduced with the improvement of measurement technique.

5.1.3 The spacing between two adjacent lines (without walls, columns, and other equipment between them) is determined based on the two equipment gauges plus a safety clearance of 100 mm. Therefore, the spacing between straight lines is different from that between curve lines. To facilitate construction, it is allowed to design several line spacing values which are not necessarily corresponding exactly to the curve radii. For example, the spacing of straight lines may be identical with the spacing of curve lines with an upper limit radius.

5.1.4 As no separate professional standard is available for gauge calculation for medium and low speed maglev transit, this code has carried out special study based on the characteristics of medium and low speed maglev transit system and given the calculation methods for vehicle gauge and equipment gauge to meet the needs of engineering.

Based on the characteristics of running system of medium and low speed maglev transit vehicles, the following key factors shall be considered in the calculation of dynamic offset (see Appendix A, Appendix B for the explanation of symbols):

1) Levitation and guidance

Equivalent vertical bouncing or rolling in dynamic changes of left and right levitation airgap that forms the effects of levitation rigidity.

① Dynamic deflection of vertical bouncing $= \pm \Delta f_{pcj}$.

② Rolling angle $= 2\Delta f_{pcj}/L$; height of rolling center $h = h_{cp}$ (height of working surface of F-shaped rail relative to surface of sliding rail).

③ ΔX_{cj}, passive guided dynamic transverse offset of levitation magnet (levitation bogie) relative to F-shaped rail, with the maximum value subject to the transverse limit devices.

④ f_{XF}, upward vertical magnitude of vehicle lifted by levitation, which is used for gauge calculation wherein the origin of vertical coordinate axis Y is defined on the sliding rail surface). It is not applicable when the vehicle is lowered down by levitation.

2) Multiple supporting suspensions for vehicle body

Each vehicle body of medium and low speed maglev transit is supported by six cap suspensions (five levitation bogies).

① #2 and #5 caps and the vehicle bodies are subject to transverse constraint and #1, #3, #4, and #6 caps and the vehicle bodies are not subject to any constraint (transverse sliding is allowed) and can generate large transverse movement required for passing the curve. Therefore the horizontal transverse movement or horizontal deflection of vehicle body relative to the levitation bogie is controlled by the characteristic parameters of ♯2 and ♯5 caps.

② For calculation section outside ♯2 and ♯5 caps (the distance to the center of adjacent levitation bogie at ♯2 or ♯5 cap is taken as n), the dynamic offset of vehicle body is calculated based on the most adverse deflection position (vehicle body shaking considered), namely there is a deflection amplification coefficient $\frac{2n+a}{a}$.

③ For calculation section within ♯2 and ♯5 caps, the dynamic offset of vehicle body is calculated based on the most adverse horizontal transverse movement (considering horizontal movement of vehicle body), namely the deflection amplification coefficient is $1\left(\frac{2n+a}{a}\right.$, where n is taken as $\left.0\right)$.

④ When passing a horizontal curve, the gauge of horizontal curve is widen based on that the centers of ♯2 and ♯5 caps coincide with the center of the line.

⑤ The height regulating valves are installed at ♯2 and ♯5 caps to control the height of air springs. Therefore the geometric offset of vertical curve is calculated based on that centers of ♯2 and ♯5 caps coincide with the center of the line, and the height of gauge of vertical curve is increased or reduced accordingly.

3) Combination of random factor and non-random factor

Random factors are combined at the root-mean-square value and haplotype non-random factor (or compound non-random factor) is combined at the linear value. For example at the central position of ♯2 or ♯5 cap, the section of vehicle body is combined at the root-mean-square value of the comprehensive transverse offset composed of ΔX_{cj} (dynamic transverse movement of levitation bogie guidance) and Δw (dynamic transverse movement of cap suspension), that is $\sqrt{\Delta X_{cj}^2 + \Delta w^2}$. Once a fault occurs, it is deemed as a non-random factor considering to the delay.

4) Deflection angle of vehicle body resulting from asymmetric loading, θ_{px}

The deflection of vehicle body on the air spring suspension relative to the levitation bogie due to asymmetric loading of passengers is a quasi-static factor (non-random). In nature, it is caused by eccentric moment of passenger loads (with reference to the subway standards, the eccentric moment is taken as 100 mm when 2/3 of the rating carrying capacity is loaded). The maximum deflection angle shall not exceed the angle resulting from the error of non-sensitive zone of the height regulating valve "$2f_2/b_s$". Therefore the vehicle body deflection angle resulting from asymmetric loading shall be calculated according to the following formula:

$$\theta_{px} = [100m_z g(1+S_2)/k_{\Phi s}] \leqslant \frac{2f_2}{b_s} \tag{2}$$

5) Rolling of vehicle body suspended by air spring

① The vehicle body suspended by air spring is subject to rolling vibration under the effects of transverse vibration acceleration and crosswind, which is similar with other traveling vehicles such as metro.

② Calculate the rolling deflection of air spring (maximum value under various factors in normal operation) with reference to the standard for gauge of metro:

$$\Delta f_{smax} = 0.5b_s \times \sqrt{[A_w \cdot P_w(1+S_2)(h_{sw}-h_{cs})/k_{\Phi s}]^2 + [m_j \cdot a_B(1+S_2)(h_{sc}-h_{cs})/k_{\Phi s}]^2} \tag{3}$$

Where, $A_w \cdot P_w$——Wind load (N);

A_w——Windward area (m²);

P_w——Air pressure (N/m²);

m_j——Calculation vehicle body weight (AW3) (kg);

a_B——Transverse acceleration (m/s²);

h_{sw}——Windward area centroid height (mm);

h_{sc}——Height of center of gravity of vehicle body (mm);

$k_{\Phi s}$——Secondary spring rolling rigidity of entire vehicle (N · mm/rad);

S_2——Additional factor for angle of inclination of gravity $= m_j g \left[(h_{sc} - h_{cs}) / k_{\Phi s} \right]$ (rad).

The calculation methods for vehicle gauge and equipment gauge are expressed in the expressions analytically in Appendix A and Appendix B.

The definition of vehicle gauge only covers the operation on flat straight line and the normal operation state. Faulty operation state is not reflected in the vehicle gauge. In this code, equipment gauge applies to the operation of vehicle on fault. The effects of curve factors on the gauge are reflected by widening the gauge of equipment on flat straight line.

5. 2 Basic Parameters

5. 2. 1 According to the main vehicles parameters in CJ/T 375 - 2011 *General Technical Specification for Medium and Low Speed Maglev Vehicles* and the prototype vehicle developed by Beijing Enterprises Holdings Maglev Technology Development Co Ltd. , the basic parameters for gauge calculation are given in Table 2.

Table 2　Basic Vehicle Parameters

No.	Item	Value (mm)
1	Calculation length of end vehicle	15000
2	Maximum width of vehicle	3000
3	Height of vehicle top from reference surface	3814
4	Track gauge	2000
5	Spacing of contact rail systems on the sides of track	2100
6	Longitudinal spacing of bearing platform of ♯2 and ♯5 levitation bogies	8220
7	Effective length of levitation bogie	2650
8	Height of current collector centerline from reference surface	700
9	Height of carriage floor from reference surface	950

The reference for the medium and low speed maglev transit vehicle is defined as " a measurement reference point that controls the size of each component of the vehicle and the relative position relationship between the vehicle and the rail. " Each R&D system of medium and low speed maglev transit system in China adopts different references. Some take the sliding surface as the reference while others take the top surface of track sleeper. The parameters in Table 2 are based on the sliding surface.

5. 2. 2 The parameters are determined based on the line parameters that the medium and low speed maglev transit vehicles may adapt to.

5. 2. 3 Two references are available for the origin of Y-axis (vertical) of the gauge coordinates for medium and low speed maglev transit in China. One takes the centerline of sliding surface as the origin, similar to the traditional rail transit, and the other takes the centerline of sleeper top surface as the origin. For the purpose of this code, the sliding surface of track is taken as the origin of Y-axis of the gauge coordinate. If the centerline of sleeper top surface is taken as the origin, coordinate conversion is required.

5.3　Structure Gauge

5.3.2　Item 3: The widening of structure gauge of transition curve section may be calculated according to TB 10003 - 2016 *Code for Design of Railway Tunnel* and the extension length is corrected based on the parameters of medium and low speed maglev transit vehicles.

5.3.3　For circular tunnel constructed by shield machine, which has a uniform aperture throughout, the structure gauge shall be designed based on the vehicle gauge and equipment gauge calculated at the minimum curve radius and maximum superelevation based on the required traveling speed.

5.3.8　Station line section structure gauge

1　The vertical elevation difference between platform surface and vehicle carriage floor shall be equal to the falling of vehicle body when the air spring is not filled.

2　The transverse gauge from the platform edge to the vehicle profile is determined with reference to Item 2, Article 5.3.8 of GB 50157 - 2013 *Code for Design of Metro*.

5.3.9　In order to ensure the safety of passengers during getting on/off, the maximum transverse gauge from the curve platform edge to the vehicle profile is controlled within 150 mm (70 mm, transverse gauge of straight platform, plus 80 mm, maximum transverse widening of curve platform).

6 Line

6.1 General Requirements

6.1.2 The main line is used for operation of train with high traveling speed and frequency, for which safety and comfort must be ensured and higher standard is required. Sidings include turn-back line, transition line, connecting line, parking line, and inlet/outlet line, which are configured for the normal operation of main line. Siding is not used for operation of train, and thus the speed requirement and standard are low. Yard line refers to the line for operations in the stabling yard. As the traveling speed of train is low, low standard is required for the yard line. Different standards are required for different types of lines in this code to meet the requirements of operation and reduce the project cost.

6.1.4 Featuring low noise, small turning radius (50 m to 75 m), and strong climbing ability (65% to 70%), the medium and low speed maglev transit line should be laid in an elevated way to improve the adaptability, reduce land acquisition and demolition, and reduce the project cost. Each medium and low speed maglev transit line should be designed to operate independently and interconnections shall be designed between two medium and low speed maglev transit lines and the medium and low speed maglev transit line and other transport lines. The plane position and longitudinal section position of the line shall be determined with due consideration on the current status and future planning of roads, ground buildings, underground lines, other structures, and cultural relics and historic sites to realize well coordination and minimize the mutual interference. The environment, landscape, topography and landform impose higher requirements and more significant impact on the elevated line and ground line. The engineering geological and hydrogeological conditions and the type of structure influence the determination of construction method, which relates to the setting of the plane of line and the burying depth of underground lines. Furthermore, the needs of operation management shall be considered. Therefore, all factors shall be taken into account in the design of plane and longitudinal section of the medium and low speed maglev transit lines to make sure the scheme is cost-effectiveness for the operation and management of the line.

6.1.5 Stations shall be located at the transportation hubs, intersections of middle and low speed maglev transit lines and other rail transit lines, and large passenger flow collecting-distributing places such as commercial, residential, sports and cultural centers. The distance between stations shall be determined according to the layout of urban rail transit network, existing and planned urban road layout, and the actual needs of passenger flow. Generally, it should be within about 1km from the central urban areas and densely populated areas, which may be increased as appropriate for the lines in surrounding areas of city.

6.1.6 In order to ensure the safe operation of medium and low speed maglev transit trains and facilitate the driver operation, operation management, and maintenance, necessary lines, signals and other signs shall be set for the whole line, stations and yard, including KM sign, half KM sign, slope sign, curve sign, blockage zone demarcation sign, speed limit sign, speed limit release sign, signs in station, departure sign, parking position sign, train stop sign, turn-back line parking position sign, fouling post, buffer stop sign, plane and elevation control signs.

6. 2　Plane of Line

6. 2. 1　The minimum curve radius of line, one of the major technical indicators for medium and low speed maglev transit, is related to the type of line, vehicle performance, traveling speed, terrain and landscape, and other conditions. To select a reasonable minimum curve radius has significant influence on the feasibility and economy of the engineering and operation, and the cost, operation speed and maintenance of the medium and low speed maglev transit project.

　　1　Theoretical analysis and calculation of minimum curve radius

　　　　1) The horizontal curve construction radius of vehicle shall be 50 m.

　　　　2) Theoretical calculation formula for minimum radius of horizontal curve satisfying the comfort requirements:

$$R_{Hmin} = \left| \frac{(V/3.6)^2 \times \cos\alpha \times \cos^2\beta}{a_y + \left[g \times \cos\beta + \frac{(V/3.6)^2}{-R_V} \right] \times \sin\alpha} \right| \qquad (4)$$

Where, R_{Hmin}——Minimum radius of horizontal curve satisfying the comfort requirements (m);

　　　　V——Traveling speed (km/h);

　　　　a_y——Unbalanced centrifugal acceleration (m/s²);

　　　　α——Cross slope angle, degree (°);

　　　　β——Longitudinal slope angle, degree (°);

　　　　R_V——Vertical curve radius (m).

　　According to the experience in the engineering of rail transit lines in China, the unbalanced centrifugal acceleration may be taken as 0. 4 m/s² at maximum.

　　The traveling speed is calculated based on the minimum curve radius. The traveling speeds at different curve radiuses corresponding to the different unbalanced centrifugal accelerations are shown in Table 3.

Table 3　Traveling Speeds of Train under Different Curve Radius (km/h)

Unbalanced centrifugal acceleration Curve Radius R (m)	a_y(m/s²)	
	0	0. 4
550	85. 4≈85	100. 7 ≈ 100
500	81. 5≈80	96. 0 ≈ 95
450	77. 3≈80	91. 0 ≈ 90
400	72. 9 ≈ 75	85. 8 ≈ 85
350	68. 1≈70	80. 35 ≈ 80
300	63. 1≈65	74. 4≈ 75
250	57. 6≈60	67. 9 ≈ 65
200	51. 5≈50	60. 7 ≈ 60
150	44. 6≈45	52. 6≈ 50
100	36. 4≈35	42. 9 ≈ 40

　　2　Other factors affecting the minimum curve radius

　　　　1) Operation safety of vehicle

Operation on the curve with small radius is adverse for the operation safety of train due to short sight distance and poor visual conditions.

2) Relationship between F-shaped rail and vehicle levitation

The levitation bogies of vehicle forms straight structural members when the train operates at a position on the small-radius curve, but "F" is curvy, and the levitation force, traction force, and guide force change with the contact area, thus affecting the normal operation of vehicle.

3) Maintenance

For the small-radius curve section, the maintenance workload increases because it is hard to maintain the track gauge and levelness and fix the geometry of curve due to large transverse force.

3 Conclusions

The horizontal curve radius of the line shall be determined as appropriate according to the nature of line, design running speed at the section, and the difficulty of project, with due consideration given on the local environmental conditions. Whether the determined minimum curve radius is reasonable will greatly influence the feasibility of project, economics of engineering and operation, as well as the application, cost, operation speed, maintenance and repair of the medium and low speed maglev transit.

6.2.2 The track panels of medium and low speed maglev transit are manufactured by machining, which makes mass manufacturing feasible for reducing the cost. A track panel module of 1.2 m is set. The line shall be designed based on the track panel module of 1.2 m and an integral multiple of 0.4 m is allowed.

6.2.3 Compound curve will increase the difficulty of survey, design, construction and maintenance. Compound curve should not be adopted generally because the train will experience significant changes in the force and transverse acceleration in short time when traveling on a compound curve, which will reduce the stability of train and the comfort of passengers. If a compound curve is used in difficult conditions, an intermediate transition curve must be set between the two circular curves with different radii to make the plane curvature radius and track superelevation change smoothly. When an intermediate transition curve is set for the compound curve, the change rate of curve radius "C" shall be identical:

$$C = R_1 \times l_1 = R_2 \times l_2 \tag{5}$$

The intermediate transition curve shall be calculated according to the following formula:

$$l_z = l_1 - \frac{R_1 \times l_1}{R_2} = l_1 - l_2 \tag{6}$$

6.2.4 Setting of cross slope

1 Theoretical calculation of cross slope value

$$\tan\alpha = \frac{\left(\dfrac{V}{3.6}\right)^2}{gR} \tag{7}$$

In the case of $0° \leqslant \alpha \leqslant 6°$:

$$\alpha \approx \frac{0.445V^2}{R} \tag{8}$$

Where, R——Radius of horizontal curve (m);

V——Traveling speed (km/h);

α——Cross slope angle (°).

2 Analysis on allowable superelevation deficiency

Since the train is subject to centrifugal force when running on a curve which affects the comfort of passengers, cross slope is set to generate centripetal force for balancing the centrifugal force. When the curve radius is given, the higher the traveling speed, the larger the cross slope is required to be set. When the required cross slope exceeds the maximum allowable cross slope (6°), an unbalanced centrifugal acceleration is generated.

For the purpose of this code, the maximum unbalanced centrifugal acceleration is taken as 0. 4 m/s² according to the design code for subways in China. The maximum superelevation deficiency allowed is 2. 3°.

6.2.5 The transition curve is mainly set to meet the requirements on the curvature of the line plane and smooth transition of the track, and meets the comfort needs of passengers.

1 Shape of transition line.

Sinusoid curve is difficult to manufacture, measure, set, and maintain due to its complex shape. According to the characteristics of sinusoid transition curve, the average superelevation slope rate of a sinusoid transition curve is half of a cubic parabolic transition curve of the same length. That is to say, to reach the same superelevation value, the length of the cubic parabolic transition curve will be two times the cubic parabolic transition curve.

The cubic parabolic shaped transition curve is convenient for survey, design, measurement, and maintenance. The horizontal curve is short, which offers good design adaptability and high flexibility. The traveling speed of the medium and low speed maglev transit vehicle is not larger than 120km/h, at which the effect of the cubic parabolic transition curve is minor and can be solved by suspension control and other means. To this end, cubic parabola shaped transition curve is adopted in this code.

2 The length of transition curve is mainly affected by the following two factors.

1) Superelevation slope rate

In the design code for subways in China, the superelevation slope rate should not exceed 2‰ and shall not be larger than 3‰ for difficult sections. The superelevation slope rate of medium and low speed maglev transit is controlled by the structure of vehicle body and the mechanical decoupling ability of bogies. Considering the special characteristics of medium and low speed maglev transit, superelevation slope rate is used in this code to limit the changes in superelevation. According to the experience of Beijing Holding Magnetic Suspension Technology Development Co., Ltd. in Tangshan test line, it is required in this code that the superelevation slope rate should not be larger than $5'00''\approx2.9\%$, and not be larger than $7'12''\approx4.1\%$ for difficult sections. Then the minimum length of transition curve is:

$$l = \frac{H}{2.9} \sim \frac{H}{4.1} \tag{9}$$

Where, l——Length of transition curve (m);

H——Actual superelevation of circular curve (mm).

2) Superelevation time

$$l \geqslant \frac{H \cdot V}{3.6 f_c} \tag{10}$$

Where, l——Length of transition curve (m);

V——Design speed (km/h);

H——Actual superelevation of circular curve (mm);

f_c——Superelevation time allowed (mm/s).

"f_c", allowable superelevation time, an indicator for the comfort of passengers, which is taken as 53 mm/s in this code.

referred to *The Subway Design* Code, and

$$l \geqslant \frac{H \cdot V}{3.6 f_c} = 0.0053 H \cdot V \tag{11}$$

3 Length of transition curve

1) Considering the analysis above, the length of transition curve is set as below:

① For $V \leqslant 50$km/h:

The superelevation:

$$H = \frac{15.73 V^2}{R} \tag{12}$$

The length of transition curve:

$$l = \frac{H}{4.1} \geqslant 18 \text{(m)} \tag{13}$$

② For 50km/h$<V \leqslant 70$km/h:

The superelevation:

$$H = \frac{15.73 V^2}{R} \tag{14}$$

The length of transition curve:

$$l = \frac{H}{2.9} \geqslant 18 \text{(m)} \tag{15}$$

③ For 70km/h$<V<4.3\sqrt{R}$:

The superelevation:

$$H = \frac{15.73 V^2}{R} \tag{16}$$

The length of transition curve:

$$l = 0.0053 H \cdot V \geqslant 18 \text{(m)} \tag{17}$$

2) If the length of transition curve is calculated in the formula above, when $l = \frac{H}{4.1}$, the calculated value is only rounded up, not rounded down. In other conditions, the calculated value is rounded up at 3 and above and rounded down at 2 and below, which shall be an integral multiple of 6 m.

3) The minimum length of transition curve is taken as 18 m, no less than the entire length of one vehicle, which is also designed to facilitate manufacturing.

6.2.6 The speed of train shall be limited when passing the turnout laterally. The connecting curve after the turnout is close to the turnout, and thus the train could not speed up quickly. Therefore transition curve and superelevation may not be set for the connecting curve after the turnout, and the radius shall not be less than the lead curve radius of turnout mainly because that the speed of train when passing by the turnout curve shall not be lower than the speed at the turnout.

6.2.7 The length of intermediate straight line between the circular curves of main line and auxiliary line and between two adjacent curves is determined mainly based on the train operation stability and passenger comfort, with the minimum no less than the length of one vehicle. Since the maximum calculation length of vehicle is 18 m, the minimum length of intermediate straight line is also taken as 18m. The length of intermediate straight line for yard lines shall not be less than the length of one levitation bogie.

6.2.8 Notes for calculation of minimum curve radius of difficult sections:

The size of curve radius of the station impacts the geometric widening. The maximum transverse widening of station, 80 mm, decides the minimum curve radius of station. The geometric widening of curve may be calculated according to the formula B. 0. 2-1 and B. 0. 2-2 in Appendix B.

Outer side of curve

$$T_a = 1000[4n(n+a)+4m(m+p)]/8R \tag{18}$$

Inner side of curve:

$$T_i = 1000[4n(a-n)-4m(m+p)]/8R \tag{19}$$

Where, $a = 8.220$ m;

$\quad n = 3.390$ m (end)/4. 110 m (middle);

$\quad p = 1.590$ m;

$\quad m = 0.575$ m.

Geometric widening at ends:

$$T_a = 1000[4 \times 3.390(3.390+8.220)+ 4 \times 0.575$$
$$(0.575+1.590)]/8R$$
$$= 20301/R(\text{mm})$$

Geometric widening in the middle

$$T_i = 1000[4 \times 4.110(8.220-4.110)-4 \times 0.575$$
$$(0.575+1.590)]/8R$$
$$= 7824/R(\text{mm})$$

Concave platform (Figure 1):

Minimum curve radius at vehicle end controlled by gauge = 20301/80 = 254 m

Transverse clearance in middle door areas = 70 + 7824/254 = 101 mm < 150 mm

Minimum curve radius of platform controlled by gauge: 254 m.

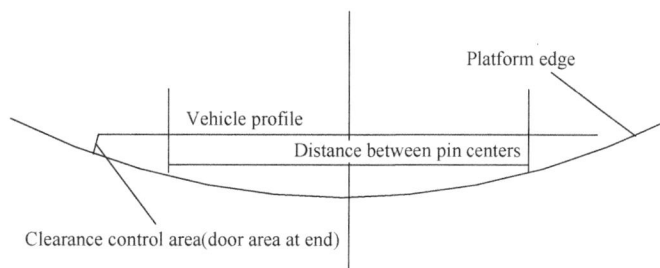

Figure 1　Concave Platform

Convex platform (Figure 2):

Minimum curve radius in the middle controlled by gauge = 7824/80 = 98 m

Transverse clearance in middle door areas = 70 + 20301/R < 150 mm

Therefore, the minimum curve radius of the platform is controlled by the transverse clearance in the door areas at end. As calculated, the minimum curve radius of platform is 300 m and the cross slope angle is less than 0.01rad.

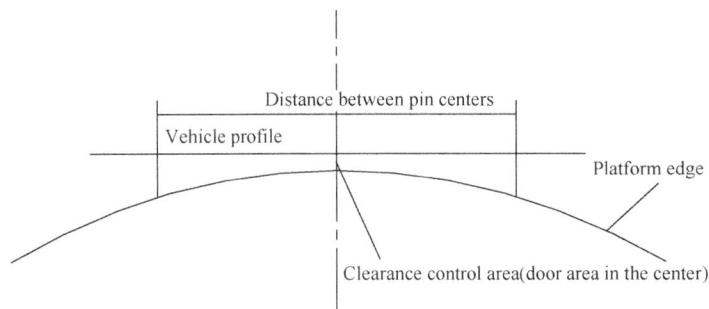

Figure 2　Convex Platform

　　The driver and station service personnel will experience poor visibility conditions when the line at the station platform section is set on a curve, which will increase the difficulty of management and compromise the operation safety. Furthermore, an excessively small curve radius will lead to excessively large clearance between the vehicle and the platform when the train stops at the curve platform, thus endangering the passenger safety. Therefore, the station shall be set on a straight line or a curve with large radius as far as possible. For the purpose of this code, the minimum curve radius within the calculation length of the station should not be less than 600 m.

6.2.9　Turnout shall be set as close as possible to the station to facilitate operation management, ensure the operation safety, and increase the performance of the line. However, a too small distance will affect the laying and installation of other equipment. It is required in this code that the turnout shall not be less than 5 m away from the end of the platform, which is determined with due consideration on the train passing ability and the technical requirements of track circuit.

6.2.10　The track at turnout has a complicated structure, which, if set on a curve, will increase the difficulty of engineering, construction and maintenance. Therefore, the turnout shall be set on a straight line.

　　To ensure that the curve or curve superelevation slope and track gauge decrease progressively and will not intrude into the scope of turnout and facilitate construction and maintenance, the shortest distance from the curve head (tail) should be 20 m for the main line and 5 m for the yard line.

6.2.11　The laying length of turn-back line and parking line for faulty train shall be determined according to the functional requirements:

　　　　1) Laying length of end-type turnback line and parking line = Length of train + Safety distance, the distance from the end of buttress girder of the front turnout to the buffer stop. The safety distance shall contain the parking error and signal visibility distance (Figure 3).

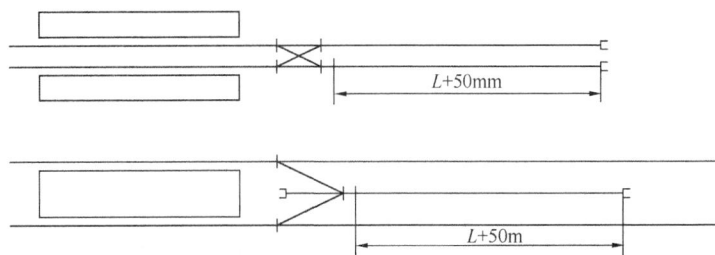

Figure 3　Type of End-type Turn-back Line

2) Laying length of through-type turn-back line and parking line = (Length of train + Parking error and signal visibility distance) + Safety distance, the distance from the end of buttress girder of the front turnout to the buffer stop. The safety distance shall contain the parking error and signal visibility distance (Figure 4).

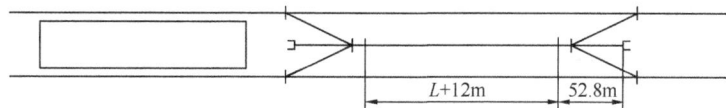

Figure 4　Type of Through-type Parking Line

6.3　Profile of Line

6.3.1　Slope reduction is not considered in the maximum gradient.

The medium and low speed maglev transit vehicles have strong climbing ability and high line adaptability. The main factor that restricts the maximum slope gradient of line is the startup of train on a steep slope in case of overload. The maximum slope gradient of middle and low speed maglev transit lines that have been put into commercial operation line in Aichi Prefecture of Japan is 60‰, while in China, the test lines in Shanghai and Tangshan are all designed with a slope gradient of 70‰ and all of them operate normally. Therefore, the maximum slope gradient of main line, auxiliary line, and yard line is generally taken as 60‰ (or 65‰ for difficult sections), and 70‰ at maximum.

6.3.2　To meet the drainage requirements, the maximum slope gradient of main line in the tunnel and cutting sections should be 3‰, while 2‰ is also allowed for difficult sections as long as the drainage conditions are met.

6.3.3　The vehicle shall keep levitation started when it is at the station. The slope of the underground station shall be as gentle as possible and meet the drainage requirements. Therefore, the slope gradient of line in the calculation length of platform should be 2‰, or a ramp not larger than 3‰ may be set under difficult conditions.

6.3.6　It is convenient and offers favorable drainage conditions to design and construct the line in the station platform on a ramp. When the conditions permit, the station shall be set on the convex part of the longitudinal section as practical as possible, that is, the train runs uphill when entering the station and downhill when getting out of the station, which helps to save energy consumption during train start and braking.

6.3.7　The turnouts of medium and low speed maglev transit are mechanical devices with high maintenance workload. Therefore the turnouts shall be set on a flat slope or a transition slope not larger than 3%.

6.3.8　The maglev transit vehicle generates additional force and additional acceleration when passing by the gradient change point. For the purpose of train operation stability, a long slope should be set. The minimum slope length shall be determined based on the effects of the two aspects to control the quantity of works and reduce the construction difficulty.

The length of the minimum longitudinal slope of the line is generally not less than the length of the long-term train, so that only one gradient change point exists along the whole length of the train to avoid the superimposed influence of the additional force at gradient change point and frequent changes of the additional force and ensure the stability of train operation. The length of the slope shall be designed that vertical curves will not overlap and are separated by a certain distance to facilitate train operation and line maintenance. For the purpose of vehicle structure and operation stability, the distance between two vertical curves shall be sufficient for accommodating 2-3 carriages, and should not be less than 40 m.

6.3.9 In order to alleviate sharp change at the gradient change point and ensure the additional acceleration generated when the train passes the gradient change point does not exceed the allowable value, vertical curve shall be set at the gradient change point.

The vehicle is equipped with clearance sensors to monitor and control the levitation height in real time, and levitation controllers to control the magnitude of levitation force, so as to reduce and control the current mutation and vehicle vibration resulting from the vertical acceleration due to the change of gradient when the vehicle passes by the gradient change point. The levitation controllers ensure the stability of levitation control when the algebraic difference of gradient at the gradient change point is less than 2‰. Therefore, it is required in this code that vertical circular curve shall be set for connection when the algebraic difference of gradient at the gradient change point is larger than or equal to 2‰. The length of the vertical curve shall be designed that one levitation bogie will not cross over three different longitudinal sections, which is taken as 5 m herein.

Although the minimum vertical curve radius allowed for the medium and low speed maglev transit vehicles is 1000 m, the vertical curve radius in the medium and low speed maglev transit project is also related to the comfort of passengers and operation efficiency.

The additional acceleration generated when the train passes by the gradient change point (that is the relationship between the vertical acceleration a_v, vertical curve radius R_V (m) and traveling speed V (km/h):

$$R_V = \frac{V^2}{3.6^2 \cdot a_V} \tag{20}$$

It is shown in the foreign documents that the range of a_v is 0.07 m/s^2—0.31 m/s^2. $R_V = V^2$ is taken in most countries, that is the value of a_v is 0.08 m/s^2. Under difficult conditions, $R_V = V^2/2$, namely a_v is taken as 0.15 m/s^2.

According to the experience in subway projects and the actual conditions of medium and low speed maglev transit, a_v is taken as 0.1 m/s^2—0.154 m/s^2 for the main line, or 0.17 m/s^2—0.26 m/s^2 under difficult conditions. Given that the traveling speed on the main line section is different from that on the station ends, the values shall be calculated according to the formula above and shall be integrals.

Line sections: the minimum radius of vertical curve is taken as 5000 m generally, or 2000 m for difficult sections.

At station ends: the minimum radius of vertical curve is taken as 3000 m generally, or 1500 m for difficult sections.

Connecting line, depot inlet/outlet line: the minimum radius of vertical curve is taken as 1500 m generally, or 1000 m for difficult sections.

Considering the difficulty in track manufacturing, the vertical curve should not overlap with the plane transition curve.

6.3.10 In order to ensure the platform levelness and passenger safety and facilitate the station engineering and construction, the vertical curve shall not intrude into the scope of station platform.

Considering the structure of turnout, the line in the scope of turnout shall keep smooth and tight. Therefore, the vertical curve shall be kept a distance from and not intrude into the scope of turnout, so as to ensure the safety of train operation and facilitate the maintenance and repair of the line.

7　Track

7. 1　General Requirements

7. 1. 1　Track structure is the main equipment of medium and low speed maglev transit system. In addition to guiding the train running direction, it also directly bears the vertical, horizontal and longitudinal loads of the train. Therefore, track structure shall have sufficient strength to support fast, safe and steady operation of the train. Meanwhile, the track structure of medium and low speed maglev transit system, as a means of public transport, shall have adequate elasticity to make passengers feel comfortable.

7. 1. 2　The track structure shall be made up of proven and technically advanced components that have passed relevant tests and authentication to ensure the technical suitability and advancement of the track structure. Meanwhile, state-of-the-art construction methods and techniques shall be used to realize good construction quality and shorten construction period.

7. 1. 3　Use of universal, proven parts and components not only reduces the design and construction efforts, but also facilitates the maintenance and repair of the track. In addition, it also helps reduce the types of spare parts to be ordered for repair and make the track appearance elegant.

The maglev transit system features long operation time and short operation intervals. Track repair can only be made within a short time when the trains are stopped at night. Therefore, the design of the track structure shall facilitate construction convenience and reduce maintenance workload.

7. 1. 4　According to Article 4. 2. 4 of GB 50057 − 2010 *Code for Design Protection of Structures against Lightning*, the lightning protection grounding resistance shall not exceed 10Ω.

7. 2　Track Panel and Composition

7. 2. 1　The introduction of standard module, commonly used in machine manufacturing and building construction, is helpful to realize standardized design, batch production, simpler installation and less cost.

7. 2. 3　Item 2: The angle between the track plane at the maximum superelevation and the horizontal plane (the cross slope angle) is determined according to the relevant test data at home and abroad as well as the parking and running requirements of medium and low speed maglev train at curved section.

Item 4: The method of realizing superelevation by elevating the outer rail for half of the superelevation and lowering the inner rail for the other half of the superelevation ensures the train runs smoothly at curved section, curved sections are easier to measure and design, and contact tracks are convenient to design and install.

7. 3　Swbstructure and Fastening

7. 3. 1　Track bearing platform made of double-cast concrete is used to connect track panels and the substructure. The construction method is simple, the construction accuracy is easy to control, and the construction duration is short.

In order to firmly connect with the substructure underneath the track bearing platform, rebars shall protrude from the top surface of the foundation and the bottom of the track bearing platform shall be chiseled.

According to the anchoring method of the current fasteners, the thickness of the track bearing platform should not be less than 130 mm.

7.3.3 Due to the particularity of the connection between the medium and low speed maglev transit track and the track beam, it is difficult to make replacement and repairs during the maintenance window period. Therefore, consideration shall be given to providing convenient conditions for the replacement of exposed parts such as bolts during maintenance and repair. For concealed components, the service life shall be along and equivalent to that of track panel.

7.4 Tectonic of Track Construction and Precision Requirements

7.4.3 Item 3: At the connection between the track bearing platform and track beam and that between the track bearing platform and underlying piers, sufficient steel bars shall be embedded in the structure according to calculation result to allow for connection.

Item 4: The connection between track bearing platform and supporting blocks shall be made of cast-in-place concrete. Therefore, the installation conditions of the supporting blocks are as follows: the pouring of the track bearing platform shall be convenient and shall ensure reliable connection between the supporting blocks and the track bearing platform. The height of the track bearing platform shall ensure that the bottom of supporting block is 50 mm to 100 mm away from the top surface of the substructure.

7.4.4 This article is proposed according to the geometric accuracy of medium and low speed maglev transit lines in Japan identified in track structure completion acceptance tests as well as the application practices of the medium and low speed maglev test line in Lingang, Shanghai and the medium and low speed maglev test line in Tangshan.

7.5 Accessory Facilities of Track

7.5.1 Sliding type buffer stops should be used at the ends of the main line, auxiliary line and test line. If being hit by train, the buffer stops will slide for some distance to effectively consume the kinetic energy of the train, thus protecting the safety of the personnel and the train and reducing personal/equipment accidents and loss.

In the case of underground lines, considering the strong support by earth and civil structures, hydraulic buffer stops involving less civil works should be used to reduce the kinetic energy of the train, protect the safety of personnel and train and reduce personal/equipment accidents and loss.

Fixed buffer stops should be used for the line sections within stabilizing yard and depot. The fixed buffer stops are characterized by simple structure, small length and low cost. Meanwhile, the speed of the train on the line sections within stabilizing yard and depot is low. The fixed buffer stops are able to consume the kinetic energy of the train, thus protecting the safety of the personnel and train and reducing personal/equipment accidents and loss.

7.6 Joint

7.6.2 According to the experience in the medium and low speed maglev test line in Tangshan, the design gap between track joints is taken as 16 mm. The size of the track joint shall be appropriately reserved during track laying, so that: (1) the installed track panels have sufficient space to release temperature stress under the control of longitudinal resistance; (2) the installed track panels form zero track joints and the track ends do not press against each other when the historical maximum track temperature is reached; (3) the track joint gaps do not exceed the structural track joint gaps and satisfy the fundamental track panel joint requirements for steady operation of the train when the minimum track temperature is reached.

7.6.3 Track joint gaps at bridge joints and bridge-abutment joints aim to simplify the interaction between bridge and track panels, which will in turn simplify the design, construction and maintenance of track panels and bridge.

7.7 Turnout

7.7.1 The main technical requirements for turnouts are proposed in accordance with CJ/T 412 – 2012 *Technical Specification for Medium and Low Speed Maglev Turnout*.

7.7.2 Item 4: The assembly deviations of turnout components are as specified in section 5.15 of CJ/T 412 – 2012 *Technical Specification for Medium and Low Speed Maglev Turnout*.

8 Track Support Structure

8.1 General Requirements

8.1.3 The project economy involves the work quantity indicators, construction, transportation and installation costs and other factors. Generally, girder bridges with a span length of 20 m to 30 m offer superior economic indicators.

8.1.4 If span length is not large, the rotation angle and deformation at the ends of simply supported beam meet the system requirements. Considering its features of good economic efficiency, convenient construction, short construction period and less impact on ground transportation, the simple supported beam structure should be considered the first choice.

8.1.5 The construction of the medium and low speed maglev transit project should not affect the implementation of urban planning and the normal operation of railways, roads and waterways. Therefore, the arrangement of the track supporting piers shall comply with the urban planning requirements. Where the maglev line crosses over railway or road, the clearance under the bridge shall meet the requirements of railway and road gauges and the structural settlement and the elevated railway height or road pavement renovation height shall be considered. Where the maglev line crosses over a navigable river, depending on the grade of waterway, the clearance under bridge shall meet the applicable requirements in the current national standard GB 50139 *Navigation Standard of Inland Waterway*.

Medium and low speed maglev lines are a part of the urban backbone transport system. In order to prevent the unsafe and even destructive impacts of floodwater scouring on the operation of maglev line, and considering the high time cost and economic cost of track structure repairs, it is specified that line sections crossing flood discharge rivers shall be designed according to the flood frequency of 1/100, and the design of large bridges and extra-large bridges involving complicated technologies and great repair difficulties shall be checked according to the flood frequency of 1/300.

8.1.6, 8.1.7

The deflection requirements of track beams have direct impact on the operation stability and passenger comfort of the train, and affect the construction cost of medium and low speed maglev lines. The deflection requirements of the track beams are determined based on the analysis and summarization of the track beam rigidity requirements of maglev lines at home and abroad and conventional wheel-track lines as well as the tests and verification according to the technical characteristics of medium and low speed maglev lines.

　1　Requirements of relevant codes or test lines on the deflection of track beam:

　　1) German design code for high-speed maglev system

See Table 4 for the requirements for vertical deflection of track beam in German design code for high-speed maglev system.

　　2) Japanese HSST system and Korean UTM system

The deflection-span ratio of the track beam of HSST-05 maglev line exhibited at Yokohama International Fair, Japan, is 1/3800. The deflection-span ratio of the track beam of the HSST-

TKL maglev line in the eastern hilly land of Japan is required to not be larger than 1/1500.

Table 4　Requirement on Track Beam Deflection in German Design Code for High-speed Maglev System

Item			Maximum deflection	Remarks
Vertical deflection	Induced by train	Single-span beam	$L/4000$	
		Continuous double-span beam with equal span length	$L/4800$	
	Induced by temperature	Single-span beam	$-L/6500$	Temperature of beam top surface is higher than that of beam bottom surface
			$L/5400$	Temperature of beam top surface is lower than that of beam bottom surface
		Continuous double-span beam with equal span length	$-L/8000$	Temperature of beam top surface is higher than that of beam bottom surface
			$L/6500$	Temperature of beam top surface is lower than that of beam bottom surface
Horizontal deflection	Induced by train	Single-span beam	$L/15000$	
		Continuous double-span beam with equal span length	$L/18000$	
	Induced by temperature	Single-span beam	$L/5800$	
		Continuous double-span beam with equal span length	$L/6960$	

At Korea Institute of Machinery and Materials (KIMM), the vertical deflection-span ratio of the track beam of test line for UTM-01 urban/inter-city maglev train is required to not be larger than 1/4000.

3) *Tentative Provisions on 200km/h Railways Shared by Both New Passenger Train and Freight Train*

See Table 5 for the vertical defection limits of track beam specified in the *Tentative Provisions on 200km/h Railways Shared by Both New Passenger Train and Freight Train* (TJSH [2005] No. 285).

Table 5　Vertical Defection Limits of Track Beam Specified in the *Tentative Provisions on 200km/h Railways Shared by Both New Passenger Train and Freight Train*

Span Length L (m)		$L{\leqslant}20$	$20{<}L{\leqslant}50$	$50{<}L{\leqslant}70$	$70{<}L{\leqslant}96$
Deflection limit	Single-span girder	$L/1000$		$L/900$	
	Multi-span girder	$L/1400$	$L/1200$	$L/1000$	$L/900$

Under the action of transverse swaying force, centrifugal force, wind force and temperature, the horizontal deflection of track beam shall not be larger than 1/4000 of span length.

4) *Code for Design of Metro*

See Table 6 for the vertical deflection requirement of beam bridge structure specified in Table 10. 2. 1 of GB 50157 - 2013 *Code for Design of Metro*.

Table 6　Vertical deflection Requirement of Beam Bridge Structure

Specified in GB 50157－2013 *Code for Design of Metro*

Span length (m)	Allowable vertical deflection
$L \leqslant 30$	$L/2000$
$30 < L \leqslant 60$	$L/1500$
$60 < L \leqslant 80$	$L/1200$
>80	$L/1000$

2　Test line rigidity requirements in China

1）See Table 7 for the deflection requirement of track beam at Shanghai Lingang Medium and Low Speed Maglev Test Base.

Table 7　Deflection Requirement of Track Beam at Shanghai Lingang

Medium and Low Speed Maglev Test Base

Item	Vertical deflection	Horizontal deflection	Maximum deflection angle
Simply supported beam	$L/3800$	$L/1300$	$1/1000$
Continuous beam	$L/4000$	$L/1800$	

2）Beijing Enterprises Holdings Maglev Technology Development Co Ltd., National University of Defense Technology, Third Railway Survey and Design Institute Group Corporation and other organizations carried out comprehensive studies on the system errors, track stability and smoothness and train operation of medium and low speed maglev system. See Table 8 for the vertical deflection limits of track beam for the medium and low speed maglev test line in Tangshan.

Table 8　Vertical Deflection Limits of Track Beam for the Medium and

Low Speed Maglev Test Line in Tangshan

Item	Deformation induced by static live load	Deformation induced by temperature
Single-span beam	$L/3800$	$L/6200$
Multi-span beam	$L/4600$	$L/7600$

Under the action of train lateral guidance force, small radius constraining force, centrifugal force, wind force and temperature, the horizontal deflection of track beam shall be less than or equal to 1/2000 of the design span length of girder. Under the action of static live loads of track beam, the vertical rotation angle of girder end should not exceed 1/1000.

For the purpose of this code, according to comprehensive consideration of the above data, the vertical deflection limits of track beam are determined as shown in Table 9. Under the action of train lateral guidance force, small radius constraining force, centrifugal force, wind force and temperature, the horizontal deflection of track beam shall be less than or equal to 1/2000 of the girder span length.

Table 9　Allowable Deformation of Track Beam

Item	Vertical deflection	Deformation induced by temperature
Simply supported beam	$L/3800$	$L/6200$
Continuous beam	$L/4600$	$L/7600$

As the rigidity indicator of track beam is closely related to vehicle design, maglev control technology and train/bridge coupling dynamics, some scholars reckon that this indicator is conservative. Given the limited project practice of commercial maglev lines at home and abroad, this indicator is yet to be optimized by future researches.

8.1.8 In order to achieve safe operation of train and passenger comfort, it is necessary to limit the minimum natural vibration frequency of the bridge. The vertical inherent frequency (natural-vibration frequency) of the bridge is the root cause of the peak value of bridge dynamic coefficient. The peak value of the bridge dynamic coefficient means the occurrence of resonance and intense vibration, which will affect the normal operation of track structure, result in concrete cracking, structural fatigue and reduced bearing capacity and even endanger the safety of bridge. For bridges with some span lengths, different structural forms and materials with different inherent frequencies may be used, but the strength and rigidity requirements must be met.

1 Minimum limit requirements of vertical natural vibration frequency specified by the relevant codes or recommend by relevant research findings

    1) Article 7.3.5 in TB 10621 - 2014 *Code for Design of High Speed Railway* (*Tentative*) specifies:

① The vertical natural vibration frequency of simply supported beam shall not be less than that specified in Table 10.

Table 10   **Vertical Natural Vibration Frequency Limit of Simply Supported Beam of High Speed Railway**

Span length (m)	$L \leqslant 20$	$20 \leqslant L \leqslant 96$
Limit	$80/L$	$23.58L^{-0.592}$

② In the case of double-line railway that is supported by concrete simply supported box girder with a span length not larger than 32 m and carries high speed train with a train length of 24 m to 26 m, if the natural vibration frequency of the girder is not lower than the limit specified in Table 11, track beam coupling dynamic response analysis may be exempted in the beam structure design.

Table 11   **Vertical Natural Vibration Frequency of Double-line Simply Supported Box Girder with a Span Length Commonly Used for High-speed railway, Allowed to be Exempted from Dynamics Check**

Span length (m) \ Design speed (km/h)	250	300	350
20	$100/L$	$100/L$	$120/L$
24	$100/L$	$120/L$	$140/L$
32	$120/L$	$130/L$	$150/L$

    2) The minimum vertical natural vibration frequency specified by the German design code for high-speed maglev lines is as follows:

$$f \geqslant 1.1 \cdot V/L \tag{21}$$

Where, V——Maximum speed of the train passing track beam (m/s);

    L——Span length of track beam (m).

2 Medium and low speed maglev test line

The vertical natural vibration frequency of girder bridge of Tangshan medium and low speed maglev test line is controlled to $64/L$. The actual lowest natural vibration frequency of simply supported beam measures 4.49Hz, and that of continuous beam measures 4.69Hz.

Therefore, this code specifies that the minimum limit of vertical natural vibration frequency is $64/L$.

8.1.10 The purpose of limiting post-construction settlement and post-construction settlement difference of abutment is to ensure that the settlement of abutment will not affect the normal operation of the train, and even if line elevation adjustment is required, the adjustment will not result in modification of bridge deck and reinforcement of bridge structure.

8.1.11 In order to ensure the standardization of track panels and minimize the number of non-standard track panels, the bridge shall be designed according to track module. In general, an integer multiple of 6 m shall be taken. In case of difficulty, an integer multiple of 1.2 m should be taken.

8.2 Loads

8.2.2 Article 4.1.2 of TB 10002 *Code for Design on Railway Bridge and Culvert* specifies: "In the design of bridge, only the combination of the main force and the additional forces in one direction (along or across the bridge) shall be considered".

8.2.3 This article is proposed in accordance with Article 4.1.3 of TB 10002 – 2017 *Code for Design on Railway Bridge and Culvert*. Considering the different probabilities of coexistence of different loads, the safety reserve measures and safety factor of the structure as well as the allowable stress of materials shall vary with load combination. The safety factor for the main force may be higher and those for additional forces and special loads may be lower. Taking the allowable stress or safety factor of the main force as the basis, products of the basic allowable stress multiplied by appropriate coefficients or safety factors may be used for other load combinations. These safety factors are also related to material properties and structure types.

8.2.4 Section 4.2.1 of TB 10002 – 2017 *Code for Design on Railway Bridge and Culvert* sets out the unit weights of the materials commonly used for bridge and culvert, including steel, cast iron, lead, reinforced concrete (with a reinforcement ratio less than 3%), concrete and rubble concrete, mortared rubble masonry, mortared stone masonry, mortared flag stone masonry, dry flag stone masonry, filled earth, filled rubble (waste ballasts), ballast, poured asphalt, compacted asphalt, unoiled wood and oiled wood.

8.2.5 Item 1: The vertical load of the train mentioned shall be determined based on the actual vehicle load and the higher load values of vehicles that have already in operation shall be used.

According to CJ/T 375 – 2011 *General Technical Specification for Medium and Low Speed Maglev Vehicles*, the maximum total weight of medium and low speed maglev vehicles is 35t, the basic length of end vehicle is 15.6 m, and the basic length of intermediate vehicle is 14.6 m. Therefore, the static load of vehicle is 23.5kN/m.

8.2.6 The dynamic effect of the vehicle's vertical load is taken to be the vertical static load multiplied by a dynamic coefficient (also known as impact coefficient). The dynamic coefficient of the bridge is related to bridge stiffness, track surface smoothness, vehicle loads, train formation, loading type and train speed. The dynamic coefficient in this code is determined according to the calculation method for high speed maglev system.

8.2.8 Item 1: According to the lateral guidance force test carried out by National University of Defense Technology on the independent levitation bogie of CMS-03 maglev train, the lateral guidance force increases with the lateral displacement of the levitation bogie. In the case of levitation gap of 8 mm and levitated weight of 6.8t, when the lateral displacement is 14 mm, the lateral guidance force will be 13.6kN; when the lateral displacement is 19.5 mm, the lateral guidance force is 18.36kN. Considering that the dynamic traverse displacement of levitation bogie relative to F-shaped rail magnetic pole is generally about 14 mm, the lateral guidance force is taken to be 20% of static load in this code.

Item 2: The dynamic lateral guidance force is generated by line geometry deviation. Its calculation formula is determined according to the dynamic lateral force of high-speed maglev line.

8.3 Structure Design

8.3.9 According to the current bridge design, it is recommended to use height-adjustable spherical steel bearing. Tensile or non-tensile bearing may be selected as appropriate.

1 Where uneven settlement of adjacent abutments exceeds limit requirement, in order to meet the line accuracy requirement, the bearing may be elevated to ensure line regularity.

2 According to the loading and structural characteristics of medium and low speed maglev track beam, under various lateral loads and the dead and live loads of curved girder, the track beam may be subjected to large torsional loads, and the bearing may be subjected to large tensile force. So, tension bearing is suitable for the track beam.

9 Station Building

9. 1 General Requirements

9. 1. 2 As a key building in the multi-modal transportation system of rail transit, the station building must be designed according to rush hour passenger flow and equipment operation demand during the passenger flow control period, so as to ensure the safety of passengers during getting on/off, quick evacuation, compact layout and easy management. The station shall be equipped with good ventilation, illumination, sanitation, disaster prevention and other facilities.

9. 1. 4 Over-peak design passenger flow means the passenger flow of the station during rush hours multiplied by the coefficient of 1. 1—1. 4, mainly considering the non-uniformity of passengers entering and leaving the station during rush hours. This Code assumes that 37%—47% of the high rush hour passenger flow happens during 20 min of rush hour, therefore 1. 1—1. 4 is adopted as the over-peak coefficient. Different countries have different situations, so they adopt different over-peak coefficients. For example, Hungary stipulates a 20% increase of the predicted rush hour passenger flow in 15 min of the rush hour, i. e. a coefficient of 1. 2, while France adopts a maximum coefficient of 1. 6.

9. 1. 6 The comprehensive utilization of above-ground and underground space around the station is a new trend in the construction of rail transit in recent years. The unified consideration of the design and supporting construction of surrounding traffic connection and above-ground and underground commercial and other facilities in combination with the construction of the station site has become a major consideration factor for station designers. For example, the combination of station entrance/exit with surrounding commercial buildings, and the interconnection of station and underground commerce are possible options. This clause only makes general provisions, and the urban and regional conditions where the station is located shall be comprehensively considered during actual operation.

9. 1. 8 The energy conservation design of station buildings shall meet the requirements of GB 50189 *Design Standard for Energy Efficiency of Public Buildings*. The energy conservation design of station heating, ventilation and air conditioning shall meet the requirements of Chapter 14 of this code.

9. 2 General Layout of Station

9. 2. 3 The planning around the station shall be investigated before the location design of station entrance/exit and ventilation shaft, which shall be set outside the road's boundary line if possible. But if they can only be set inside the road's boundary line due to external control conditions, the permission of relevant planning departments shall be obtained. Besides, the ventilation shaft shall meet the distance requirements on sensitive buildings according to the requirements of EIA report.

9. 2. 4 The station is a crowded building and has a very close relationship with other traffic organizations on the ground. Therefore, a square for passenger flow gathering and distribution shall be set in front of the entrance/exit of the station. The square shall be connected with other traffic forms around it, and its area and dimensions shall be determined according to specific conditions. As an important interchange facility between rail transit and municipal road traffic, P+R stabling yard set beside stations in suburbs and outskirts may effectively reduce the road traffic pressure in the city center.

9.3 Station Plane

9.3.1 The determination of parking error is related to the driver's proficiency in manual driving or the advanced level of automatic parking equipment. The generally adopted parking distance inaccuracy is 1 m—2 m, and if platform screen doors are used, the parking error must be controlled within ±0.3 m.

9.3.2 The calculation formula specified in Article 9.3.2 of GB 50157 *Code for Design of Metro* is as follows:

Width of island platform:

$$B_d = 2b + n \cdot z + t \tag{22}$$

Width of side platform:

$$B_c = b + z + t \tag{23}$$

$$b = \frac{Q_{board} \cdot \rho}{L} + b_a \tag{24}$$

$$b = \frac{Q_{board\ and\ alight} \cdot \rho}{L} + M \tag{25}$$

Where, b——Width of side platform (m), the greater of the calculation results of formula (24) and formula (25) taken from formula (22) and formula (23);

n——Number of transverse columns;

z——Thickness of longitudinal beam (including decorative layer) (m);

t——Sum of widths of each group of stairs and escalators (including space reserved between longitudinal beams) (m);

Q_{board}——The design passenger flow of one-side boarding during over rush hour of each train during long-term or passenger flow control period (person);

$Q_{board\ and\ alight}$——The design passenger flow of one-side boarding and alighting during over rush hour of each train during long-term or passenger flow control period (person);

ρ——Crowd density at platform, 0.33 m²/person to 0.75 m²/person;

L——Calculation length of platform (m);

M——Distance from the edge of the platform to the inner side of the platform screen door, and the distance shall be 0 if there is no platform screen door is provided (m);

b_a——Width of safety protection belt of platform, which is taken as 0.4; it is replaced by M when platform screen doors are used (m).

Taking the greater value of formula (24) and (25) means:

Formula (24): before the arrival of the train at the station, the passengers waiting for boarding can only stand within the safety belt, during which the calculation width of the side platform is the width required for standing by passengers waiting for boarding plus the width of the safety belt.

Formula (25); after the arrival of the train at the station, the boarding and alighting passengers exchange and the safety belt has been used.

When the platform screen door is used, the value of b_a in formula (24) is replaced by M, the distance from the edge of the platform to the inner side of the column of the platform screen door. When the platform screen door is not adopted, the value of M is zero.

The final calculation width of the platform shall be the greater value under the above two different working conditions. For stations with large passenger flow tidal phenomenon, the formula under the above two different working conditions can yield obviously different results.

The width b of island platform shall be calculated according to the passengers going up and down respectively for upward and downward routes. The values of b are generally not equal. It is appropriate to take larger values and make symmetric arrangement for the sake of appropriate architectural layout.

Q_{board} and $Q_{board\ and\ alight}$ in the formula are the design passenger flow of one-side boarding during rush hour of each train of long-term or passenger flow control period and the design passenger flow of one-side boarding and alighting during rush hour of each train of long-term or passenger flow control period. In the calculation, they shall be converted into the design passenger flow within high rush hour departure interval of long-term or passenger flow control period.

Due to the different conditions of different cities and different line conditions in the same city, the values of ρ may vary, but the values of ρ for the same line shall be consistent.

9.3.4 The design of the elevated station shall be as simple and unobstructed as possible. Considering the medium and low speed maglev transit station has higher platform floor and track bed surface, the space under the platform plates may be fully utilized in the architectural design. Except for the facilities necessary for the boarding, alighting and train-waiting of passengers, as well as operation management, other rooms shall not be located in the public area on the platform floor.

Considering the ventilation condition of elevated station, air-conditioned waiting rooms may be provided for some special passengers (the elderly, weak, sick, disabled, pregnant, and infants, etc.).

9.3.5 According to climatic conditions, open station shall be equipped with rain and snow shielding measures at both ends of the station platform, and the urban landscape requirements and summer ventilation shall be considered during its size and style design. In northern areas, elevated stations in the middle of the road shall take measures to prevent ice from falling to pose threats to the safety of vehicles under the stations.

9.3.8 Article 7.3.2 of GB 50490 - 2009 *Technical Code of Urban Rail Transit* stipulates that "the size of the station concourse, platform, entrance/exit corridor, pedestrian stairs, escalators, ticket offices, ticket gates (machines) and other parts of the station shall match with the passing capacity. In case of accident or disaster, the predicted maximum passenger capacity of one incoming train and the passengers waiting on the platform shall be evacuated to the safety area within 6 min".

Emergency evacuation time:

$$T = 1 + \frac{Q_1 + Q_2}{0.9[A_1(N-1) + A_2 B]} \leqslant 6(\text{min}) \tag{26}$$

Where, Q_1——Number of passengers on the train (person);

$\quad$ Q_2——Number of passengers on the platform (person);

$\quad$ A_1——Escalator capacity[person/(min $\cdot$ each)];

$\quad$ A_2——Pedestrian stair capacity [person /(min $\cdot$ m)];

$\quad$ N——Number of escalators;

$\quad$ B——Total width of pedestrian stairs (m).

Based on the concept of "human-oriented", more and more escalators are used to connect the platform floor and the station concourse floor. Therefore, it is necessary to use escalators for emergency evacuation. If only pedestrian stairs are used for emergency evacuation, the size of the station shall be greatly expanded. Therefore, the power supply for escalators must be upgraded from the original Grade II load to Grade I load. Besides, the descending escalator shall have the function of changing into ascending direction (the ascending escalator of the elevated station shall have the function of changing into descending direction).

The probability that one escalator is damaged and unable to run shall be considered in the calculation, and the capacity of ($N-1$) escalator and pedestrian staircase shall be reduced by 10%. "1" in formula (26) is the reaction time of human beings.

9.3.9 This article is formulated by reference to 9.3.7 of GB 50157 - 2013 *Code for Design of Metro*.

The arrangement of ticket vending machines shall conform to the passenger entry stream line, and there shall be a gathering space in front of the ticket vending machines for passengers to queue. If the direction of ticket buying queue is vertical to the direction of passenger flow entering or leaving the station at the entrance and exit, and the ticket vending machine is located near the middle span of the outer wall in the equipment management room, the range of 2.0 m outside of the ticket vending machine should not intrude into the projection line of the entrance/exit corridor. When the ticket vending machine is located near the side span of the outer wall in the equipment management room, the range of 3.0 m outside of the ticket vending machine should not intrude into the projection line of the entrance/exit corridor. When the direction of ticket buying queue is parallel to the passenger flow direction and the ticket vending machine is located near the side span of the outer wall in the equipment management room, the distance between the outside of the ticket vending machine and the entrance/exit corridor shall not be less than 1.2 m.

9.3.17 This article is formulated by reference to Article 9.3.9 and Article 8.3.15 of GB 50157 - 2013 *Code for Design of Metro*. Equipment and management rooms of underground station shall be reasonably and compactly arranged to reduce space waste and save project investment. The main management rooms shall be centrally arranged to facilitate the adoption of effective fire control measures.

"The fire pump room should be located beside the main corridor in the occupied area of equipment and management room or beside the evacuation exit passage in the equipment area" in this article aims to ensure that personnel entering and leaving the fire pump room can reach the outside of the building without passing through other rooms or spaces.

9.3.20 This article is illustrated as follows:

1 During the operation of elevated stations, passengers often fall down due to rain and snow falling in from both ends of the station. Therefore, effective preventive measures shall be taken at both ends of the station.

2 The vibration and piston air due to train entering and leaving the station may cause the decoration parts to fall off, resulting in the interruption of train operation or safety accidents, therefore, the vibration and piston wind shall be fully considered in the design process.

3 During the roof design of elevated station, safety measures for the maintenance personnel during the roof maintenance conducted by operation department shall also be considered, in order to avoid unnecessary safety accidents.

9.4　Station Environment Design

9.4.2　The station is a place for transportation and traffic distribution, especially for underground station, as a closed and narrow space, the smoke generated by combustion will pose great harm to the evacuation of passengers. In addition to higher fire resistance rating required for the structure, the decoration for the station must adopt non-combustible materials (Class A). Although the materials for fixed service facilities in public areas with small volume and small total amount are difficult to reach Class A in practical application, they shall be flame retardant materials at minimum.

Currently, wear-resistant materials such as granite and vitrified bricks are widely used as decoration materials for station floors, therefore, attention shall be paid to skid resistance. The anti-skid performance of floor materials of elevated stations and stations with semi-open awnings in particular shall be emphasized on. For elevated platforms without platform screen doors, more attention shall be paid to open stairs, walkways and steps. In particular, the materials such as granite and glazed floor tiles should not be used for the safety protection belts at the platform edge.

Safety glass such as tempered glass and wire glass shall be used for the platform screen doors, advertising light boxes, customer service centers and other places in the station, where glass material is used, in order to avoid injury to passengers when broken.

9.4.3　Article 7.3.27 of GB 50490 - 2009 *Technical Code of Urban Rail Transit* stipulates that: "Lighting or light-retaining evacuation signs shall be set on the places such as platform, public areas of the station concourse, escalators, evacuation corridors, exits, stair corners of the station. Evacuation signs with adjustable indication direction shall be set up in the section tunnel".

GB/T 18574 - 2008 *The Passenger Service Signs for Urban Rail Transit* stipulates the safety signs, guidance signs, location signs, comprehensive information signs and accessibility signs for urban rail transit.

As public buildings, medium and low speed maglev transit stations must be equipped with safety signs, guidance signs, location signs, comprehensive information signs and accessibility signs.

9.5　Station Entrances and Exits

9.5.1　This article is formulated in accordance with the requirements on station entrance and exit and evacuation capacity in Article 56 of the *Construction Standard for Urban Rail Transit Projects* (JB [104] 2008) and Article 9.5.1　of GB 50157 - 2013 *Code for Design of Metro*.

9.5.4　The underground traffic buildings have higher requirements on flood control than ordinary ground buildings, but the high indoor and outdoor elevation difference at entrance/exit causes inconvenience to passengers and increases the construction cost of the project. The ground elevation of entrance and exit of underground station shall be 300 mm—450 mm higher than the outdoor ground in general. When the elevation does not reach the local flood prevention height, flood prevention sluice shall be added, and the height of the sluice may be determined according to the local highest water level.

9.6 Ventilation Shaft and Cooling Tower

9.6.2 This article is formulated in accordance with Article 9.6.2 of GB 50157 − 2013 *Code for Design of Metro*.

Item 1: The main purposes of the specification on the distance between the air vents of the ventilation pavilion: prevent short circuit of air inlet and air outlet flow which affects the air inlet quality during normal operation; prevent short circuit of smoke exhaust and air inlet which cause smoke backflow in case of fire. Combined ventilation pavilions, scattered high ventilation pavilions, and ventilation pavilions combined with ground buildings usually have air vent set on the side. The ventilation pavilion with air vents opened on the side are distinguished from those with the air vents set on the top in terminologies of the distribution of external air flow smooth fields, therefore, the air vent spacing shall be specified separately.

9.6.4 This article is formulated by reference to Article 9.6.4 of GB 50157 − 2013 *Code for Design of Metro*. The air inlet pavilion in this article means the air inlet pavilion that needs to be put into use in case of fire. If it does not need to be put into use in case of fire, the provisions of this article may be exempted.

In case of fire, the entrance/exit is not only the evacuation route, but also the air supplement route for mechanical smoke exhaust. If the entrance/exit is too close to the opening of smoke exhaust pavilion, the evacuation of personnel will be affected or the smoke will flow backward into the station. Therefore, the distance between the entrance/exit and the opening of smoke exhaust pavilion shall follow the same standard as the opening of air inlet.

9.7 Stair, Escalator, Elevator, Platform Screen Door

9.7.3 This article is formulated in accordance with Article 9.7.6 of GB 50157 − 2013 *Code for Design of Metro*: "The horizontal distance between the outer edge of the escalator handrail belt and the decorative surface of the parallel wall or edge of the floor opening shall not be less than 80 mm. The horizontal distance of the outer edge of handrail belts between two adjacent escalators arranged in crisscross or parallel manner shall not be less than 160 mm. When the outer edge of the handrail belt is less than 400 mm from any obstacle, collision prevention safety devices shall be installed. "

9.7.15 Each sliding door shall be able to be manually opened or closed by the station attendant on the platform; each sliding door shall be able to be manually opened by passengers on the track side.

9.7.16 In consideration of the situation that the train fails to stop in place for some reason, and all double sliding doors fail to align with the passenger compartment doors of the train and provide access for boarding and alighting, emergency doors must be set for passenger evacuation.

9.7.19 In order to ensure the safety of passengers, screen doors shall be equipped with safety signs. In order to ensure the quick operation of the station staff, usage marks shall be provided.

9.7.21 According to Article 4.3.6 of CJJ 183 − 2012 *Technical Code for Platform Screen Door System of Urban Railway Transit*, sliding doors shall have obstacle detection function, and should be able to detect steel plate obstacles larger than 5 mm (thickness) × 40 mm (width).

9.8 Accessible Facilities

9.8.3 Article 3.7.1 and Article 3.7.2 of GB 50763 − 2012 *Code for Accessibility Design* proposes specific requirements for the waiting hall of accessible elevators and the elevator cage.

9.8.4 This article is formulated by reference to Item 1 of Article 3.7.1 on the waiting hall of accessible elevators of GB 50763 − 2012 *Code for Accessibility Design*, which stipulates that "the depth of waiting hall should not be less than 1.5 m, and the depth of waiting hall for public buildings and places with hospital bed elevators should not be less than 1.8 m" and Article 9.8.4 of GB 50157 − 2013 *Code for Design of Metro*, which stipulates that "the depth of waiting area in front of the accessible elevator should not be less than 1.8 m, and in case of restricted conditions, the elevator door of the waiting area may face the track area, but the waiting area in front of the door shall not intrude into the width of side platform within the calculation length of the platform".

9.9 Transfer Station

9.9.3 The transfer station has relatively large passenger flow. In order to avoid the disturbance between the transfer passenger flow and the passengers entering/leaving the station and the congestion in front of the entrance/exit gate machine of the station, transfer within the pay area shall be preferred. The passengers do not need to re-enter the station after leaving it for transfer, therefore, the time and cost can be saved, the efficiency can be improved, and the transfer is made more convenient and faster, which reflects the "people-oriented" spirit.

9.9.4 This article is formulated based on subway construction experience and Article 9.9.4 of GB 50157 − 2013 *Code for Design of Metro*. Margin on both sides of the transfer nodes is reserved to leave fine adjustment allowance for lines and stations during the implementation of line transfer.

9.10 Economize Energy of Building

9.10.4 The heat transfer coefficient of the retaining structure is an important index to measure the thermal characteristics of buildings, and it is related to the building materials used in the retaining structure. Most of the above-ground stations adopt retaining structure with large heat transfer coefficients such as glass curtain and aluminum veneer, and the platform is sultry due to direct sunlight on the roof, therefore, heat insulation measures shall be taken.

9.10.5 Due to the high construction cost, underground station is generally designed as two-storey station. If three-storey station is adopted in case of restricted conditions, the length of the station shall be controlled to reduce the construction cost.

10 At-ground Structure

10.1 General Requirements

10.1.1 As medium-to-low-speed maglev transit lines is restrained by vehicle structure, power supply mode, and track plane flatness requirement, at-ground track bed structure should not be used at the sections with complex geology, uncontrollable post-construction settlement, high groundwater level, frost-prone subgrade and other unstable factors. At-ground track bed structures (buttress structure) have been adopted for medium-to-low-speed maglev lines in Japan and the pilot medium-to-low-speed maglev line in China.

10.1.2 The key to the success or failure of at-ground track bed structures lies in the control of settlement. The main risks are derived from the uncertainty of subgrade and the quality and variability of filling materials. So geological survey work shall be strengthened. It is required that the geological survey work shall be able to accurately ascertain the geological conditions of subgrade and the properties of the filling materials, and provide the necessary geological data for the evaluation of the deformation potential of the subgrade and track bed structure. Since the subgrade and corresponding technical requirements of the at-ground line structure are closer to the subgrade of buildings, it is stipulated that the spacing of the cross sections for geological survey shall not be more than 50 m and the geological observation points on the cross section shall not be less than 3 points, in line with the subgrade geological survey practices of buildings and oversea maglev transit lines. At transition sections and complex sections with settlement transition requirements, the geological observation points shall be appropriately increased and geophysical survey shall be conducted between geological sections. Where problems are found, conduct timely resurvey. Comprehensive survey techniques shall be adopted to verify and compare with each other.

10.2 Design of Support Structure and Subgrade

10.2.3 The requirements of at-ground structure for settlement and deformation especially non-uniform settlement are strict. Generally, local settlements shall be within the adjustable range of fasteners, and the uniform settlement in a large range shall maintain the smooth vertical curve of maglev line. For fasteners with the adjustment height of 30 mm, only 20 mm can be adjusted after deducting the construction error of $+6$ mm and -4 mm. Considering that the track structure needs to be reserved with a deformation margin of 5 mm when the train is running, the allowable settlement of the track bed during the actual operation is only 15 mm, which is the upper limit of local adjustment. For the range within 20 m, according to the experience of Germany, the allowable settlement is 20 mm. For uniform settlement in a larger range, in accordance with the data from Germany, the allowable residual settlement is 3 times of the adjustable range of fastener for the settlement of track bed, and German standard specifies twice of such adjustable range, that is 30 mm.

Non-uniform settlement of at-ground structure$\leqslant$20 mm/20 m。

The faulting of slab ends caused by the differential settlement between at-ground structure and bridge or tunnel (abutment or slab) ≤5 mm.

For the deflection angle caused by settlement difference on the transition section between at-ground structure and bridge or tunnel, it is stipulated to not be more than 1/1000 in Shinkansen plate track line project of Japan and stipulated to not be more than 1/500 in Germany technical standard for ballastless track of high-speed railway. Therefore the deflection angle of at-ground structure should be controlled no more than 1/1000. The requirements of gradual transition and deflection angle of settlement at transition section also focus on the control of non-uniform settlement.

10. 2. 4 This code is mainly based on the experience in domestic ballastless track and relevant foreign standards. Because the foreign control indicators are different from the traditional indicators in China, it is not conducive to the introduction of foreign mature technologies. Theoretically, K_{30}, E_{v2} and E_{vd} have a certain relationship, but due to the nonlinear nature of soil and the difference of test methods in operating procedures and error influencing factors, there is a lack of reliable corresponding relationship. Therefore, multi-indicator control is conducive to the introduction and absorption of foreign experience. On the other hand, it is also conducive to actual operations. Among these parameters, the provisions on deformation modulus E_{v2} and dynamic deformation modulus E_{vd} are mainly based on the technical requirements of German railways.

10. 2. 6 China is a vast country with large differences in climate, geology and natural factors. The current professional standard TB 10001 *Code for Design of Railway Earth Structure* listed the upper and lower limit values for the slope rate of cutting slope. The specific design shall be selected within the upper and lower limit values in accordance with the results of field investigation and analysis, and the slope height. The steeper value can be selected for the low slope, protective slope or slope with rock mass structure which is conducive to stability, otherwise select the slower value.

10. 3　Structure of Side Slope Retainer

10. 3. 2 This article is proposed in accordance with the practical experience of railway and subway track bed retaining projects as well as GB 50157 − 2013 *Code for Design of Metro* and TB 10025 − 2006 *Code for Design on Retaining Structures of Railway Subgrade*.

Item 1: In addition to gravity retaining wall, the most suitable type can be selected from various retaining types according to the specific topographic, geologic, hydrologic and engineering technical conditions. No matter which type is selected, it shall meet the requirements of economy, rationality and construction and maintenance convenience.

The selection of building materials for retaining structure can be determined according to the structure type. For gravity retaining wall, the adoption of concrete or rubble concrete shall be considered. For other retaining structures, in addition to the use of reinforced concrete, different materials shall be considered for different types of structure. Adopt the geogrid, reinforcement, concrete bands or bands of other materials as the tie bars of reinforced soil retaining wall, and adopt the steel rods with good weldability and extensibility as the tie bars of anchor rod retaining wall and anchor plate retaining wall. As the above materials are buried in the filling materials, the durability and corrosion resistance shall be ensured.

Item 2: It is emphasized that the engineering geological conditions and hydrogeological conditions of the mountain and subgrade shall be explored during the design process so as to make the design conform to the reality. The confirmation of the physical and mechanical properties of the subsoil is mainly to avoid placing the same track bed on the subgrade with great difference in physical, mechanical properties and compressibility, and to avoid non-uniform settlement of the track bed.

Item 5: Rainwater infiltration will reduce the mechanical indicators of wall back earth filling or soften the subgrade, and greatly reduce the stability of retaining structure, so that it is very important to conduct the drainage and water separation measures to ensure the stability of retaining structure. In addition, measures also need to be taken for the shoulder wall to avoid water overflow. Therefore, the sections with retaining structure shall be coordinated with subgrade drainage facilities to form a sound drainage system.

10.4 Drainage and Protection

10.4.2 In accordance with Article 13.1.8 and Article 13.1.9 of TB 10001-2016 *Code for Design of Railway Earth Structure*, hydrological computation of subgrade drainage shall be in accordance with Appendix F of this code, based on the catchment area, surface shape, surrounding topography, geological conditions and climatic characteristics of each section. The design parameters and computation methods shall be determined according to the local engineering experience.

The structural dimensions of drainage facilities shall be determined by calculation and according to local experience.

10.4.3 In accordance with Item 9, Article 13.2.10 of TB 10001-2016 *Code for Design of Railway Earth Structure*, the distance between the inner edge of the gutter at cutting top and the cutting top should not be less than 5 m. If reinforced anti-seepage measures are taken in the gutter, the distance shall not be less than 2 m.

10.4.5 In accordance with Item 4, Article 13.2.10 of TB 10001-2016 *Code for Design of Railway Earth Structure*, the water in the side ditch of the cutting shall not be discharged through the tunnel. If the drainage is difficult, the length of the tunnel is less than 300 m, the drainage ditch of cutting outside the tunnel has a low water flow and a low mud content, make study and comparison to make the decision.

11 Elevated Station Structure

11.1 General Requirements

11.1.1 To meet the needs of construction program and ensure the safety of structure, the strength, rigidity and stability calculations for construction and operation stages shall be incorporated into the design.

11.1.2 The travel lane structure may be deemed as part of the elevated structure in the section where it is separated from other structures of the station and thus a "bridge-station" structure is formed, for which the seismic design shall follow the current national standard GB 50111 *Code for Seismic Design of Railway Engineering*. For other structures of the station, the current specifications for building construction apply.

11.1.5 The structural members of elevated station can be classified into two types: structural members significantly impacted by train load, e.g. track beam, transverse beam supporting the track beam, columns supporting the transverse beams, and the foundations of sub-structures of columns; and general building structural members lightly impacted or even not impacted by train load, e.g. beams and plates of platform and general longitudinal beam. As the train load varies greatly from the general building loads, the provisions in this chapter shall apply to the structural design of the latter type of structural members of elevated station.

For integrated "bridge-station" structure, the station houses and other buildings shall be designed according to the current design specifications for buildings and structures, while the transverse beams supporting the track beam, columns supporting the transverse beams, and foundations of columns which are significantly impacted by the train load shall be checked according to the current specifications for the design of railway bridges and culverts in addition to the building specifications above.

11.2 Loads

11.2.2 With reference to Article 9.2.2 of GB 50458 – 2008 *Code for Design of Straddle Monorail Transit*, the standard value for live load of the station concourse, platform, ladder, and overpass shall be taken as 4.0 kN. The live load of equipment room shall be determined based on the weight, installation and transportation requirements, and operating state of the equipment, and shall not be less than 5.5 kN. The standard value of live load of other buildings shall be taken according to the current national standard GB 50009 *Load Code for the Design of Building Structures*.

11.3 Structure Design

11.3.1 According to Article 58 of JB [104] 2008 *Code for Construction of Urban Rail Transit Project*, the safety level of the main structure and the key structural members connected to it shall be Level Ⅰ.

11.3.2 Where the track beam supports or is rigidly connected to the station structure, platform beam, and other structural members of the station, or rigidly connected to the track beam bridge to form an integrated "bridge-station" structure, the track beam and supporting structures shall be deemed as beams in the section, while for other structural members, the calculation and structure shall follow the current national standard GB 50010 *Code for Design of Concrete Structures* and other applicable codes or standards for structural design of buildings.

11.4 Seismic Design

11.4.1—11.4.7 According to the relevant provisions of the current national standard GB 50157 *Code for Design of Metro*, the seismic design of elevated station with double transverse columns shall comply with the current national standard GB 50111 *Code for Seismic Design of Railway Engineering*. However in the actual structural design of elevated station, the current national standard GB 50111 *Code for Seismic Design of Railway Engineering* is mainly used for such structures as railway bridge and tunnel, instead of reinforced concrete frame structure. Therefore the seismic design may follow the current national standard GB 50011 *Code for Seismic Design of Buildings* so that the design may be carried out. Furthermore as it is difficult to comply with both of these two different standards, in the actual design, the current national standard GB 50011 *Code for Seismic Design of Buildings* is taken as the main standard and some indicators such as structural displacement, deflection, and crack control level are required to comply with the more stringent ones in the two standards.

It is required in Article 6.1.5 of GB 50011 - 2010 *Code for Seismic Design of Buildings* that type B buildings shall not adopt single-span frame structure. A double-span structure with double transverse columns shall be adopted where conditions permit. Single-span structure with double transverse columns is widely taken at present, for which the seismic performance shall be designed according to the requirements of the current national standard GB 50011 *Code for Seismic Design of Buildings* and meet the requirements of Section 11.4 herein. For the single-column station, no sufficient study is available although there are some engineering examples in China. Therefore, this form is not recommended, especially it shall not be taken in high-intensity areas unless adequate demonstration and special research are carried out.

11.5 Tectonic Requirements

11.5.2 As the medium and low speed maglev transit has high requirements for settlement, height-adjustable spherical steel bearing are preferred.

11.5.4 It is generally concerned in the current operation of elevated stations that it brings in difficulties in the structure maintenance, cleaning, and component replacement especially it is impractical to carry out routine maintenance for curved roof with complex form, in particular necessary conditions for carrying out such work are not reserved. Therefore in the design, anchors and other facilities shall be provided in appropriate positions to be used for securing of safety facilities during maintenance. Alternatively steel ladders, sliding ladders, temporary anchors and other facilities which are accessible by the maintenance personnel shall be set for the elevated structure and ceiling structure as needed.

11.6 Structure of Platfond, Entrances and Exits

11.6.1 The roof structure of the station generally requires a large span, which involves various construction disciplines, construction types, and structural changes. Therefore, the structural design should cooperate with the construction disciplines as much as possible to adopt a plan that is more favorable to the structural force.

11.6.6 The overpass at entrance/exit generally adopts steel structure, for which comfort check is necessary. For large-span structure, the vertical seismic action shall be considered according to the current national standard GB 50011 *Code for Seismic Design of Buildings*.

12　Underground Structure

12.1　General Requirements

12.1.1　Open-cut foundation pits can be classified into two types: pit excavated by side slope method and that excavated by retaining wall method. The foundation pit retaining walls include anchored shotcrete bracing, soil nail wall, gravity retaining wall and piles, diaphragm wall and so on.

12.1.3　The construction of underground structures inevitably has an adverse impact on the surrounding environment and may be close to or very close to the existing buildings (structures). In some cases, they may penetrate the existing underground buildings, structures or rail transit structure. Meanwhile, the impact of planned urban buildings (including planned urban rail transit) shall also be considered. Therefore, the design of underground structures of medium and low speed maglev transit system shall minimize the adverse impact on environment during and after construction, while considering the influence of surrounding environment changes brought by urban planning.

12.1.4　Interval tunnels can be built by open-cut or undermining method depending on the buried depth of the line and the actual environmental conditions. For underground station, open-cut method shall be given priority. However, where the existing roads on site are not allowed to be occupied, the cover and cut-bottom up method may be used. Where it is needed to alleviate the impact of construction on ground traffic or it is needed to meet the ground construction requirements as early as possible, the cover and cut-top down method may be used. Where the site conditions are unsuitable for open-cut excavation and the stratum conditions permit, the undermining excavation method may be used if the ground traffic cannot be interrupted.

12.1.5　This article is proposed in accordance with Article 11.1.6 of GB 50157 - 2013 *Code for Design of Metro*.

Item 1: The main structure of the underground structure of medium low speed maglev transit system refers to the structural members that directly or indirectly bear the loads of strata and running vehicles to ensure the structural stability of medium and low speed maglev system. The structural members that cannot be replaced during use refer to the members that directly bear the equipment load and crowd load of medium and low speed maglev transit system and that cannot be replaced during use or their replacement during use may affect system operation. The above structural members shall be designed for a service life of 100 years to ensure system safety within the system's design life.

Item 2: Minor structural members that can be replaced during use mainly refer to structural members installed at non-key positions in underground structure, the replacement of which will not affect the normal operation of system functions. These members shall be designed in principle for a service life of 50 years.

The retaining structures, which do not act as the main force bearing structures during system operation, mainly refer to the enclosing piles, enclosing walls and other earth retaining structures in foundation pit retaining structure. The retaining structures shall be designed to meet the functioning requirements during construction without considering the durability requirements. However, if the load bearing capacity of retaining structures (such as cast-in-place pile and diaphragm wall) needs to be considered in design, the requirements on durability of materials and structures in this code shall be met.

The preliminary shotcrete bracing of tunnels built by mining method (including simple anchored shotcrete and shotcrete bracing with steel arch) may be considered as temporary bracing due to small sectional thickness, poor impermeability and hard-to-control construction quality and stability.

Item 3: Temporary structures mainly refer to the enclosing piles, enclosing walls and other earth retaining structures in foundation pit enclosing structure. They are not the main force bearing structures during system operation, so their design only needs to meet the usage requirements during construction period.

12. 1. 6 The durability of underground structures is mainly related to the use environment, materials, structure type, cracks in concrete, construction quality and the maintenance quality during use. The durability design includes:

1 Determining the design lives of the structure and the structure members and the category and grade of environment action.

2 Carrying out conceptual design that is conducive to alleviating environment impact, including structure type, arrangement and pattern.

3 Selecting concrete materials and rebars and proposing the durability and quality requirements of the materials.

4 Determining the thickness of concrete cover according to the durability requirements.

5 Setting structural measures such as waterproofing and drainage.

6 Proposing the concrete crack control requirements.

7 When necessary, proposing multiple protective measures and additional anti-corrosion measures to prevent serious environmental effects.

8 Proposing the construction techniques and quality acceptance criteria in line with durability requirements.

9 Proposing the maintenance and inspection requirements during the use of the structure.

12. 1. 7 According to experience in metro structure design, the loads of some underground structures are not yet clear, it is immature to design all underground structures by using the limit state method based on probability theory. According to Article 11. 1. 8 and the Article Explanation on the determination of applicable underground structure design code and method in GB 50157 – 2013 *Code for Design of Metro*, the underground structures may be designed in accordance with the relevant national, professional or local codes for the design of civil engineering structures, which are determined based on the usage conditions and load characteristics of the structure. If the loads are clear and conditions permit, limit state method should be used. If the loads are unclear or conditions do not permit, the structure may be designed according to the damage stage or using the allowable stress method. When there are mature engineering cases with similar usage conditions, loads, structure type, structure dimensions, buried depth and geological conditions, the structure may be designed by the project analogy method. The codes used for the design shall be indicated in the design documents.

12. 1. 8 In the design of underground structures, the changes in gauges, structural members and clearance between structural members of the medium and low speed maglev transit system due to construction errors, structure deformation, settlement and other factors shall be considered.

12.1.9 The aim of overall dynamic analysis of coupling effect among maglev vehicles, tunnel structure and earth is to determine whether the performance of maglev vehicle, track and tunnel is satisfactory under soft soil condition, such as the influence range of dynamic loads of maglev vehicles, the settlement as result of dynamic loads and the safety and comfort of vehicle operation.

12.1.10 For the track beam foundation of medium and low speed maglev line, it is required that the even settlement shall be 30 mm, the uneven settlement shall be $\leqslant$20 mm/20 m, the differential settlement shall be $\leqslant$5 mm, and the deflection angle shall be $\leqslant$1/1000. Therefore, the track support structure needs to be determined according to the specific conditions.

12.1.11 This article is proposed based on metro design experience in accordance with Article 11.1.12 of GB 50157 - 2013 *Code for Design of Metro*.

Where the requirements of this article cannot be met, analysis shall be made in combination with the engineering geological, hydrogeological and environmental conditions of the tunnel and whether to take necessary engineering measures shall be determined based on the analysis results.

12.1.12 The anti-float safety factor of the immersed tube tunnel shall not be less than 1.20.

12.2 Loads

12.2.1 In view of the complexity and variability of underground works, the most unfavorable combinations of possible overall or local structure loads must be calculated based on the actual conditions in accordance with the relevant provisions on classification and combination of loads in the selected applicable design code.

12.2.2 Stratum pressure, water pressure and other loads are the main forces undertaken by underground structures. Influence factors such as work conditions, construction techniques and the clearance to adjacent underground works shall also be considered, which may be determined in combination with the existing experiments, tests and studies on similar projects.

12.3 Engineering Material

12.3.1 According to the engineering practice of metro projects, the use of reinforced concrete underground structures is conducive to improving durability. The main force bearing members of underground structure, especially those directly in contact with stratum, shall be made of reinforced concrete. For the members in the tunnel (including both major and minor load-bearing members), other structure materials and types may be used as appropriate, including steel-concrete composite structures (such as steel pipe reinforced concrete structure, steel rib reinforced concrete structure and composite members), pure metal structure and other materials. The materials used shall meet the durability requirements.

12.3.2 The minimum strength grades of concrete in Table 12.3.2 are determined in view to meet structural design requirements. To meet the durability requirements of the structures, these strength grades shall also be corrected according to GB/T 50476 *Code for Durability Design of Concrete Structures*. According to the design experience of metros, in order to reduce the shrinkage stress and temperature stress of overlong underground concrete structures, the design strength grades of cast-in-place concrete structures should not be adjusted upwards to higher grades except for members such as column or longitudinal beam.

12.3.6 Anti-corrosion treatment methods include electro-galvanization, hot-dip galvanization, and zinc-based chromate coating.

12.4 Structure Type and Inner Wall

12.4.2 Open-cut Inner wall.

1 Prefabricated lining has the advantages of high industrialization level and fast construction and has been widely used in the metro station and interval tunnels in the Soviet Union. The members of fabricated structures shall be joined together as a whole on site to facilitate waterproofing and earthquake resistance and to improve the ability of the tunnel to resist uneven longitudinal settlement.

2 Foundation pit bracings such as diaphragm wall and cast-in-place piles are utilized as a part of the main structure. This not only saves project cost, but also reduces resource consumption and meets the sustainable development requirement. Most of the open-cut metro stations in China are designed according to this principle. In this case, there are three types of side walls in main structure: single wall, composite wall and compound wall.

    1) Single wall: The retaining structure is directly used as the side wall of main structure, not as the lining wall bearing loads. Most single walls are cast-in-place diaphragm walls. The joints between wall segments need special treatment. Generally, in case where bottom-up method is used for construction, flexible waterproof joint may be used. In case where up-bottom method is used for construction, rigid waterproof joint or integral joint capable of transmitting vertical shear force may be used. Cast-in-place piles should not be used as the independent side walls of main structure, because they have no structural linkage with each other, poor integrity and unreliable waterproof performance.

    2) Composite wall: As a part of the side wall of main structure, the retaining structure constitutes a superimposed structure together with lining wall. Structural and construction measures shall be taken to ensure smooth transmission of shear force through the superimposing interface. The composite walls are deemed as a whole. This type of retaining structure is often designed as diaphragm wall.

    3) Compound wall: As a part of the side wall of main structure, the retaining structure constitutes a composite structure together with the lining wall. Shearing force and bending moment cannot be transmitted between walls and only normal pressure can be transmitted. The retaining structure may include diaphragm wall, cast-in-place bored piles or artificial hole-dig piles. An isolating layer or an enclosed waterproof layer may be applied between the enclosing wall and lining wall. For separated cast-in-place piles used as foundation pit bracing, although transmission of tensile force between the piles and lining wall can be realized by tierebars, the piles are still considered as compound wall because the interconnection is weak. In aquifers, waterproof curtain are generally required on the outer side of cast-in-place piles, so the water and earth pressure during construction is undertaken by the enclosing wall. In the design for long-term use, factors such as waterproof curtain failure and groundwater flowing-around should be also considered, in which case the water pressure is imposed on the lining wall.

The type of side wall has a great influence on project cost, structure loading, construction and use. Therefore, it shall be determined through technical and economic comparisons in combination with the usage requirements, the type of retaining structure, the actual engineering geological and hydrogeological conditions and the site conditions. Where single wall is used, the durability of underground concrete wall poured in mud shall be properly justified. Otherwise, in the design of composite wall or compound wall, the transfer of external loads towards lining structure during long time use due to degraded performance and declined rigidity of wall materials shall be considered.

12.4.3 Lining structure of tunnels built by shield method.

1 The type of lining of tunnels built by shield method shall be determined according to factors such as engineering geological and hydrogeological conditions, functional requirements and lining fabrication technique. In the case of pre-fabricated lining structure, double-layer lining may be used, which features better waterproofing and anti-corrosion performance, higher strength and rigidity, less construction errors and lower noise and vibration level. However, the double-layer lining needs a long construction period and high construction cost. As long as the usage and load bearing requirements are met, single-layer lining is preferred.

2 Pre-fabricated linings are made of reinforced concrete, steel, cast iron or the combinations of these materials. At present, with the advantages of convenient fabrication, high strength, good durability and pressure resistance and high economic efficiency, reinforced concrete linings are most commonly used. In addition, the use of high-precision sheet steel forms ensures the dimensional accuracy of the lining. Steel segments, cast iron segments or steel-reinforced-steel composite segments are used only at the positions subjected to complicated loads such as gaps and rings.

3 To facilitate the construction of interval tunnel between side-platform stations, a double-circle shield tunnel has emerged in recent years, in which the lining is of a double-circle structure with a center column. Compared with the traditional two-track large-diameter shield tunnel, the double-circle shield tunnel has the advantages of sufficient space utilization and less subgrade settlement and is especially suitable for interval tunnels beneath narrower streets.

12.4.4 Structural lining of tunnels built by mining method.

1 In view to make full use of the compressive strength of lining materials, improve the bearing capacity of structure, reduce construction difficulty, simplify engineering measures, ensure the stability of surrounding rocks and protect the ambient environment, horseshoe-shaped cross section shall be preferably used for tunnels built by mining method, which is especially necessary for those in surrounding rocks of IV to VI grades featuring poor geological conditions.

However, in actual projects, due to constrains of construction process requirements or construction conditions, even in V—VI grade surrounding rocks, straight wall arch structure or the flattop straight wall structure may be used sometimes.

In the case of maglev stations in grade I—III surrounding rocks, the straight wall arch structure may also be used in order to make full use of the underground space.

2 The integrated lining is a lining structure widely used in tunnels built by mining method and is supported by long-term practical experience. Capable of restraining the deformation of surrounding rock, giving full play to the self-supporting ability of surrounding rock, and adapting to loading changes after completion of tunnel, composite lining has broad application prospects in metro tunnels built by the mining method. It is especially suitable for tunnels suffering poor geological conditions or shallow buried tunnels and generally can be used in II—IV grade surrounding rock.

3 Considering the high difficulty in controlling construction quality and the uncertainty in ensuring structure durability, currently anchored shotcrete lining should not be used in interval tunnels and underground stations where trains, people and equipment concentrate.

12. 5 Structure Design

12. 5. 1 Item 1: The design standards, structural systems, and load conditions of the underground structures may vary during the construction phase and normal operation phases.

Item 4: It is proposed in accordance with Item 5 of Article 11. 6. 1 in GB 50157 – 2013 *Code for Design of Metro*.

Factors to be considered in the calculation sketch of structures:

1) In the structural analysis, the calculation mode and sectional calculation parameters selected for the double-layer lining shall correspond to its force transmission characteristics in order to reflect the actual stress conditions of the lining;

2) Necessity for analysis on the actual loading process of structure:

Except the open-cut structure built by side slope method, mine tunnel built by full face excavation method, and the tunnel built by single-circle shield method, the underground structures of urban rail transit mostly have the following characteristics:

① The main force bearing members of the structure are generally serving both as temporary and permanent structures, and their structural form, components composition, rigidity, support conditions and load conditions keep changing during the formation process of the structure.

② The stresses of the structure forces are closely related to the construction method, excavation sequence, and engineering measures. Especially for the large underground station constructed by mining method, the excavation, primary support, secondary lining, and disassembly of temporary partitions are carried out in an alternating way. The conversion of stress of the structural system is frequent and complicated.

③ New structural members are constructed under the existing deformation and stress of the structural system, and thus the load effects are continuous.

Because of the above characteristics, it is general that the most adverse condition of stress on some key parts of the structural system does not occur in the use stage of structure after completion. Therefore, the traditional calculation method in which the loads are imposed at one time after completion and the influences of construction process are not considered, or the analysis method which omits the continuity of stress on the structure although the influence in the construction stage and the load changes are considered, could not reflect the actual stress conditions of the structure, and thus the design based on such calculation and analysis are unsafe. Therefore, it is required in this item that the internal stress and deformation shall be analyzed according to the actual loading process of the structure.

12. 5. 2 Item 7: Two methods are available at present for the analysis of stress during the operation stage of open-cut structure, in which one considers the influences of construction process and the other does not consider such influences. For the former one, the stress of the structure in the operation stage is taken as the continuation of that in the construction stage and the stress and its development process during the whole stress process of the structure from construction beginning to long-term operation are considered. For the latter method, the stress in the construction stage of the structure is separated from that in the operation stage during the analysis and calculation, that is, the stress and deformation in the two stages are considered as unrelated completely. Calculation experience shows that whether the influence of the construction process on the stress of the frame structure during use is considered will have great influence on the calculation results. Although the analysis method considering the influence of the construction process is complicated, it can reflect the continuity relationship of the structure stress in the operation stage from that in the construction stage, and the actual stress process of the structure. With the latter method, the reinforcement is more economical. Generally this analysis method should be adopted in the construction drawing design stage. While the former method may be used in the preliminary design stage to select the sectional parameters of the structure.

Item 8: According to GB 50010 *Code for Design of Concrete Structures*, the superimposing interface of superimposed plates shall be a rough surface with the roughness no less than 4 mm. For the superimposed plates subjected to large loads, reinforcing bars extending into the superposed layer should be provided. In the early rail transit projects in Shanghai, shearing reinforcement has ever been preinstalled in the underground wall, which, however, increased the construction difficulties. According to the Shanghai standard DGJ 08 - 109 *Urban Rail Transit Standards* and based on the comprehensive calculation theory and practical experience, the superimposed interface of underground wall is not provided with shearing reinforcement after chiseling, and the allowable shear stress of the superimposed interface is taken as 0. 7 MPa.

Paragraph 1) of Item 9: The safety level standards of foundation pits in different cities in China vary with geographical conditions. The maximum ground settlement, horizontal displacement control requirements for enclosing wall, and the environmental protection requirements also vary. Therefore the local codes and specifications for construction of foundation pits in the cities or regions may be taken as reference.

Paragraph 2) of Item 9: The stability check items of foundation pit shall be determined according to the type of retaining structure and the geological and hydrogeological conditions of the site. Refer to Table 12.

Table 12　Foundation Pit Stability Check Items

Type of support	Overall instability	Anti-slip	Anti-tilting	Internal instability	Anti-uplift (Ⅰ) (soil upwelling under enclosing wall)	Anti-uplift (Ⅰ) (soil upwelling above enclosing wall)	Anti-piping or anti-percolation	Anti-surging of confined groundwater
Protective slope	△	△	—	—	—	—	—	○
Soil nailing	△	△	△	△	—	—	—	○
Gravity retaining structure	△	△	△	—	△	—	△	○
Retaining piles and walls	○	△	△	—	△	△	△	○

Notes: 1　△—It shall be checked, ○—Checked when necessary;

2　Where the pile or wall type retaining structure is provided with one support (or anchored cable), overall instability check shall be carried out.

Notes for stability safety coefficients:

1 Existing formulas for the calculation of excavation stability are mostly based on the subsoil stability concept of shallow foundation, which is not exactly the same as that of deep and large foundation pits or those with retaining structures. In addition, due to the limitations in the test section, some stress states that directly affect the true state of soil during the excavation process could not reflect the influences of soil unloading or precipitation on the soil properties in various parts. Besides, the focus on the foundation pit stability in each city varies with the geological conditions. Even if the formulas are same, the values of some coefficients and the shear strength of the selected soil layers are different. Therefore the values for the foundation pit stability safety coefficients must be taken according to the local experience.

2 The uplift of bottom soil during the excavation process will cause deformation of the soil outside the excavation and the settlement of the ground. Therefore in the calculation of foundation pit stability, the safety factors of some check items are related to the protection level of foundation pit.

For example, in the Shanghai standard DG/T J08 – 61 *Technical Code for Excavation Engineering*, different safety factors shall be taken for anti-overturning stability of excavation bottom and anti-overturning of retaining structure shall be taken based on the safety grade of foundation pit. In the Shanghai standard DGJ 08 – 109 *Urban Rail Transit Design Standard*, the anti-lifting safety factor K_s shall be determined according to the environmental protection level of foundation pit.

Paragraph 4) of Item 9: The support is taken as one part of the main structure to save the project investment and reduce resource consumption. Comparison of several methods:

Single wall: No additional lining wall that participates in the structural stress is provided, and the retaining structure is directly taken as the side wall of the main structure. The underground continuous diaphragm wall is mostly used. Such structure could not offer satisfactory structural waterproofing effects and good structural durability.

Composite wall: Serving as a part of the side wall of the main structure, the composite wall is combined with the lining wall to form a superimposed structure, and structural construction measures are taken to realize shear force transmission on the superimposed surface. After the superposition, the two are regarded as an integral wall. The retaining structure is mostly formed by diaphragm wall, which offers poor waterproofing effects and is subject to crack.

Compound wall: Serving as a part of the side wall of the main structure, the composite wall is combined with the lining wall to form a superimposed structure. Shear force and bending moment could not be transmitted between the wall surfaces. Instead, only normal pressure may be transmitted. The retaining structure is only required to satisfy the foundation pit support requirements. Such structure offers good waterproofing effects, large rigidity, and good durability despite of poor cost-effectiveness.

Paragraph 5) of Item 9: Determine the maximum crack width limit according to the durability requirements and the category of structure environment.

12. 5. 3 Paragraph 3) of Item 5: The construction axis and design axis errors of the tunnel include construction error, measurement error, structural deformation, and line axis fitting error.

12. 5. 4 This article is drafted with reference to Article 11. 6. 6 of GB 50157 – 2013 *Code for*

Design of Metro.

Item 1: Judgment of stability of primary support.

The stability of primary support for the tunnel of single-route and double-route lines with an excavation width less than 10 m may be judged by using the method in Appendix F of TB 10003 – 2016 *Code for Design of Railway Tunnel*. For tunnel with large-span transition line and the station structures, the stability of primary support may be determined through special study.

Item 2: Design parameters for shotcrete primary support and composite lining.

For the tunnel of single-route and double-route lines, the design parameters may be determined by taking the project analog method based on the applicable codes and engineering practices. Under the special terrain and geological conditions (such as shallow burial, bias, swelling wall rocks, or surrounding rocks with excessive ground stress) and for the tunnel or station structure with large span, the design parameters of the primary support shall be determined through theoretical calculation for the main force bearing structure.

The primary support for earth tunnel may adopt forepoling, grill steel frame or steel arch support, reinforced mesh and shotcrete. The design requirements are as follows:

1 The thickness of the primary support shall be 200 mm—350 mm.

2 For the steel arch support used in primary support, reinforced grille is preferred. The spacing of steel arch supports shall be 500 mm—1000 mm and the diameter of main reinforcing bar in the reinforced grille should not be less than 18 mm.

3 Single-layer reinforced mesh should be provided on the inner side when the thickness of primary support is not larger than 300 mm, while double layer reinforced mesh should be provided on the inner side when the thickness of primary support is larger than 300 mm.

4 The sections of primary support shall be reliably connected.

Item 3: Design of secondary lining.

1 Besides of the requirements in Item 2 of this article, the external loads borne jointly by the primary support and secondary lining for the structures that are shallowly buried in Quaternary soil layer, buried in rheological or swelling wall rock, for which the secondary lining shall be constructed in advance or the external load increases after construction of secondary lining, shall also be considered, and the pressure values summarized from the actually measured data on site for the existing composite lining of the structure shall be taken as the calculation load of secondary lining.

2 For the large-span station structure or bi-arch structure for which the primary support and secondary lining are constructed in an alternating way, take the stratum-structure model or load-structure model according to the structural characteristics and stress transmission characteristics between the primary support and secondary lining, and determine the stress conditions of secondary lining based on the analysis on construction process.

3 Since the shotcrete could hardly satisfy the durability requirements of underground maglev transit project, it is necessary to reinforce the secondary lining to meet the durability requirements of the structure constructed with mining method. Therefore, in the stress analysis on the composite lining during long-term service, the transfer of the external load to the secondary lining after the rigidity degradation of the primary support shall be considered.

4 Considering the uncertainty of the external loads and their distribution under shallow burial conditions and in V — VI surrounding rocks, and the possibility of urban groundwater level, the secondary lining should adopt reinforced concrete structure for the purpose of safety.

12.6 Tectonic Requirements

12.6.1 Item 1: Considering the vast territory and highly different geological conditions and climatic conditions in China, the standards for setting deformation joints may be set flexibly in each region. For example for subway stations, generally inducing joints are set to take the effects of temperature induced deformation into account.

12.6.3 Table 12.6.3 "Minimum Cover Thickness of Outmost Reinforcing Bars under General Environment" is given based on the practical experience in metro projects.

13 Structure Waterproof

13.1 General Requirements

13.1.2 Waterproof design for medium and low speed maglev transit line shall place priority on prevention, use multiple preventive measures combining rigid and flexible waterproof layers, full make use of local conditions and focus on comprehensive treatment.

13.1.3 Excessive water seepage in underground station and the sections where electromechanical equipment is concentrated will greatly affect passenger's safety and equipment operation. According to metro construction and operation experience, the underground station structure of medium and low speed maglev shall reach waterproof grade I, while the underground interval tunnels and liaison channel structures shall reach a waterproof grade II to satisfy essential application needs.

13.2 Self-waterproof of Concrete Structure

13.2.1 Impermeability grade of waterproof concrete is determined according to tests on plain concrete samples and the dense rebars making up the main structure of underground station tunnel has an adverse effect on concrete anti-seepage performance. Therefore, impermeability grades shall not be less than P8 to ensure satisfying waterproof performance of underground construction.

13.3 Waterproof for Underground Station Structure

13.3.3 The Article was proposed in line with Table 12.5.2 of Article 12.5.2 as stated in GB 50157 – 2013 *Code for Design of Metro*. Waterproof works for underground structure excavated by open cut method are designed for main and detail structures. Main structures mostly use the self-waterproof concrete for waterproofing, which is a common practice. One or two waterproof layers shall be additionally provided for waterproof works of Grade I. One waterproof layer may be added according to geologic, environmental and practical conditions for waterproof works of Grade II. Such requirements are necessary as underground structure is affected by water corrosion and carbonization for a long time while waterproof concrete is absolutely watertight material. Structural durability will be enhanced if the design of structure to keep hazardous substances from the underground structure is taken into account. Wholly-covering waterproof layer or cement-based permeable crystalline waterproof material coated outside main structure will effectively prevent corrosive medium of underground water from corroding underground structure and delay carbonization process to enhance structural durability. Waterproof measures shall be tailored to meet requirements of different waterproof grades of construction joint, post-cast strip and deformation joint. More waterproof layers are required for a higher waterproof grade to tackle the problem of high joint seepage, ensure prudent construction and overcome weaknesses as the waterproofing workload at joints is relatively less than that at the main structure.

13.3.9 The Article was proposed in line with Table 12.6.1 of Article 12.6.1 of GB 50157 – 2013 in *Code for Design of Metro*. Waterproof measures on tunnels built by mine tunneling method is generally constructed with composite lining for overall waterproofing, which needs an interlining flexible waterproof layer in addition to its self-waterproofing. Composite lining is generally composed of primary support made of anchored shotcrete waterproof concrete, interlining flexible waterproof layer and secondary die casting waterproof concrete lining.

Anchored shotcrete retaining structure is mixed with a performance-reliable and convenient composite swelling agent to provide concrete spray layer with controllable swelling ratio for compensating volume contraction arising from setting and hardening, to finally reduce and avoid shrinkage cracks, block seepage channels and thus realizing self-waterproofing of shotcrete.

The interlining waterproof layer is generally provided with a buffer and guidance pad on its back. The pad shall be laid without bolt holes to protect the waterproof isolating layer from damage and improve waterproofing effect.

For the buffer layer paved before waterproof layer, plastic round washers shall be firstly fixed on the base layer with blind nails. Interval of plastic round pads: 500 mm to 800 mm for vault; 800 mm to 1500 mm for side wall. The pads are laid in quincunx style. Less or no pads may be laid on the bottom board.

Waterproof board shall be laid without nails and gradually welded with plastic round pads duringlaying. Coiled materials shall be welded by automatic walking-type plastic welder so that the air inflation pressure between double welds can reach and keep at 0. 15 MPa for 5 minutes.

Secondary die casting should be made of shrinkage-compensating waterproof concrete of an impermeability grade higher than or equal to P8.

13. 4　Waterproof for Tunnel Structure

13. 4. 6　The Article is proposed in line with Table 12. 8. 2 of Article 12. 8. 2 of GB 50157 – 2013 *Code for Design of Metro*. Multiple waterproof protections are considered necessary for lining waterproofing of tunnels built by shield method. Multiple waterproof protections include stratum treatment, self-waterproof lining structure, sealing of joint grooves and bolt holes, embedded grooves and other waterproof measures.

Stratum treatment reduces the permeability of stratum around tunnel by filling in grout. This may lower the pressure of underground water flowing into the tunnel and thus greatly lessen the water flow.

The fabrication of lining segments shall be strictly checked according to related quality standards. Lining segments delivered to construction site shall be sampled for waterproof and anti-seepage test.

Waterproof sealing pads plastered into grooves are the first but important waterproof protection measure for joints. They shall be made of materials with high elasticity, excellent deformation adaptability and aging resistance and the capability of withstanding the relative displacement and stretching value (design value) in circumferential direction and longitudinal rib plane under certain water pressure (design value) while keeping leakless. For example, EPDM, neoprene, water swelling rubber and other waterproof sealing materials.

Caulking serves as an auxiliary prevention for joint waterproofing. Shape and dimensions of caulking grooves shall be tailored to meet requirements of specific works and the selected caulking materials which shall have less contractibility, excellent durability and watertightness and gas tightness to better adapt to the structure-induced deformation. Common caulking materials include elastic cements, modified epoxy, polysulfide rubber and polyurethane.

Assembled lining segments are commonly found with water seepage at screw holes. So the bolt holes in longitudinal and circumferential lib surfaces of the joints shall be treated. The treatment procedures are as follows: fabricate the bolt hole on the side of cavity rib into a taper shape, mount sealing washers made of neoprene or water swelling rubber (the type of washer shall match the type of bolt hole), and screw up and compact the bolts in longitudinal and circumferential rib planes to realize waterproofing. The sealing washer shall be resistant to oil, water and aging.

14　Ventilationing, Air Conditioning and Heating

14. 1　General Requirements

14. 1. 2　Article 8. 4. 1 of GB 50490 - 2009 *Technical Code of Urban Rail Transit* stipulates that the internal air environment of urban rail transit system shall be controlled by means of HVAC and shall be in accordance with the following requirements:

　　1　During normal operation of the train, ensure that the temperature, humidity, airflow and air quality of the internal air environment of the transit system meet the physiological requirements of personnel and the normal operation needs of the equipment.

　　2　When the train is blocked in an interval tunnel, there shall be effective ventilation at the blockage point.

　　3　When the train catches fire in an interval tunnel, effective ventilation shall be available at the place of fire.

　　4　Where there is a fire in the public area or in the equipment and management rooms of maglev transit station, effective smoke exhaust and ventilation shall be carried out.

14. 1. 3　Most of medium and low speed maglev transit systems are built at an elevated or ground level, so natural ventilation should be given priority. Mechanical ventilation or air conditioning system may be used when natural ventilation is insufficient.

14. 1. 4　The ventilation and cooling capacity of ventilation and air conditioning system for medium and low speed maglev transit depends on ridership and rail capacity. The long-term planned ridership and rail capacity shall be larger than the near-term values and match with the capacity of ventilation and air conditioning equipment. If long-term capability is used as the initial design basis, it will result in excessive initial investment. Therefore, the ventilation and air conditioning system of medium and low speed maglev transit system shall be designed according to the maximum ridership and rail capacity, but equipment installation shall be implemented by stage according to the actual needs of each stage.

14. 1. 6　In order to ensure traffic safety, HVAC equipment and smoke exhaust system shall not be installed above track. Effective anti-falling measures must be taken if they have to be so installed.

14. 2　Design Standards

14. 2. 1　In the case of stations of elevated lines and ground lines, where air conditioning system is installed in station concourse, the temperature in the station concourse shall be somehow lower than the outdoor air temperature, so that passengers can feel the temporary coolness when entering the station concourse from the outside. To this end, the design temperature of station concourse in summer shall be 29 ℃ to 30 ℃.

　　The design ambient air temperature for tunnel ventilation in summer is taken as the average ambient air temperature of the hottest month over the past 20 years, rather than the design ambient air temperature for ventilation of ground buildings in summer. This is because underground structure is different from ground building. The underground line enclosing structure and the surrounding soil have large heat capacity and high thermal inertia. Therefore, the average ambient air temperature of the hottest month better reflects the actual condition.

The requirement "For underground stations, when the station adopts a ventilation system, the calculation summer air temperature in the station should not be higher than the outdoor calculation temperature by 5 ℃" is proposed in accordance with the *Hygienic Standards for the Design of Industrial Enterprises* and the metro operation experience. The underground stations feature high heat dissipation demand and passengers go in and out in a hurry, so it is similar to workshops and light-duty operations workplaces with large heat dissipation.

The minimum temperature in the underground station is defined in accordance with the relevant standards for ground buildings; it shall not be lower than 12 ℃.

14.3 Underground Station and Tunnel

14.3.1 Considering underground lines are relatively isolated from ambient air, in order to keep good air quality in underground line, the air inside the tunnel shall be directly exchanged with the ambient air to ensure effective discharge of dirty air and smooth intake of fresh air.

14.3.4 According to design and operation practices of metro projects, where station has no platform screen door or is provided with half-height platform screen door, piston air has a great influence on the air environment in the station. Installing piston air discharge shaft or bypass ducts at both ends of the station can significantly reduce the impact of piston air on the air environment in the station.

14.3.9 Rooms where gas fire extinguishers are used need to be ventilated during normal use. In the event of fire accident, fire extinguishing gas will be sprayed to extinguish the fire. Therefore, a mechanical ventilation system shall be provided to achieve forced ventilation and eliminate the fire extinguishing gas and various harmful indoor gases generated by combustion. The gases must be directly discharged to the ground.

14.3.11 This Article stipulates: When ventilation systems of end line or turn-back line equipment and management rooms need to induce draft from tunnel, the air inlet shall be set on the side the train enters the station, where inlet air is relative fresh, and the air outlet shall be set on the side the train exits, so that exhaust air can be brought by the train to interval tunnel and discharged through the ventilating ducts in the interval tunnel or the piston venting well of the next station, therefore reducing the impact on the air environment of the station.

14.4 Ground and Elevated Station

14.4.1 The station concourses and platforms of elevated lines and at-ground lines are built above or on the ground. Interconnection with ambient air in architectural form shall be considered, which is conducive to using natural ventilation to eliminate residual heat and residual humidity and thus simplifying the ventilation and air conditioning system, reducing construction cost and saving energy.

14.4.5 The purpose of this article is to prevent large amount of cold air from entering the station due to piston effect.

14.5 Cooling Source, Water System and Heating Source

14.5.2 Item 3: Item 2, Article 6.3.7 of GB 50736 – 2012 *Design Code for Heating Ventilation and Air Conditioning of Civil Buildings* sets out the specific requirements on the ventilation of refrigerator room.

Item 4: This item is proposed in accordance with Item 5, Article 8.10.1, of GB 50736 – 2012 *Design Code for Heating Ventilation and Air Conditioning of Civil Buildings*.

14.5.7 The stations of both elevated and ground lines of medium and low speed maglev transit system are generally independent of other buildings on the ground. If heating is required in station, the local urban utility heat supply network shall be used as much as possible to simplify the station heating system and realize reliable heating effect and less operation and maintenance efforts. If a separate heat source is built, it will bring a series of problems in operation, management and maintenance and may result in cost increase.

14.7 Air Duct, Air Shaft and Air Pavilion

14.7.2 In order to prevent the dust, debris and other foreign objects near air inlet pavilion from being raised by the outlet air of air outlet pavilion and sucked into the underground line via air inlet, it is required that the air inlet pavilion should be on the windward side of air outlet pavilion. For the convenience of exhaust air the opening of air outlet pavilion should keep clear of the local most frequent wind direction in the year.

15 Water Supply and Drainage

15.1 General Requirements

15.1.2 According to the *Law on Water Pollution Prevention and Control*, the provincial, autonomous region and municipality-level governments may formulate local water pollutant discharge standards for the items not covered in the national water pollutant discharge standards, and impose more stringent standards for those already covered in the national standards. The local discharge standards shall apply to any discharge to the water bodies for which local pollutant discharge standards are available.

15.2 Water Supply

15.2.1 In order to reduce the project cost and ensure the reliability of water supply and water quality, the urban tap water supply system shall be preferred for the medium and low speed maglev transit. At the suburbs or urban-rural junctions where it is impossible to connect to the urban tap water system, a well may be drilled to serve as the standby water or new tap water supply system or reliable ground water source may be taken in consultation with the local planning authority.

15.2.2 Item 3: In order to alleviate the water shortage in many areas in China, municipal sewage treatment plants are constructed in some cities and municipal reclaimed water (for miscellaneous use) pipe network is formed along the urban roads to supply water for flushing, greening, garden landscape, road spraying to which human is not exposed. With lower treatment cost than tap water, the price per ton of reclaimed water (for miscellaneous use) is far lower than the tap water. Reclaimed water may be deemed as a reliable, low-cost, energy conservation and environmentally friendly non-drinking water source. If the municipal reclaimed water (for miscellaneous use) with acceptable quality is available in the vicinity, such water shall be used for flushing, greening, cooling water make-up, road flushing, etc. of the medium and low speed maglev transit as far as possible. Separate quality water supply system shall be used for the tap water and miscellaneous water systems of the project, and separate water metering devices must be installed.

In order to ensure the system safety of domestic water and prevent misuse and drinking, the miscellaneous water system shall not be connected with the drinking water pipeline. Where a short pipe or nozzle is installed on the pipe of miscellaneous water system, both Chinese and English signs indicating "Not for Drinking" shall be set at the water point to remind the working personnel or passengers not to drink the water, thus ensuring safety and reliability of water use.

Item 4: The water supply for vehicle base and stabling yard shall be led from the municipal water supply system as practical as possible. Where two water intake pipes are available from the municipal tap water system and the pressure is acceptable for the outdoor fire hydrant at the most unfavorable point, the production and living water supply systems should be shared by the outdoor fire water supply system in order to reduce the number of water supply networks to be laid in the vehicle base. However, it is required by some urban water supply companies in China that the outdoor production and living water supply systems must be separated from the outdoor fire water system. Therefore, the comments from the local municipal water supply departments shall be obtained for the arrangement of outdoor production, living and fire water systems.

15.2.3 The consumption of flushing water shall be determined according to the current national standard GB 50157 *Code for Design of Metro* with reference to the experience in metro design and operation in China.

15.2.6 Item 1: Generally one or two main water intake pipes are led from the municipal tap water system to supply water for the production, living and fire water supply systems of the station, and then one water pipe may be connected from the main intake pipe.

Item 5: Less flushing water taps are set for the flushing water of station concourse, platform, and section tunnel (on the branch pipe of fire hydrant) because they are infrequently used. According to the operation of metros in China, the station concourse and platform are usually cleaned by mopping, instead of flushing, while the section tunnel may be flushed by water at an interval.

Item 7: The water supply pipe running through the substation, communication signal room, station control room, and power distribution room might cause equipment failure or damage due to water leakage.

Item 8: Insulation and anti-condensation measures need to be taken for the pipes. Expansion on heating and contraction on cooling shall be considered for metal pipe. For long-distance pipe, stability shall be considered, the bends shall be designed by calculation, and buttress shall be provided if necessary. The pipes of ground and elevated stations shall be buried as practical as possible.

Item 10: The living water pipe shall meet the requirements in the current national standard GB/T 17219 *Standard for Hygienic Safety Evaluation of Equipment and Protective Materials in Drinking Water*.

15.3 Drainage

15.3.2 Where possible, the wastewater from local and temporary drain pump houses should be drained into the drainage ditch of the line. The main purpose is to reduce the length of pipe and the project cost. Note that the drain pump shall not be excessively large and the outlet flow of lifting pipe shall be in the same direction as the water flow of drainage ditch of the line so that the outlet pressure water will not come out of the drainage ditch.

15.3.3 Item 5: For the elevated section, open entrance/exit, open air shaft, and tunnel opening which are subject to rainwater intrusion, the amount of drainage shall be calculated based on the local storm intensity, so as to determine the scale of drain pump station, performance of the drain equipment and the diameter of drainage pipe reasonably. The amount of drainage of rainwater shall be calculated according to the intensity of 50-year return period rainstorm and the design rainfall duration shall be determined by calculation.

16　Power Supply

16.1　General Requirements

16.1.1　The power supply system of medium and low speed maglev transit is an integrated power supply network supporting each load in the transit system via substations along the line.

16.1.2　In the power supply system of medium and low speed maglev transit, centralized power supply mode, distributed power supply mode or centralized-distributed hybrid power supply mode may be used for external power supply.

The centralized power supply mode is an external power supply mode in which a high voltage substation (or power supply switching station) is specially built to supply power to rectifier substation and lighting and power substation. The distributed power supply mode is an external power supply mode in which urban MV power sources are introduced in a distributed manner to supply power to rectifier substation and lighting and power substation. The hybrid power supply mode is an external power supply mode in which rectifier substation and lighting and power substation are mainly served by high voltage substation (or power supply switching station), while urban MV power sources are introduced as supplementary where appropriate.

16.1.4　According to the capacities of rectifier substation and lighting and power substation in medium and low speed maglev transit system, their reasonable supply voltage ranges from 10 kV to 35kV. 10 kV power supply network has lower equipment cost but higher line loss. 35 kV power supply network has lower line loss but higher equipment cost. 10 kV and 35 kV are the commonly used transmission and distribution voltage levels in China. In some regions in China, however, 20 kV is being promoted, for this voltage level features lower equipment cost, lower line loss and other advantages within a certain capacity range.

16.1.5　Power loads shall be graded according to power supply reliability requirement and the degree of political and economic losses or impacts of power interruption. Interruption of power supply to traction system, communications system, signal system and fire protection system will directly affect the normal operation and safety of maglev train. Therefore, power loads such as traction system and fire protection system are defined as Grade I power loads. Loads such as power equipment and lighting devices may be classified as Grade I load, Grade II load or Grade III load.

16.1.6　Two LV busbar sections from two non-parallel transformers of the same lighting and power substation may be used as duplicate power supply to Grade I loads.

16.1.8　Actual operating experience suggests that electrical faults cannot be confined to a certain range. Therefore, emergency power sources shall be those electrically independent of utility power grid, such as battery, diesel generator, etc. The "special feeder lines independent from normal power sources in power supply network" refer to the lines that would not have power interruption at the same time as normal power sources.

16.1.9　According to the importance of maglev transit project, all substations within medium and low speed maglev transit system have Grade I and Grade II loads, so the power supply shall be designed according to this code.

16.1.10　The MV power supply network in power supply system is generally composed of power cables. In order to ensure the reliability of power supply, the MV cables are usually configured in duplicate (one active and one standby) to satisfy the power demand after first fault in supply line. The MV cables are light load lines during normal operation and their aging process is slow and service lives are long. So, it is neither economical nor convenient to lay the MV cables by stage.

16.1.11　The traffic density and traction power load of maglev train is the highest during peak commuting hours. Therefore, the traction load calculation shall be based on the peak commuting hours. Prediction of ridership in the initial stage of project contains some uncertainties. So, considering the potential rapid growth of ridership, it is recommended that the capacity of the rectifier unit at rectifier substation be designed according to the planned long-term load.

16.1.12　Item 3: When the rectifier substation of vehicle maintenance base or stabling yard shuts down due to fault, the contact line of vehicle maintenance base or stabling yard shall be powered by the rectifier substation or contact line of the main line. Whether it is suitable to use the rectifier substation of vehicle maintenance base or stabling yard to power the main line relies on the actual power supply demand and the power supply capacity of rectifier substation of vehicle maintenance base or stabling yard. If the rectifier substation of vehicle maintenance base or stabling yard is capable of supporting the power supply demand of the main line, it may be considered to support main line in such way.

16.1.13　The nominal voltage of contact line is determined in accordance with Article 4.3.2 of CJ/T 375 - 2011 *General Technical Specification for Medium and Low Speed Maglev Vehicles*. However, DC 750V is also used in some urban rail transit systems in China and may be used depending on the specific conditions, but such requirement shall be specified when placing order for the vehicle.

For short-distance maglev transit lines in tourism areas, the nominal voltage of contact line may be designed as DC 750V.

When DC 3000V is used under special conditions, the parameters and technical conditions of the traction power supply system shall be determined through profound studies, tests and assessment on maglev vehicles.

16.1.14　Harmonics may generally bring the following harms to power system:

1　Harmonics lead to additional harmonic loss of components (such as induction motor and synchronous motor) in utility grid and decline in efficiency of power generation, transmission and consumption equipment.

2　Harmonics affect the normal operation of electrical equipment. In addition to harmonic losses, the impacts of harmonics on the motor also include mechanical vibration, noise and overvoltage, which in turn result in local extreme overtemperature of transformers as well as overtemperature, insulation aging, service life decrease and even damage of capacitors, cables and other equipment.

3　Harmonics may result in local parallel resonance and series resonance in utility grid, which will amplify the effect of harmonics, greatly increase the harms indicated in items 1 and 2, and even cause serious accidents.

4　Harmonics may cause malfunction or action failure of relay protection and automatic devices and may make electrical measuring instruments inaccurate.

5 Harmonics may generate interference with adjacent communications systems, ranging from noises compromising communication quality to data loss hindering normal operation of communications system.

In order to reduce the above-mentioned hazards of harmonics, measures shall be taken to control the distortion rate of sinusoidal voltage waveform of the grid caused by the harmonics from DC traction system and non-linear electrical equipment. The control indicators shall comply with the current national standard GB/T 14549 *Quality of Electric Energy Supply Harmonics in Public Supply Network*.

16.1.15 Train's regenerative braking energy may be absorbed by resistor, absorbed by resistor and inverter, inverted and absorbed by MV network, or stored in capacitor. Which absorption method should be used shall be determined according to comprehensive technical and economic comparison.

16.1.16 Reactive power compensation shall be designed to reach overall balance. To realize an overall power factor above 0.9 and meet the reactive power compensation requirement of the system, capacitor compensation devices capable of automatic switching may be provided on the 0.4 kV side of lighting and power substations for distributed compensation, or a reactive power compensation device (SVC or SVG) may be provided at the high voltage substation for centralized compensation. However, the one-time investment in the above two schemes is different. Which scheme should be used shall be determined through technical and economic comparison based on the actual condition of power supply system.

16.2 Substation

16.2.1 Hybrid substation can reduces the number of auxiliary facilities, cuts down construction cost and facilitates maintenance and management.

16.2.2 The quantity and arrangement of high voltage substation (or power supply switching station), rectifier substations and lighting and power substations along the line shall be determined by calculation in accordance with the actual work conditions of the line. The determination considerations shall include various technical requirements, economic rationality, long-term demands of power supply system, operations management, environmental coordination and transportation convenience.

16.2.3 With rapid development of science and technology and in response to the need for reducing staff to improve efficiency in China, automation and communication technologies have being advancing and become increasingly mature. Unattended operation mode has been gradually accepted as a common operation management mode of power system and rail transit substations.

16.2.4 In order to save initial investment and reduce operating costs of maglev project, the quantity and capacity of main transformers in high voltage substation may be determined according to the planned near-term load. But the civil engineering design of the high voltage substation shall be based on the quantity and capacity of main transformers determined according to the planned long-term load.

16.2.5 To assess the harmonics generated by the traction power supply system of medium and low speed maglev transit, a harmonics monitoring system should be provided on the power supply side of high voltage substation, and harmonics control devices may be added depending on the specific conditions.

16.2.6 If the quantity and capacity of transformer-rectifier units determined according to near-term design load are significantly different from the figures determined according to long-term design load, the transformer-rectifier units may be installed by stage; otherwise, the quantity and capacity of transformer-rectifier units may be designed according to long-term design load.

In order to ensure the normal operation of the train after rectifier substation stops operating due to fault, the adjacent rectifier substation shall be able to support the power supply loads of the stopped one.

16.2.8 According to the operation experience of metros in China, the capacity of distribution transformer of lighting and power substation shall ensure that when one transformer goes out of service, the other transformer is able to support the Grade I and II loads within its scope of power supply. This is conducive to meeting the reliability requirements of power supply system, cutting down project cost, increasing the load rates of distribution transformers during normal operation, and realizing more economic operations.

16.2.13 To facilitate operation, maintenance and management, the production houses of substation shall be arranged centrally and arrangement by storey is allowed.

16.2.15 The requirement on duration of DC operating power supply after AC power loss varies with the operation mode of substation. Considering that medium and low speed maglev transit generally employs unattended substations, the duration of DC operating power supply is taken to be 2h.

16.2.17 Item 1: The integrated automation system of substation can be classified into substation-level management layer, network communication layer and equipment bay layer. The equipment bay layer is a comprehensive system that integrates control, protection, measurement and communication and is able to serve as a remote terminal unit.

Item 2: The integrated automation system of substation generally communicates with the power dispatching system at control center via a channel provided by communications system and works with the power dispatching system to realize PSCADA.

Item 3: The integrated automation system of substation, through carrying out local control at substation or executing remote control commands, realizes on/off switching of circuit breakers and electrical disconnectors, control of on-load voltage regulating device, on/off switching of protection function, switchover among protection settings, release of blockage, on/off switching of automatic devices and other functions.

Item 4: The integrated automation system of substation shall use standard interfaces and open protocols for easy access to PSCADA system.

Item 5: The online system fault self-inspection includes patrol inspection and fault diagnosis of software and hardware in the system. The hardware fault diagnosis shall be detailed to panel level.

16.2.21 If DC incoming line is equipped with disconnector, reverse current protection device shall be installed as the short-circuit protection measure for DC incoming line and rectifier unit.

16.2.26 Short-time overload caused by the non-permanent fault of contact line and the unfavorable characteristics of traction load has a high probability of triggering protective actions. Automatic reclosing device may be installed to avoid unnecessary power failures.

16.3 Traction Power Network

16.3.1 The contact line system of medium and low speed maglev transit is a DC power supply system that supplies electric energy to maglev vehicles. As it is not equipped with standby power supply facilities, it shall have good electrical and mechanical performance to meet the technical requirements of the system.

The contact rail system is mainly composed of contact rails, support members, insulating components, connecting parts and electrical connectors. Each of the components shall have good electrical and mechanical performance. The main functions of contract rail system are as follows:

1 Contact rail: As the main component carrying electric current, the basic function of contract rail is to ensure that power supply system supplies electric energy to maglev vehicles via current collector.

2 Support members: members supporting the contact rail.

3 Insulating components: including electrically sectionalizing components and electrically insulating components.

4 Connecting parts: The parts connecting any adjacent sections of contact rail.

5 Electrical connectors: Connecting parts that enable power supply system to supply power to contact rail system via cables.

Item 4: Where vehicle turns back along return line, the positive and negative poles of contact rail shall be reversed in time to meet the polarity conversion requirement of current collector.

Item 5: The current collection modes of contact rail include the current collection on lateral side, current collection at top and current collection at bottom. Which mode should be used in project shall be determined through technical and economic comparison in combination with the structural and current collection requirements of the current collector. Current collection on lateral side is recommended.

16.3.10 The current collection face of contact line and the current collector of maglev vehicle constitute a friction pair. The material of current collector shall match with that of the current collection face of contact line to realize good current collection effect and expected service life.

16.4 Cable

16.4.1 For power cables and control cables laid underground, low-smoke and halogen-free flame-retardant cables shall be used with the purpose of reducing the adverse impact of harmful gases on human body during fire. In order to ensure power supply to emergency lighting and fire-fighting facilities during fire, the power supply cables of emergency lighting and fire-fighting facilities, if they are laid in an exposed manner, shall be low-smoke, halogen-free, fire-resistant copper core cables or mineral-insulated fire-resistant cables.

16.4.2 Medium and low speed maglev transit generally needs a large number of cables, which may be laid in very different ways (e. g. , many cables need to be laid via conduit). Many project practices have proved that 3-core cables with a large cross sectional area are hard to lay and can be easily damaged during construction. According to experience, cables with three or more cores usually have a cross sectional area larger than 150 mm^2 and are generally difficult to lay, so single-core cable is recommended.

16.4.4 The main purpose of this article is to protect the safety of maglev vehicles and equipment.

16.4.8 The main purpose of orderly arrangement of cables is to facilitate operation, maintenance and management and reduce the electrical interference intensity of weak-current cable circuits.

16.4.10 The purpose of this article is to prevent such an incident that cable metal sheath is damaged by the short-circuit current from conductor.

16.4.13 The purpose of this article is mainly to consider the axial force of cables generated due to thermal expansion and contraction.

16.5   Power and Lighting

16.5.1 Emergency lighting includes evacuation lighting and standby lighting. Evacuation lighting mainly consists of exit identification light, direction identification light and evacuation light.

16.5.3 The dedicated power supply line refers to the distribution circuit from the LV switchgear cabinet of substation to fire-fighting (fire prevention) equipment or the distribution circuit of the last distribution box in fire-fighting (fire prevention) equipment room. According to the actual firefighting needs, after firefighters arrive at fire site, they must cut off the non-fire power supply to prevent fire from spreading along distribution line and avoid electric shock. If fire and non-fire power distribution lines are mixed, the firefighters have to cut off all power supplies in which case the fire-fighting equipment cannot operate normally. Therefore, the distribution line of fire-fighting equipment should be laid separately from those of other power and lighting equipment. In addition, to prevent misoperation and to facilitate firefighting, the fire power distribution equipment shall be marked with red character signs that are easy to identify in emergency.

16.5.4 The active load of power and lighting equipment can be calculated by multiplying the equipment capacity with a demand coefficient. The calculation is very simple and it is the earliest and the most common method for active load calculation. The formula for calculating the active load by using the demand coefficient method is as follows:

$$P_{30} = K_d P_e \tag{27}$$

Where, P_{30}——Calculation active load;

   K_d——Demand coefficient;

   P_e——Total capacity of power and lighting equipment.

16.5.10 Group control of lighting offers flexible lighting control at station concourse and platform of underground station. It allows the operator to keep on only a part of lamps as necessary, which is conducive to energy conservation.

16.5.11 According to Section 6.1 "Emergency Lighting" in GB/T 16275 - 2008 *Urban Rail Transit Lighting*, the duration of power supply to evacuation lighting and standby lighting shall not be less than 60 min.

16.6   Power Monitoring

16.6.1 At present, automation technologies are developing rapidly. To adapt to such development, in the design of PSCADA system, the development demands shall be fully considered in terminologies of equipment type selection, system integration and function configuration.

16.6.2 Item 1: Remote control can be classified into point selection control, station selection control and line selection control.

Item 2: The PSCADA system shall be able to carry out real-time monitoring of the operating status of power supply system equipment through data channels. The scope of monitoring mainly includes switching acts, faults, operations, alarms, record of abnormity alarms, statistical reports, parameter variation curve, limits inspection, overload record, maximum and minimum current and maximum and minimum voltage. The diagnosis results may be interrogated as needed or periodically sent to the backend host computer of substation and the dispatch center. In this way, dispatch center can timely grasp and deal with the incidents and alarm events of power supply system and accurately issue dispatch commands to eliminate the faults.

Item 3: The scope of monitoring includes the various operating parameters and power quality parameters of the high voltage substation (or power supply switching station), rectifier substation, lighting and power substation, contact line equipment and switches within the power supply system.

Item 4: Post disturbance review (PDR) means that the incident-related data before and after the incident is stored to allow data extraction for comprehensive analysis and judgment of the cause of the incident. The system allows users to set the related information for PDR, such as incident name, trigger condition, pre-incident time and post-incident time. During operation of the system, the relevant parameters will be followed up in real time according to the presetting. Once PDR conditions are met, the system will start up the PDR function. User is allowed to view the relevant data via incident analysis tool. The trend of each relevant parameter at the time of incident is displayed in form of a curve to reproduce the "incident scene", providing important data for incident analysis.

Item 6: The report printing covers the automatic timed printing, interrogated printing, alarm and statistical data printing, and screen printing as well as printing of daily and monthly reports on energy consumption statistics.

Item 7: The system shall provide several grades of password and shall allow modification of passwords to ensure operation security.

Item 8: The system shall be capable of fault self-inspection and automatic maintenance.

16.7 Grounding

16.7.1 The exception is that DC switchgear cabinet, rectifier cabinet, contact rail disconnector cabinet, brake energy absorption device and ancillary equipment need to be electrically insulated and their exposed conductive parts should be grounded through protective devices, rather than directly grounded.

16.7.6 To protect the electrical safety of people entering/exiting the train, maglev station and vehicle base shall be equipped with vehicle safety grounding devices, and the grounding resistance shall not exceed 4 Ω.

16.7.7 To prevent safety hazards such as physical injury to maintenance personnel during maintenance work, the contact rail of the repair work line within vehicle maintenance base shall be equipped with reliable grounding devices and be well grounded.

17　Communication

17.1　General Requirements

17.1.2　Although prompt and timely communication is necessary in the event of accident or disaster, an additional communications system for disaster prevention and rescue in addition to the normal communications system will incur much higher investment, and the equipment could not maintain good conditions if they are in standby for long. To this end, the communications system shall be designed to provide prompt and timely communication for operation management, command, and monitoring and quality services for passengers under normal circumstances, and in the case of disaster or accident, it shall be used as a means of emergency response and disaster relief.

17.1.8　Some equipment and materials of the dedicated communication, civil communication access system, and public security communications system share the same functions, e. g. transmission system, CCTV system, and cables. Where the conditions in construction, use, and operation permit, they may be integrated so as to reduce system investment and operation cost.

17.1.9　The integrated system consists of collinear and star type structures.

17.1.10　In order to protect the safety of vehicles in operation and the equipment and facilities set along the line, all trackside communication equipment and facilities and on-board antenna devices shall satisfy the gauge requirements.

17.2　Transmission System

17.2.1　As the infrastructure of communication network, optical cables, once constructed, are hard to extend despite of the long service life. With the technical development and construction of electromechanical system, the demand for optical cables will see a rapid growth. Besides the present needs, the optical cable shall also be provided with reserve capacity to adapt to the long-term needs.

17.2.2　In order to fundamentally improve the reliability of optical cable communication and prevent complete communication interruption due to the failure of one optical cable, the optical cables for medium and low speed maglev transit shall be laid separately along different routes to form a self-healing protection ring through information transmission, thus improving the network security.

17.2.6　To prevent the longitudinal inductive potential on the metal enhancement and metal sheath from accumulating, it is required that the metal sheath and metal reinforcement on both sides of the optical cable joint are insulated from each other. Insulating connectors shall be used for the optical fiber led in to prevent the inductive current from flowing into the station and affecting the equipment and personal safety.

17.5　Broadcasting System

17.5.3　According to Item 6 of Article 8.2.2 in GB 50490 - 2009 *Technical Code of Urban Rail*

Transit. "The Public Address System shall enable the dispatcher of control center and the on-duty operators at stations to broadcast the information on train operation, safety, and guide to the passengers, and issue work instructions and notices to the service personnel. Disaster prevention broadcast shall have priority over train operation broadcast."

17.5.7 The power amplifier and the load of the public address system are temporarily connected by the switching control cabinet. According to the actual conditions of the project, one standby is provided for N power amplifiers (N: less than or equal to 4) which are designed to switch automatically. Under the $N+1$ standby based configuration mode, N main power amplifiers and one standby power amplifier, together with the automatic detection and switching devices, are set on one standard 19-inch rack. The automatic detection and switching device detects the working status of the power amplifiers on the rack in a realtime way, and switch between the main and standby power amplifiers automatically once it discovers any fault.

17.6　Clock System

17.6.3 Beidou satellite time system shall be prioritized where the conditions permit.

17.7　Image Monitoring System

17.7.1 Surveillance cameras shall be installed in the following places: fare collection hall, concourse, upward and downward platforms, escalators and other public places, and the places with firefighting equipment, turnout equipment and substation equipment installed.

17.8　Radio Communication System

17.8.3 The radio system for ground line, elevated line, vehicle base, and stabling yard should adopt space wave for radio wave propagation, while for the tunnel, leaky coaxial cable or directional antenna radiation mode should be taken.

17.8.5 The radio system shall be designed with the call, storage, and monitoring functions required for the dispatch to meet the demand for radio-based dispatch.

17.10　Public Mobile Communication Access System

17.10.1 According to the construction experience in civil communication of metro project, the construction method of the civil communications system is determined by the owner and the telecommunication operator through negotiation. The civil communications system mainly offers the wireless coverage, supporting facilities, introduction conditions and usage conditions of the telecommunication operator network, and the wireless base station and the like are provided by the telecommunication operator.

17.11　Public Communication System

17.11.1 The public communications system is installed to meet the communication requirements of public security department for the middle and low speed maglev transit, and needs to connect with the urban public security system which has different requirements. The system shall be built based on practical principles with due consideration given on the economic and technical factors.

17. 12　Office Automation System

17. 12. 1—17. 12. 5　This section takes reference to the Section 16. 9 of GB 50157 – 2013 *Code for Design of Metro*. The system design shall be sufficiently negotiated with the operation organization or department and the system size shall be considered in a comprehensive way.

17. 13　Power Supply System and Grounding

17. 13. 1　The communication equipment shall be powered as Grade 1 load. When one circuit of the system in operation is faulty, the system is automatically switched to the other. At present, the electromechanical systems are generally powered by UPS, and it is also the case that the communications system power supply is integrated with the power supply of other weak current systems. In addition to the requirements of this clause, the integrated communications system power supply shall satisfy the reliability and availability requirements to ensure quality and uninterrupted power supply. According to Article 8. 2. 3 of GB 50490 – 2009 *Technical Code of Urban Rail Transit*, "the backup power supply time of the communications system shall not be less than 2 h".

18　Operating Control System

18.1　General Requirements

18. 1. 2　This section sets out the composition of the Automatic Train Control system in two aspects, ground control and train control, and requires that the Automatic Train Control system shall be provided with necessary fault monitoring and alarm equipment and should be installed with maintenance monitoring subsystems as needed, so as to improve the integrity.

18. 1. 3　The Automatic Train Control system is a key control system for maglev transit. In order to ensure the safety of train operation and improve the service quality of maglev transit, stringent requirements shall be imposed on the reliability, availability and safety design of the Automatic Train Control system and equipment. The reliability, availability, and safety-related indicators shall match up with the technical development of the Automatic Train Control system.

18. 1. 4　The equipment, circuits and interfaces of MATC system which are involved in the train operation safety must follow the fail-safe principle. The system R&D and production processes shall be subject to safety inspection and safety certification, and the system and equipment may only be applied in practice after being approved. Although the R&D and application of ATP system and interlock system and equipment also follow this principle, most safety certifications are carried out by international institutions. Domestic certification methods and authoritative certification organizations have yet to be improved.

Fail-safe is the persistent goal of the safety technology for operation control. Failure of fail-safe shall be an event with minimal probability. In other words, unsafe event is probable when the Automatic Train Control system/equipment fails. The principle of "fail safe" shall run through the entire life cycle of the Automatic Train Control system/equipment and relate to the entire process of product research, design, manufacture and application.

18. 1. 5　This section depicts the role of the Automatic Train Control system in train operation command and control. The automatic train control techniques are developed based on the continuous improvement of train operation command level, participation in operation management, and improvement of train operation efficiency to ensure the safety of train operation. The functions of ATS, ATO, ATP, and CI subsystems are fully set out in this article.

18. 1. 6　The MATC system is directly related to the operation efficiency. The metro in operation at present has reached the maximum speed of 120 km/h, the minimum train interval of 90s, and the rush hour train departure interval of more than 30 pairs. Although the medium and low speed maglev transit is at the early stage, the Automatic Train Control system shall be designed with higher standard to adapt to the long-term demand and the operation under various train formation and high density.

18. 1. 7　In the design of MATC system, due consideration shall be given to the electromagnetic influence in the operating environment. They shall pass safety test and satisfy the safety and reliability requirements.

18. 1. 9　As the safety key of the Automatic Train Control system, ATP and CI systems are considered as the safety products which must be configured. The safety integrity level (SIL) of ATP and CI systems shall be taken in the range of $10^{-8}/h$—$10^{-9}/h$ according to European standard.

18.1.10 The on-board equipment of the Automatic Train Control system shall follow the vehicle gauge while the station and trackside equipment shall follow the equipment gauge. It is necessary for ensuring the safety of train operation, personal safety of passengers, and the safety of operation equipment.

18.1.12 The Automatic Train Control system equipment shall include the protection facilities installed on the elevated line to protect the maintenance personnel. The arrangement of such facilities shall be coordinated with the urban landscape.

18.2 Maglev Automatic Train Control (MATC) System

18.2.1 The medium and low speed maglev transit is featured by high train traveling speed, short station spacing, and significant changes in line slope and curve, which necessitates frequent train starts and stops and result in high workload and fatigue of the driver. Besides, in order to ensure energy conservation operation of train, regulate the operation order, carry out operation adjustment, improve the operation efficiency, and reduce the workload of drivers and dispatchers, the MATC system for the trains on the main line of medium and low speed maglev transit shall include the ATS, ATP, ATO and CI subsystems to meet the actual control needs, which will play important role in improving train operation efficiency and ensuring operation safety.

18.2.2 With high carrying capacity, the quasi-moving block and moving block MATC systems may adapt highly to the changes in passenger volume and improve the utilization efficiency of the line, realizing highly efficient and energy conservation operation. Furthermore the train control mode is similar to the non-linear characteristics of train operation, which is better suitable for the technical states of various trains. With higher technical level, it will welcome great development potential.

18.2.5 The Automatic Train Operation (ATO) mode and unmanned driving mode help improve the train operation efficiency and realize automatic operation adjustment, thus reducing the workload of drivers and service personnel and the staffing needed. However, unmanned driving involves multiple factors such as line and station configuration, vehicle, train operation organization, and depot configuration and no sufficient experience is available in China. Therefore the unmanned driving system should only be applied according to the user requirements when adequate research is carried out to obtain experience.

18.2.6 Fallback mode of the Automatic Train Control system includes several modes: automatic control degraded to manual control, central control degraded to station control, enabling all functions degraded to partial functions. Under the current technical development, failure of the MATC system/equipment may lead to serious operation problems. Especially when CBTC system is used, if fallback mode is unavailable, the operation safety upon system failure will be impacted and the operation would not be recovered after the failure. To this end, the system shall be designed with in-depth back-up operation mode and perfect system failure recovery function. Downgraded operation and the specific requirements shall be determined based on user needs and the reliability, availability, and safety of the system equipment. The operation efficiency of degraded trains is low. The train interval is generally 3 min to 6 min depending upon the level of fallback mode. Fault recovery means that when the system encounters any level of failure, it could be repaired to restore the ability of train tracking and control as soon as possible, thus improving the utilization of full functions of the system and ensure the safety of operation.

18.3 Automatic Train Supervision (ATS) System

18.3.1 The functions of ATS mainly include:

1 Offer HMI interface;

2 Monitor and display the train position and the communication between various parts of ATC;

3 Adjust the train operation to keep responsive to the train diagram or the instructions given by the dispatcher of the train control center, and modify the system operation parameters;

4 Control the stop time at station;

5 Make reasonable control of train operation and realize energy conservation operation;

6 Collect data to generate management reports;

7 Generate passenger guiding information text;

8 Automatic fault management;

9 Section block and releasing;

10 Train diagram (timetable) preparation and management;

11 Automatic adjustment of train operation, and adjustment with dispatcher intervention;

12 Operations and data logging and statistics;

13 Automatic drawing or copy of actual operation route of train;

14 Monitor the train operation and equipment state;

15 Display and recovery of system or equipment fault.

18.3.5 Train route control is one of the major functions of ATS. Taking the route as the main object, the interlocking table lists all routes related to train operation and the relationships between the routes, between route and turn-out, and between route and signal. The interlocking table shall be generated as the operation requires and will be taken as important basis for the design of interlocking equipment. The operation timetable and train identification number are the basis for correct treatment of train route and realizing route control.

18.4 Automatic Train Protection (ATP) System

18.4.1 The ATP system shall integrate the safety functions and train integrity inspection functions, and be responsible for the safe operation of the train. The main functions of ATP equipment include:

1 Prevent conflicting operation of trains;

2 Prevent the conflict resulting from incorrect rotation/setting of turn-out;

3 Prevent passenger injury caused by accidental opening of door, train rolling, or other factors;

4 Prevent damage to the train or line due to overspeed (beyond the speed limit or instructed speed);

5 Monitor overspeed;

6 Constantly monitor the position of the train in the entire system by using the vehicle-ground two-way communications system;

7 The safety distance refers to the shortest distance required for safe parking that shall be kept between the trains;

8 The turn-out interlocking shall be designed to ensure the turn-out will not rotate when the train passes by. The train is allowed to enter the turn-out section only when it is confirmed that the turn-out has been arranged and locked at the correction position;

9 Arrange and block the route and monitor the operation of the train at route convergence or diversion point;

10 Limit the speed of the train according to the requirements of train operation safety and speed limit of the line;

11 Control the direction of train operation;

12 Monitor the direction of train operation in the entire system;

13 Monitor unmanned train operation and turn-back;

14 Rolling protection;

15 Provide vehicle door control safety interlock;

16 Monitor the system management center and the emergency stop button at the station;

17 Train integrity inspection.

18.4.3 Train stop resulting from the overspeed protection or fault of ATP system belongs to safe action. Faults like train overspeed, interruption of vehicle-ground continuous communication, interruption of train integrity circuit, and unexpected moving of train are considered as major faults involving the train operation safety, and safe stop by way of forced braking belongs to safe measures for train operation.

18.4.4 Forced stop control performed by ATP includes different modes such as all normal brake modes or emergency brake mode. The emergency brake control shall be taken as the ultimate control mode. For the purpose of train operation safety, brake release shall not be allowed during the parking process. The brake may only be released by the driver after performing the required operations after the train is stopped.

18.4.6 ATP is a control system that takes the equipment as the main object of safety protection. The in-train information of on-board equipment is an important part of ATP on-board equipment. ATP is a safety protection mode under the control of the driver. The in-train information offers correct, reliable information display following the fail-safe principle, which is taken as the basis for train operation of the driver.

18.4.7 Generally relay interfaces are used between the ATP on-board equipment and the vehicle appliances, and relays are used for physical isolation. If other types of interfaces are used, proper isolation measures shall be taken to prevent against interface fault that affects the normal operation of equipment.

18.5 Automatic Train Operation (ATO) System

18.5.4 The ATO system satisfies the comfort requirements in the control process mainly relying on the rate of change of acceleration and de-acceleration during the traction, idling, braking control and the conversion among various operating conditions. To meet the rapidity requirements, the time required for the control process should be short. Under the control of the ATO system, the train runs at the speed that is most close to the recommenced speed value by ATP to minimize the train operation time and improve the operation quality. The punctuality requirement is put forward to realize stable train interval and punctual riding time.

18. 6　Computer-based Interlocking (CI) System

18. 6. 1　The CI system is one of the main systems required for the operation safety of train. With the development and evolvement of CI techniques, the system is required to deliver increasingly high safety and redundancy. A redundant structure of $2\times$"2 out of 2" or "2 out of 3" could meet the requirements of the CI system in terminologies of safety and availability.

18. 6. 2　This article sets out the basic principles for going through the route formalities based on the interlock table, which is also the fundamental principal for guaranteeing the route safety. Refer to the relevant technical specifications for interlocking.

18. 6. 4　The normal modes for route release include release at one time and release by section. In order to shorten the train tracking interval, route release by section should be adopted for the Automatic Train Control system.

18. 6. 6　The platform emergency stop button is mainly used to perform emergency operations when any condition that endangers the train operation safety and personal safety occurs to the track in the station and the above space, so as to prevent the train from driving into the station and avoid dangerous accident. It belongs to safety concept and action.

18. 6. 7　Under the automatic station blocking mode, the wayside equipment of ATP inspects the idle section between stations automatically, for which the station blocking formalities are gone through manually. Under the given manual driving mode, if the station blocking formalities are not cancelled after the train departs as instructed by ground signals, it forms automatic station blocking mode. The coverage of blocking should include the platform area of the next station.

18. 6. 10　The CI system is of the major system used to ensure the safety of train operation. In order to avoid incorrect operation and ensure train operation safety, all operations of the CI systems must be subject to secondary confirmation.

18. 7　Base of Vehicle and Stabling Yard

18. 7. 2　Item 3: Whether the stabling yard is wholly or partially incorporated into the control scope of Automatic Train Control system shall be determined depending upon its size and operating nature. The stabling yard may also be incorporated into the control scope of ATS as needed.

18. 8　Others

18. 8. 1　Item 1 and Item 2: The Automatic Train Control system is closely related to the train operation safety, improvement of operation efficiency, and the train operation command. Therefore the power supply for the Automatic Train Control system shall be continuous, stable, and reliable.

18. 8. 2　It is required in the technical specifications for integrated earthing of passenger dedicated line in China that the earthing resistance shall not be larger than 1 Ω. The earthing resistance value selected decides directly whether the system equipment may be protected effectively in the case of lightning stroke. For the purpose of high safety and high reliability of maglev Automatic Train

Control system, fixed earthing busbar shall be provided in the central control room and section control room and the earthing busbar shall be connected with the integrated earthing electrode. The internal earthing of equipment, cabinet retaining structure, cable shield and armor, and metal structures shall be led to the indoor earthing busbar and the earthing resistance shall not be larger than 1Ω.

18.8.3 Connection with external power source, equipment power source, power cable and fiber cable connected outdoors, and outdoor electrical equipment shall all be provided with reliable lightning protection measures. The lightning protection earthing cable shall be connected to the earthing electrode in a route as short as possible.

18.8.4 The Automatic Train Control system equipment shall adapt to the electromagnetic environment of medium and low speed maglev transit, and be provided with proper anti-electromagnetic interference measures. The metal enclosure of equipment cabinet, and the metal net in the wall, ceiling, and floor constitute an electromagnetic shielding net to prevent interference of external electromagnetic signal and external radiation of indoor electromagnetic signal.

18.8.7 This article requires that for special environment, the equipment and facilities shall be designed and produced to meet the requirements of the actual environmental conditions on the site, and the applicable scope of dustproof, waterproof, anti-corrosion, temperature and relative humidity of the equipment shall meet the site conditions of the project. In the areas subject to rats and other pests, proper protection measures shall be taken for the equipment and cables, and the holes and openings of equipment room shall be sealed.

18.8.8 In principal, the circuits of Automatic Train Control system shall be laid separately from the power line. However, due to the conditions of maglev transit lines, it could not offer large clearance whether the Automatic Train Control system circuits are laid in crisscross or parallel with the power lines. With the improvement of the MAT and safety protection technique, and anti-interference capability, the spacing between Automatic Train Control system circuit and power line may be determined with reference to the current national standard GB 50157 *Code for Design of Metro*.

19 Elevator, Escalator and Autowalk

19.1 Elevator

19.1.3 The three-party intercom system among maglev station control room, lift car and control cabinet or machine room can meet the operational needs of elevator. The necessity of designing a five-party intercom system depends on the characteristics of the specific project.

19.1.8 In the event of fire, in order to ensure smooth fire evacuation, fire elevators must be treated as Grade I power load.

19.1.9 This article is proposed in accordance with Article 25.2.9 of GB 50157 - 2013 *Code for Design of Metro*.

19.1.10 Construction practice of metros suggests that some elevators are difficult to be designed at a rated load capacity larger than 800kg. According to Article 25.2.10 of GB 50157 - 2013 *Code for Design of Metro*, the rated load of elevators for medium and low speed maglev transit shall not be less than 800kg.

19.2 Escalator and Autowalk

19.2.1 Escalators and moving walks can be classified into standard type and public transport type according to their structural characteristics. For medium and low speed transit, escalators and moving walks of public transport type shall be used.

According to the Explanation of Article 25.1.8 of GB 50157 - 2013 *Code for Design of Metro*, heavy-duty public transport escalator and moving walk are defined as follows: escalators and moving walks that are able to continuously run for at least 20h per day, or 140h per week and are able to run continuously at 100% braking load for 1h in every 3h.

19.2.2 With the view of low carbon emission, environmental protection and energy saving, escalators and moving walks with variable frequency speed control shall be used.

In order to ensure normal operation in the event of disaster, fire evacuation escalator must be treated as Grade I power load.

19.2.9 To ensure operational safety, it is recommended that escalators and moving walks should use local control system. Where station-level control is used, operations are allowed only when operation safety can be ensured.

19.2.10 Item 2, Article 8.9.2 of GB 50490 - 2009 *Technical Code of Urban Rail Transit* stipulates that "The escalator shall be of heavy-duty, public transport type. Its gearing devices, structural members and decorative parts shall be made of non-combustible materials or low-smoke, halogen-free, flame retardant materials."

20 Automatic Fare Collection System

20. 1 General Requirements

20. 1. 1 Short-term and long-term over-peak hour passenger flows are that short-term and long-term rush hour passenger flows to be expected by the station multiplied by the ultra-peak coefficient of 1. 1 to 1. 4.

20. 1. 2 Availability usually includes the capacity to support expected machine halt (refers to events that are arranged in advanced including system upgrade, daily maintenance and disaster preparedness drill) and unexpected machine halt (refers to the unavailability of some equipment of the system or the entire system due to unexpected external causes).

Reliability usually refers to the reliability of the system, which is the probability of continuous operation of the system in case of internal failures of hardware equipment or the capability of application software in failure alarm, self-diagnosis and self-recovery.

Maintainability means that the system is easy to maintain and the maintenance cost is low. The maintainability is the technical base for normal, safe and stable system operation.

Extendibility includes the vertical extension of the system, which is capable to expand businesses by increasing equipment quantity and enhancing processing performance or by modifying and upgrading software and adding new application software modules.

Security means that it is equipped with an integrated security system for both hardware and software, which is the assurance of safe operation system.

20. 1. 3 In case that station is in the state of emergency, AFC system can be manually or automatically linked with FAS, and the retention device of automation ticket checking machine shall be in the state of clearance. If this provision is not strictly implemented and AFC system is not linked with FAS, in case of any fire disaster in the station, the incapability of automation ticket checking machine to evacuate crowds or the continuous ticket selling of ticket vending machine will result in accumulated and crowded passenger flow to further cause serious consequences to the safety of passengers' lives and their properties.

20. 1. 4 "All operation modes" mainly refer to: Passengers are allowed to rapidly buy tickets, get in or out of the station under normal circumstances; passengers in the station are cleared and released when the rail train is blocked; one-way ticket that is not used in the station may be extended; The ticket checking machines at all entrances and exits are available under the control of station attendants during emergent evacuation so that passengers can be rapidly evacuated.

Operation modes mainly include normal operation mode and degraded operation mode.

Normal operation mode means that the system runs automatically in this mode, which mainly includes the modes of regular service, operation ending, service suspension, equipment failure, and testing as well as offline operation.

Degraded operation mode refers to the degraded operation modes adopted in the system under a variety of abnormal circumstances during operation, which mainly includes the modes of train failure, inbound/outbound check exemption, time check exemption, date check exemption, over-travel check exemption and emergency.

20.1.6 In case that the communication outage with central computer system occurs, the station computer system shall be capable of offline operation, at least 30 days' data storage and information exchange between central computer system through backup media. It shall also be capable to automatically upload all data into central computer system immediately after communication is recovered.

In case that the communication outage with station computer system occurs, the terminal equipment of the system should be capable to work standalone and store data. The terminal equipment shall be capable to store at least 50,000 pieces of most recent transaction data and 7 days' equipment data. And it shall be capable to upload the data into station computer system immediately after communication is recovered.

20.1.7 The system equipment shall be capable to continuously run for 24 hours. The battery standby time of the uninterrupted power supply for line central computer system and station computer system should not be less than 1h and 0.5h respectively. In case that the power supplies of two transit lines automatically switch or momentary power failure occurs, the system equipment shall be capable to run normally, in the meanwhile, the terminal equipment of the system should be capable to complete the last current operation and ensure the integrity of events during power failure.

20.1.9 AFC system shall be interfaced with related systems, which mainly include communications system, FAS, monitoring and control system and clearing center.

20.2 Management Mode and Type of Ticket

20.2.2 In accordance with the construction program of medium and low speed maglev transit line, the central computer systems of multiple medium and low speed maglev transit lines can be firstly integrated with local fare clearing system of medium and low speed maglev, and then accessed to the fare clearing system of local urban rail transit.

20.3 System Composition

20.3.3 Functional workstations mainly refer to the workstations of security, clearing, audit, maintenance and statistics. The maintenance workstation should be located in the maintenance area of AFC system in the maintenance base, and the remaining workstations should be located in the corresponding functional departments of control center.

20.3.5 Banknote processing module shall be equipped with the sensors of laser, magnetic, ultraviolet, color transmission and reflected light, which are capable to detect magnetic banknote number, magnetic security thread, paper and patterns marked with fluorescence, to accept 4th and 5th editions of RMB banknotes and the RMB banknotes that will be newly issued afterwards, to machine-readably identify anti-counterfeiting features of banknotes and to accept internationally universal banknotes. Banknote processing module shall also have the function of temporary storage.

20.4 System Function

20.4.4 Paragraph 6) in Item 1: The metal shell of station terminal equipment shall be reliably grounded to ensure the personal safety of staff and passengers.

Item 4: In case that the station is in a critical situation, all ticket checking machines should be initiated and opened through the computer system of the station, emergency button or the local control of ticket checking machine to ensure that passengers are allowed to rapidly leave payment area without any barriers.

20.5 Terminal Equipments Allocation Rules

20.5.2 With a view to the processing capacity and practical utilization of the equipment, the calculation parameters of Station Terminal Equipment are recommended as follows: Automation ticket vending machine: 4 pieces/min to 6 pieces/min; semi-automation ticket vending machine: 6 pieces/min to 10 pieces/min; automation ticket checking machine: 25 people/min to 30 people/min (door type).

20.6 Others

20.6.1 The Ethernet transmission channel between fare clearing system and all line central computer systems should be provided by superior communication transmission network that connects all line control centers.

21　Fire Alarm System (FAS)

21.1　General Requirements

21.1.2　FAS shall automatically control the relevant firefighting and disaster relief equipment when fire is confirmed. However, in medium and low speed maglev system, some routine ventilation and air conditioning equipment is also used as smoke prevention and exhaust system and functions under both fire and normal work conditions. The supervision and control scope of BAS totally satisfies the automatic control requirement of FAS. To avoid repetitive configuration of supervision and control facilities, reduce cost and facilitate management, this article specifies that BAS may be used for automatic control of the smoke prevention and exhaust system that also serves as routine ventilation and air conditioning equipment. The equipment configuration of BAS providing automatic control shall comply with the current national standard GB 50116 *Code for Design of Automatic Fire Alarm System*.

21.1.3, 21.1.4　They are proposed in accordance with Article 7.3.14 and Article 7.3.15 of GB 50490 – 2009 *Technical Code for Urban Rail Transit*.

21.2　System Composition and Function

21.2.1　With the development of computer and communication network technologies and the massive application of computer software technologies in modern fire protection field, the structural forms of FAS have been diversified, and the automatic fire alarm technologies have become increasingly intelligent. In view of the traffic characteristics of urban rail transit, FAS should be designed with two control levels, centralized management at control center and distributed control at stations, that is, FAS is mainly composed of center-level supervision and control layer, station/vehicle base/stabling yard supervision and control layer, field fire detectors, fire automatic control devices and the associated communication networks and interfaces. This enables the fire information from any point within the control area and all instructions from management centers across the maglev line to be quickly, unimpededly transmitted throughout the line, achieving early detection and rescue of fire incidents.

In case where an integrated supervisory and control system is provided, the supervision and control layers of FAS may be merged with the integrated supervisory and control system in view to save cost and facilitate operation. However, such merge needs to be approved by local fire authority.

21.4　Layout of Fire Detector

21.4.3　Item 2: This item is proposed in accordance with Article 19.4.5 of GB 50157 – 2013 *Code for Design of Metro*.

Item 3: This item is proposed in accordance with Article 19.4.7 of GB 50157 – 2013 *Code for Design of Metro* to specify the positions of fire detectors at control center and vehicle base.

21.4.5　This article is proposed in accordance with Article 19.4.9 of GB 50157 – 2013 *Code for*

Design of Metro. This article specifies that, in the design of FAS, both automatic and manual triggering devices shall be provided, that is, where fire detectors are configured in FAS, a number of manual fire alarm devices shall also be provided. The purpose is to further improve the reliability of FAS and the accuracy of fire alarms.

21.4.6 This article is proposed in accordance with Article 19.4.11 of GB 50157 – 2013 *Code for Design of Metro*. Considering the characteristics of urban rail transit, it is not recommended to use audible alarm device in public activity areas for passengers. The purpose is to prevent disordered scenarios and secondary disasters and facilitate orderly passenger evacuation in case of fire.

21.6 Power Supply and Cabling

21.6.2 FAS plays a key role in fire monitoring, alarming and extinguishing of medium and low speed maglev system. Nevertheless, unexpected power interruption will lead to loss of fire monitoring, alarming and extinguishing. So, FAS's power supply must be configured as Grade I power load and emergency power supply is also necessary.

21.6.4 Item 1: When fire occurs in underground sections or at underground line, smoke is difficult to exhaust and people in such environment are at high risk of suffocation. Therefore, in order to protect life safety, FAS cables used in underground section and lines shall be low-smoke and halogen-free.

22　Building Automation System(BAS)

22.1　General Requirements

22.1.1　BAS shall be provided for the medium and low speed maglev transit in order to build good and comfortable travelling environment, protect the safety of passengers, reduce energy consumption, and improve the level of operational management. The BAS shall be designed in the principles of decentralized control, centralized management, and resource sharing.

22.2　Principle of System Design

22.2.2　For the underground line with four stations and three sections or above, in case of train fire in the section, the central level computer shall control the tunnel smoke control equipment between the two adjacent stations to perform the smoke control mode. Where the underground line has three stations and two sections or less, in case of train fire in the section, the station level workstation may control the tunnel smoke control equipment between the two adjacent stations to execute the smoke control mode.

22.2.3　Article 8.7.7 of GB 50490 - 2009 *Technical Code of Urban Rail Transit* requires that "The station equipment shared by the smoke control system and the normal ventilation system shall be under the centralized control of the BAS. Reliable interfaces shall be set between the BAS and fire monitoring and alarm system. FAS issues the fire mode command while the BAS executes the fire control program in priority. "

22.3　Basic Function of System

22.3.1　Under normal conditions, the BAS monitors the electromechanical equipment, detects and statistically analyzes the environmental parameters, controls the ventilation and air conditioning equipment to improve environmental comfort and ensure energy conservation operation, calculates the operating conditions of equipment to optimize operation and complete statistical management, alarm management, trend management, and event management in the normal mode. In the case of fire, the BAS system executes the disaster protection and blockage mode.

22.3.3　This article is proposed in accordance with Article 8.7.3 of GB 50490 - 2009 *Technical Code of Urban Rail Transit* and Article 21.3.3 of GB 50157 - 2013 *Code for Design of Metro*.

When the train catches fire in the section, it shall be preferred to drive to the station ahead for disaster relief. Only when the train is forced to stay in the underground section due to power loss, the central level workstation will issue the fire control mode command based on the fire location reported by the driver via radio communication and the signal about the train location in the section provided by ATS. The BAS of the station adjacent to the fire section will execute the smoke control mode.

For train blockage in the section, the adjacent station level BAS performs the blockage ventilation mode and the air flow direction shall be consistent with the train travelling direction.

22.4 Basic Requirement for Hardware

22.4.1 Industrial control system shall be used for the BAS to ensure normal operation in the environment of the medium and low speed maglev transit. For the field equipment, dustproof, anti-corrosion, moisture-proof, mildew-proof, and anti-vibration control equipment suitable for industrial environment shall be considered. For the monitoring of emergency ventilation and smoke control system, redundant PLCs and redundant field industrial bus structure shall be adopted to improve system reliability. Redundant configuration shall be taken at the main links to improve the fault tolerance capacity of system.

22.5 Basic Requirement for Software

22.5.1 In addition to the software of operating system, the application software of BAS mainly includes central-level application software, station-level application software, DCS or PLC application software, communication interface software, database generation and management software, human-machine interface software, system configuration software, system maintenance and diagnostic software, communication management, and network management software.

22.7 Cabling and Grounding

22.7.3 The power line and signal line of the BAS shall be isolated to avoid mutual interference.

23　Integrated Supervisory and Control System

23.1　General Requirements

23.1.3　For the definitions of integrated system and interconnected system, refer to GB 50636 – 2010 *Technical Standard for Urban Rail Transit Integrated Supervision and Control System Engineering*. The PSCADA discipline and the building automatic discipline integrated into ISCS are the main parts of ISCS. Whether to integrate FAS into ISCS will be decided by the local fire authority. In this code, it is recommended that FAS should be integrated into ISCS.

23.2　System Setting Requirements

23.2.1　The functional requirements of operation management vary with the operation management mechanism of maglev line. In the design of ISCS, the system configuration shall be determined according to the specific functional requirements.

23.2.5　The integrated subsystems should be connected to the station network equipment of ISCS, while the interconnected systems should be connected to the communication processors of ISCS.

23.3　Basic Function of System

23.3.4　Item 2: Fire may occur in trains, tunnels and stations of medium and low speed maglev transit system. In case of fire in an interval tunnel, central ISCS will issue command to the ISCSs and the building automatic system of two adjacent stations according to the positions of the fire and the train, so as to start the tunnel fans at both ends of station, identify the smoke exhaust direction, guide passengers to safely evacuate, and start the station fire broadcast system and passenger information system to issue fire information, and allow display of the fire scene at OCC. When a fire occurs at a station, FAS will transmit fire alarm information to both the building automatic system (BAS) and ISCS of the station. BAS will start the station's exhaust fans, and at the same time, the station ISCS will start the station's fire broadcast system and passenger information system to issue fire information and allow display of the fire scene at OCC.

23.4　Requirements of Hardware

23.4.1　ISCS mainly monitors electromechanical systems and equipment, which are closely related to the operation safety of maglev line. Electromechanical systems and equipment in stations are complicated, so the ISCS needs to have high safety, reliability and maintainability. This article is proposed for this reason.

23.4.2　The network equipment, real-time server, history server and communication front-end processor are the main elements of ISCS. If they are in single configuration, the system will not work properly in the event of failure. Therefore, redundant configuration is necessary and generally 1+1 redundancy is used.

23.4.3　Article 6.0.3 of GB 50636 – 2010 *Technical Standard for Urban Rail Transit Integrated Supervision and Control System Engineering* stipulates: " Station-level ISCS shall be mainly composed of network equipment, server, workstation, communication processor, UPS, integrated backup panel (IBP) and printer. Among them, the network equipment, server and communication processor shall be in redundant configuration. The servers and workstations at vehicle base may be used as the backup center of ISCS".

23.6 System Performance Index

23.6.1 Uplink real-time response data refers to equipment status change data, including changes of digital quantities and changes of analog quantities. The status change response time refers to the period from the time when the interface between ISCS and external system receives data to the time when ISCS's human-machine interface updates such data. The status change response time does not include the duration the data is processed by the systems or devices outside ISCS. The downlink real-time control data refers to the control commands issued by ISCS, including the remote control and other control operations on local equipment. The control command response time is the period from the time when operator issues control command at workstation to the time when the control command is sent to the external interface of the controlled equipment. The control command response time does not include the processing time outside ISCS, such as the command execution time of the equipment.

23.6.2 Item 1: The real-time server switching time refers to the period from the time when the real-time server on duty fails to the time when standby real-time server is completely put into operation instead of the failed one and all functions of ISCS restore to normal. The allowed switching time of history server shall include the switching time of commercial database. The redundant task module switching refers to the switching between task module on duty and task module on standby.

Item 3: The time for switching to redundant communication processor refers to the period from the time when the communication processor on duty fails to the time when standby communication processor is completely put into operation instead of the failed one and all functions of the communication processor restore to normal. The redundant task module switching refers to the switching between task module on duty and task module on standby. This response indicator does not apply if there is no dedicated communication processor configured.

23.7 Power Supply, Protection Against lightning and Grounding

23.7.2 ISCS may share a common online UPS with other weak-current systems, provided that the UPS can support at least 1 hour's emergency power supply to ISCS.

23.8 Equipment Room and Arrangement

23.8.3-23.8.5 These articles are proposed in accordance with Article 9.3 of GB 50636 - 2010 *Technical Standard for Urban Rail Transit Integrated Supervision and Control System Engineering*.

23.9 Laying of Cable and Conduit

23.9.2 Since maglev stations and control centers are exposed to complicated electromagnetic interferences, anti-interference measures shall be considered in the laying of cables. For example, ground the cable tough or protective steel conduit, and use shielded cables.

24　Operation Control Center

24. 1　General Requirements

24. 1. 1　Given the complex relationships among the objects to be monitored and controlled, it is necessary to attach great importance to the monitoring, control, operation, and centralized management of, as well as the safety and reliability in the medium and low speed maglev transit operation. In order to ensure safe, reliable and efficient operation of the trains and systems and enable the operators to carry out comprehensive and centralized monitoring and management on the operation process, an OCC with the required environment, conditions and scale shall be established to enable operation command, dispatch, and control.

24. 1. 2　The OCC should be located at a central place that is near the medium and low speed maglev transit line, stations, and the objects to be monitored and controlled, facilitates the operation management of the whole line and interconnection with other urban traffic networks, and gives consideration to multiple lines to shorten the distance to the medium and low speed maglev transit lines, reduce the project and pipeline investment and the operation management costs, and facilitate the organization of repair and handling under emergency conditions.

The OCC may either serve for a single medium and low speed maglev transit line, or shared by several medium and low speed maglev transit lines. The medium and low speed maglev transit line may also share the OCC with other urban rail transit lines.

24. 1. 3　To realize comprehensive monitoring, control, coordination, command, dispatch and management of all operating vehicles, stations and sections of the medium and low speed maglev traffic line, the OCC shall be equipped with the central level equipment of signal system, FAS, BAS, AFC system, and communications system so that the dispatchers may take advantage of these equipment to perform centralized monitoring and management and other basic functions on the whole operation process of medium and low speed maglev transit.

24. 1. 4　Functioning also as the disaster prevention and emergency command center of the line (or lines), the OCC shall have the functions required for disaster prevention and emergency command. The disaster prevention and emergency command centers of multiple lines shall be able to realize information exchange and information sharing. The operation coordination of line network and the functions and composition of disaster prevention and emergency command center shall be planned uniformly.

24. 1. 5　The design of the OCC shall adapt to the engineering conditions and operation management system. The overall layout shall be designed with due consideration on the safety and reliability, facilitate operation, maintenance, and management, and reduce the operation cost. The setting of OCC varies greatly with the project location, climatic conditions, route planning, scope of monitoring and management, number and level of system equipment, and the required functions for overall operation. So the design shall be based on the actual conditions of the project and the size, level, operation management mode and decoration standards shall be determined economically and reasonably according to the number of specific equipment and room for future development should be reserved as new technologies, equipment, and new processes may be promoted and new systems or equipment may be installed in future.

24. 2　Function Section and General Layout

24. 2. 1　The OCC may be classified into operation monitoring area, operation management area, equipment area, and maintenance area by function. As the associated functional area for the central control room, the operation monitoring area enables running monitoring, operation, dispatch and command. The operation management area enables operation dispatch management, technical management, as well as production and work management. The equipment area is used to store the central level equipment of each system. The maintenance area is used for the maintenance and repair of the central level equipment of each system. The operation monitoring area shall be close to the equipment area to reduce the pipes and cables to be laid. The equipment area and maintenance area shall be adjacent. The division of functional areas shall be based on the actual operation mode and management mode.

24. 2. 2　The operation monitoring area shall be taken as a separate safety zone and have the functions required for operation monitoring, operation, control, coordination, command, dispatch, management and duty for the whole line (or lines). The central control room and emergency command room shall be set up in the operation monitoring area. A buffer area with security facilities (visual access control devices to prevent unauthorized entry) shall be provided for it. In the operation monitoring area, shift handover room, printing room, necessary duty and management rooms as well as living and sanitation facilities should be provided to reduce the off-post time of the dispatchers.

24. 2. 3　Equipment layout and design of systems in central control room.

Item 1: The equipment in the central control room shall be arranged in a tidy, compact, neat, and orderly manner to provide convenience for observation, operation, maintenance, and ventilation to build good environment for the dispatchers and operating equipment and facilitate the movement and evacuation of dispatchers.

Item 2: The overall layout of mimic panels and dispatch consoles in the central control room shall be based on the needs of train operation dispatch and command and facilitate the communication among train operation dispatcher, power dispatcher, BAS dispatcher (and disaster protection dispatcher), maintenance dispatcher (or duty assistance when working as the information dispatcher and passenger transport dispatcher concurrently; they may be set up separately where needed) and the general dispatcher (Shift Director);

Item 4: The mimic panels for the systems should be set up uniformly. Adequate operation space and maintenance space must be provided in front of and behind the mimic panels and dispatch consoles, and space for near-term and long-term development shall also be reserved. The passage shall be wide enough for personnel entering and leaving, contacting, and equipment repair. For the passage behind the mimic panel, the width should be larger than 1. 5 m when its length is less than 10 m, larger than 1. 8 m when its length is larger than 10 m and less than 20 m, and larger than 2. 0 m when its length is larger than 20 m. For the passage leading to the back of the mimic panel from the lateral sides, the width should be larger than 1. 5 m to allow for personnel and equipment access. The area behind the mimic panel may be set up as a separate zone.

Item 6: When the equipment is arranged in a sector shape by layer, taking the central position of the sector as reference, the vertical angle should be 15° and the horizontal angle should be 120° to give reasonable angle of view and meet the ergonomic needs.

Item 7: When the central control room is designed to be used for multiple lines, the functional areas may be divided by line, namely the train operation dispatch system, power dispatch system, and BAS dispatch consoles of each line are arranged together. When the central control room is designed to be used for multiple lines and these lines are greatly correlated and mutually influenced, the functional areas shall be divided by line, that is, the train operation dispatch console, power dispatch console, and BAS dispatch console of each line are arranged respectively in a centralized manner.

Item 8: The dispatch console shall be designed ergonomically for the operators to observe conveniently, so as to reduce their workload, improve their reaction speed, and minimize incorrect operation. There shall be nothing in the top that may hinder the line of sight for normal observation of the mimic panels.

24. 2. 4　Equipment layout and design in equipment areas.

Item 1: The equipment areas shall provide conditions for the installation, operation and maintenance of the central-level equipment of each system. The layout in the equipment rooms shall be neat, compact, beautiful, and tidy and provide conditions for observation, operation and maintenance, as well as ventilation and lighting to create good operating environment for the equipment.

Item 2: The equipment rooms may take different layouts. They may adopt system or line based division, enclosed or open layout, and centralized or decentralized arrangement or a combined mode depending upon the actual conditions.

1) When the OCC is designed to be used for one line and the equipment areas are arranged in a decentralized manner, the equipment room and UPS room for each system shall be arranged in a decentralized way.

2) When the OCC is designed to be used for one line and the equipment areas are arranged in a centralized manner, the equipment rooms and UPS rooms for each system shall be arranged in a centralized way while the auxiliary system equipment shall be arranged according to the actual conditions.

3) When the OCC is designed to be used for several lines, the central level monitoring and control of each system is designed to be independent of each other, and the equipment areas are arranged in a decentralized manner, the equipment for the same system of several lines shall be arranged on the same floor to provide convenience for operation and management of the discipline.

4) When the OCC is designed to be used for several lines and an integrated automation system is set up at the central level, the equipment areas shall be arranged in a centralized way. Different systems of the same line shall be arranged in the same equipment room on the same floor to facilitate operation, maintenance, and management, and the equipment and passage should be separated by glass curtain wall to facilitate observation and management.

5) Advantages and disadvantages of various division and layout modes:

By system: advantage-facilitate management of each discipline; disadvantage-inconvenient for phased implementation and energy conservation operation.

By line: advantage-facilitate phased implementation and energy conservation operation; disadvantage-inconvenient for management by discipline.

Enclosed layout: advantage-relatively small equipment room, high fire protection and isolation safety; disadvantage-inconvenient for management.

Open layout: advantage-relatively large equipment rooms, convenient for observation and management and emergency response since the equipment and passage are separated by glass curtain wall; disadvantage-poor fire protection and isolation safety.

Centralized arrangement: advantage-relatively large equipment rooms, facilitate observation and management and fast emergency response; disadvantage-poor fire protection and isolation safety.

De-centralized arrangement: advantage-relative small equipment rooms, high fire protection and isolation safety; disadvantage-inconvenient for management.

24.2.5 The operation management area shall enable technical management and production management on the central-level operation of medium and low speed maglev transit, in which the management rooms such as director room, operation management technical room, operation diagram editing room and operation management room should be set up. When the central control room is arranged in a relatively high floor, a visit room separated by glass curtain wall should be established in the upper rear mezzanine of the main dispatch console of the central control room. Teaching facilities should be provided in the visit room. The rooms above may be set up separately or combined according to actual needs.

24.2.6 Functions like system commissioning, maintenance test, as well as storage of spare parts and tools, shall be available in the maintenance area. So system commissioning room, maintenance test room, spare parts room and tools room should be set up. The system commissioning room and maintenance test room may be shared by all systems provided that they shall meet the requirements of the maintenance procedures for replacement repair or that below minor repair. The spare parts room and tools room may be shared by all systems or set up individually for each system depending upon the actual needs.

24.2.7 Equipment layout and design in auxiliary equipment area.

Item 1: In the auxiliary equipment area, the auxiliary facilities and functions such as power supply, ventilation, air conditioning, fire protection, automatic fire extinguishing, water supply and drainage shall be available and the management, office, operation, tools, maintenance, and duty rooms should be set up.

Item 2: Auxiliary facilities such as the power supply system, LV power distribution system, air-conditioning system, water fire-fighting system and water supply and drainage system in the auxiliary equipment area should be arranged at the ground floor, 1st basement, or 2nd basement. The ventilation system and automatic fire extinguishing system should be set in the places close to the users. Ventilation duct or water pipe shall not pass through the power supply system room and LV power distribution system room. Independent pipe shaft shall be set for the water system. The rooms for each system shall be set up according to actual needs.

In the auxiliary equipment area, rooms and power supply, fire-fighting, smoke prevention and exhaust, and isolation facilities shall be reserved according to the characteristics of equipment rooms and office management rooms for communication, network, and public security and other purposes of medium and low speed maglev transit.

24.3 Building and Decoration

24.3.1 As one of the most important buildings for the operation and management of medium and low speed maglev transit, the OCC must be highly safe and reliable. To ensure the overall safety, the OCC should be set up as an independent and separate building, rather than being integrated with other functional buildings. When it is indeed necessary to integrate it with other buildings, the OCC shall have its own entrance/exit (including elevators) and fire access. The central control room and system equipment rooms should not be directly adjacent to the building where the function is unknown. Instead, isolation and buffer room or isolation belt shall be set up between them and reliable fireproof and explosion-proof isolation facilities must be provided.

24.3.2 To prevent lightning interference, the central control room and equipment rooms should not be located in the top floor or basement of the building.

24.3.3 Requirements on central control room.

Item 1: The central control room shall meet the technical requirements of the technical process. The scale, level, decoration standards, and room size shall be determined economically and reasonably according to the route planning, scope of monitoring and management, quantity and level of system equipment, and the actual conditions of the project. The interior decoration color relates directly to the mood of operators, working environment and lighting effects. The color of the interior floor, wall and ceiling should be coordinated with that of the indoor equipment. The whole color of the room should be soft, bright and comfortable.

Item 3: Passage shall be set among the dispatch consoles in the central control room. The central control room shall be provided with at least two accesses leading to the outside. The size of the door shall be adequate for the access of the operators and the handling of indoor equipment and maintenance equipment. Generally at least one door of 1.2 m in width, 2.3 m in height, and opened outwards shall be set, provided that threshold shall not be installed. The rooms shall be protected against dust and rodent and meet the requirements of the current fire protection codes and regulations.

Item 5: The central control room shall be installed with anti-static raised floor that is fixed securely and easy to disassemble. The floor shall be tight, flat, clean, dust-proof, easy to clean, and avoid glare. A space no less than 0.45 m shall be set beneath the floor to allow for relatively free laying of cables. The wall in this space shall be decorated with dust-proof materials and consideration shall be given on the system pipeline interface of dispatch consoles, power sockets for the systems and other purposes. At the installation location of equipment, foundation or embedded parts shall be provided on the ground because the equipment may not be installed directly on the raised floor.

Item 6: Ceiling should be provided in the central control room. In the mezzanine on the ceiling, ventilation ducts and cables may be laid, so it must be convenient for the installation of lighting fixtures and access of maintenance personnel. The ceiling should be made of light, fireproof, moisture proof, sound absorbing, ash-free and dust-proof materials. The ceiling shall be tight to prevent insects and rats. The ceiling shall be designed to coordinate with the arrangement of vents, lighting fixtures, and FAS smoke detectors. The upper part of mimic panel may be sealed and treated to be coordinated with the ceiling to keep the room neat and beautiful.

24. 3. 4 The structural design shall meet the load requirements for equipment transportation, hoisting and installation. For heavy load positions in the equipment areas, such as the equipment transportation route, location of equipment lifting point, and the lifting point, the bearing capacity and fixing and lifting devices shall be set according to the installation requirements when the equipment is heavy.

24. 5 Cabling

24. 5. 2 Vertical cabling mode shall be taken between different floors of the OCC. The vertical cables should be laid in cable shaft. The heavy-current cables should be laid in different cable shaft from the weak-current cables with a certain distance reserved between them. The cable shaft on each floor shall be adequate for personnel entry, project implementation, maintenance and inspection, fire isolation and FAS detector installation and maintenance.

24. 5. 3 The cables and wires on the same floor shall be laid horizontally and should be installed in cable mezzanine (of floor, ceiling, raised floor). Cable tray or cable trough shall be set by layer and section according to the specific conditions of the mezzanine to separate the heavy-current power cable from the weak current cable and keep a certain distance between them. When ground (floor) mezzanine is used for cabling, the auxiliary system such as ventilation system and FAS should be placed in the cable mezzanine. The cables between the OCC and the medium and low speed maglev transit line should be laid in cable tunnel to facilitate maintenance, repair, and expansion.

24. 6 Power Supply, Protection Against Lightning and Grounding

24. 6. 1 The OCC shall be provided with a separate lighting and power substation to supply reliable power, in which two power transformers are installed and connected with two mutually independent power supplies. The requirements on Grade I, Grade II, and Grade III loads in the OCC shall be met. When one transformer is out of operation, the other transformer should meet the requirements of all Grade I and Grade II loads. The power supply for automatic train control, PSCADA, FAS, BAS, AFC, communications, and automatic fire extinguishing and other systems in the OCC, and that for the lighting, emergency lighting, smoke prevention and exhaust systems in the central control room and other important equipment rooms shall be treated as Grade I load, the air conditioning system shall be taken as Grade 2 load, and others as Grade 3 load.

24. 7 Ventilationing, Air Conditioning and Heating

24. 7. 1 In order to reduce the equipment failure of each system, the temperature in each equipment room should be controlled at around 24 ℃ all the year around. The temperature and humidity may be controlled according to the specific conditions, but shall be kept within the range of 15 ℃—32 ℃ and 45%—85% respectively. The temperature change in each equipment room should not exceed 3 ℃ per hour to prevent condensation. The recommended temperature in the central control room is 18 ℃—28 ℃ because the operators work at high efficiency and low error rate under such temperature.

24. 7. 4 The mode and parameters of ventilation and air conditioning system should be monitored and controlled by the BAS. The division with the FAS shall be clearly defined.

24.8 Lighting and Emergency Lighting

24.8.1 The OCC shall be equipped with general lighting and emergency lighting, which should be under centralized control. Energy saving lighting fixtures with good heat dissipation effects, long service life, and convenient for maintenance and replacement should be used and shall conform to the current national standards GB 50034 *Standard for Lighting Design of Buildings* and GB/T 16275 *Urban Rail Transit Lighting*. The layout of the lighting fixtures should be coordinated with the building decoration and equipment layout.

24.8.2 Design of lighting system of central control room.

Item 3: Where projection type mimic panel is used in the central control room, the illumination should be 100 lx—150 lx in front of the mimic panel and at 0.8 m of the operation console above ground, and local lighting should be provided. The panel area shall be as dark as possible in the protection mode provided that the contrast in the central control room shall not be excessive.

24.8.3 Table 4 in GB/T 16275 – 2008 *Urban Rail Transit Lighting* gives the standard values of general lighting applicable to different places of urban rail transit. Temporary local lighting may be installed in the equipment rooms where greater illumination is required.

24.9 Fire Protection and Security

24.9.1 As the first-class protection object, the OCC shall be provided with automatic fire alarm, BAS, fire accident broadcast, automatic fire extinguishing, water fire protection, and smoke prevention and exhaust system. Important electrical equipment rooms shall be equipped with automatic fire extinguishing system. The smoke prevention and exhaust system shared by the ventilation and air conditioning system shall be linkage controlled by the BAS. For a large OCC used for multiple lines, the central control room shall be equipped with water spray, water mist or other suitable automatic fire extinguishing system to be determined in consultation with the local fire department according to the relevant fire protection regulations.

24.9.2 In the OCC, a fire control room shall be set up to accommodate the operation consoles or workstations of FAS, BAS, and fire accident broadcast system. The fire control room shall be attended all the day to monitor and manage the fire safety of the building.

The fire control room should be located at the main entrance/exit of the first floor of the OCC, and dedicated fire telephone communicating with the central control room shall be set up.

24.9.3 The OCC should be installed with security systems such as CCTV and access control to monitor and automatically record the entrance/exit, rooms and main passages in each area. Different types of automatic doors opened by ID key or password should be installed. Important rooms should be provided with alarm and detection devices to prevent unauthorized entry.

24.9.4 The OCC should be provided with a watch room as needed, in which the operation consoles or workstations of the CCTV and access control system should be set up and 24 h attendance shall be arranged to monitor and manage the safety of the building. The watch room should be combined with the fire control room.

25 Vehicle Base

25.1 General Requirements

25.1.1 Vehicle base mainly completes the following tasks:

1 Vehicle running and servicing tasks;

2 Routing patrol inspection, regular maintenance and urgent repair of civil construction facilities and electrical and mechanical equipment/systems;

3 Staff training and job operations examination;

4 Daily management, training, supervision, on-site commanding and implementation of rescue;

5 Logistics support for office work and daily life.

25.1.2 Vehicle bases are large-scale construction projects with high construction cost and are mostly at-ground projects. Therefore, this article emphasizes staged implementation of a general plan. The station tracks, buildings and mechanical and electrical equipment shall be designed according to near-term demands, while the size of land use shall be determined according to long-term demands. Since the near-term plan and long-term plan of vehicle base are closely related to each other, it is required to plan and arrange the main tracks and main houses of vehicle base in the determination of long-term land use. In addition, some facilities, such as buildings and equipment for carrying out vehicle workshop repairs, may be constructed by phase according to a general design, provided that the process layout will not affect the normal production and surrounding environment in the future expansion or addition. This is to avoid long idle period of buildings and equipment.

Regarding the number of marshaled vehicles, the maglev vehicles are expensive, so the number of marshaled vehicles is designed according to near-term plan to increase the utilization rate of vehicles.

25.1.6 In order to meet the requirements of fire protection, vehicle base shall have at least two accesses to external roads so that fire engines can enter the fire scene from different directions in the event of a fire.

The medium and low speed maglev transit lines are relatively independent and transshipment cannot be realized via tie lines. Whether to build a separate access road depends on the specific project conditions and comprehensive technical and economic comparison. Road transport within depot is the first choice, and a special design of the road is needed, in which the open-air or indoor loading and unloading requirements should be considered.

25.2 Function, Scale and General Layout of Depot

25.2.2 According to the existing experience and lessons in urban rail transit operations and in view of the characteristics of medium and low speed maglev vehicles, the stabling yard, even without a dedicated temporary repair line, should at least allow for temporary repair and replacement of roof-mounted air conditioner, vehicle doors and some equipment at vehicle bottom. Where conditions permit, the stabling yard may be designed to allow for temporary repair and replacement of bogies.

25.2.3 According to existing experience in metro operations, the number of maglev trains to be serviced may be calculated according to the following formula:

$$N_{\text{to be serviced}} = N_{\text{in use}} + N_{\text{in repair}} + N_{\text{standby}} \qquad (28)$$

Where, $N_{\text{to be serviced}}$——Number of maglev trains to be serviced at vehicle base;

$N_{\text{in use}}$——Number of maglev trains in use;

$N_{\text{in repair}}$——Number of maglev trains in repair;

N_{standby}——Number of standby maglev trains, may be considered as $0.1\ N_{\text{in use}}$ to $0.06\ N_{\text{in use}}$.

It is recommended that the standby train ratio should be taken as 10% in the early stage of commercial operation and 6% in long-term. Urban rail transit projects in China are usually designed with fewer trains in early operation stage. However, after commercial operation, many lines experience a sudden increase of passenger flow and the actual standby vehicle ratio declines to zero, resulting in high operation pressure and risk. Therefore, where the reduction of initial investment conflicts with the reduction of operation risk, priority shall be given to the latter.

The number of maglev trains to be serviced at vehicle base may be designed according to the formation plan for the initial years. This is mainly because maglev trains are expensive and one-time procurement will increase the initial project cost.

25.2.4 Scheduled maintenance refers to all work required to maintain the intended functions of maglev system. It mainly includes regular inspection, maintenance and repair, status monitoring, and regular replacement of components (and parts). Its main tasks include patrol inspection, maintenance and repair. The patrol inspection mainly includes inspection, diagnosis, function inspection and determining whether to carry out maintenance after system defects are found. The maintenance work mainly includes measurement, comparison, inspection, adjustment, cleaning, lubrication, and determining whether to carry out maintenance after system defects are found. The repair work mainly includes replacement of parts and repairs (such as overhaul, minor repairs, component repairs, etc.), as well as unscheduled non-emergency repairs. Scheduled maintenance is generally carried out on a regular basis. During operation, scheduled maintenance shall be optimized as needed to minimize adverse effects in operation.

Unscheduled maintenance mainly includes urgent repair and non-urgent repair of faults. The nature of repair is determined by an online diagnostic system. The online diagnostic system monitors the running status information of the system, judges whether to conduct urgent repair of emergency fault, and generates fault report.

The repairs of medium and low speed maglev transit vehicles can be classified into daily inspection, weekly inspection and maintenance, monthly inspection and maintenance, regular repairs, intermediate repair, and overhaul (see Table 13). The maintenance cycle may be tentatively determined according to Table 14.

Table 13 Repairs of Medium and Low Speed Maglev Vehicles

Repair	Description	Repair duration (day)
Daily inspection	General inspection carried out on a daily basis	—

Table 13 (Continued)

Repair	Description	Repair duration (day)
Weekly inspection and maintenance	Inspection and maintenance carried out on a weekly basis	0. 5
Monthly inspection and maintenance	Whenever the vehicle has travelled 10,000 km or the vehicle has not travelled 10,000 km but one month has passed since the last monthly inspection and maintenance	2
Regular repair	Whenever the vehicle has travelled 120,000 km or the vehicle has not travelled 120,000 km but one year has passed since the last regular repair	10
Intermediate repair	Whenever the vehicle has travelled 600,000 km or the vehicle has not travelled 600,000 km but five years has passed since the last intermediate repair	20
Overhaul	Whenever the vehicle has travelled 1,200,000 km or the vehicle has not travelled 1,200,000 km but ten years has passed since the last workshop repair	35

Refer to Table 14 for an instance of main tasks and cycles of different repairs. The specific repair tasks and cycle must be determined according to the vehicle maintenance manual provided by vehicle supplier.

Table 14　Scopes of Repairs of Medium and Low Speed Maglev Vehicle

Maintenance category	Tasks	Cycle
Routine maintenance	Inspection before and after operation (including skirt board, safe braking device, current collector, magnet module, etc.)	Daily inspection
	Daily cleaning of interior of train cars	Daily inspection
	Daily cleaning of exterior of train cars	Weekly inspection and maintenance
	Weekly visual inspection of vehicle doors and interlayer structures at vehicle bottom	Monthly inspection and maintenance
	Monthly visual inspection of levitation/guidance modules and their connectors, air springs and their rockers, air conditioner, etc.	On a regular basis (every about 120,000 km)
Maintenance and tests	Maintenance of batteries	Every three months (about 30,000 km)
	Maintenance of air circuit system	Every six months (about 60,000 km)
	Functional tests on gap measurement unit, positioning sensor, magnet control unit, DC chopper, inverter, battery fan, current collector, vertical positioning system, etc.	On a regular basis (about 120,000 km)
	Mechanical or electrical adjustment of corridor doors, magnet module supports, etc.	On a regular basis (about 120,000 km)
Replacement	Replacement of most mechanical and electrical equipment in vehicle (such as gap measuring unit, magnet controller, on-board control unit, diagnosis equipment, linear motor current rectifier, current collector, etc.)	During intermediate repair or temporary repair depending upon faulty condition
	Replacement of car couplers	On a regular basis (about 240,000 km or 360,000 km)

Table 14 (Continued)

Maintenance category	Tasks	Cycle
Replacement	Replacement of smog alarm system, air spring, rubber bumper, etc.	Intermediate repair
	Repair of faulty parts	Irregular temporary repair
	Inspection of welds at importance parts such as vehicle's structural members and levitation chassis, etc.	On a regular basis (or 120,000 km)
Overhaul	Dismantling of vehicles for inspection and repair, replacement of important mechanical structural members that have fatigued, complete cleaning and paint repair of vehicle.	Overhaul

25.3 Facilities for Vehicle Running and Service

25.3.2 There are contact rails on both sides of track beam in running shed, and their height is within the reach of human. In order to ensure the safety of personnel in the shed, safety protection facilities are necessary. Disconnector or sectionalizer must be installed in the front of the shed and there shall be optical or audible signal at the time of energization.

25.3.4 Paragraph 1) in Item 4: The safety distance of dead-end vehicle wash line, 10 m, is determined in accordance with the *Code for Railway Technical Management*. Where shutting operations are carried out on dead-end line, there shall be a safety distance of 10 m at the end.

Paragraph 2) in Item 4: The additional length of 12 m required for the signal equipment of run-through vehicle wash line includes vehicle parking error (2 m) and the additional length for installing the signal equipment (5 m on either side).

25.4 Facilities for Vehicle Repaire and Maintenance

25.4.2 In the additional length of 18 m: the front end of train is 6 m from end wall, the rear end of train is 6 m from buffer stop (including the buffer stop and the relevant structure), and the buffer stop is 6 m from end wall. In this article, the work safety distances of different line sections in the shed and the access needs of personnel and equipment are fully considered. If it is necessary to store some accessories, tools and parts removed from vehicle at the rear end of vehicle bumper, the length of the shed may be increased in combination with the process design requirements. The length of shed shall be determined taking into consideration both the modulus requirement of column spacing and the maintenance process requirements. The maintenance techniques and supporting tools of medium and low speed maglev train will become increasingly mature with the development of technology, and their layout may vary accordingly.

26 Disaster Prevention

26. 1 General Requirements

26. 1. 1   Domestic and foreign statistics show that dozens of disasters such as fire, flood, windstorm, icing and snow, lightning, power outage, shutdown, and man-made accidents may occur to the urban rail transit, among which fire is most frequent and causes most significant casualties and economic losses. Therefore, prevention against fire shall be taken as the primary task in the disaster prevention design of medium and low speed maglev transit and comprehensive, advanced and reliable fire prevention facilities shall be taken.

26. 1. 2   The fire protection system shall be designed based on the consideration that one fire accident occurs at one time for both one line and the transfer station of two or more lines. It is determined based on the experience in the construction and operation of urban rail transit of over 40 years in China, with reference to the relevant foreign documents.

26. 1. 3   Considering the difficulties in fire extinguishing in the underground station, this code requires that commercial premises shall not be set up in the passenger evacuation area in the hall, platform floor, and passenger evacuation passage of the underground station, so that the passengers may evacuate to a safe place quickly in the event of fire accident.

26. 1. 4   Underground commercial premises are generally subject to higher fire risk because there are more flammable materials, due to which the fire protection standards are greatly different from those required in this code. It is necessary to ensure the commercial premises may be effectively isolated under emergency conditions, and proper measures may be taken according to different fire conditions.

26. 2 Building Fire Prevention

26. 2. 1   According to Article 7. 3. 14 of GB 50490 – 2009 *Technical Code of Urban Rail Transit*, the fire resistance rating of underground works, entrance/exit passages, and air shafts shall reach Class 1, while that of the ground buildings at entrance/exit, at-ground stations, elevated stations, and elevated line section structures shall not be lower than Class 2.

26. 2. 2   The control center is the dispatch and command center that is used to ensure the normal operation of one or several rail transit lines and respond to disasters. According to Article 7. 3. 15 of GB 50490 – 2009 *Technical Code of Urban Rail Transit*, the fire resistance rating of the control center buildings shall reach Class 1. Separate access passage shall be set up for the control center if it is integrated with other buildings.

26. 2. 4   Item 1: "Other parts" refer to the equipment and management rooms in the station, provided that the area of fire pump house, sewage and wastewater pump houses, toilet, washroom, drinking room, and pure air shafts may not be counted into the areas of fire compartments.

Item 2: The development of urban rail transit from single-line to line network necessitates more and more transfer stations. According to Article 7. 3. 18 of GB 50490 – 2009 *Technical Code of Urban Rail Transit*, "when the transfer stations for multiples lines share one station concourse public area, and the area is greater than 2. 5 times the public area of one standard single-line station, necessary fire protection measures shall be taken through fire performance design and analysis". In the provision, "2. 5 times the public area of one standard single-line station" means that when the public area of line A is 2000 m² and that of line B is 1800 m², take 2. 5 times the line A, that is, 5000 m².

Item 3: This item is proposed in accordance with Article 7. 3. 16 of GB 50490 - 2009 *Technical Code of Urban Rail Transit*.

26. 2. 10 This article is proposed in accordance with Article 28. 2. 3 of GB 50157 - 2013 *Code for Design of Metro*.

Item 1 and Item 2: When one station is provided with two or more separate station concourses, each hall shall have two exits leading directly to the at-ground space because if only one exit is set, the exit may be blocked by smoke in the case of fire, causing serious casualty.

Item 3: Two safety exits are required for the equipment and management rooms of underground station because if only one exit is set, the exit may be blocked by smoke in the case of fire, causing serious casualty. Besides, attended fire compartment shall be provided with one exit leading directly to the at-ground space to serve for rescue concurrently. For unattended fire compartments, two safety exits leading to another fire compartment are allowed.

Item 4: This article is proposed because if the entrances and exits are in the same direction, congestion may be caused during evacuation when the clear distance between them are excessively small, causing serious casualty.

Item 5: Shafts, escalators, elevators, and fire accesses are not allowed to be used as safety exits for evacuation because they could not offer adequate evacuation capacity in the case of fire, and thus accidents such as blockages and trampling may be caused. Fire access could not be used as safety exit because it is specially used for the fire firefighters to enter the station for firefighting. The cross-track passage between two side platforms cannot be used as safety exit because it is within the same fire compartment.

Item 6: This article is proposed because the transfer passage of underground station is generally not installed with safety exit leading directly to the outside and it will cause great impact on the passenger evacuation on the other side if it is used for evacuation.

26. 2. 11 This article is proposed in accordance with Article 28. 2. 7 of GB 50157-2013 *Code for Design of Metro*.

26. 2. 16 When the train is likely to catch fire in the underground tunnel and cannot be dragged to the station, the passengers may evacuate from the side doors of the train, and then to another tunnel quickly and safely through the connecting passage between the two tunnels.

26. 3 Water Supply for Fire Protection and Extinguish Fire

26. 3. 2 Item 1: This article is proposed in accordance with Article 8. 5. 2 of GB 50490 - 2009 *Technical Code of Urban Rail Transit*. When the municipal tap water pipeline is of dentric type, the fire water supply is poorly reliable. Once the fire water is interrupted, it will be adverse for firefighting of the fire fighters. To this end, it is necessary to store adequate fire water in the fire water pool of the underground station.

Item 2: This item is proposed in accordance with Article 23. 4. 7 of GB 50458 - 2008 *Code for*

Design of Straddle Monorail Transit, which specifies that "the fire water supply system of at-ground or elevated stations shall comply with the current national standard GB 50016 *Code for Fire Protection Design of Buildings*". However, in the revised edition, GB 50016 – 2014 *Code for Fire Protection Design of Buildings*, fire water supply is not covered, instead, the fire water supply requirements are put forward in GB 50974 – 2014 *Technical Code for Fire Protection Water Supply and Hydrant Systems*. Therefore the fire water supply of at-ground or elevated stations shall comply with the current national standard GB 50974 *Technical Code for Fire Protection Water Supply and Hydrant Systems*.

26.3.3 According to Article 28.3.5 of GB 50157 – 2013 *Code for Design of Metro*, the underground sections (including the connecting line and inlet/outlet line) connected with underground station shall be installed with fire hydrant system. According to Article 8.5.3 of GB 50490 – 2009 *Technical Code of Urban Rail Transit*, the interval tunnel more than 200 m in length shall be installed with fire hydrant system.

26.3.5 It is proposed in accordance with Article 28.3.7 of GB 50157 – 2013 *Code for Design of Metro*.

Item 1 and Item 2: The water of fire hydrants in the underground section shall be supplied from the adjacent underground station, and the water supply system of fire hydrants in the underground station and underground section shall form an annular water supply pipeline network.

Each underground station should be provided with two water supply pipes led from the urban ring pipeline network to supply water for the station plus two adjacent half sections or the station plus one section length, depending upon the fire pump head, ground elevation of two adjacent stations, and other factors. If only one water supply pipe may be connected from the urban tap water system to the underground station, the division of water supply ranges shall be identical with that of the station with two water supply pipes if the station has a fire water pool. If the adjacent station fire water source serves as backup, the two stations shall be assigned with the same water supply ranges.

Item 3: Whether to install connecting pipe for the fire hydrant pipes shall be determined by comprehensively considering various factors such as water supply safety, fire pump head, length of pipe in the section, pressure and safety of the pipeline, and the laying of over-track pipe.

26.4 Smoke Prevention, Smoke Exclude and Emergency Ventilation

26.4.1 Foreign literature shows that most casualties in the fire accident are resulting from fainting, poisoning, and suffocation caused by smoke. Article 28.4.1 of GB 50157 – 2013 *Code for Design of Metro* and Article 23.7.1 of GB 50458 – 2008 *Code for Design of Straddle Monorail Transit* put forward the provisions on the smoke prevention, exhaust, and emergency ventilation system of underground line. Therefore the underground line of medium and low speed maglev transit shall be provided with smoke prevention, exhaust, and emergency ventilation system.

26.4.3 The available space for ventilation and air conditioning system is limited in the underground station and line section tunnel. Due to their large cross-section, it is difficult to arrange the pipes of ventilation and air conditioning system and considering the large area required for the ventilation equipment room, an additional equipment room will be needed if a separate smoke prevention, exhaust and emergency ventilation system is installed. It is impractical in some cases. In the actual projects, the smoke prevention, exhaust and emergency ventilation system is generally integrated with the normal ventilation and air conditioning system, in which case, the latter shall be provided with reliable fire protection facilities to guarantee safety and ensure timely and effective smoke prevention, exhaust and emergency ventilation in case of fire. A reliable control system must be designed to ensure fast switching from normal ventilation and air conditioning mode to the smoke prevention and exhaust mode in the event of fire.

26.4.4 In the underground station and line section tunnel, the three main areas subject to fire include tunnel, station concourse and platform, as well as equipment and management rooms. Different requirements are imposed on them according to their actual situations.

1 When a fire occurs in the line section tunnel, the smoke shall be exhausted in a direction opposite to the direction of passenger evacuation and fresh air with positive pressure shall be supplied towards the direction of passenger evacuation to form a push-and-pull smoke prevention and exhaust system.

2 When a fire occurs to the station concourse or platform, perform mechanical smoke exhaust and ensure to supply fresh air with positive pressure at the entrance/exit and the passengers shall evacuate toward the ground.

5 When a fire occurs to the equipment and management rooms, mechanical smoke exhaust can be performed. Rooms with gas fire extinguishing devices shall be installed with air exhaust and supply system.

Emergency ventilation is applicable mainly when the train stops and is blocked in the line section due to faults other than fire. It takes time for the passengers to wait for troubleshooting or evacuate to a safe place in an organized manner. During such time, the train and passengers generate huge amount of heat although the piston effect is lost because of stop of the train and the air conditioners of the train could not work as well. Thus the temperature keeps rise and the passengers will feel uncomfortable. In such case, mechanical ventilation must be taken to supply and exhaust air for the accident position to reduce the air temperature in the tunnel and ensure the normal operation of the air conditioner of the train. For this purpose, this article requires that the emergency ventilation is used to supply air to the accident site.

26.4.5 This article is proposed in accordance with Article 8.4.7 of GB 50490 - 2009 *Technical Code of Urban Rail Transit* and Article 28.4.8 of GB 50157 - 2013 *Code for Design of Metro*. According to the experience in metro construction, in order to control the smoke within a reasonable area, realize the smoke exhaust function effectively, reduce the civil works and space required for the equipment, simplify the composition of system and equipment, and reduce the size of equipment, the floor area of each smoke compartment in the public area of station concourse and platform should not exceed 2000 m².

26.5 Communication for Disaster

26.5.1 For the alarm to be sent to the fire authority as soon as possible when a fire occurs, the program-controlled telephone of public communication for the medium and low speed maglev transit shall have the function of automatic switching to the local telephone network "119" upon a fire alarm. Besides, in order to ensure the rescue is organized effectively, wireless communication devices shall be provided for the rescue personnel to communicate with each other on the ground and under the ground.

26. 6   Disaster Prevention Power Supply and Evacuation Indicator Sign

26. 6. 1   To avoid the effects of failure of main power distribution line on the power supply of fire protection equipment, automatic switching devices shall be installed for the last power distribution box. In the case of fire, equipment not for fire-fighting purpose must be switched off to prevent accident expansion while the power supply for firefighting equipment shall be kept on to ensure the fire extinguishing and rescue work proceed normally.

26. 6. 2   According to Article 6. 1. 2 of GB/T 16275 – 2008 *Urban Rail Transit Lighting*, the emergency lighting system shall be capable of working continuously for no less than 60 min.

26. 6. 3   In order not to affect the disaster relief and rescue due to misoperation, the power distribution equipment for disaster prevention shall be provided with obvious signs to facilitate operation in emergency cases.

26. 6. 4   Survey in multiple cities suggests that fire accidents resulting from improper design and installation of illuminators are frequent. According to Article 28. 6. 4 of GB 50157 – 2013 *Code for Design of Metro*, the high temperature parts of illuminators shall be provided with fire prevention measures when they are close to any combustible.

26. 6. 5   This article is proposed in accordance with Article 28. 6. 5 of GB 50157 – 2013 *Code for Design of Metro*.

26. 6. 6   This article is proposed in accordance with Article 28. 6. 6 of GB 50157 – 2013 *Code for Design of Metro*.

26. 7   Evacuation Platform

26. 7. 1   According to item 2 of Article 7. 3. 24 in GB 50490 – 2009 *Technical Code of Urban Rail Transit*, longitudinal evacuation platform shall be set up in the elevated section of straddle monorail transit and maglev transit.

26. 7. 2   The minimum width of longitudinal evacuation platform is proposed in accordance with Table 5. 2. 2 in GB 50157 – 2013 *Code for Design of Metro*.

26. 7. 3   The height of longitudinal evacuation platform shall be lower than that of the floor in vehicle, taking into account the most adverse condition when the train is under non-levitation status and the air spring is not loaded. The curved section shall be adjusted according to the curve radius and super-elevation setting.

26. 9   Other Disaster Alarms

26. 9. 2   In addition to fire, the medium and low speed maglev transit may be subject to the earthquake, windstorm, heavy rain, snow, and other disaster weather. In the principle of "prevention first", the system shall be equipped with alarm function.

26. 9. 3   National and regional earthquake monitoring centers are available to provide earthquake forecast information. The maglev transit system shall be designed with the function of receiving the forecast and alarm from the local earthquake forecast department to make early preparation. If the local earthquake forecast has formed a regional network, the maglev transit system shall connect to the network to receive earthquake disaster information. In such case, separate earthquake alarm equipment may not be provided for the maglev transit system.

27 Environment Protection

27.1 General Requirements

27.1.1 According to the relevant provisions of the *Regulations on Environmental Protection Management of Construction Projects* [No. 253 Directive of the State Council (1998)], the environmental protection facilities for construction projects must be designed, constructed and put into operation simultaneously with the project. The environmental protection facilities must be accepted by the environmental protection authority that has approved the environmental impact report before they are put into use. For construction projects that are built and put into use by phase, their environmental protection facilities shall also be accepted by phase.

27.1.3 The environmental protection measures of medium and low speed maglev transit system refer to environmental protection measures during operation period. At the line sections, stations, substations, depot and stabling yard of at-ground and elevated lines, the pollution control measures for the noise, vibration, water pollution, ecological damages and other pollutions from maglev train, equipment and ancillary facilities are dominated by noise reduction and wastewater treatment measures. The main measures for noise reduction include acoustic barriers and sound insulating walls.

27.1.4 The environmental protection facilities shall be designed according to long-term design service life and conditions for building future environmental protection facilities shall be reserved according to the planning for land use along maglev line. The design service lives of environmental protection facilities shall be consistent with the design service life of maglev line, that is, design shall be made according to long-term planning, but construction may be implemented by phase.

27.2 Noise

27.2.2 The maglev lines should generally make use of the existing transit corridors, and be parallel with existing railways and highways. Use of newly-built transit corridors should be avoided. The maglev lines shall keep clear of the areas where noise sensitive areas and important sensitive buildings exist or are under construction or planned. If such areas cannot be avoided, an appropriate clearance shall be kept, and the natural noise reduction effect of surrounding street shops and green belts shall be fully utilized.

27.2.4 Item 1: This Item is proposed according to the following bases: Article 3.1 in GB 9672 – 1996 *Hygienic Standard for Waiting Room of Public Transit Means*, which stipulates that the noise level limit for waiting room of public transit system is 70 dB(A); Item 3, Article 29.1.2 in GB 50157 – 2013 *Code for Design of Metro*, which stipulates that in the absence of trains, the equivalent noise level of station platform and station concourse shall not exceed 70 dB(A); Table 3.0.1 ("Noise level limits of workplaces") in GB/T 50087 – 2013 *Code for Design of Noise Control of Industrial Enterprises*, which stipulates that the background noise levels in main control room, central control room, communication room, telephone switchboard room, fire protection duty room, offices, conference rooms, design rooms and laboratories shall not exceed 60 dB(A).

Item 2: According to GB 14227 – 2006 *Acoustic Requirement and Measurement on Station Platform of Urban Rail Transit*, the maximum allowable noise level of maglev train at the time of entering and exiting station platform is 80 dB(A).

27.2.5 Item 2: The applicable noise reduction measures include: acoustic barrier, sound insulating wall, sound insulating corridor and sound insulating window, which shall be selected according to the positional relationship between sensitive building and maglev line and the structural characteristics and type of sensitive building.

27.2.6 Item 1: According to GB 12348 – 2008 *Emission Standard for Industrial Enterprises Noise at Boundary*, the environmental noise levels at the boundary of industrial enterprises shall not exceed the limits in Table 15.

Table 15　Noise Emission Standards for Industrial Enterprises

Category	Scope of application	Equivalent sound level, L_{eq}[dB(A)]	
		Daytime	Night
0	Health resort, superior hotel, villa area	50	40
1	Residential, cultural and educational areas	55	45
2	Residential-commercial-industrial hybrid area and central business district	60	50
3	Industrial areas	65	55
4	Areas on either side of trunk road	70	55

Noise control measures that may be taken in the maintenance workshops within depot and stabling yard include: equipment vibration damping pad, acoustic shield, acoustic louver, sound insulating window, etc.

27.3　Vibration

27.3.1 Limits for vertical Z-axis vibration levels [dB] in various types of urban areas stipulated in GB 10070 – 88 *Standard of Environmental Vibration in Urban Area* are shown in Table 16.

Table 16　Limits for Vertical Z-axis Vibration Levels [dB] in Various Types of Urban Areas Stipulated in GB 10070 – 88 *Standard of Environmental Vibration in Urban Area*

Area	Limits	
	Daytime	Night
Special residential areas	65	65
Residential, cultural and educational areas	70	67
Hybrid area and central business district	75	72
Industrial area	75	72
Areas on either side of trunk road	75	72
Areas on either side of trunk railway	80	80

27.4　Air Polution

27.4.1 The maximum allowable emission concentration and blackness of boiler air pollutants stipulated in GB 13271 - 2001 *Emission Standard of Air Pollutants for Coal-burning Oil-burning Gas-fired Boiler* are shown in Table 17.

Table 17 Maximum Allowable Emission Concentration and Blackness of Boiler Air Pollutants
Stipulated in GB 13271 - 2001 *Emission Standard of Air Pollutants for*
Coal-burning Oil-burning Gas-fired Boiler

Type of boiler		Area	Dust (mg/m^3)	SO_2 (mg/m^3)	NO_x (mg/m^3)	Flue gas darkness (Lingeman blackness, grade)
Coal-fired boiler	Natural draft boiler	Class I area	80	900	—	I
		Class II and III areas	120			
	Other boilers	Class I area	80			I
		Class II area	200			
		Class III area	250			
Oil-fired boiler	Light diesel oil, kerosene	Class I area	80	500	400	I
		Class II and III areas	100			
	Other fuel oils	Class I area	180	900	400	I
		Class II and III areas	150			
Gas-fired boiler		All areas	50	100	400	I

Note: This table applies to boilers built since January 1 2001.

See Table 18 for the maximum allowable emission concentration of cooking fume and the minimum removal efficiency of fume purifier according to GB 18483 - 2001 *Emission Standard of Cooking Fume*.

Table 18 Maximum Allowable Emission Concentration of Cooking Fume and Minimum Removal
Efficiency of Fume Purifier according to GB 18483 - 2001 *Emission Standard of Cooking Fume*

Size	Small	Medium	Large
Maximum allowable emission concentration (mg/m^3)	2.0		
Minimum removal efficiency of fume purifier (%)	60	75	85

According to the *Atmospheric Pollution Prevention and Control Law*, for items not covered by national atmospheric pollution emission standards, the people's governments of provinces, autonomous regions, and municipalities are allowed to issue their local emission standards. For items covered by national atmospheric pollution emission standards, the people's governments of provinces, autonomous regions, and municipalities are allowed to issue more stringent local emission standards. Where atmospheric pollutants are emitted to areas with local emission standards, the local emission standards shall be observed.

27.4.2 China has issued nine national standards for hazardous materials from decorative materials. These standards include GB 18580 through GB 18587 *Indoor Decorating and Refurbishing Materials* and GB 6566 *Limits of Radionuclides in Building Materials*. The decorative materials of medium and low speed maglev stations shall comply with these standards.

27.4.3 This article is proposed in accordance with the national standard GB 9672 - 1996 *Hygienic Standard for Waiting Room of Public Transit Means*.

27.5 Effluent

27.5.1 According to the *Water Pollution Prevention and Control Law*, for items not covered by national water pollution discharge standards, the people's governments of provinces, autonomous regions, and municipalities are allowed to issue their local discharge standards. For items covered by national water pollution discharge standards, the people's governments of provinces, autonomous regions, and municipalities are allowed to issue more stringent local discharge standards. Where water pollutants are discharged to areas with local discharge standards, the local discharge standards shall be observed.

27.6　Electromagnetic Environment

27.6.2　The national standard GB 8702 – 2014 *Controlling Limits for Electromagnetic Environment* has stipulated the public exposure limits for electric, magnetic and electromagnetic fields of 1 Hz to 3 GHz.

Appendix A Calculation Methods of Dynamic Vehicle Envelope and Equipment Gauge for Beeline Section

Table 19 gives some example values for vehicle gauge calculation parameters of medium and low speed maglev transit.

Table 19 Example Values for Vehicle Gauge Calculation Parameters of Medium and Low Speed Maglev Transit

S/N	Symbol	Description	Reference value
1	ΔX_{cj}	Dynamic traverse displacement of levitation chassis relative to the magnetic poles of F rail (mm)	± 14 mm
2	ΔM_{BX}	Transverse manufacturing error of maglev vehicle (mm)	± 5 mm
3	ΔM_{BY}	Vertical manufacturing error of maglev vehicle (mm)	± 10 mm
4	$\Delta \omega$	Normal transverse deformation of maglev vehicle relative to levitation chassis at ♯2 and ♯5 track bearing platforms at straight line sections (mm)	± 15 mm
5	δ_w	Vertical wear of skid (mm)	2 mm
6	f_{1dx}	Empty-to-load elastic deflection change of levitation chassis (mm)	2 mm
7	f_2	Height adjustment error of air spring (mm)	± 3 mm
8	Δf_{pcj}	Dynamic variation of levitation air gap of magnetic pole (mm)	± 3 mm
9	Δf_{smax}	Deflection of air spring due to lateral roll (maximum value in the presence of various factors during normal operation) (mm)[1]	± 20 mm
10	$\Delta f'_{smax}$	Dynamic deflection of air spring due to floating and sinking (mm)	± 30 mm
11	ΔM_{qc}	Upwarp/downwarp of vehicle pin (mm)	3 mm
12	Δ_c	Transverse deviation of F rail centerline (mm)	± 3 mm
13	δ_c	Vertical deviation of F rail centerline (mm)	± 2 mm
14	Δh_1	Transverse height difference of F rail (mm)	1.5 mm
15	Δ_e	Transverse elastic deformation of F rail (mm)	1 mm
16	δ_e	Vertical elastic deformation F rail (mm)	2 mm
17	Δh_2	Transverse elastic height difference of F rail (mm)	1 mm
18	a	Longitudinal spacing between ♯2 and ♯5 track bearing platforms of levitation chassis (mm)	8220 mm
19	n	Center distance between design section and ♯2 and ♯5 track bearing platforms of the adjacent levitation chassis (mm)	3390 mm
20	h_{cs}	Height from the upper supporting surface of air springs and the rail surface (mm)	335 mm
21	ΔM_{tX}	Transverse manufacturing error of levitation chassis (mm)	± 2 mm
22	ΔM_{tY}	Vertical manufacturing error of levitation chassis (mm)	± 1.5 mm
23	R	Horizontal curve radius (depot line) (m)	50 m
24	R_V	Vertical curve radius (minimum) (m)	1000 m
25	θ_{ac}	Maximum cross slope angle of F rail (°)	8°
26	θ_{dc}	Superelevation deficiency rate	0.04

Table 19 (Continued)

S/N	Symbol	Description	Reference value
27	V	Maximum running speed of vehicle (km/h)	120 km/h
28	f_{XF}	Levitation height (mm)	8 mm
29	Δf_{SD}	Decline due to underinflated air spring or rise due to overinflated air spring (mm)	45 mm
30	Δf_{sk}	Out-of-control limit of unilateral levitation gap (mm)	11 mm
31	$\Delta X'_{cj}$	Transverse geometric extreme displacement of magnetic pole (mm)	14 mm
32	L	Track gauge (mm)	2000 mm
33	Δf_{hq}	Vertical deflection of skid (mm)	0 mm
34	h_{cp}	Height of F rail acting surface relative to sliding rail surface (mm)	78.5 mm
35	b_s	Transverse spacing of air springs (mm)	2020 mm
36	θ_{px}	Offset angle (maximum) of vehicle as a result of asymmetric arrangement of passengers (rad)②	$2f_2/b_s$
37	$\Delta \omega_{max}$	Maximum transverse deformation of vehicle relative to levitation chassis at ♯2 and ♯5 track bearing platforms (mm)	±25 mm
38	a'	Longitudinal spacing of ♯1 and ♯6 track bearing platforms of levitation chassis (mm)	13700 mm
39	n'	Center distance between the design cross section and ♯1 or ♯6 track bearing platforms of levitation chassis (mm)	650 mm
40	L_{xfj}	Effective length of levitation chassis (mm)	2650 mm

Note: ① Deflection of air spring due to lateral roll (maximum value in the presence of various factors during normal operation):

$$\Delta f_{smax} = 0.5 b_s \times \sqrt{[A_w \cdot P_w(1+S_2)(h_{sw}-h_{cs})/k_{\Phi s}]^2 + [m_j \cdot a_B(1+S_2)(h_{sc}-h_{cs})/k_{\Phi s}]^2}$$

Where, $A_w \cdot P_w$ ——Wind load(N);

A_w ——Windward area(m²);

P_w ——Wind pressure(N/m²);

m_j ——Design weight of vehicle (AW₃)(kg);

a_B ——Transverse acceleration(m/s²);

h_{sw} ——Centroid height of windward area(mm);

h_{sc} ——Height of center of gravity of vehicle(mm);

$k_{\Phi s}$ ——Anti-roll rigidity of secondary springs throughout vehicle(N · mm/rad);

S_2 ——Additional coefficient of gravity angle $= m_j g[(h_{sc}-h_{cs})/k_{\Phi s}]$(rad).

② Offset angle (maximum) of vehicle as a result of asymmetric arrangement of passengers:

$$\theta_{px} = [100 m_z g(1+S_2)/k_{\Phi s}] \leqslant 2f_2/b_s$$

Where, m_z ——2/3 passenger capacity (AW₂)(kg).

Table 20 shows the gauge control coordinates within straight line sections based on the reference values in Table 19 and the calculation method given in this Appendix A. Figure 5 shows the diagram of the gauges.

Table 20 Coordinates of Gauge Control Points within Straight Line Section

Vehicle profile control points							
Control point	0	1	2	3	4	5	6
X	0	620	800	800	890	890	1133
Y	3814	3782	3760	3724	3688	3551	3432
Control point	7	8	9	10	11	12	13
X	1274	1354	1399	1483	1495	1500	1500
Y	3216	2932	2732	2132	1832	1532	967

Table 20 (Continued)

Vehicle profile control points							
Control point	14	15	16	17	18	19	20
X	1500	1494	1470	1391	1480	1480	1236
Y	438	338	338	-308	-344	-853	-853
Control point	21	22	23	24	25	26	27
X	1236	1050	1050	1130	1130	1080	1080
Y	-796	-796	-585	-585	-322	-322	-302
Control point	28	29	30	31	32	33	34
X	917	917	1140	1140	720	720	0
Y	-302	-102	-102	24	24	-5	-5
Vehicle gauge control points							
Control point	$0'$	$1'$	$2'$	$3'$	$4'$	$5'$	$6'$
X	0	666	846	925	1013	1010	1230
Y	3871	3839	3817	3767	3693	3572	3464
Control point	$7'$	$8'$	$9'$	$10'$	$11'$	$12'$	$13'$
X	1386	1460	1500	1570	1575	1573	1560
Y	3216	2932	2732	2132	1832	1532	967
Control point	$14'$	$15'$	$16'$	$17'$	$18'$	$19'$	$20'$
X	1548	1541	1517	1411	1500	1502	1214
Y	438	291	291	-293	-329	-863	-863
Control point	$21'$	$22'$	$23'$	$24'$	$25'$	$26'$	$27'$
X	1214	1050	1050	1109	1109	1059	1059
Y	-806	-806	-571	-571	-332	-332	-312
Control point	$28'$	$29'$	$30'$	$31'$	$32'$	$33'$	$34'$
X	896	897	1120	1120	740	740	0
Y	-312	-88	-88	22	22	-15	-15
Equipment gauge control points							
Control point	$0''$	$1''$	$2''$	$3''$	$4''$	$5''$	$6''$
X	0	700	880	1078	1164	1157	1393
Y	3896	3864	3842	3760	3688	3551	3432
Control point	$7''$	$8''$	$9''$	$10''$	$11''$	$12''$	$13''$
X	1521	1585	1619	1668	1663	1651	1619
Y	3216	2932	2732	2132	1832	1532	967
Control point	$14''$	$15''$	$16''$	$17''$	$18''$	$19''$	$20''$
X	1589	1577	1553	1421	1510	1515	1200
Y	438	242	243	-279	-314	-873	-873
Control point	$21''$	$22''$	$23''$	$24''$	$25''$	$26''$	$27''$
X	1200	1050	1050	1100	1100	1050	1050
Y	-816	-816	-560	-560	-342	-342	-322
Control point	$28''$	$29''$	$30''$	$31''$	$32''$	$32_1''$	$32_2''$
X	887	887	1110	1110	865	865	750
Y	-322	-80	-80	20	20	0	0
Control point	$33''$	$34''$					
X	750	0					
Y	-30	-30					

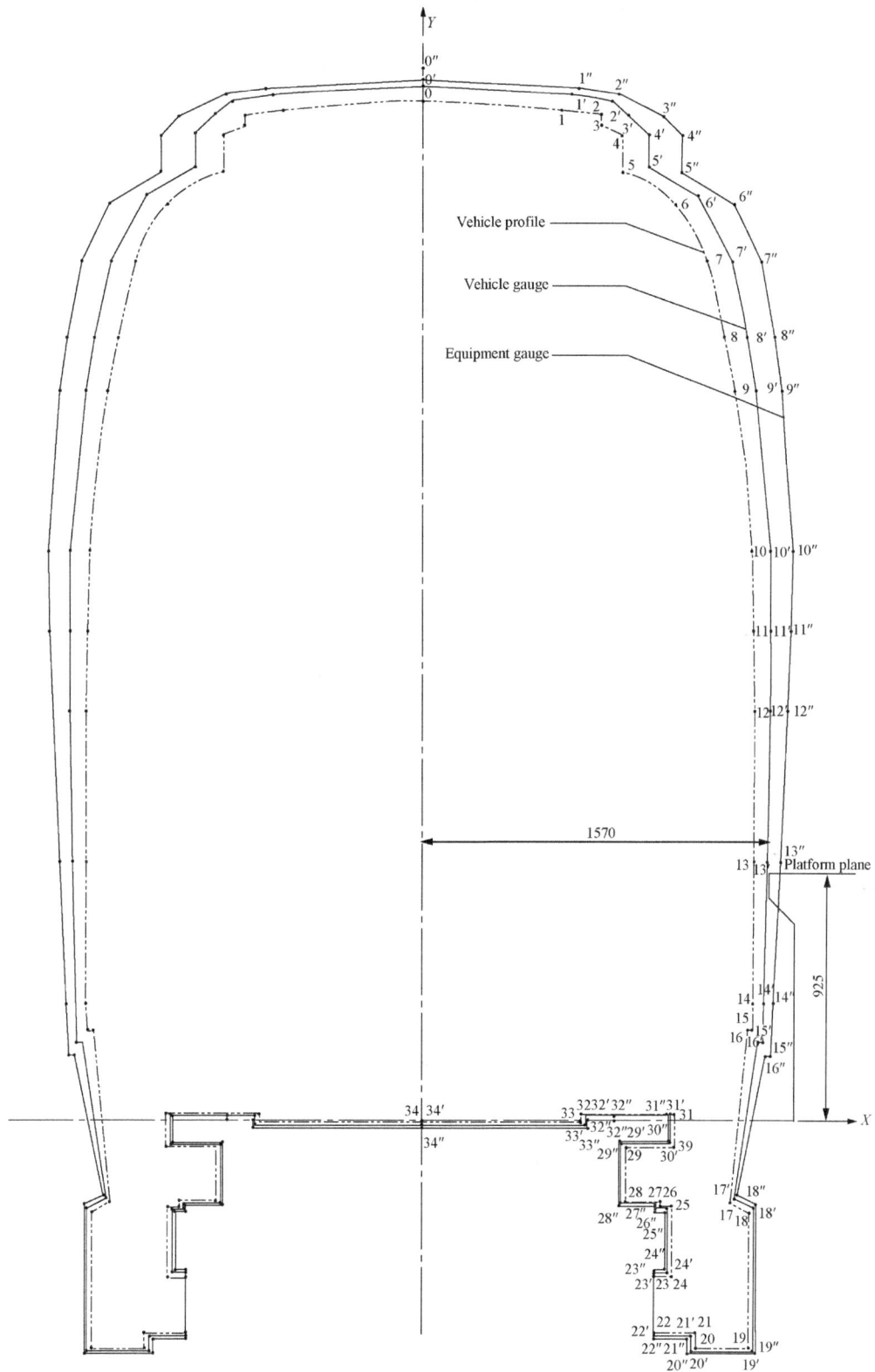

Figure 5　Gauges within straight line sections